Out of Our Minds

Out of Our Minds

Reason and Madness in the
Exploration of Central Africa

Johannes Fabian

The Ad. E. Jensen Lectures
at the Frobenius-Institut,
University of Frankfurt

UNIVERSITY OF CALIFORNIA PRESS
Berkeley · *Los Angeles* · *London*

University of California Press
Berkeley and Los Angeles, California

University of California Press, Ltd.
London, England

Library of Congress Cataloging-in-Publication Data

Fabian, Johannes.
    Out of our minds : reason and madness in the
exploration of Central Africa : the Ad. E. Jensen
lectures at the Frobenius Institut, University
of Frankfurt / Johannes Fabian.
       p.   cm.
    Includes bibliographical references and index.
    ISBN 0-520-22122-2 (alk. paper).—
    ISBN 0-520-22123-0 (pbk. : alk paper)
      1. Ethnology—Africa, Central—
Fieldwork.   2. Ethnologists—Africa,
Central—History.   3. First contact of
aboriginal peoples with Westerners—Africa,
Central—History.   4. Africa, Central—
Discovery and exploration—German.
    5. Africa, Central—Discovery and explo-
ration—Belgian.   6. Africa, Central—
Description and travel.   I. Universität
Frankfurt am Main. Frobenius-Institut.
II. Title.
GN17.3.A352 F33 2000
967—dc21   99-088221

Manufactured in the United States of America

09 08 07 06 05 04 03 02 01 00
10 9 8 7 6 5 4 3 2 1

For Gabi and Anna,
who give me a home to return to

Contents

Illustrations

Preface and
Acknowledgments

This book has kept me busy during more than a decade. Its subject matter never ceased to intrigue me, and it is a safe bet that a study of tales about travel to central Africa will have at least some of the fascination for contemporary readers that its sources had for readers about a century ago. Joseph Conrad's *Heart of Darkness* continues to fire artistic imagination and has inspired extraordinary works, from Francis Ford Coppola's film *Apocalypse Now* to Sven Lindqvist's study *"Exterminate All the Brutes"* (1992; trans. 1996), while books such as Adam Hochschild's *King Leopold's Ghost* (1998) have won popular and critical acclaim.

Out of Our Minds plays in a different arena. It is about the continued struggle of anthropology with its colonial inheritance. On a personal level—I admit from the start—it is also yet another attempt to get even with a discipline that has us believe, today more than ever, that it is not really a discipline (in the sense of a regime of controls and constraints). I should have known better after my experience as a graduate student at the University of Chicago in the early sixties. At twenty, before I came to the United States, I had read Marx's early writings and was smitten with his angry brilliance. Later I found in Critical Theory a contemporary idiom that helped me develop what I had learned from Marx. But I was far removed from the intellectual scene of Frankfurt, Berlin, or Paris. In Chicago, Theory with a capital *T* was in high fashion, and the dream of elevating ethnography to "ethno-science" excited many minds. I had to confront a local variety of Parsonian sociological scholasticism (with echoes of Radcliffe-Brown and forebodings of Lévi-Strauss), brilliant yet somewhat mad in its ambition. Science stood triumphant in "new archeology"; in human prehistory and evolution and in linguistics, one breakthrough followed another. Students had to assimilate all these developments in an incredibly short time. No wonder I experienced my graduate studies as an intellectual boot camp. I survived and became a professional contributor to a discourse on other peoples that, on the whole, prided itself in having got rid of people, real living persons, and of otherness that makes us be ourselves, so as to be able to explain actors and their identities. Theories gyrated in an empty space: no sound or wind in our faces, no bodies that could tire or ache, sweat or shiver. And history was called social change. What had brought this on? Theoretical progress bought, I realized much later, at the price of the progressive disembodiment of reason and knowledge.

When I began to do fieldwork in Africa, it was no problem at all to write disembodied anthropology, because in effect *I* was disembodied. Yet somehow I always knew this was wrong (perhaps because I had received an antidote in the example of Paul Schebesta, my first ethnology teacher and a famed explorer of the Bambuti, who had crisscrossed the Ituri forest with a caravan). To keep my own sanity, as well as that of my discipline, I had to question and subvert the seeming convincingness and elegance of anthropology's findings. There are many ways to do this, and I have tried a number of them.

In this book I undertake a voyage back to the time when those we might consider proto-ethnographers traveled to faraway places. Though fieldwork eventually established anthropology as an academic profession and gave anthropologists the authority of those who had "been there," its institutionalization promoted the disembodiment of knowledge. Yes, fieldwork put anthropology on empirical ground, and I am among those who cannot conceive of anthropology without it. It is also true that ethnographic research became "scientific" to the extent that it was submitted to a regime of censorship, abstention, and discipline (that word again!). But the desired effect was only on the surface. The triumph of logic and rationality, the clever architecture of theoretical edifices, and the cunning methods devised for novice researchers do not make science. What they do promote is ascetic withdrawal from the world as we experience it with our senses. In the end, science conceived, taught, and institutionalized in such a manner is sense-less.

To gain a critical understanding of this development, we need to go back to its beginnings. (That was not why I got started on this project, though it may turn out to be what it accomplishes.) But how relevant to the critique of anthropological practices is a story of exploratory travel carried out by about twenty persons, when only two of them were to become professional anthropologists (and unique in their field, at that)? The answer hinges on the connections between imperial colonialism, exploration, and ethnographic research.

By the end of the seventies, it began to dawn on many anthropologists that the hallmark of modern anthropology—relatively extended, sedentary fieldwork in settings that were as yet relatively undisturbed, whether it took the form of deep immersion into a living context (and a ritual of professional initiation) or work under conditions that approached those of a laboratory—was a mythical beast: a utopian ideal at best, propaganda at worst. The posthumously published diaries of Bronislaw Malinowski, still ritually cited as the inventor of modern ethnographic research, were a wake-up call: there he revealed himself as a figure bearing more than an incidental resemblance to Conrad's heroes and villains (as George Stocking observes in his masterful essays on the "ethnographer's magic" [1992, 17]). Edward Evans-Pritchard and Marcel Griaule, as it turned out, were more embroiled in mundane colonial realities than we once thought. Many of the towering figures of American anthropology (Ruth Benedict, Margaret Mead, Gregory Bateson, and others) worked in the field with theoretical agendas and methods devised to contribute to the "war effort" during World War II and the Cold War in the fifties.

The sixties brought radical change when former colonies—many of them classical "fields" of ethnographic research—engaged in struggles for independence or were, often as soon as the goal was attained, drawn into a maelstrom of postcolonial conflicts that has kept them spinning to this day. As a result, certainties developed during colonial times began to crumble and sometimes went to pieces, among them the ethnic units of observation—what we used to call tribes or clans—that gave fieldworkers a place to settle in. Anthropology found itself, sometimes literally, "on the road again." Travel was rediscovered not only as an interesting historical subject but also as a predicament of postmodern anthropology. It is now becoming a key metaphor, a figure of thought, in

theory-building. What travel meant when scientific explorers began producing knowledge about vast regions such as central Africa—the sense
it had or, more often, did not have—merits close attention, especially in
view of what I believe is an imminent danger of disembodied postcolonial theorizing.

In the introduction I give an account of the course this project has taken.
Here I would like to express my gratitude to those who helped me along
the way. A stay as Visiting Scholar at the Getty Center for the History
of Art and the Humanities, Santa Monica, in 1990–91 enabled me to
get a first grasp of the corpus of travelogues that would become the
sources of this study. With Suzanne Preston-Blier I shared not only an
untiring research assistant, Elizabeth Cameron, but many thoughts and
the pleasant life our families were privileged to lead under the skies of
southern California. Other Fellows endured and encouraged my explorations of reason and madness, foremost among them Mogens Trolle
Larsen and Mario Torelli, whose company I have missed ever since. In
the years that followed, many colleagues and their departments allowed
me to try out embryonic versions of this study. I thank them collectively,
since the list of names and places would be long and probably incomplete. I have a standing, and growing, debt to the Africana Library and
its staff at Northwestern University, a place to which I return as often
as possible.

   I had the honor of presenting a first version of this book as the Ad. E.
Jensen Lectures of 1997–98 at the Frobenius-Institut of the University
of Frankfurt. I thank Karl-Heinz Kohl for inviting me, and especially
Beatrix Heintze, whose extraordinary knowledge of the colonial history
of Angola and beyond helped me clarify certain complex issues and find
documentation I would otherwise have missed. During a stay at the In-
ternationales Forschungszentrum für Kulturwissenschaften in Vienna, in
the spring of 1998, I found the time to prepare the manuscript for publication and the leisure to have long conversations with my friend Bogumil Jewsiewicki. Of course, I could not have done my work without support from the Faculty of Political and Social-Cultural Sciences and my
colleagues at the Department of Anthropology at the University of Amsterdam.

   My thanks go to James Clifford and, again, to Bogumil Jewsiewicki,
who read the manuscript for the University of California Press and offered encouragement and detailed critique. I am sure they will understand that I cherished the first but could not on all points live up to their

expectations regarding the latter. Finally I want to express gratitude and respect to the editors at the press: Monica McCormick for steering the manuscript through the process of acceptance, Rose Vekony and especially Edith Gladstone for valiant struggle with my prose.

Xanten, September 1999

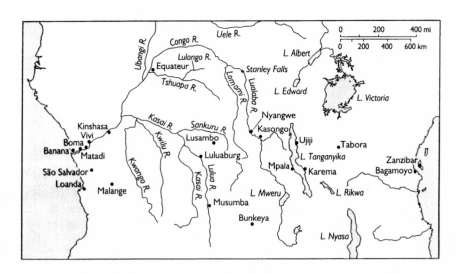

Map of central Africa, showing the main places named in the travelogues.

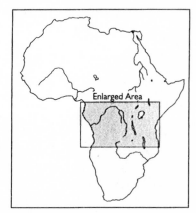

Enlarged Area

ONE

Introduction

When I retrace the steps that led me to embark on this project, I must begin with a few remarks about my previous work. Trained in anthropology, I have done field research and written about contemporary African culture in the urban and industrial region of Shaba, in southeastern Zaire.[1] Disciplinary divisions and the strong sociological outlook that characterized even cultural anthropology may account for the fact that it took years before I realized I needed to place my work in the context of colonial history. Knowledge of the colonial past was essential for me to understand, among other things, a problem that intrigued me more and more: how did it come about that Swahili, a language that had its origins on the east coast of Africa, would emerge, in different variants, as both a tool of Belgian colonization and a "weapon of resistance"— that is, as the common medium through which displaced labor recruits and other immigrants created spaces of freedom for the vital and complex popular culture I first encountered in the sixties?

Sometime in the late seventies I began to search more purposefully for evidence of a colonial history of Swahili. I looked for early vocabularies, grammars, phrase books, and primers written for use in the Congo Free State, which became the Belgian Congo in 1908. It turned out that the earliest instances of these genres of linguistic appropriation could be found (often as appendixes) in travelogues, and by chance, in the library of my institute, I came upon a truly remarkable example of such writing, Jérôme Becker's *La vie en Afrique* (1887). I thus decided to begin my project with a study of the uses of Swahili in this account of expeditions carried out for King Leopold's International African Association. For the sake of contrast, I also analyzed a contemporary account of missionary travel from the east coast to the Great Lakes, the White Fathers' *A l'assaut des pays nègres* (1884). I presented the results in a rather recondite long essay or small book, *Language on the Road* (1984), and this could have been the end of that particular excursion into history and literary interpretation. But the larger project of a colonial history of Shaba Swahili, which I had originally envisaged as not much more than an annotated bibliography, turned into a story that had to be told (*Language and Colonial Power* [1986; reprint 1991]).

A number of questions that came up in the course of my readings for these studies kept intriguing me even after the results were published. For instance, I could not let go of certain strange assertions that had got me hooked on Becker's account in the first place. Much like other early travelers (and later anthropologists), this author flaunted his authority by liberally larding his story with Swahili terms and phrases. This was an interesting feature, though not exceptional in itself. What made it so gripping was a comment of Becker's, in a chapter where he assumes the stance of the linguist: "The African, by the way, gets along with a very restricted choice of vocables. Three or four hundred words make up his usual glossary" (Becker 1887, 2:51).

This claim struck me as nonsense, even if it was meant to apply to a reduced variant of Swahili, a kind of trade language. Because I had by then formed a high opinion of Becker as a proto-ethnographer, the statement also made me mad, mad enough to comb the two volumes for Swahili terms and phrases that Becker himself used in the French text. What I found was that his own demonstrated knowledge of the language and the generalizations he asked us to accept contradicted each other. I was able to compile a Swahili vocabulary, interspersed in the French text, of more than four hundred terms and more than one hundred phrases (names, greetings, fragments of conversation, quotations).[2] Considering that all this evidence must be assumed to present only part of Becker's actual competence in the language (let alone that of his African interlocutors), I could only conclude that Becker was "out of his mind" (as I put it to myself) when he labeled Swahili a poor language and even insinuated, by the singular phrase "the African," that such poverty reflected reduced communicative capacities or needs on the part of its speakers. This, as best I can recall, was my first inkling of the insights that would later crystallize in the title of the present study.

Other travelogues and early ethnographic reports of roughly the same period and region as Becker's opened another route that eventually converged with this line of thought. At the time I still had no clear program for systematic research, but my reading evoked an image, diffuse yet lively. There was something curious about a topos, presumably shared by these writers, their contemporary readers, and, I would maintain, most present-day readers as well, a topos that was to become emblematic for the history of exploration in the last third of the nineteenth century: that of the encounter between a European explorer, the intrepid leader of an expeditionary caravan and emissary of science, and the African chief, a local ruler (real or presumed) cast in the role of a representative of his society and culture and invariably identified as either a political friend or foe of European penetration. In numerous instances—sometimes explicitly noted, sometimes to be inferred from descriptions—the African potentate appeared in a state of more or less advanced inebriation, caused by drinking vast quantities of beer, palm wine, or mead and occasionally made worse (or better?) by smoking hemp. But what about his European guest? Though I cannot cite from the sources anything that would directly correspond to the reported states of African rulers (after all, explorers would not be likely to depict themselves in such a fashion), there is overwhelming indirect evidence that European travelers seldom met their hosts in a state we would expect of scientific explorers: clear-minded and self-controlled. More often than not, they too were "out of their minds" with extreme fatigue, fear, delusions of grandeur, and feelings ranging from anger to contempt. Much of the time they were in the thralls of "fever" and other tropical diseases, under the influence of alcohol or opiates (laudanum, a tincture of alcohol and opium, was the principal drug used to control acute and chronic dysentery), high doses of quinine, arsenic, and other ingredients from the expedition's medicine chest. Luc de Heusch's *roi ivre* took on new meaning for me,[3] and I thought there might be interesting material in these travelogues for a paper to be titled "Travel as Tripping."

As my initial enthusiasm about this discovery subsided—I began to doubt that I could come up with more than a somewhat sensationalist, muckraking, but in the end negligible piece—I kept mulling over possible wider implications. By 1990, I had collected my thoughts sufficiently to present them in a paper (unpublished) that was also a proposal for research. Here, assembled from my notes, is the gist of the emerging project: in popular as well as traditional scholarly opinion, the encounters that took place during European expansion were exemplary enactments of our civilization. They were guided by self-denying missionary zeal and philanthropic compassion, as well as by a taste for travel and adventure, often combined with scientific curiosity. To be sure, the motives that brought individual travelers to Africa must be judged against a collective background that entailed territorial expansion, the pursuit of military power, commercial greed, and the need to find raw materials and investment opportunities for accumulated capital—not to mention the demands of an emerging "media industry" in search of stories to sell.

In all these explanations, the terms and the nature of the encounters with those about to be colonized are supposedly determined by motives and goals contained in (and therefore controlled by) faith and reason, as well as political and economic imperatives. This "containment" makes for histories of precolonial or colonial encounter that are predictable, their conclusions inescapable. As a result, the history of Western expansion becomes a celebration of said motives and goals, even in the writings of those who criticize, on moral or political grounds, the blatant misuses of power that were the soul of imperialism. As we have come to realize, many condemnations of imperialism have been predicated on acknowledgment of its success.

One strategy adopted in recent years to counteract that self-fulfilling prophecy is to accumulate evidence for resistance to conquest and to write about that. This is a necessary task, and much more needs to be done to carry it out.[4] But what will such efforts show? That imperialism was weaker than the image it liked to project, or less organized, or less rational? That the colonized reacted, survived, hung on? In that case, what We assert about Them is still but a function of what we assert about ourselves. Even if we can point to deception, misrepresentation, and perhaps blindness in these encounters of exploration, conquest, and exploitation, that is not likely to shake in any fundamental way the belief in the basic rationality, and hence necessity, of Western expansion.

A truly radical critique needs to address the very concept of rationality, especially the built-in tendency of that concept to present itself as outside and above historical contexts. To this end, I would like to pursue another strategy, showing that the actual encounters that paved the way for imperial rule or established it in embryonic form were often inherently contradictory—indeed, anarchic—so much so that their true nature had to be concealed or, better, negated by projecting to the world images of a purposeful *oeuvre civilisatrice*: intrepid explorers mapping the unknown; saintly missionaries offering their lives for the salvation of pagans; heroic military men vanquishing an enemy that always outnumbered them; unselfish administrators toiling for the public good; and so forth. This colonial hagiography cannot simply be dismissed as pious legend. It represents a discourse that must be interpreted by reading it backward—from the rationalizations and glorifications to that which was thought to be in need of rationalization and glorification.

Intrepid, heroic, courageous: these were but some of the obligatory adjectives preceding the noun *explorer.* In the illustrations of travelogues, those verbal flourishes parallel pictorial ones: the traveler's quasi-military garb, his faraway gaze, his proud and determined posture. He rides or walks ahead of his caravan; a few porters and guards are recognizable, while the rest blend into a file that gets smaller and smaller until it disappears in the landscape. In these representations of explorers, traces of which we all have stored in our childhood memories (well, all of us above a certain age), the myth of science as an arduous battle for victory over self and nature has been condensed and concentrated; it is always available for consumption in a diluted form. The myth of scientific exploration, inasmuch as it supports our concept of ethnography, has come to us as an extract as well as an abstract of the experiences and practices it invokes. As an abstraction, the myth is in need of the kind of critique that addresses the limits and faults of representation; it calls for deconstructive literary analysis. As an extract, the myth contains "active ingredients" whose potency continues to affect modern ideas and practices of ethnography. It needs, if I may extend the pharmaceutical metaphor, an antidote, one distilled not from presumedly superior "modern" ethnography but from a contemporary counterstory—one contained in the accounts of scientific travel and exploration we are about to consider.[5]

In describing the myth, I may of course have projected my own preconceptions and stereotypes of African exploration. I acquired them, as many educated people have, through the powerful images created and widely circulated in travelogues and the countless rehearsals of these images in literature, art, and the media, as well as through mindless repetition of opinions about the impact of travel and exploration on the formation of anthropology. Recent critical discussion and revision in the literature on colonial travel brought certain doubts into focus and convinced me that an epistemological history of ethnography will prove essential to our understanding of the role of anthropology in the coming century, and of the need for its continued existence.[6]

Mary Louise Pratt prefaces her critical study of imperial travel writing with a personal story, much as I have done here. She recollects the image and myth of Livingstone with which she grew up in her family and speaks of the "redundancy, discontinuity, and unreality" of such images in the literature on travel. The present study joins hers and other recent efforts to overcome the "numbing repetition" of stereotypes. I agree with Pratt's description of what needs to be done.

> The effort must be, among other things, an exercise in humility. For one of the things it brings most forcefully into play are the contestatory expressions from the site of imperial intervention, long ignored in the metropolis; the critique of empire, coded ongoingly on the spot, in ceremony, dance, parody, philosophy, counterknowledge and counterhistory, in texts unwitnessed, suppressed, lost, or simply overlain with repetition and unreality. (1992, 2)

My approach differs in a few ways. I emphasize contradiction rather than contestation, though the two are of course related, and I do cite many examples of resistance. My aim is also more limited, because I address my critique to anthropology and, within anthropology, to ethnography, which is but one of the practices that originated with "imperial intervention." And I have certain reservations about adopting two of Pratt's theoretical concepts, "transculturation" and the "contact zone." Still, I hope that our efforts will be perceived as complementary.

There is a consensus among cultural anthropologists that ethnography, as empirical research that produces knowledge, justifies our claims to the status of an academic discipline. Modern practices of ethnography were developed from premises, activities, and conventions that guided scientific travel and exploration in the late nineteenth century. I do not subscribe to the widespread opinion that Bronislaw Malinowski instituted fieldwork as an obligatory practice. Others had carried out research in situ before him, and much of his theoretical orientation derived from the positivism inspired by Auguste Comte or Herbert Spencer, figures influential to the generation of explorers who preceded academic anthropologists.

Leszek Kolakowski (1969) characterized the classical, positivist understanding of science that also informed scientific exploration as "a collection of prohibitions concerning human knowledge" (9), expressing a "normative attitude" (2) that can be summed up in four rules.

1. The rule of phenomenalism: "We are entitled to record only that which is actually manifested in experience" (3).[7]

2. The rule of nominalism, stipulating that "we may not assume that any insight formulated in general terms can have any real refer-

ents other than concrete objects" (5). Thus conceived, knowledge production is essentially classification—Foucault's "taxonomic" episteme.

3. The rule *"that denies cognitive value to value judgments and normative statements"* (7; original emphasis). In my understanding, this proscription would also apply to what I will call ecstatic elements in the production of knowledge.

4. The rule expressing belief in the "essential *unity of the scientific method,"* that is, "the belief that methods for acquiring valid knowledge, and the main stages in elaborating experience through theoretical reflection, are essentially the same in all spheres of experience" (8).

Travel began to serve ethnography more directly to the extent that the latter became methodologized and professionalized, a development studied in depth and detail by Justin Stagl (1995). Trips and voyages turned into expeditions (a term that, after anthropology was recognized academically, coexisted for a long time with "fieldwork"). The professional travelers we call explorers were among those whose practices established modes of knowledge production (and of knowledge representation) that continue to inform present-day conceptions and practices of field research. This connection between travelers and anthropologists, however, is seldom stated and hardly ever analyzed; when touched upon, it is often dismissed by positing clear distinctions that never existed.

In the travelogue—the genre that preceded, often contained, and sometimes paralleled the ethnographic monograph—scientific travelers cultivated images of themselves and of the pursuit of scientific knowledge that appealed to a wide public. Typically, the traveler was depicted as an individual, often solitary, agent, fully in control of himself and others. Psychologically, morally, and intellectually, he was equipped to carry out the assigned task, unless impeded or prevented by persons, events, or conditions beyond his control. Self-control required "other-control," which above all meant maintaining distance from the country to be explored and its people. This distance was kept with the help of varying amounts of protective equipment and varying degrees of withdrawal. Self-control called for "abnegation," an ascetic virtue, fueled by the knowledge that exploration in all its respects must be subject to the norms and injunctions of science. To cite but one of many modern examples of such an ascetic stance, here is how Claude Lévi-Strauss put it in *Tristes tropiques:* "To get to that which is real it is necessary first to repudiate lived experience, though it may later on be reintegrated in an objective synthesis stripped of all sentimentality" (1955, 63).

Taking a view diametrically opposed to Lévi-Strauss's, I hope to demonstrate that, especially in their first or early contacts with unfamiliar cultures, the emissaries of imperialism got to "that which is real" when they permitted themselves to be touched by lived experience. More often than not, those instances involved them in quandaries and contradictions, in moral puzzles and conflicting demands. What I find striking, and worthy of much more attention than it is usually given, is that explorers frequently overcame these intellectual and existential problems by stepping outside, and sometimes existing for long periods outside, the rationalized frames of exploration, be they faith, knowledge, profit, or domination. This "stepping outside" or "being outside" is what I call the ecstatic. In German, my first language and the one that intrudes whenever I struggle with the philosophical meaning of concepts, we have phrases like *außer sich sein,* "to be beside oneself," and *aus sich herausgehen,* which my dictionary translates as "to come out of one's shell." They elaborate further the meaning I am after: ecstasis can be an act as well as a state.

To avoid getting lost in a cloud of connotations, let me give some precision to the concept by rejecting most of the current meaning of ecstasy as nonrational, erratic, escapist, perhaps enthusiastic behavior (such as that described in, say, studies of cults and movements). Ecstasis, I shall assume, is not so much a kind of behavior but a dimension or quality of human action and interaction—one that creates a common ground for the encounters that will be the subject of this study. Unlike empathy (a concept frequently evoked in reflections on ethnographic fieldwork), ecstasis is neither a moral quality nor a psychological attitude; it is an epistemological concept. In the context of exploration, ecstasis was a "condition of possibility" for the meetings between Europeans and Africans to result in anything more than physical collision. Ecstasis, in a nontrivial understanding of the term, is (much like subjectivity) a prerequisite for, rather than an impediment to, the production of ethnographic knowledge.

In recent anthropology there has been much criticism of the disembodied scientific mind. The importance of gender has been recognized; senses other than vision have, as it were, been rehabilitated, emotions have received attention, and the body as a site of knowledge has been rediscovered. In the perspective opened up by these developments, a critical study of the objective conditions that determined knowledge of the Other as reported in travelogues and early ethnographies must consider the effects of alcohol, drugs, illness, sex, brutality, and terror, as well as the role of conviviality, friendship, play, and performance. Included in this approach are the sounds, movements, and objects that made up performances—music, dance, art, material culture, whatever mediated encounters and made it possible for the participants to transcend their psychological and social boundaries. Not only do the travelogues we shall examine offer plentiful documentation of all these elements, they also contain surprisingly articulate statements regarding their significance.

PROBLEMS OF PRESENTATION

In 1990–91 I enjoyed the luxury of a stay at the Getty Center for the History of Art and the Humanities, including a part-time research assistant who kept me supplied with books from libraries in the Los Angeles area. By the end of that year I had read thousands of pages, accumulated hundreds of pages of notes and excerpts, and established a list of topics and key words. At that point, however, I had to set the study aside to work on another book (Fabian 1996), and only in 1996 could I finally close the remaining gaps in my reading of the sources. It occurred to me then that I had spent at least as much time on this undertaking as on previous field research projects and the resulting publications. But for all the reading done, all the exciting ideas recorded, all the carefully organized notes, and all the opportunities I'd had to test the material in lectures and conversations, I had never before run into comparable problems in envisaging the shape of the book to be written.

Eventually I had to fall back on setting down a preliminary table of contents. I managed to find a sequence for the topics that were important and capable of bringing together what was dispersed in the sources. My account would move from description to analysis to critical reflection. But then I began to doubt whether filling those rubrics with prose would serve my intentions. What, I asked myself, would prevent this study from becoming just another book on travel? It could only be the evidence of ecstasis in exploration, of lack of control, of an inability to follow plans and carry out schemes, as well as a capacity to go beyond plans and schemes. How can the ecstatic in the making of knowledge be given a fitting literary form?

Since I am not a writer gifted with, say, Michael Taussig's knack for collage,[8] I had to consider other possibilities. A tempting one, given the wealth of material, was to divide my presentation between an account of proto-ethnographic knowledge processes in the positivist-ascetic vein and a counterstory made up of striking instances of ecstasis. In the end I made limited use of this strategy, realizing that alternation between examples and counterexamples would quickly grow old and essentially reduce the argument to anecdote.

Another possibility was to search for "proof" that the very accounts these explorers gave of their endeavors contradicted, in fact destroyed, the myths of objective science and its ascetic servants. The elements of the myth would generate the topics, beliefs, and assertions to be disposed of one after the other. However, though debunking myths is what critical analysis tries to achieve and is also one of my goals in this project, it is not all that I hope to accomplish.

My larger goal is to use the exploration of central Africa as a historical detour toward critical reflection on the processes of ethnographic knowledge. To that end, I strive to lead the reader through the past without compromising the primacy of the epistemological critique addressed to the present. The connection between history and epistemology (a dangerous one if we remember the positivist tenet that a science is legitimated by the history of its successes) is perhaps best understood if we accept that a discipline, in order to be critical of itself, needs a history not only of its findings but also of its ways of searching, that is, of the practices of knowledge production and presentation. That this latter history should, in this case, resemble an ethnographic treatise was inevitable. Much of ethnographic writing, starting with the travelogues we examine, has been presented, though rarely directly, as responses to research questions set down in such authoritative works as the famous *Notes and Queries*. A critical, historical study formulating notes and queries on an ethnography that was inspired by *Notes and Queries* probably cannot avoid resembling the target of its critique.[9]

Beneath superficial resemblances is a more fundamental issue: the dialectical nature of ethnographic knowledge. Before I began to write the present study, I had argued in an essay on ethnographic mis- and non-understanding that we must acknowledge negativity as a condition of knowledge, as a subject of critical reflection on knowledge, and as an element in the (re)construction of processes and practices of knowledge production (Fabian 1995). Every positive assertion about science and knowledge should be confronted with its negations and contradictions; every feat of science with defeat; every gain with loss.

Yet to show this negative dialectic at work is but the first step toward a more important aim. Positivists will admit defeat and loss; what they will not accept is the presence and inevitability of the ecstatic in our practices of knowledge production: the necessity of being out of our minds as well as being in control of our aims and methods. I anticipate the objection that nowadays positivism is, if anything, a straw man; an adversary stuffed and sewn by the opponent and therefore no adversary at all. Still, in intellectual debates we always address adversaries not so much as they are but as we construe them; that is the difference between discursive and real fights. Setting up straw men is how we get arguments going. The more I think about vital questions regarding the history of my discipline—especially its connections with colonialist and imperialist politics—the closer the links become between positivist conceptions of science and imperialism. If I am fighting a straw man, this is a formidable one.[10]

THE TEXTS

The selection of texts was guided by themes that grew out of my reading and subsequently refined by narrowing the geographical area and the historical period to be covered. I decided early on not to include authors such as Livingstone, Cameron, Stanley, Schweinfurth, Nachtigal, and Emin Pasha, whose lives and works are covered by many popular and scholarly biographies and secondary studies. I sought out travelogues off the beaten path, works that are known, if at all, only to specialists. Becker's account (1887) was my first, purely serendipitous find; I was struck by the wealth of information it conveyed and the literary quality it displayed. When I mentioned my discovery to a Belgian colleague, he directed my attention to a book that is in many respects a companion piece.[11] Its author is Camille Coquilhat (1888), whose intelligence, sensitivity, and flair for writing—reminiscent of Joseph Conrad—rival Becker's (Coquilhat and Becker were contemporaries and mutual admirers).

I then took up the writings of German explorers of central Africa: Paul Pogge (1880), Curt von François (1888), Hermann Wissmann (1889, [1890], 1891), and Wissmann and his associates (1891). A valuable help in sorting out the connections among German expeditions, as well as those between German and Belgian endeavors, was the complete series of *Mittheilungen der afrikanischen Gesellschaft in Deutschland* (hereafter *MAGD*), published by the African Society in Germany, the sponsor of most of these expeditions. *MAGD* appeared between 1878 and 1889, when the society was dissolved. Only after I had completed a first draft of this study did the travelogues of three contributors to *MAGD* (Büttner 1890, Schütt 1881, and Wolff 1889) and the posthumously published letters of a fourth (Böhm 1888) become available to me. Therefore, most of the quotations from their reports come from *MAGD* rather than from those books.[12] Leo Frobenius (1907) and Emil Torday (1913, 1925) are the most recent authors in my selection. Torday and his companion M. W. Hilton-Simpson (1911) were included because their travels partially overlapped with those of Frobenius and Wissmann and could not have been undertaken without approval and support from the Congo Free State.

Intrigued by Becker's extraordinarily harsh rejection of Joseph Thomson's two-volume travelogue (1881), I eventually added that work to my list. Thomson had joined a British expedition sponsored by the Royal Geographical Society.[13] It was nevertheless connected to the Belgian and German operations as an attempt not to be outdone in the work of exploration. Thomson was twenty-four when his expedition returned— gloriously, as we are told. His is in many ways the freshest of the accounts, full of interesting observations reported without guile; his youthful impetuousness and Scots radicalism made him come up with statements that need to be taken with more than a grain of salt, yet I found myself wanting to excerpt entire pages. When the draft of this study was almost completed, I decided to pick some of the most striking passages, which I now present, without direct comment, as epigraphs throughout the book.

I also include Hermingildo Capelo and Roberto Ivens (1882), whose account resembles Thomson's in many respects. Their expedition was organized to safeguard Portuguese interests in view of German activities in the area, and their travel routes crossed those of several authors in our corpus. Their travelogue contains a wealth of eminently quotable statements and observations. I refer to it occasionally and quote a few irresistible excerpts.

With few exceptions, the texts I have chosen have not been available in English. Extensive quotations, in my own translation, will make at least fragments of these sources accessible to English-speaking readers.

The mainly Belgian and German sources that are the focus of this study cover an area that became the target of exploration during a distinctive period. Sponsorship by the International African Association and its German affiliate gave the various expeditions an institutional focus (more about this in chapter 2). This is not to say that these sources cover all exploratory activities that went on in that area during the thirty years between roughly 1878 and 1908. I do not include several reports by marginal or temporary members of German-sponsored expeditions (Lux 1880 and Soyaux 1879; both authors briefly traveled with Pogge) or books published by individual travelers who had little or no connection with the activities reported in the main corpus (for instance, Casati 1891; Chavanne 1887; Dupont 1889; Mecklenburg 1909; and Wiese 1983 [originally in Portuguese, 1891]). Nor do I include, with the exception of Coquilhat, authors whose main activities were military, commercial, or administrative (such as Alexandre Delcommune, who devotes nearly a thousand pages to these themes in his 1922 memoir). By the same token I exclude literature on the "exploration" of Katanga whose real purpose was breaking resistance to the incorporation of that area into the Congo Free State.

Since my critique of ethnography in its early manifestations is also a historical study, I have taken care to respect historiographic standards. However, for practical reasons alone, I was unable to cover two kinds of sources that historians would normally consult. One consists of the vast and diffuse material found in contributions by these authors to newspapers and illustrated magazines of the period; the other is the private correspondence and the unpublished diaries and expedition logs preserved in German and Belgian colonial archives. Though I did not consult these sources directly, the authors made use of their letters and especially their diaries when they wrote their travelogues. In some instances, often amounting to substantial parts of a travelogue, they state that they are simply copying their journals, letters, lectures, and other documents.

To concentrate on published, widely circulated travelogues implies a generic choice, which in this case amounts to what philologists used to call a *lectio dificilior,* a "more difficult reading" that makes a virtue of the shortcomings of a corpus of texts.[14] Presumably, much of the information I am after—especially evidence for the uncontrolled, ecstatic aspects of ethnographic knowledge production—that might be found in unpublished letters and diaries would have been filtered out of travelogues addressing a popular readership. It is hard to tell how much censorship was formally exercised by those who sponsored exploration, but that it existed, given the fact that these travelers were also in the business of gathering political, economic, and military intelligence, cannot be doubted. To such outside control we must add self-imposed restrictions, which reveal themselves when we compare what different writers wrote of the same expedition. That a wealth of often astounding information nevertheless passed all these filters can only strengthen the arguments I intend to build on these sources.

TIMES AND SPACES

Ranging from the last quarter of the nineteenth through the first decade of the twentieth century, the sources cover an important period in the exploration of central Africa. In 1873 the Deutsche Gesellschaft zur Erforschung des äquatorialen Afrikas (German society for the exploration of equatorial Africa) was founded. Perhaps the most influential promoter of this organization was the German ethnologist Adolf Bastian, who had written about his travels to the center of the old Kongo kingdom as early as 1859 and would also publish in 1874 the first substantial report on German exploration of the Loango coast. The next important date was 1876, the year when Leopold II of Belgium convened the Geographical Conference of Brussels, attended by eminent travelers and presidents of geographical societies, as well as several important financiers, from most major European countries. The announced purpose of the conference was to pool existing knowledge about Africa and promote the gathering of new knowledge. The published declaration, however, defined the goals more concretely. An organization was to be created "to attain the goal of the Brussels conference, that is, to scientifically explore the unknown parts of Africa, to facilitate the opening of routes along which civilization can penetrate the interior of the African continent, and to seek means to suppress the black slave trade in Africa" (*Exploration* 1 [1876]: 4–5).

The most palpable and consequential result of the meeting was the founding of the International African Association (hereafter IAA). When this organization was first proposed at the Brussels conference, its awkward but more revealing name was Association internationale pour réprimer la traite et ouvrir l'Afrique centrale: the international association to curb the slave trade and open central Africa. With headquarters in Brussels and national committees in many European countries as well as in the United States, the IAA ostensibly served to raise funds and coordinate the many projects of exploration that were planned or under way, so as to avoid conflict and duplication, and generally facilitate travel through the establishment of what the king in his invitation had called *stations hospitalières, scientifiques et pacificatrices*—hospitable, scientific, and pacifying stations. In the resolutions of the conference the third adjective was discreetly omitted; it was too early to name ulterior goals openly.[15]

A few months after the Brussels conference, still in 1876, a German affiliate of the IAA was founded under the name Deutsche Afrikanische Gesellschaft (German African society). Since this society and the Deutsche Gesellschaft zur Erforschung des äquatorialen Afrikas shared members of the board and were pursuing similar goals, they merged in 1878 to become the Afrikanische Gesellschaft in Deutschland (African society in Germany). The new entity proclaimed central Africa, especially the Congo Basin, the target of its operations. Both the IAA and the German association sponsored German travelers to the region—a confused situation reflecting the increasing intensity of the "scramble for Africa."

During the Berlin Conference of 1884–85, the IAA mutated into the Congo Free State, and the imperial powers named much of East Africa between the coast and the Great Lakes, as well as parts of West and Southwest Africa, German colonial possessions. In 1887, citing the fact that the conditions of research had changed with "the German Empire becoming active in African politics," the Afrikanische Gesellschaft in Deutschland decided to dissolve itself. The decision became valid by imperial decree in early 1889.[16] Finally, in 1908, the Congo Free State, up to then a private possession of King Leopold II, became a colony of Belgium.[17]

All the principal sources reported activities during the period just described, but not all their expeditions were covered in the travelogues I selected. One of the most difficult tasks in preparing for this study was getting a reasonably clear picture of the trajectory of all major expeditions, of their duration, and of their leadership (which changed often, because of high mortality among the travelers; see the appendix). Though this book examines only travel documented in substantial travelogues (and in reports to *MAGD,* a quasi-official bulletin of central African exploration), references in our sources show that aside from officially sponsored expeditions, there was "heavy traffic" in central Africa. Travelers of all sorts—private scholars and artists, adventurers and hunters, traders and nonaffiliated missionaries, not to mention literate Arabs,[18] Indians, Africans, and perhaps others—might have left records I did not consult.

In a narrow sense of the term, the central Africa that was to be explored was practically identical with the Congo Basin. It became the de-

clared target of operations at a time when some of the geographical rid-
dles that had occupied learned societies and the public around the middle of the century—the sources of the Nile and the location of the Great
Lakes—had been solved by explorers, before the beginning of our designated period. The travels of Richard Burton and John Hanning Speke,
Georg August Schweinfurth, David Livingstone, and Gustav Nachtigal
had shown that the center of Africa was accessible from the north as well
as the south. Verney Lovett Cameron's expedition and Henry Morton
Stanley's tour de force proved that the continent could be crossed from
east to west. They also marked a shift in motivating exploration,[19] with
geographic curiosity overshadowed by political and economic imperial
interests. Exploration of unmapped space turned from a universalist project into the pursuit of knowledge in the service of European nation-states
(closely watched and often supported by the United States).[20] Leopold,
whose true intentions did not become public for a few years, was extremely clever to stage his conference as a pooling of intelligence and a
spectacle of peaceful collaboration among nations. Obviously, this national orientation would affect the perception of space for exploration
and its demarcation; it also encouraged the glowing patriotism our authors often displayed.

But the national orientation had a deeper significance as well. As we
know from the history of anthropology and sociology, two theoretical
paradigms dominated scientific thought in the latter part of the nineteenth century. Most vociferous was evolutionism, which ostensibly provided the foundation for a universalist, natural-history approach to human diversity; less obvious, but equally pervasive, was the consolidation
of nation-states, reflected in the emerging modern theories of culture and
society. Geographic space to be discovered and explored turned into a
laboratory in which scientific assumptions were to be tested, as well as
into a territory that was to be occupied. That both the laboratory and
the territory had to be desired and imagined before they were "opened
up," as it was put at the time, accounts for the peculiar mixture of fact
and fiction that characterizes our sources. It is important for a dialectical understanding to realize that, notwithstanding all the protestations
to the effect that the light of science was to remove the darkness of fiction about central Africa, the tension between imagination and observation, between desire and disinterested research, between devotion to
ideals and the pursuit of pragmatic goals, had to be maintained if exploration was to be initiated and carried out. It was as a catch basin of
all these features—personal, scientific, economic, and political—not just

as a geomorphological feature, that the Congo Basin can be said to have defined the space for exploration that united the various accounts we will examine.

The image of a space that was simply there to be entered was, of course, part of the myth of exploration. Yet even public calls for support of African exploration—for instance, those issued by the German societies in 1873 and again in 1878—contradicted this image.[21] They signaled the need to break the "tough resistance" this continent had put up to European attempts at penetration. The authors of the first call went so far as to state that Europeans themselves were in part responsible for the obstacles to exploration and that their ignorance of Africa was self-inflicted: "It would be an honorable task for our time, and its humanist aspirations, to regain knowledge that was lost for Europe through the slave trade, its heaviest guilt. And wherever such goals were to be reached, the German people have always stood in the first line" (Bastian 1874–75, 1:xi).

Such was the power of the metaphor of the basin, a vessel waiting to be filled, that the notion of central Africa as an empty space that had only to be reached in order to be put on the map could nonetheless be sold to the European public. The enterprise of exploration was ridden with contradictions even before it really got under way. When it did, the protagonists of our story came to realize sooner or later—though they dearly wanted to believe in the myths that had made them volunteer for African exploration—that "the interior" had remained mythical and unknown for so long because of political rather than merely geographical reasons. Acting quite rationally, African (and to some extent Arab-Swahili) populations and their rulers had brought trade between the interior and the coasts under their control. Naturally, they resisted what they recognized as attempts by Europeans to break their monopoly on trade and communication with areas of economic interest in the interior. Central African geography was geopolitics, a fact already expressed by the Brussels conference when it declared the Arab slave trade a crime to be fought in the service of humanity.

DRAMATIS PERSONAE

In the chapters that follow I will rely heavily on quotations from the sources. The reader will be confronted with and perhaps—until the protagonists' statements and my comments bring them into focus—confused by the names of a score of travelers. To introduce them, I add a list with brief biographical information for each, compiled from standard sources (among them obituaries in *MAGD*, entries in *Deutsches Coloniallexikon, Biographie coloniale belge,* Essner 1985, and Heintze 1999).[22]

Bastian, Adolf (b. Bremen, June 26, 1826; d. Port-of-Spain, Trinidad, February 3, 1905). A physician and later professor of ethnology at the University of Berlin and director of the Royal Museum of Ethnology, which he helped found. In 1851–59 he traveled around the world as a ship's surgeon (in Africa visiting the Congo and São Salvador), and in 1861–65 he undertook scientific travels in Asia. He founded the Deutsche Gesellschaft zur Erforschung des äquatorialen Afrikas in 1873 and was a mentor and sponsor of German exploration of central Africa. He resumed his travels in 1873, first to the Loango coast and then to the Americas, the islands of the Pacific, Australia, Southeast Asia, and finally the West Indies, where he died. A prolific writer and major theoretician, he was one of the outstanding anthropologists of the nineteenth century.

Becker, Jérôme (b. Calmthout, August 21, 1850; d. Antwerp, April 30, 1912). A lieutenant transferred to the Institute of Military Cartography. In 1880, as a member of the IAA Third Expedition, he departed for the first of three stays in Africa. He returned to Belgium in 1883 but left for Zanzibar that same year to lead the IAA Fifth Expedition. In mid-1885 he resigned his command for health reasons. In 1888 he traveled to the lower Congo as an agent of the Congo Free State. Appointed a liaison officer with Hamed bin Mohammed el Murjebi (called Tipo Tip), he remained loyal to his Arab-Swahili friends when the Belgians embarked on their anti-Arab campaign. He fell into disgrace with the authorities and left their service to explore on his own, accompanied by Arab friends, reaching the area north of the Uele River before returning to Europe in 1890. During the following decade he traveled widely to North Africa, America, and the West Indies, but his later years were clouded by accusations of financial misconduct and of the attempted murder of his much-admired commander Captain Jules Ramaeckers; he was exonerated by a military tribunal. He died in Antwerp from cerebral bleeding after a fall.

Böhm, Richard (b. Berlin, October 1, 1854; d. "Katapäne in Urua," March 27, 1884). A zoologist and specialist in ornithology, he received his doctorate at the University of Jena under the theoretician of evolution Ernst Haeckel. Recruited by the famous explorer Gustav

Nachtigal, he became a member of the German East African Expedition in 1880. A bullet wound incurred during a punitive expedition organized from the Belgian station Karema became badly infected, and he took months to recuperate. He then joined Paul Reichard on a trip to northern Katanga, where he died of fever.

Buchner, Max (b. Munich, April 25, 1846; d. Munich, May 7, 1921). He began his travels as a ship's surgeon. In 1878–81 he headed the German expedition to the Lunda; after 1884 he had a short colonial career in Togo and Cameroon. In 1887 he was named director of the Ethnological Museum in Munich. Conflicts with his superiors and problems of health led to his early retirement in 1907.

Büttner, Richard (b. Brandenburg an der Havel, September 28, 1858; place and exact date of death unknown [1928–35]). Trained as a botanist and mineralogist, he traveled in the lower Congo between 1884 and 1886 as a member of the German Congo Expedition. In 1890–91 he headed a research station in Togo. Afterward he became a secondary school teacher in Berlin.

Capelo, Hermingildo do Carlos de Brito (b. Palmela, Portugal, 1841; d. Lisbon, May 4, 1917). As a naval officer he participated in various expeditions to Angola, Mozambique, Guinea, and China. With Roberto Ivens, and for some of the time with Alexandre de Serpa Pinto, he was a member of expeditions to explore the Congo-Zambesi watershed (1877–79 and 1884–85). He later worked in cartography and served three Portuguese kings as aide-de-camp.

Coquilhat, Camille (b. Liège, October 15, 1853; d. Boma, March 24, 1891). A lieutenant who, like Becker, was transferred to the Institute of Military Cartography, he joined the Upper Congo Expedition in 1882. He founded and served at several stations along the river and accompanied Stanley to the Bangala. He returned to Europe in 1885 but went back to the Congo the following year to lead a relief force to the embattled station of Stanley Falls. Wounded upon arrival, he grew ill on the way back and returned to Europe to recuperate and write his book. He traveled in Switzerland and Egypt and became a close collaborator of King Leopold II. In 1890 he returned to the Congo as vice-governor-general; he died a year later at Boma.

François, Curt von (b. Luxembourg, December 2, 1852; d. Berlin, December 1931). A lieutenant and member of the Wissmann expedition of 1883–85. In 1888 he led an imperial expedition to explore the Togo hinterland and in 1889 served as commander of the *Schutztruppen* (colonial forces). Until his retirement from the colonial service in 1895, he was a leading figure in crushing African resistance in German Southwest Africa (today's Namibia).

Frobenius, Leo (b. Berlin, June 29, 1873; d. Biganzolo, Italy, August 9, 1938). A largely self-educated ethnographer, he worked at several ethnographic museums before leading twelve expeditions to Africa, the first to the Congo Free State in 1904–6 with the artist Hans Martin Lemme. A successful fund-raiser and friend of influential people (among them the former kaiser Wilhelm II), he created his own research facility, the famed Frobenius-Institut, which was originally planned for Munich but established in Frankfurt am Main. From there he propagated his theories of *Kulturmorphologie* and published a large number of studies. He began teaching at the University of Frankfurt in 1932 and became director of that city's museum of ethnology in 1934.

Ivens, Roberto (b. São Miguel, Azores, June 6, 1850; d. Dafundo, January 28, 1898). As a career officer in the navy, he saw India, São Tomé, and South and North America. He traveled with Capelo through Angola (1877–79) and from Angola to Mozambique (1884–85).

Kaiser, Emil (b. Zerbst, Germany, December 7, 1855; d. Lake Rikwa, November 1882). A topographer and astronomer with a doctorate from the University of Bonn, he was a member of the German East African Expedition.

Pechuël-Loesche, Eduard (b. Zöschen, near Merseburg, July 26, 1840; d. Munich, May 29, 1913). A member of the German Loango expedition (1874–76), initially recruited by Bastian. In 1882–83 he assisted Stanley during the exploration and occupation of the Congo that preceded the establishment of the Congo Free State. After 1886 he had an academic career, retiring for health reasons in 1912 from the University of Erlangen, where he had been a professor of geography.

Pogge, Paul (b. Zierstorf, December 27, 1838; d. São Paulo de Loanda, Angola, March 26, 1884). After law studies and a period managing his parents' farm, in 1865 he went on a hunting trip to Natal and the Cape. He later offered his services as a hunter for an expedition organized by the Deutsche Gesellschaft zur Erforschung des äquatorialen Afrikas. Accepted as a volunteer by Bastian, he arrived with four others in Loanda in February 1875. The commander, Major Alexander von Homeyer, and the others soon returned to Europe for health reasons, and Pogge alone completed the assignment to reach the Lunda capital, returning to Germany in 1876. In 1880 he was back in Africa, accompanied by Wissmann, to head an expedition to found a station at the Lunda capital. Suffering from a painful infection of the jaw, he got as far as Nyangwe on the Lualaba. Wissmann continued to cross the continent while Pogge returned to the station he had founded on the Lulua River. His health forced him to travel back to the coast, where he died before he could leave for Europe.

Reichard, Paul (b. Neuwied, December 2, 1854; place of death unknown, 1920). Trained as an engineer, he joined the German East African Expedition in 1880 as a volunteer, traveling at his own expense. After unsuccessful attempts at establishing scientific stations near Tabora in Tanzania, the expedition directed its activities westward to Lake Tanganyika and beyond, as far as Katanga. Reichard returned as its sole survivor in 1886.

Schütt, Otto H. (b. Husum, Germany, January 6, 1843; place and date of death unknown). A former topographer working in railway construction for the Ottoman Empire, he was recruited by the German association in Aachen (Aix-la-Chapelle) to continue the work of Pogge's first expedition. His 1878–79 expedition, on which he was accompanied by Paul Gierow, almost reached Luba country but had to return under pressure from the Lunda. Back in Europe, he immediately took up service for the Japanese government and left the publication of his travel account to an editor, Paul Lindenberg.

Thomson, Joseph (b. Thornhill, February 1858; d. London, August 2, 1895). He began his 1878 journey to the Great Lakes as the companion of Keith Johnston and, after the latter died, led this expedition sponsored by the Royal Geographical Society. Another trip followed, in 1883–84, to the Masai region and Lake Victoria. In 1885 he traveled on the Niger, in 1888 in southern Morocco, and in 1890–91 in South Africa.

Torday, Emil (b. Torda, Hungary, 1875; d. London, May 9, 1931). While in the service of the Compagnie du Kasai, he first made contact with the British Museum (and his later collaborator and coauthor T. A. Joyce) in 1904. In 1906 he left the company and returned to England, where he organized an expedition sponsored by the British Museum (accompanied by M. W. Hilton-Simpson and the artist Norman Hardy). Returning to England in 1909, he worked on his publications and began to study medicine. During World War I he became an enemy alien and was put under house arrest. He lost his property when his native town became Romanian and he refused to take up citizenship. He died after undergoing surgery.

Wissmann, Hermann (von) (b. Frankfurt an der Oder, September 4, 1853; d. Weissenbach, Austria, June 15, 1905). A lieutenant of the Prussian army, he joined Pogge on his second expedition in 1880–83. When health problems forced Pogge to return to Loanda, Wissmann continued to the east coast, a trip counted as the first crossing of the continent from west to east. In 1883–85 he headed another expedition to explore the Kasai region. He left Africa for health reasons but returned in 1886 to accomplish a second crossing of the continent from west to east in 1887. Afterward he served as imperial commissioner in German East Africa and was a leader in defeating the Bushiri uprising. In 1895–96 he was governor of German East Africa; he retired for reasons of health. He later traveled to Siberia and South Africa and lived as a country squire in Styria, where he died of a self-inflicted wound from a hunting gun. His death was ruled accidental by a court.

Wolf, Ludwig (b. Hagen, January 1850; d. Ndali, Dahomey, June 26, 1889). After traveling for the North German Lloyd as a ship's surgeon, he served as a military physician before joining the 1883–86 Wissmann expedition. He became the expedition's leader in 1885. From 1887 on he was employed in the German colonial service and charged with the exploration of the Togo hinterland. He died of fever or poison on one of his missions.

Wolff, Wilhelm Albert (called Willy) (b. Berlin, March 6, 1852; place and date of death unknown). A member of the German Congo Expedition, 1884–85. After reporting on his trip and his opinions on colonial policy, he seems to have cut his ties with German colonial and ethnological circles. His travelogue was dedicated to King Luís I of Portugal, and he received a Portuguese decoration. He later practiced as an ear, nose, and throat specialist in Berlin.

TWO

Travel, Exploration, and Occupation

A few years ago, when Europe was stirred by the striking adventures of some of our later travellers, Livingstone, Stanley, and Cameron, and united, with royalty at its head, to form an International Association for the opening of Africa, a general belief arose that at last a new era of hope for the Dark Continent had been ushered in. Anticipations of civilizing centres dotted over the length and breadth of its vast area, were held by the most sanguine. Few corners were to be left unveiled. Everything that was good and great in Europe was to be transplanted to African soil, and under the nurturing care of International pioneers to be reared and developed. Travellers and other scientific men were to receive every assistance. Trade was to be introduced and developed; and of course Christianity, of what ever creed, was to be fostered and encouraged.

What has really been the result? Some years have passed, and as yet we have only the sublimely ridiculous spectacle of united Europe knocking its head idiotically against a wall, betraying an utter inability to grapple with the difficulties of the case, and making itself the laughing-stock to the benighted negroes whom it undertook to enlighten. (2:275)

OPERATIONS: THE EXPEDITION

Put as simply as possible, exploratory travel was movement through space. But nothing turns out to have been simple about it as soon as we ask who and what moved (leaving aside for the moment the how and the why). Before and even during the trip, traveling was an operation: personnel, supplies, and equipment had to be recruited, acquired, and put to work. Where can we expect to get a clear picture of the logic and

As noted in the Introduction, all epigraphs are from Thomson 1881. They are cited throughout by volume and page number only.

rationality of travel if not from the logistics of expeditions? Conversely, if the operations defy logic and lack rationality, even in enterprises considered successful, these fundamental flaws mark the first dent in the myth of scientific exploration.

EXPLORERS

> Among the prospective travellers whom we met, the
> most notable of all was a Belgian, full of infinite graces
> and smiles, charmingly dressed, and quite irresistible
> with the ladies, especially when he let forth his soul in
> passionate song. He was further marked by his pro-
> found ignorance, both of the work and the country be-
> fore him. But that was nothing! As he said, his king
> had need of him in his philanthropic and enlightened
> designs for the opening of Africa. His Majesty had
> said, "Go to Zanzibar, and organize a caravan to travel
> in the interior." That was sufficient for him, and with-
> out considering such trivialities as whether he was fit
> for duty or not, he had at once set off. (1:25)

Let us begin with the image of the solitary European leading his caravan. I have already hinted at the probability that this stereotype was if not created then reinforced by the literary genre of the travelogue, whose typically single author inevitably emerges as the protagonist and hero of the story told. We see this same pattern in accounts of expeditions in which two or more Europeans participated (with one remarkable exception, the expedition of Capelo and Ivens, to be discussed in chapter 10). But how does this heroic posture appear when considered in light of the operational planning that preceded and accompanied travel?

The Germans and the Belgians, though united by the charter of the IAA, had different views on what was required, at least in the beginning. The German affiliate stated in its by-laws, under "means to reach the goal," that exploration was to be accomplished "by sending out and supporting scientifically educated travelers, especially solitary travelers [*Einzelreisende*]" (*MAGD*, no. 1 [1878]: 3). Because this position is nowhere explained or argued and was soon abandoned, we can only speculate on its reasons. It is safe to assume that an organization led by the likes of Nachtigal and Bastian, who both epitomized the figure of the great traveler, would have envisaged the future of African exploration as a continuation of past practices. Furthermore, at their inception, the

German sponsoring organizations had a pronounced scientific orientation and could, in the spirit of the time, be expected to have stressed individual scholarship. The German term *Forscher* (or *Afrika-Forscher*)
was less specific than its English and French equivalents, *explorer* and
explorateur. Chemists experimenting in their laboratories and philologists deciphering ancient texts also were *Forscher.*

A little further in the same issue of *MAGD,* however, the challenge of
African travel is said to consist of "breaking resistance." Planning is
therefore described in military language (with talk of "bases of operation" [18]). This blatant contradiction with the image of the solitary traveler devoted to science did not seem to bother those who wrote the general and programmatic statements.

The Belgians paid their tribute to the towering figures of Livingstone
and Stanley but decided to "rationalize" (actually, to militarize) travel
by sending out teams of explorers. Among the members of these expeditions were physicians, scientific specialists, experienced hunters, and
men of great practical experience. They were headed by officers on leave
from the army. Hierarchy, the division of tasks, and the structure of command were well defined when the teams left for Africa. The nomenclature reflected this emphasis on organized collectivity: Belgian expeditions
were usually referred to by numbers (first to fifth), whereas most of the
German ones bore the names of their leaders.

By the time when Becker reported from the IAA Third Expedition
(1880–81), it was clear that the agents of exploration were groups, not
individuals. Because these groups were small and their tasks demanded
that their members remain in close contact, the imperatives of rational
organization often clashed with the dynamics of group life. Conflict man-
agement, in modern parlance, became one of the many responsibilities
of expedition leaders. Early on in his *La vie en Afrique,* Becker admiringly records the admonitions of his superior, Captain Ramaeckers, who
tells his associates of the psychological problems that are bound to arise
when a few Europeans must live together day and night:

> Fatigue, discouragement, illness, and—how shall I put it?—amour propre can
> get you into unfortunate situations of estrangement. Whatever happens must
> be accepted and anticipated. Here is what I propose to write into our partic-
> ular code of travel: at the slightest misunderstanding, at the smallest hard
> word or injury that could lead to an altercation, you have the right to abstain,
> during three days, from any direct communication beyond what the service
> requires. Such a period of time is sufficient for any man who has his heart in
> the right place and is endowed with common sense to examine matters from
> a point of view that will show them in their true light. (1887, 1:52)

Becker's story contains little evidence that the rule was applied much in practice. He quoted it because it appealed to his imagination and allowed him to express his conviction that the harmonious functioning of a team must not be achieved at the expense of the individual, and that the individual must remove the causes of conflict, not by the moral act of obeying a code but by attaining a *véritable point de vue*—that is, by regaining his sense of reality.

Later on we will dwell in more detail on Becker's capacity to live with contradictions. Here I would like to quote two passages from an appendix to his work (a memorandum on "training schools for exploration and colonization" addressed to an international congress on "hygiene and acclimatization" in Berlin). They show that, in spite of (or because of?) his experiences with teamwork, Becker ultimately endorsed the ideal of the solitary traveler. Summing up remarks on the necessity for the traveler to master all sorts of crafts, he states,

> You could almost say that in Africa you need to proceed against the direction taken by our present civilization, in the sense that instead of keeping to the division of labor, you must, on the contrary, bring everything to a practical synthesis. The white man, being far away from European or American amenities, must be self-sufficient in everything that is necessary to assure his settlement, his defense, and his continuance. (2:492–93)

Though this seems merely a practical recommendation, actually Becker is invoking the classic idea that travel to faraway places is time travel into the past. To travel in Africa is to go to where our present civilization came from, socially and culturally, if not geographically. The person who embarks on a journey to Africa must collect and keep together what modernity has rent apart. The whole enterprise is "a utopia," he says, alluding to Fourier. He then comes up with a truly remarkable, in my view epistemological, defense of the individual explorer.

> To the statisticians of science who, from above, delve into questions of exploration and draw general deductions from complex and sparse elements provided to them by simple travelers who sometimes failed to see their significance, many of the observations I bring together [i.e., in this travelogue] without much order may seem useless. But I repeat: in Africa the tiniest detail takes on enormous importance, often overturning all purely theoretical expectations.... On this mysterious continent, which social interest (correctly understood), will, and curiosity drive us to conquer peacefully, everything is matter for personal exploration. (495)

In his influential essay on ethnographic authority, James Clifford attributes a "vision of ethnography as both scientifically demanding and heroic" to a much later time (naming Malinowski, Mead, and Griaule as examples [1988, 30]). Was Becker prophetic, or was he describing the solitary traveler as an already existing role—one that anthropologists would also play when they began to do fieldwork? That by the time Becker made these pronouncements hardly anyone involved in exploration could still believe in peaceful conquest—Becker himself had been involved in armed conflict and military operations—is another of the contradictions that seem to have fed rather than destroyed the myth of the scientific traveler.

When Ramaeckers spoke of a code of travel, he had in mind individual standards, not a public set of regulations, since there was none beyond the recommendations dispersed in the many manuals of travel that circulated at the time.[1] Still, the notion of a code reflects an incipient professionalization of travel (a process obviously relevant to the emergence of professional ethnography). This trend is most apparent when our authors feel the need to define their activities in contrast to those of other Europeans who roamed Africa at the time.

Again, Becker gives one of the most explicit statements on the professionalization of travel (and incidentally confirms our thesis on mythical images). He formulates a typology of the explorer that deserves our full attention:

> There are first the intrepid travelers, following an irresistible calling, relying on instinct, who forge ahead and never shy away from an obstacle, as if they believed themselves invulnerable. Those are the demigods, who, though they often become martyrs by their generous daring, like Prometheus in Greek myth, shine eternally in the Pantheon of Science.
>
> Then come those who simply by nature are enterprising and curious, have a passion for struggle, and are infatuated with the Unknown. What they seek in faraway places are emotions or new spectacles; among them are both the daredevil and the artist, but we are indebted to them for valuable information.
>
> Then there is the man of ambition, who wants to amount to something, and the social loser who is not content with being nothing.
>
> Finally, we have the soldier, the seaman, and the merchant, persons who don't care about danger and who, by their constitution and profession, have confidence in their star.
>
> I do not include in this list the simple adventurer, motivated by personal interest, who, as a sort of bandit of progress, seeks accreditation from whatever flag as a shield for his dubious operations.
>
> In sum, what we have is not recruitment based on selection but many active, determined volunteers, often just fortunate. There are very few true travelers, ones who combine the complex aptitudes that only a reasoned and complete system of education could develop. (1887, 2:495–96)

While advocating the professionalization of travel, Becker still clung to the image of the heroic traveler. Some of the most telling expressions of the ideal of selfless heroism may be found in his long refutation of Thomson's acerbic attacks on IAA operations, whereby Belgian travelers were "wandering like lost sheep in the wilderness, paralyzed by fevers, deserted by their men, in trouble with the natives, and plundered by their own porters" (Thomson 1881, 1:40; see Becker 1887, 2:109–35). The impression we get from Becker's bungled defense of what did after all turn out to be a bungled oeuvre is that these IAA people had to dream of heroism and selfless abnegation; otherwise they could never have kept working for an enterprise whose lies and contradictions they were too intelligent to overlook.

Becker gained his experience on expeditions that started from the east coast. His colleague and fellow officer Coquilhat, who was part of operations starting on the west coast, likewise conveys a process of professionalization in his opinions on the traveler. In the conclusions to his work he points to the limits of exploration. Even in the late phase about which he reports (the few years preceding the establishment of the Congo Free State, in 1885), only about a twentieth of the territory to which he was assigned was explored, in the sense of actually being inspected and controlled. Therefore, "the reader has an idea of the embarrassment felt by travelers when they have to respond to questions of minute detail that are posed to them when they return to Europe" (1888, 470). With unusual candor he admits his own limitations: "The longer I lived in a district, the more things I discovered that had to be learned there. I still often smile at opinions I pronounced at the beginning of my stay in the Congo.... Serious men cannot be careful enough about the superficial judgments voiced by passing travelers, unless they are dealing with learned specialists who rely on the science in which they are competent" (471).

Such statements point back to the German position we commented on at the beginning. The true explorer, the *Reisende* or *voyageur*, unlike the passing traveler, has a personal calling and exercises a profession.

AUXILIARIES AND INTERMEDIARIES

The camp formed a circle of neat houses, built in the coast fashion, surrounding the store-house, where my goods were located, and where the headmen dwelt as a guard. Everything was surprisingly clean, and the circle

> gave evidence of being swept up each day. In expecta-
> tion of my return, a cool, commodious hut had been
> built for me, under the shade of a tamarind-tree. The
> goods were all found to be safe. Chuma had acted with
> much care and moderation, in spite of his somewhat
> extravagant character. The only fault I had to find was
> that he had carefully selected all the bales with fine
> cloths in them, and being of a very gallant nature, with
> a soft side toward the female sex, he had been some-
> what lavish in his gifts to such Iendwe damsels as had
> the good fortune to attract his attention. I found that
> he had earned great popularity among the natives; and
> immensely to my amusement, I heard myself described
> as "Chuma's white man," as if I was some curiosity
> which that illustrious gentleman was exhibiting for
> the benefit of the benighted natives of the interior.
> (2:205)

Solitary explorers never traveled alone. That such an indisputable fact should hardly have affected the mythical image is among the most glaring contradictions in travel writing, so much so that it tempts us to write it off as another example of the damage ideology can do to reason. But such contradictions produce important insights when we consider not so much why they arise but how they are maintained and met with various "solutions." With regard to expeditionary travel as an operation, the sources agree that the most difficult, complex, and arduous task was that of organizing a "caravan," that is, of recruiting and keeping African helpers, without whom none of the feats of exploration could have been accomplished. The travelogues abound with reports, complaints, and recommendations on this subject.

Transportation, a logistical task par excellence, was of course the principal preoccupation of all travelers. The number of required personnel was a function of variables such as the distance to be covered, the time available, and the amount of trade goods, food, and supplies that needed to be carried, to say nothing of unforeseen events, accidents, and local geographical and political conditions that were impossible to calculate in advance. Eventually, experience values were established that allowed, for instance, Becker to describe in his "*Vade-Mecum* du voyageur en Afrique" (1887, 1:455–90) the "organization of a caravan of 200 men and 100 guns ('minimal quantities for one year's stay')."[2]

The varying auxiliary personnel of an expedition (numbering from as few as a dozen to several hundred persons) caught the explorers in networks that were highly structured and intricate. Typically, the major division of labor was between armed soldiers (*askari,* led by *akidas*) and unarmed porters (*pagazi,* led by *nyamparas*).[3] A named hierarchy of functions existed within each group. Simple as it sounds, this arrangement was a constant source of conflict and trouble. Members of the two categories, sometimes even those in the same category, were recruited from different ethnic groups. The soldiers' group, usually consisting of Zanzibaris, tended to be more stable than that of the porters. The latter group often included a core of "professionals," most often Nyamwezi and "Loangos," with additional members hired only for part of the trajectory that led through their own country. How strongly predefined these groupings and functions were became visible when the travelers made occasional attempts, mostly futile, to shift at least part of the porterage tasks to the soldiers. Similar problems arose when the soldiers had to be kept busy during long stops or at IAA stations.

Next came the category of domestic personnel: cooks, valets, and gun bearers, many of them children. When I began reading the sources, I did not take the term "boy" too literally (the word is used in English in many French- and German-language texts). When the text specifically mentioned eight-year-olds, for instance, I attributed their employment to the traveler's peculiarities. But it soon became clear that the role of children in exploration was considerable. Much of what our authors learned about Africa indeed came "out of the mouth of babes." Far from a mere whim, hiring boys was an accepted (and expected) practice, in the east as well as in the west. Pechuël-Loesche reports from the Loango coast that these child-servants were known by a special name (*muléka;* plural *miléka*) and notes that "especially for the scientific explorer (*Forscher*), a good Mulék is irreplaceable" (1907, 67). Often travelers would acquire these children as slaves (as did Pogge, Coquilhat, and Becker). Coquilhat mentions "my two little domestic servants, Katembo and Katchéché, who were bought back from the Arabs" (1888, 119). His use of the French term *racheter* rather than *acheter*—buying back rather than simply buying—refers to a usage popular especially among Catholic missions and may even imply that he found his servants at a mission station. The practice of buying slave children with the intent to free them—of course not immediately; first they had to be educated by means of useful labor—made it possible for the staunchest opponents of slavery to profit from the trade.

Becker also has much to say about the intelligence, inventiveness, and loyalty he found among his domestic boys. When he confronts one who had run away after being separated from his best friend, he gets as a response "an argument that flattened me. 'You say that we are free when we serve the whites. Well, I did as a free man does. I ran away.' The little ones here are more clever than the grown-ups. I'll have to remember this!" (1887, 2:33). Capelo and Ivens categorically state: "African children are, beyond all compare, more intelligent and more agreeable than African adults. Little fellows of five years old often do such clever things and display such an amount of reasoning power as to cause both wonder and admiration." They go on to attribute this to the freedom African children enjoy, whereas European children receive "spiritual training at the hands of an ascetic, who oftentimes fills the imagination of a child with stupid, senseless fears." When African children grow up, however, they become "sly, distrustful, covetous, and above all, stupid," which, they surmise, is the result of "the outrageous habits of alcohol-drinking and hemp-smoking" (1882, 2:168). Behind these gratuitous generalizations is an experience probably shared by most travelers who made African children part of their domestic sphere: the children served as invaluable conduits of information about the often brutal reality travelers faced in carrying out the intrusive work of scientific exploration and at the same time offered a psychological buffer against this reality.

Among African auxiliaries, domestic servants were closest to the white man and claimed a status frequently contested by soldiers and porters. The interpreters, guides, and general intermediaries who were hired as the need arose would in turn insist on their superiority vis-à-vis the domestic servants. Most often they were ethnic outsiders or half-castes; some were literate Moslems or Christians who had acquired competence in European and African languages in a prior career of service with expeditions. In later chapters we will meet several of these interpreter-guides, but here I would like to introduce one of the most remarkable among them.

David Kornelius Bardo (often simply called Kornelius or Cornelius) served the German Congo Expedition initially led by Lieutenant Eduard Schulze. When that expedition split up into several caravans, Kornelius became attached to Büttner, from whose travelogue it is clear that this extraordinary African explorer of Africa held a crucial role in the German enterprise. Here is how Büttner describes meeting Kornelius.

> When we went ashore in Accra we were, to our surprise, addressed in German by a black dressed like a gentleman, who wanted to take up service in our expedition. First Lieutenant Schulze informed himself about this person in the factories and hired the man, who called himself David Kornelius Bardo, aged around forty and at the time the owner of two houses and a sizable busi-

ness in Accra. Kornelius hailed from Cape Coast and had received a rather good education at the Basel mission. Through this mission he had come to Europe, where he spent several years in various countries and employments. After his return to Africa he served the mission as a teacher. Later he accompanied a certain white trader on his trip up the Niger and finally served in the British campaign against the Ashanti. (1890, 4–5)

Kornelius more or less managed the affairs of Büttner's caravan. Büttner tells of him interpreting or leading negotiations, preaching to the local population, and teaching former mission students (122, 124). He acquired a young wife, a present from the Yaka chief, and came to be known as "*mundele ndombe,* that is, black white man, or a black man with the knowledge, the habits, and the status of a white man" (156, 115). In spite of his obvious importance, however, we learn very little about him. On the last page of his travelogue Büttner only parenthetically mentions his farewell to his "faithful companion Kornelius, who, I am prepared to attest, was the only honest black I saw in West Africa" (282–83).[4]

One of the most conspicuous oddities in reports on expeditions is, with some significant exceptions, the explorers' failure to acknowledge the presence and role of African women in these operations.[5] Many soldiers and porters traveled with their wives, who brought along at least some of their smaller children. Both soldiers and porters also had passing relations with local women at the IAA stations and sometimes fairly lasting relations in places where the caravan stopped for longer periods.

The logistical importance of African women was apparent in the 1850s to Francis Galton. They fed and cared for their husbands; usually they would walk ahead of the caravan and have dinner ready by the time the men reached their stopping place (see also Becker 1887, 1:147). Often they would roam the countryside and gather vital intelligence regarding the availability of food, the mood and attitudes of the local population, and the current political situation. They helped the traveler maintain authority and discipline. Coquilhat notes that one way to control the male members of an expedition is through their women (1888, 83). He also mentions that the Zanzibaris learn local languages through their "private relations" and generally acknowledges the diplomatic services women render in matters of *affaires étrangères* (90, 123). Here are Becker's comments on the presence of women.

Nothing, by the way, gives more animation and life to the itinerant band. Here [in Africa], as everywhere, the ladies are curious. They do extremely well when it comes to gathering information and rumors, which often can be used with great profit. During the march or at the stopping place nothing es-

capes them, and the finesse with which they establish contacts is outright remarkable. You can be certain that a traveler who comes back with a rich harvest of information and ethnographic studies (*études des moeurs*) owes these
for the most part to the women in his escort. (1887, 1:147)

It is tempting to picture the expedition as a series of concentric circles
surrounding the travelers—first the domestic staff, then the soldiers, the
porters, and the wives or temporary partners of soldiers and porters. But
it would be wrong to assume that this order reflects a scale of decreasing logistical importance. The European-centered expedition often performed its information-gathering tasks at the periphery. Moreover,
though our writers accord great importance to their heroic feats in assembling and keeping together the personnel of their expeditions—rely-
ing, so they imply, solely on their own judgment and experience—they
also give ample evidence of the existence of a veritable travel industry.
It operated on both coasts and was run mostly by Asians (Indian and
Arab) and Europeans who were in the business of financing and outfit-
ting caravans departing for the interior; they often also took care of hiring the personnel (keeping them, in some instances, on their payroll). On
the east coast in the early eighties, the French-Indian firm of Sergère and
Sevua (or Sewa), which had done business with Stanley, was notorious
for controlling and driving up the cost of expeditions. German travelers
complained about this, and Becker initially shared their disdain for these
entrepreneurs. Once he worked with them and got to know them personally, however, he noted many positive impressions of both these gentlemen and the services they provided.[6] Comparable services, though apparently not considered exploitative, were performed for caravans taking
the western approach, especially by the Portuguese brothers Saturnino
and Custodio de Sousa Machado, who resided in Malange.[7]

By and large, these entrepreneurs set the prices for labor and goods.
Furthermore, they often provided expert guides and served as the clear-
inghouse for information on routes and roads, changing demands for
trade goods, and current political situations. Thus, the notion that expeditions were, in terms of logistics, exclusively metropolitan European
operations is clearly erroneous, even if some travelers projected such an
image (perhaps to prove their competence and justify costs to sponsors
and the public). As soon as expeditions were organized they became—
apparently often unbeknownst to their leaders—part of existing networks and structures of communication. None of the caravans described
in our sources ever left the beaten path, geographically, socially, and politically speaking, as we shall see at the end of this chapter.

POWERS AND POTENTATES

> He is old, tall, and very stout and bloated-looking,
> with bleared eyes, as if perpetually intoxicated. Alto-
> gether he looks the very type of a savage potentate. On
> each side of him stood a pot of *pombe* [beer made from
> grain], in a beautifully made basket with a cover. In
> front of him sat a little boy who held the tube through
> which he ever and anon recreated exhausted nature by
> sucking up the *pombe*, on which he almost entirely
> lives. (1:298)

When caravans finally got on their way—generic descriptions of such departures were part of most of the travelogues—travelers had to face difficulties that sometimes outranked the problems of logistics. As they entered new regions, they had to deal with local rulers of varying stature and legitimacy. Even without the expeditions' own political goals or assignments, local politics would have been a factor affecting travel.

It is not easy to reconstruct the scene as it would have appeared to contemporaries. One premise of exploration was to match ignorance of central Africa with the expectation that this region was a political vacuum, nothing but "geography." Much of the history of exploration consists of discovering that no such thing was the case. When they began to plan operations, the IAA and its affiliates knew that access to the interior depended on authorities who ranged from village headmen to powerful rulers such as the Mwant Yav of the Lunda (in the south) or recent usurpers like Mirambo in Unyamwezi (in the east). Also to be contended with were interest groups ranging from Afro-Portuguese traders to Swahili merchants and colonists, all of whom had got to the center of the continent before the Europeans began to organize their exploration.

To deal as equals with some of those rulers who controlled regions several times the size of Belgium was not an idea the imperial powers seriously entertained. Letters from European royalty, carried and exchanged, were never more than gestures (and occasions to mock African inexperience with international diplomacy's codes and conventions). It could not have been otherwise. The nation-states of Germany and Belgium could not regard any of the African political entities as equal partners. That role was reserved for other European nation-states that had similar interests in Africa—and for the Europeans' most serious competitors, the Arab-Swahili. The founders of the IAA expressed moral indignation but in fact gave away their ultimate motives when they defined its most pressing task as repression of the slave trade. Though Europeans

negotiated abolishment of the slave trade with the sultan of Zanzibar—
one example of a political solution—even contemporaries had few illusions regarding the ultimate aim of antislavery campaigns: removal of
the Arab-Swahili as economic (and cultural) competitors.

Because there were reasons to keep silent about political assignments,
the politics of travel in central Africa was usually discussed as a strictly
logistical problem: as a matter of the quantity of trade items or local
currency to be carried, calculated on the basis of expected tolls, tributes, and presents required to ensure safe passage; and as a matter of
arms and ammunition necessary to look imposing enough and to use
when necessary. Again there were vexing problems of balance between
traveling light and being vulnerable to attack and extortion, on the one
hand, and carrying sufficient equipment and weaponry, on the other.
The same events and relations—obligatory presents, imposed fees, hostile attacks but also certain kinds of excessive hospitality—that explorers experienced as an inevitable nuisance connected with African travel
were the ones that brought them in touch with African people (not only
with rulers and their emissaries). Most travelers would have agreed that
the operational requirements of travel to central Africa fit the summary
of experiences noted by Capelo and Ivens.

> On comparing notes about the scenes we had recently passed through, since
> our plunge into the interior, the character of receptions, the pretensions of
> these pseudo-monarchs, the cupidity of the *macotas* [minor dignitaries], the
> impudence of the interpreters, the open-mouthed astonishment of the on-
> lookers, and the absurdity of many of the speeches, we arrived at the con-
> clusion that it was far the wiser course for the explorer to act the part of the
> laughing than the weeping philosopher, for that whilst in the former charac-
> ter he might pass through many difficulties unscathed, in the latter he would
> probably go to the wall. (1882, 1:183)

COMPETITION AND CONNECTIONS

> My national pride revolted at the idea of a Belgian ex-
> pedition overtaking and perhaps passing us. The men
> were at once convened and the business stated to them.
> Such a thing they declared they would not endure,
> though they marched till they fell on the road. They
> were ready to start in the middle of the night. So great
> indeed was the enthusiasm, that they turned the place
> into a very pandemonium, forming a procession round
> the village, firing guns, and shooting, thoroughly
> alarming the entire district. (1:196–97)

The mythical image of solitary heroism shone on the explorer and on his expedition or caravan as well. Strictly speaking, one European (Pogge, Buchner, Thomson, for instance) led only a few expeditions. But, with one exception, all the travelogues had a single narrator, not counting quotations from other works or documents. The explorer as hero is above all the author as hero. Exceptionally, Capelo and Ivens figure as coauthors and found ingenious solutions to the problem of a double narrative subject (more about this in chapter 10). Furthermore, the writers tended to make their tour a unique and self-contained enterprise, hence to deemphasize two facts: a caravan was seldom alone when it traveled, and it benefited from many preexisting connections among European travelers and African auxiliaries and intermediaries.

Even before the period of activities we cover came to its height, traffic was at times heavy, both along the eastern and the western routes of access. European caravans met other European caravans, as well as African, Swahili, and Afro-Portuguese trading parties of varying size. Sometimes European travelers joined the latter; often it was the other way around. In return for information and local expertise, small operators joined well-armed European expeditions for protection. Logistically, to operate several expeditions simultaneously had advantages, for instance, when leaders met, exchanged information, and gave each other material or moral support. Of course the density of traffic also encouraged those who provided materials and services to increase their prices. Demand and supply regulated the cost of travel in a market the Europeans did not control.

Apart from contacts made in meetings and joint travel, historical connections that do not fit images of solitary pursuits also had effects on the operation of expeditions. There are several reports of "chance" encounters between two or more Europeans who turn out to have met previously or even shared part of their past in Europe. Wissmann, writing from Malange on May 28, 1881 (that is, at the beginning of his first trip as Pogge's companion), gives a vivid example. Notice that this occasion represents a kind of structural opposite to the emblematic encounter between Stanley and Livingstone. Wissmann had not been searching for Buchner and could not—even jokingly—coopt Stanley's "Mr. Livingstone, I presume?"

> On February 8, I had a most curious encounter when I rode out to meet Dr. Buchner on his way back from Muata Jamvo [the Mwant Yav]. In 1874 we both had an extended, forced stay at the Magdeburg citadel [a military prison], because of a duel. We had adjoining rooms and shared quite a few

memorable experiences. We had not seen each other since, and now we came upon each other on the edge of civilization, once again under such unusual circumstances. Dr. Buchner most kindly gave me his maps and research notes and I also owe him much gratitude for instructing me in the use of instruments. (*MAGD* 3, no. 1 [1881]: 72)

On the same day Wissmann, Pogge, Buchner, and von Mechow with his companions Bugslag and Theus came together for a party to celebrate the kaiser's birthday and to exchange information and experiences.[8] Buchner (on his way from Malange to the Lunda) and von Mechow (traveling from Loanda to Malange) had met Capelo and Ivens the year before. With Buchner the Portuguese travelers had a pleasant conversation and exchange of information; von Mechow could not speak Portuguese and conversation was difficult (Capelo and Ivens 1882, 2:42–44 [see a picture of the meeting with Buchner on 43], 223).

Von Mechow's role in the German operations never became clear to me. But his mention of companions is an occasion at least to signal that both the Belgian and the German expeditions also employed European craftsmen who did not leave written accounts and therefore do not figure in our story. For instance, the gunsmiths Schneider and Meyer and Bugslag, a ship's carpenter, traveled with Wissmann's second expedition. Bugslag's contribution, especially, does not seem to have been limited to his technical services (Wissmann 1891). Significantly, we never learn the first names of these men—an indication of their lower social class and of strict hierarchical relations within a team of explorers.

Whether or not our authors emphasized the military aspects of their activities, most of them shared a military background (a recent experience, given their youth). It gave them a culture of habits and skills and set the hierarchical form of their expeditions. Belgians as well as Germans experienced problems when internal conflict or external events disturbed these basically military arrangements. The German Congo Expedition more or less disintegrated after its leader, Lieutenant Eduard Schulze, died of fever in 1885.

In sum, most of our travelers represented a professional type, the officer. In leading their expeditions, they went through the same motions. They differed in degrees of tact and sensitivity and in their national and ethnic cultural background—Becker, for instance, repeatedly stresses his Flemish identity—and in their abilities as writers, yet they produced remarkably similar accounts of their travels. The exceptions only confirm the rule.

Possibly even more consequential for the conduct of expeditions was a continuity among certain auxiliaries. Professionals like most of their employers, many of them had become specialized in serving European explorers. The headman of the Johnston-Thomson caravan was the same Chuma who had served Livingstone and brought his body to the coast. Thomson draws a detailed portrait of Chuma and precedes it with an extraordinary statement worth quoting.

> The vague expression of "the Expedition," "we," or the more egoistical "I," is very apt to swallow up a subordinate's individuality and valuable services, throwing him into the background, where he is more than likely to be forgotten. To obviate such a fate for the invaluable headman of the East Central African Expedition, let me anticipate the thread of my narrative while I bring him specially under the reader's notice. (1881, 1:31)

Becker's affectionate obituary for his servant Daimo (1887, 1:228–29) is one of the few appreciations of African auxiliaries that compares to Thomson's monument for Chuma. Becker mentions Zaidi, a former boatman with Stanley, being hired as a cook for their expedition (69). He also knows of a certain Mabruki Speke, who had served in an expedition led by Roger and Burdo and, as his name indicated, went all the way back to the Speke and Grant expedition of 1860–63; he may have been part of Stanley's expedition searching for Livingstone (187n. 1). Later, Becker counts among the personnel of Karema station a certain Tchéo, former chief of Burton's escort, which must refer to the Burton-Speke expedition of 1857–59 (2:222).[9]

On the west coast a similar story obtained: the same Afro-Portuguese interpreters and guides served in several expeditions. In both approach routes the exploration of central Africa relied on preexisting connections, formed by individuals and their shared histories of involvement. Such connections linked European travelers with other explorers and with their African auxiliaries; we must assume they acted among auxiliaries as well. One thing seems certain: the "solitary traveler" was never physically alone. Perhaps that was why mental solitude became a topos of travel writing.

During almost half of the period we selected, exploration from the west was carried out, in Frobenius's words, "in the shadow of the Free State."[10] Did the organization of a growing number of internationally recruited state agents, I asked myself, change the practices of exploratory travel sponsored by the IAA? I found no discernible line separating accounts that report on travel before or after 1885. Loosely speaking, Becker and Coquilhat, Wissmann and Frobenius—respectively—reported similar experiences and problems. They often thought and wrote alike and, when they differed, did so for reasons unrelated to the official recognition of Leopold's Congo Free State.

MOVEMENT: THE CARAVAN

As a rational operation, an expedition faced intricate logistical problems and was a maze of links and connections, internal and external. It was conceived as a scientific and humanitarian enterprise but its sponsors were associations that more or less openly served imperial and capitalist interests. In Africa, the complexities of the local political and economic situation multiplied those stemming from the expedition's motives and aims. Our general sketch of the expedition as an operation should quash any remaining impulse—encouraged by the myth of scientific exploration—to equate the rational with the straightforward or, for that matter, clear conceptions with simple execution. And we might wonder (with Taussig 1987, ch. 11) if travelers experienced the enterprise's complexities as anxiety-producing and projected the "jungle" within onto a largely metaphorical wilderness outside. Or if perhaps they registered the complexities as a frightful thing inside, an *incubus* (as Thomson speaks of it in a passage to be quoted presently).

If there was *structure* in expeditions, to present it we need to avoid "repetition and unreality" (see Pratt 1992, 2; and the earlier reference to her). Exploration can be viewed as a series of *events*. This is why we now turn from operation to movement. An expedition moved as a caravan.[11] Travel as movement, however, included stillness as well as motion; in fact, as we shall see, stillness was by far the predominant state. Going to places occupied much less time and perhaps less energy than being in places.

MOTION

> It is impossible to describe the pleasant feeling of exhilaration which took possession of me on finding myself on the march with so small a band. I felt as if, free and unfettered, I once more roamed alone on my own Scotch hills. I revelled in the sense of deliverance from the soul-wearing cares and troubles of a large caravan, which, like an incubus, hangs round a traveler's neck, and stifles all pleasure by the anxiety it gives rise to. When he would prefer knocking about unfettered in this place and in that, in search of something new or fascinating, he must ever keep on beaten tracks. (2:20)

If we want to appreciate what exploratory travel involved and how it proceeded, we must set it against powerful images of travel as motion from here to there, from one place to another. One such image is the *Einzelreisende,* the agent who knows his destination; his caravan is but the means by which the destination is reached. Yet even a cursory glance at the many reports of how caravans moved from place to place makes us realize that, in order to maintain our beloved visions, we would have to keep actual relations standing on their head. Granted, expeditions usually had instructions that gave them targets to reach. But existing routes largely determined how exactly and how fast they got there. It was these routes—navigable rivers and trade routes—that "moved" a caravan; the condition of routes was a decisive factor determining direction, speed, and distances covered.

Getting to places depended, furthermore, on the habits and rules established for caravan travel—a kind of caravan culture—which the explorers found when they arrived in Africa. These rules could seldom be changed or bent (this subject will have our attention in chapter 3). Even more important, we must keep in mind that a caravan never consisted only of human bodies in motion. There were several different kinds of bodies and things, each of them with different abilities or requirements as regards motion.

In received iconography, the people who traveled with the explorer marched in a single file. Many of the leaders adopted military principles and organized a caravan such that it had a vanguard, one or several main columns, and a rear guard. In practice, it rarely kept that order. Soldiers made up only part of the personnel. They may have been armed and uniformed but—at least in these early times before there were colonial armies—most of them were unused to military drill and unlikely to move in an orderly fashion for a long time. Porters were even less amenable to discipline. As we saw before, they often were a mixed bunch of different ages, physical constitutions, and mental attitudes to their work. Fatigue, illness, and the need to redistribute loads after frequent fugues and desertions further contributed to making a caravan's movement erratic. Women and children too went along but were not supervised by the Europeans or their African assistants. They were free to roam the countryside in search of food and information. Often they attracted local hangers-on while the men sought comfort and distraction, however briefly, in the villages they passed through. In other words, a caravan should be envisaged more as a swarm than a file.

The household staff was probably most closely supervised, also because its tasks often included carrying the European's arms, scientific and camping equipment, personal effects, and kitchen utensils. In some cases, not infrequent but not the rule either, a special crew was required to carry the explorer in a *tipoy*, the African sedan chair. But more often a leader, in order to keep control, had to move within the caravan and, in search of game, occasionally into the surrounding country.[12] In most cases, an explorer's daily form and state of health varied greatly and were bound to affect the whole enterprise.

Next in the category of bodies, caravans almost always included animals, often a veritable menagerie of them. Some travelers used riding oxen (on the southwestern approach) or donkeys (on the eastern approach); they seldom used horses. The animals, too, were a source of problems, depending on the terrain, availability of fodder, and state of health. Still other animals were taken along for food: goats, sheep, cattle, and fowl that had to be herded or carried. Finally, most travelers kept pets—mostly dogs but also parrots, monkeys, and even a tame ostrich.

Animals offered one of the most striking examples of the tragicomic in the exploration of central Africa. As part of the second expedition organized by the Brussels committee of the IAA (departure via Zanzibar in 1879), someone convinced King Leopold II to order an experiment with elephants as beasts of burden. What really inspired this extraordinary experiment (described by Becker in an appendix to the first volume of his work) was expressed, in a fine example of mercantile reasoning, by Colonel Maximilien Strauch, Leopold's man in charge of his colonial projects. In a report dated March 1, 1880, Strauch stated that, if this experiment succeeded,

> one would soon be able to see groups of domestic elephants rapidly traveling the routes on which today negro caravans arduously drag along under their heavy loads. Then our trade goods, no longer subject to such exorbitant expenses, can be offered to the natives at a price that will not dampen their desire, their use will spread and, from luxury articles which they are at the moment, they will change into necessities. Traffic will grow and, since progress calls for further progress and generates the resources for its own realization, will soon create new ways of communication and more and more rapid means of transportation. Then the elephant will, as one has said, no longer be just the precursor of the tramway and the locomotive. It will be the one who has made them possible by preparing the clientele they absolutely need. (Becker 1887, 1:435)

Eventually, the IAA was to establish a station where captured elephants would be tamed. Because domesticated animals could not be found in

Africa, in this first experiment four elephants were acquired in India and shipped, together with their mahouts, to the East African coast. M. Carter, a British subject in the service of the IAA, was in charge of the enterprise. Problems began when the beasts, after months at sea, had to be lifted from the ship's hold by a system of pulleys and put down into the water at some distance from the shore. The operation was witnessed by a great part of the European colony who had come from Zanzibar to watch the spectacle. All four of the animals made it to shore and joined up with an expedition led by Captain Emile Popelin. Two elephants died before the caravan arrived in Tabora, another one expired in view of Karema station, and the head elephant died seven months later.

Becker's brief summary of the episode has detailed medical bulletins on the circumstances of each demise and information we lack for most of the human auxiliaries who succumbed en route during these expeditions, the name of each animal: Mahongi, Naderbux, Sosankalli, and Pulmalla. In a lengthy conclusion, he analyzes the reasons of failure (noting, among others, that the Indians had sold the IAA the "castoffs of the stables of Poona"). Contradicting Strauch, he thinks steam will play a decisive role before experiments with elephants yield returns (1:433–37, 442–44).

Besides bodies, many other things moved with a caravan. Just how many different objects an expedition carried was one of my most amazing discoveries when I began to search for factors and circumstances in scientific exploration that could be said to control the traveler rather than the other way around. There were exceptions, such as Pogge and Wissmann, who decided to travel light (at least on their 1880 expedition) and did not even bring along camping equipment. There was also much variation in what travelers thought necessary or could afford. But one striking continuity among a number of expeditions into central Africa is their material culture of exploration, that is, an obligatory set or repertoire of things to take along on the passage into the Unknown. One of the most widely read lists and manuals was published in 1855: Francis Galton's *The Art of Travel: or, Shifts and Contrivances Available in Wild Countries*—a title I always loved.

The state of the art during the period we cover was set down by Becker in his traveler's vade mecum (1:455–90). He calculated the cost and described the composition of the personnel of a caravan ("of 200 men and 100 guns"). Then he listed denominations of money, measures, and weights, current prices for merchandise, arms, foodstuffs, and camping equipment at Zanzibar (for the year 1883). He also discussed the distribution of loads, packing, and keeping and checking an inventory. Under the headings "merchandise for tolls, wages, and reserves," "provisions of food and current use," "kitchen and table equipment," "camping gear," "clothing," "toiletries and articles of hygiene," "medicines, material for dressing wounds, and so forth," "precision and scientific instruments," "books and stationery," "arms and ammunition for the traveler," "arms for the caravan," Becker named more than two hundred different items and categories of items! Granted, he described an ideal caravan. He insisted, however, that his estimates, for one year, were "minimal quantities" (455).

Wissmann, ready to depart from Malange to the interior, listed the trade goods carried by a caravan that had to make do with scant funds. The quantity of things still is impressive enough: 600 pieces of striped calico in 32-yd. lengths; 100 pieces of the same, but of the worst quality; 100 pieces of cotton fabric in 40-yd. lengths; 400 lbs. of gunpowder in 3-lb. vats; 400 lbs. assorted glass beads; 120 yds. red flannel; 24 flintlock guns; 12 colored umbrellas; 200 lbs. of salt, and sundry small things (1889, 11–12). Another list was given by Capelo and Ivens, containing only items they handed over to Serpa Pinto when the latter split from their expedition (1882, 1:xlviii–xlix). Later they faced a situation where they had to get rid of much of their equipment for lack of carriers. Among the items they threw into a river were "articles for our personal use...carefully arranged in Europe...at the time they were packed in the Bazar du Voyageur in Paris" (2:210).

To be added to this panoply are, of course, the items that were collected en route: geological, botanical, zoological, and anthropological specimens and, above all, "ethnographic objects" that will have our attention later (some explorers also traded in ivory as a sideline). All these things had to be carried and constantly controlled; theft, careless handling, the effects of heat and humidity, damage caused by mold, insects, and rodents were among the constant preoccupations of the well-equipped explorer. Packing, unpacking, and repacking, made necessary by rain, river crossings, desertions, and other assorted incidents, were among the most time-consuming chores of exploration. Thus, the *Expedition,* a term that in German also refers to a shipping company and its activities, takes on literal mundane meaning beneath its heroic image.

STILLNESS

> As a real white man had never before visited Mahenge
> I must stay a few days to give his subjects an opportu-

nity of seeing me and studying my appearance and customs. To this I entered an energetic protest.... [But] as
a pioneer of civilization, and a living example of the
blessings of ample clothing and frequent washing, I
was constrained to bow to the inevitable and stay.
(1:183)

Founding "hospitable and scientific stations" was, remember, one of the
tasks given to IAA expeditions. It is natural to think of stations being established, or reached, at the end of a voyage. What is difficult to recon-
cile with the image of the intrepid traveler is the fact that much, probably most, travel was stationary. On the average, caravans actually moved
only during 3 to 5 hours per day. The number of traveling days varied
greatly; about 15 days per month would have been considered re-
spectable. Let us assume that a given expedition covered 2,000 km in
one year and a typical daily trip covered about 20 km. That would mean
(2,000 km divided by 20) 100 days in travel; the balance, 265 days, at
rest (or not in motion).

Many reasons and causes made a caravan cease to be in motion. First,
there was the physical condition of the European, especially when he was
alone. With virtually no exception, travelers repeatedly became too ill to
travel, even to be carried. Then there was the health of the porters, each
of whom had to carry loads of 60 lbs. or more. This factor alone limited
traveling time, depending on the terrain, the season, and the availability
of food. Furthermore, in the latitudes where these expeditions traveled
they had about twelve hours of daylight. Within that time the caravan,
which we may well compare to a traveling circus, had to break and make
camp. Each of these chores took several hours, following well-established
routines that travelers found impossible to speed up, except if there was
imminent danger. Frequently, departure was delayed by deserters who
had to be hunted down (often without success), by the aftereffects of
feasting during the night, by disputes over the distribution of loads, and
by the discovery of theft committed by nocturnal visitors or members of
the caravan. Occasionally (but less often than readers imagined), attacks
by marauding hyenas, lions, or leopards interrupted the much-needed
rest, also causing delays the next day.

All this forced idleness was a minor nuisance compared to the delays
caused by various payments and attending negotiations that expeditions
had to make along the much-traveled routes they took most of the time.
The rates for tolls or tributes (called *hongo* in the east) were generally
known but never exactly fixed. But cashing in on travelers was only part

of what the locals were after. They were curious and often decided to explore the explorers. These transactions would require ceremonious visits and countervisits and the exchange of gifts. Some authors liked to depict these occasions as annoyances caused by greedy village potentates, often drunk and always given to crafty deception. Yet clearly these forced halts were chances for a caravan to get to know the local population—and such, after all, was presumably one of the aims (or means) of exploration. Why were these occasions generally detested by the European travelers? More about this later.

Less productive ethnographically, and even more daunting than the payment of *hongo,* were river crossings that required the caravan to be ferried. Africans who provided that service expected some haggling over the price with the trade caravans they were used to. Often they were scared of a heavily armed European expedition and simply disappeared, or else the display of wealth they witnessed raised their expectations to unreasonable levels. Sometimes a shortage of dugout canoes (the usual means of river travel) made the task painfully slow. Depending on the season, even small rivers and streams could be difficult to cross and quite dangerous.

Most expeditions kept the name of expedition when they became stationary. As happened during Pogge's first trip to the Lunda capital, they might be forced to spend long periods of time at the point of destination. Or perhaps when they had fulfilled their assignment, they had to set up an IAA post or station (for instance, at Tabora and Karema in the east and at the many stations along the Congo or at Luluaburg on the Lulua River toward the west).

EXPLORATION AND POLITICS

> "The Warua were not accustomed to these ways; they
> were not to be hurried in finding guides; they preferred
> to do things quietly and according to custom. They ex-
> pected travelers when they came to their village to
> pitch their tents, take refreshment, and rest awhile;
> then go on and speak to the chief, and see and be seen
> by the people. This was the way they were accustomed
> to..."
>
> Kilonda's harangue surprised me very much. It was
> so well put together, and indicated so much latent
> strength. The appeal to their customs was put very
> strongly; and for the first time in my travels I felt I had
> got among a powerful tribe, who would require to be

> treated with the utmost care and circumspection if we
> would avoid getting into trouble. (2:124–25)

The plot thickens. Matters get more and more complicated as we try to step carefully through the many issues that come up even in this first attempt to get a general picture of exploratory travel. Are we now at the end of the road, and should we leave our sources at a point where exploration and discovery were replaced by—or turned into—occupation and colonization? That would make us disregard a substantial portion of most of the travelogues and some of them altogether, such as Coquilhat's story of getting control of the Congo and its riverain regions (1888) or Frobenius's report on travel in a more or less "pacified" Congo Free State (1907).

Both travel and stay, motion and stillness—we argue—shaped these expeditions. This would be a truism, except for the realization that, while movement defined expeditions ideologically, in practice stops took up by far the larger portion of the total time spent. (In light of this, talk of modern field research's distinctive progress over earlier travel—extended stays replacing impressionistic encounters—loses much of its plausibility.)

All the accounts on which we draw show that travelers wanted or needed to settle in. Desire was behind the occasions, sought and cherished by most travelers, for interrupting the often dreary trek by a mise-en-scène of bourgeois European domesticity and by demonstrations of serious scientific work: reading instruments, making observations, querying informants, and above all writing (the last chapter will look at the traces such occasional settling-in left in the very form or genre of presentation in a given travelogue).

Necessity came into play whenever politics dictated a considerable stay in one spot. Even if the ultimate purpose of these expeditions had not been to prepare central Africa for imperial occupation, the travelers could not have kept their dealings with the population to the kinds of exchanges we described above. Wherever they went they moved on political territory: either Arab-Swahili traders and colonists or African rulers of various stature and ambition claimed their stakes of power. Protestations of friendly intention and pure scientific motives were irrelevant because the mere presence of armed caravans led by Europeans made for situations that had to be addressed and resolved. Sometimes this happened by violence; more often by encounters, performative events whose pomp and circumstance demanded time and leisure. Both sides had to gauge the importance of these events by figuring out the real or assumed political clout of the participants in such meetings. What started out as negotiation over a passage sometimes turned into a stay lasting days or weeks, urged upon the travelers by their African hosts for reasons ranging from hospitality and curiosity to use of their guests in intricate local plays for power. Especially in the east, Swahili merchants and representatives of the sultan of Zanzibar showed themselves masters of the game.

The politics of travel were further complicated by the fact that in all the territories through which expeditions had to travel, Africa was in the midst of spectacular processes of change. In the west Portuguese colonial rule was disintegrating, and in the east the success of Arab-Swahili colonization was accompanied by the formation of new African supraregional (proto-)states led by the likes of Mirambo in Unyamwezi, Kalamba Mukenge in the Kasai, and Msiri in Katanga. In the interstices of power there operated armed "bandits"—Becker calls them "brigands"—highly mobile gangs of ethnically mixed composition, most notorious among them the famous *rugaruga* (lit., those who operate on the fly), sometimes loosely attached to a ruler, ethnic group, or locality.[13] There was even a commercial variety of banditry. Men whom Becker calls ivory *courtiers* (brokers) specialized in intercepting trade caravans before they reached the coast and offering seemingly good prices for their wares, which they then sold at great profit in Bagamoyo or Zanzibar (1887, 2:22). Today we would interpret this state of anarchy as the concomitant of economic and political modernization; for the imperial powers, especially in Belgian colonial discourse, all this was a proof of African savagery in need of salvation by their *oeuvre civilisatrice*.

All the Belgian and some of the German expeditions had, as we saw, the assignment to establish "hospitable and scientific stations," a task they fulfilled with varying fervor and success. Stations introduced a new dimension to exploratory travel; travelers, however temporarily, had to settle down. New logistical problems had to be solved: dwellings and furniture, stables, warehouses, and fortifications required materials and labor; gardens and fields had to be planted to ensure food supplies in an attempt to become as independent as possible from fickle local markets subject to periodic shortages or resistance (which the Europeans experienced as extortion). Stations also changed political relations with African rulers, albeit not as drastically as we might imagine. Many of the encounters en route had already been given a measure of permanence through ritualization and legalization. Pacts of blood brotherhood, enacted according to rules preestablished by African custom, were made and celebrated. Written contracts were "signed" by illiterate rulers, often drafted and duly witnessed by literate intermediaries. Because Europeans lacked as yet the power to occupy these lands militarily, they could found stations only by obtaining concessions to land and rights of access. While the travelers took these agreements as legally binding once and forever, Africans saw them as rituals requiring, as most rituals do, repetition or at least maintenance in the form of repeated proofs and enactments.

"Life at a station" became a separate chapter in reports and manuals of exploration. The operational tasks of an expedition now included maintaining permanence and continuity. African staff willing to settle had to be recruited; succession had to be organized among European heads, many of whom regarded their station as a personal achievement and were loathe to leave when their term expired or when they were given new assignments. Nor did travel stop once explorers settled down. Visits to Swahili or Portuguese trade centers and to African rulers became necessary to ensure supplies and keep supply routes open. Imperceptibly, these movements turned (especially in the Belgians' case) from apparently innocuous attempts to extend a sphere of influence into military campaigns and pacifying, often punitive expeditions. Exploration reached the end of the road and turned into colonization.

DISCOVERING THE TRODDEN PATH

> I was very much pleased with the Arabs at the head of this caravan. They certainly were not the brutal monsters we would be inclined to imagine on learning that they left their slaves to die of starvation, or to live on roots and grasses. At the risk of being misunderstood, I cannot but describe them as almost courteous gentlemen, with as humane and kindly feelings on the whole as are found in the average European. (2:74)

The myth of African exploration filled our mind with images of scientific heroism; it also spread confusion and promoted amnesia. On the topic of confusion, our reading of travelogues and ethnographies probably encouraged us to overlook differences between exploration and discovery: between getting to know better, or differently, areas already known and coming upon the novel and unknown. The travelogue as a story of success feeds on such confusion. But even more impressive has been the myth's ability to cause us—and often those who were part of the enterprise of exploration—to forget that expeditions traveled trodden paths, literally and metaphorically.

Belgium and Germany had their expeditions depart from both the east and the west coasts, as Great Britain had done in an earlier phase with Cameron and Livingstone (though strictly speaking, Livingstone came from the south; by 1880 or so the southern and northern approaches to the Congo Basin had been ruled out by the IAA and its German affiliate). France also entered from both directions, with Pierre-Paul-François-Camille de Brazza in the west, the abbés Debaize and Loyet in the east, to mention only names that show up in our travelogues. Among the missions, Protestants entered central Africa at first predominantly from the west (English and American Baptists and other denominations). The Catholics began their "attack on negro lands" from the east (Holy Ghost Fathers and White Fathers). In some cases our accounts slight the support explorers received from missionaries: the relations Thomson had with Protestant missionaries in the region of the Great Lakes or Büttner on the lower Congo and in Angola, to name but two examples. And in other cases missionaries took on the role of explorers (most notably Grenfell; see von François 1888).[14]

Both western and eastern approaches followed paths trodden by earlier Portuguese and Arab travelers. Afro-Portuguese and Afro-Arab (Swahili) traders and entrepreneurs (not to forget the east coast's Indian capitalists) gave our explorers logistical support, geographical and cultural knowledge, and means of communication, among them vehicular languages—trade and work idioms that were not their native languages—without which exploration would have been impossible and probably unthinkable. In fact, the prefix *Afro-* should remind us that, on the ground, no one prepared and facilitated the famous "penetration" of the continent more than Africans themselves, economically, with the slave and ivory trade's long-standing links to the world market; mentally, with the political structures and spheres of influence they set up to assure them an independent role in this network of exchange and often violent competition.

Many of our sources explicitly stated how much European travelers owed to the existing network of trade routes and centers set up by the Arab-Swahili who reached the upper Congo around 1860. When Wissmann came to one of these centers, Nyangwe, he admiringly described the town, its market, and the large plantations. But his comments show the contradictions in the colonial mind—at once giving and withholding recognition.

It cannot be denied that the Arabs, wherever they settle, initiate a certain cultural improvement which, however, they pursue purely egotistically and in such an inconsiderate manner that, though it is carried out energetically to their own advantage, it is anything but a blessing for the natives. Among all the improvements that strike one here in Nyangwe almost nothing was transmitted to the surrounding tribes of natives. Given the fact that the settlement has been in existence for a long time this must, however, be in part ascribed to the indifference of the negro. (1889, 179)

Relations with the Arabs were not limited to logistical support—they included lasting personal friendship as well as intellectual exchange. Explorers gathered specific information about Africa and an Arab-Swahili perspective on their own findings (definitely not limited to a crusade against slavery, a cause many travelers recognized as propagandistic and hypocritical). Replaying a scenario first propagated in the fifteenth century—when Portuguese seafarers made their way along the coast of Africa, sent to outflank Islam by searching for the mythical kingdom of Prester John—our authors cast their enterprise as a confrontation between the West and the Orient and as a competition between two visions of colonization. Entry through the Arab-Swahili sphere mobilized in almost all the travelogues a plethora of images and stereotypes described by Edward Said in his *Orientalism* (1978). The consequences of this epistemic complex deserve a separate study on themes such as the explorers' view of their arrival in Africa as a clash between Occident and Orient overlaid by other oppositions: coast and interior, civilization and savagery. It would have to analyze how European travelers dealt with clashes between the image of brutal slave traders and the genuinely hospitable, urbane hosts most Arab-Swahili turned out to be in practice. Or how explorers reconciled the ideological creed of European superiority with the admiration and envy they felt at the Arab-Swahili colonial method and their often excellent relations with Africans.

Of course, on the ground explorers rarely had time to indulge in such theoretical reflections; they faced the crude facts of imperialist competition with Arab-Swahili influence. In central Africa such competition came to a head in the military defeat of the Arab-Swahili.[15] When the Congo Free State achieved this in the early 1890s, colonial propaganda predictably celebrated it as a victory over the slave trade. To the Arab-Swahili and even to some European contemporaries, it meant the betrayal of trust and friendship. Apparently untroubled by *mauvaise conscience* in their later careers, Coquilhat and some of his early associates, and Wissmann, took part in the breaking of African as well as Arab-Swahili resistance to imperial conquest. Only Becker, it seems, always stood by his friendship with Tipo Tip. "Arabophile" opinions caused Becker to fall from grace with his sponsors and eventually ruined his colonial career.

THREE

Living and Dying

Expedition and caravan, planning and operation, moving and stopping, scientific investigation and politics—in each conceptual pair the second activity came after the first, and the entire string represents the process from discovery to colonization. Yet even the bare outlines of the enterprise we sketched in the preceding chapters make it clear that, from the beginning, European exploration of Africa had a rationality that was anything but linear and logical. The ideas and practices evoked by each pair of terms were also sources of tension—gathering the whole project into a net of contradictions and casting the myth of a heroic quest in the service of science against the harsh conditions of exploration reported in the same sources that cultivated the myth.

As a verdict this may sound definitive enough to suggest closing the books on an illusion that seemed harmless when it inspired youthful dreams or even when it informed notions of science in the service of a better, more complete understanding of humankind. There are reasons, however, for keeping the books open. A myth exposed is not a myth conquered. A myth of the kind we have in mind here (using the term in its diffuse, nontechnical meaning of an unfounded yet powerful story) is never a simple falsehood. Be it dream or nightmare, the exploration of central Africa is still with us whenever we recall it in popular memory or academic historiography.[1] More important—and this is a working assumption of our study—we anthropologists (and other researchers) are connected to this period through habits of producing and representing knowledge about Africans. That these habits were formed more than a century ago and may be looked at "historically" does not remove them from the agenda of a critique of the present state of our discipline.

Unlike theoretical paradigms, racial and cultural stereotypes, and colonial ideologies—all of them imposed from above—habits grow from experience. Habits determining what European and African actors experienced, and how, when, and where, accumulated in the drama, or the tragicomedy, of exploration. Such a perspective "from below" is what we attempt to open up in this and the following chapters. Because it was filtered through narratives where European travelers tell *their* story, information on what Africans experienced will be scarce and indirect; but when we put the dispersed bits and pieces together a picture emerges of the realities of exploration on the ground.

TIME AND TIMING

> This preliminary trip was of undoubted value to us in many ways. It corrected our mistaken notions concerning African travelling. It enabled us in some degree to measure our individual capabilities for the work we had undertaken. It helped us draw a pretty accurate line between the possible and the impossible in exploration, and thus was the means indirectly of saving much precious time. (1:62)

All expeditions were rushed, because in "all great and extensive enterprises in central Africa, the true chance of success lies in the rapidity with which they are performed" (Capelo and Ivens 1882, 1:337). Not all explorers subscribed to this view. Jérôme Becker, who has already emerged as the most quoted among our witnesses and will continue to be one of our key informants, chose a remarkable title for his travelogue when he called it simply *Life in Africa*—travel as a way of life. Above all he wanted to convey a sense of the practice of exploration and incipient colonization (though he was not averse to discussing contemporary theories and formulating a few of his own). From Becker we know that life in Africa had a life of its own. Executing the grand schemes of imperialism and living up to the myths of exploration was not what got the explorer through the day. Given the "geographical" nature of the enterprise and a deep-seated cultural propensity to think of research and the production of ethnographic knowledge in spatial terms, we can easily overlook the importance of time and timing that animated exploration.

What, to formulate a first question, was the explorers' sense of time as history? Pogge's diary of his trip to the Lunda (1880) and Schütt's partly questionable travelogue (1881) appeared in a series called Beiträge zur Entdeckungsgeschichte Afrikas (Contributions to the history of the discovery of Africa). It seems odd to call a book, published only a few years after the events it reports, a contribution to history. But at that time, exploration *was* history, because it *made* history. To understand such consciousness we need to take exploration and the encounters it involved as events. Imperialism as well as science had to happen if they were to produce the expected results. If the wider purpose of our project could be titled a *critique of imperialist reason,* one point of comparison with Kant's *Critique* would be to give attention to the perception of Africa (*aesthetics* is the term Kant used). But our target is imperialist reason at the front line, rather than in boardrooms and compendia. Therefore, *unreason* should be sought at the points of articulation between experience and judgment, description and prescription, travel and writing, not only on the grand level of imperialists' designs and deceptions.

On that grand level, incidentally, we sense change and development during our period. Take, for instance, the editorial pronouncements in *MAGD,* the bulletin of the German association. In 1879 they stressed time and timeliness (after all, the political background was the "scramble for Africa").

> Because in most recent times the opening up of regions offering such prospects, once initiated, proceeds as a rule with surprising speed, it is likely that very soon different nations will make efforts to secure their commercial interests a part in the expected success....Even in cases where [this effort] is not at all directed toward occupation, the members of a given nation that made the first discovery of a certain region will tacitly be granted precedence in its further exploration and exploitation. (*MAGD,* no. 2 [1879]: 59)

With space largely desired and imagined, uncontrolled events could happen. But five or six years later the goal was in sight. Time and timeliness—and the need to beat the competition—were no longer at issue; there was more and more talk about space and territory. Now the principal concern was with localizing exploration, which meant assuming authority and control in the face of local resistance. As exploration turned into occupation, place—or controlled space—became more important than events. In that sense, exploration, as it shaded into colonization, became less "historical," less conscious of time as timing. Explorers began to take the "long view." Becker, reflecting on the work of the missions, at one point states that the only way to civilize Africa is through agriculture, commerce, and industry. "But the element even more indispensable than money and science is time, *magister rerum*" (1887, 1:308).

But back to exploration as event. On the ground, keeping an expedition on track was, first of all, a matter of keeping time as measured by clocks. Exact time was required for astronomical, meteorologic, and topographic calculations. The chronometer, Capelo and Ivens say in conclusion to a long passage praising this instrument, "is an indispensable adjunct, and the explorer who goes to Africa without one will soon find it simply impossible to do his work" (1882, 2:207). Becker recounts the last-minute setting of the expedition's chronometer before departing from Zanzibar and notes that the instrument was "handed to a trustworthy man, generally a soldier and always the same" (1887, 1:38). Capelo and Ivens were naval officers and knew how to use their excellent instrument made by "Mr. Dent of London" (1882, 2:205). Other explorers were less well equipped, or less competent; some even lost count of the calendar. Commentators on Pogge and Wissmann's topographic and meteorologic observations found "that Pogge and Wissmann, already at the beginning of their journey, had got confused about the date. When he arrived in Tabora, Wissmann found that he was a day behind. Pogge, at one place in his diaries, called July 28 a Sunday, though it was de facto a Friday" (*MAGD* 4, no. 4 [1885]: 272n.).

Paul Gierow, who accompanied Schütt on the German Congo Expedition, has an entry in his published diary, dated November 12, 1878, which indirectly expresses anxieties about "losing time" that other travelers must have shared. In Kimbundu, an outpost of the Lunda empire and a trading town and former slave market, he met a deported European, a small trader who had become dependent on African *Handelsneger* (probably the German translation of *pombeiros*, Afro-Portuguese traders). "People here," he notes, "had three completely different dates: while in reality we wrote the twelfth of November, one of them swore it was the fourth, another the nineteenth of November; the days of the week they had lost altogether" (*MAGD* 3, no. 1 [1881–83]: 112).

Keeping correct time and dates had, apart from its scientific importance, also social significance. All expeditions celebrated certain holidays such as Christmas, New Year's, the king's or emperor's birthday, and others. These were important occasions for Europeans to recall their mission and to stage their Europeanness by dressing up, sharing elaborate meals, and spending time exchanging memories of life back home. On the western approach, days of rest for the caravan were also set by the

European calendar. In sum, clock and calendar were the umbilical cord to civilization.

Dispersed throughout our sources, we also find statements testifying to qualitative, phenomenological awareness of time (as fast or slow, full or empty, exciting or dull). Daily life during an expedition was routine punctuated by events. Departures and arrivals were usually described with special attention and relish. En route, celebrations and illness broke routine. Attacks of fever could become a timekeeper of sorts "because *Omma* [Swahili *homa:* fever] is usually characterized by its regular punctuality" (Becker 1887, 1:317). One recurring topos was that of critical "moments." Wissmann, for example, reports an incident when he had to intervene in a brawl among porters who were under the influence of palm wine: "Moments such as this are very dangerous for the European, because it has often happened that senseless rage turned against the caravan's leaders and resulted in the murder of the whites" (*MAGD* 4, no. 1 [1883]: 42). Coquilhat concurs, reflecting on a similar critical situation: "In such a circumstance, to lose my sangfroid, even for a second, could have been my perdition" (1888, 230–31).

Time can slow down to a point where Europeans must resort to remedies. Here is how Coquilhat solved the problem: "In order to distract myself and find something to do, I plunge into action, feverishly putting together furniture.... And while I am working... time passes quickly" (178). But later he is at pains to dispel an impression he thinks is common in Europe: of yawning boredom for heads of stations in central Africa, "being isolated and inactive!" He insists that routine can have the contrary effect.

> In the evening, after supper, I study tomorrow's program; I reflect on the situation; I take a walk through camp and have conversations at the blacks' sleeping places, something which is quite instructive; finally I place the guards, and during the night I interrupt my light sleep, making the rounds two or three times. Since the mind is kept busy by incessant activity and by worry about so many obligations I stay in full vigor. My life reaches its maximum of intensity, and many of my European friends would never suspect this. (243)

Buchner, invoking one of the incongruities that beset exploration, complains that routine occupations may in fact be so time-consuming as to endanger the traveler's principal task, which is to record his observations and follow up on certain projects, in this case language studies: "If only I had more time and was not so terribly tired when I have the time! My traveling apparatus [*Reiseapparat*] absorbs too much of my capacity for work" (*MAGD* 2, no. 1 [1880]: 49).

All the travelers complain about lack or loss of time. Sometimes they regret not having more time to deepen their observations and inquiries; more often they lament the time it took to get and keep a caravan organized, the slowness of progress, detours that needed to be made for political or logistical reasons, delays caused by natural or human obstacles. They hated waiting and invariably tried to fill time experienced as empty with various chores. In fact, we get the general impression that activities that make up ethnography—observing, inquiring, conversing, noting—would hardly have taken place without forced or otherwise unplanned stops during the journey. That the production of ethnographic knowledge, a proclaimed aim of travel, was often forced on our explorers and, in this sense, suffered rather than pursued, is among the paradoxes that gave exploration its somewhat demented character.

A deeper problem affects ethnographic research generally: it has to do with the limits of characterizing exploration as a way of life. After all, travel remained an enterprise that had to be carried out during a limited time, often too under the pressure of new or changed orders from the sponsors or simply because of the shortage of funds. In this light, we need to look at the exchange of gifts, a classic ethnological theme that all the sources record as one of the major nuisances plaguing travel to central Africa. Capelo and Ivens have one of the most explicit statements to that effect.

> Following the vicious system in operation throughout Africa, of not selling anything to the European but making him a present of it, they extort from him in turn all his goods and effects, bit by bit, until the unhappy man finds himself under the necessity of refusing all presents, and thus giving birth to serious questions affecting the customs and prejudices of the country. (1882, 1:116–17)

For most authors, these practices were nothing but payments of tributes or tolls. African conceptions that defined them as exchange of presents were, if at all, acknowledged ironically, devalued by quotation marks: they expressed African rulers' typical deviousness and greed. Rare are the occasions when the travelers book the long negotiations surrounding such exchanges—what to give to whom and when; how to match presents received—as anything but a loss of time.

Pogge has an epic account of a seemingly endless traffic of gifts when he records the repeated "extortions" inflicted on him by the Mwant Yav and his sister during his protracted stay in the Lunda capital. The strain caused by such occasions had a double cause: the encounter of two cultures and the intrusion of science, exercised in limited projects, on the daily life of Africans. Especially when they relished such interruptions, as they obviously often did, Africans used gifts to buy time and establish mutual obligations. Europeans may have found the exchange useful but always saw it as limited to making connections and getting contracts signed, seldom as opening a space for more thorough ethnographic inquiries.

COPING WITH THE TROPICS

HYGIENE

> It is a well-known fact that the only way to resist successfully the enervating effects of a humid tropical climate is by constant exertion, and by manfully fighting the baleful influence. The man who has nothing to do, or won't do what he has to do, is sure to succumb in a few months, and degenerate into an idiot or a baby. He becomes the helpless victim of manifold bilious troubles, and is continually open to attacks of fever, diarrhoea, or dysentery. His mental energy flies with his physical, till any sustained thought is impossible, and to pass the time he must dose night and day, except when he is grumbling and defaming the climate. Hard constant work is the great preserver. Sweat out the malaria and germs of disease, and less will be heard of the energy-destroying climate of the tropics. (1:123)

By now, little should be left of images we may have held of exploratory travel as movement controlled by the traveler. True, most expeditions kept to the planned routes or could justify the unplanned routes they had to take; they covered their trajectory more or less within the time allotted to them. After all, their efforts made it possible to write histories of exploration as stories of accomplishments ranging from work well done to heroic exploits. But even the most self-congratulatory accounts could not overlook the death toll for the "opening up" of central Africa. There were many reasons why the sponsors and commentators, presumably the public, and even our authors had little difficulty making death, ultimate rupture, part of narratives that related continuity and fulfillment. Europeans had several hundred years of experience with the deadliness of tropical Africa. Recent advances of medicine notwithstanding, nineteenth-century expectations of mortality also differed from ours. And most of our story's protagonists either came directly from the military or viewed their earlier military careers as a preparation for travel in

Africa: premature death was part of such a way of life. On the loftier levels of colonial discourse, more or less thoroughly internalized by the travelers, death figured as a noble sacrifice, as a price well worth paying for the victory of science and civilization.

But glorification, even celebration, of death had its other side in a truly Foucauldian regime of controls that affected life in the tropics in its minute details and down to the depths of a person's psyche. By the time the expeditions we describe were carried out, such a regime had become articulated around the concept of hygiene. Hygiene meant something that was both much deeper and more encompassing than what went later by that name.[2] Our first glance at contemporary conceptions comes from Becker, reporting from Tabora.

> Here I follow a very hygienic regime. Up at dawn, after having taken my bath, I take excursions to villages nearby. I can be seen in the fertile valley of Kou-yara, in the region of Ou-Ganga, surrounded by light brown rocks, at Itourou where the father and brother of the famous Tipo Tip make their home, gun over my shoulder, notebook in my hand. Covering long stretches, I pick up and bring back a lot of small game, ethnographic observations, and a robust appetite. (1887, 2:20–21)

Hygiene was needed, as everyone agreed, to meet the African environment's extraordinary demands on the European traveler. Temperature and humidity were subject to abrupt change, and road conditions varied all the time, as did the density of the vegetation obstructing travel and the level of streams and rivers. In the east, dry and wet seasons were more pronounced than in the west, and accounts of travel from the east coast to the interior abound with tales of horror and suffering when expeditions had to cross unpopulated stretches of swamp land or arid savanna. Adequate protection of the body became a foremost concern, and many writers recorded their experiences and offered advice on anything from boots and hats, tents and raincoats, to bedding and underwear. Many complained about having made the wrong choice of clothes and camping gear from the goods offered by specialized manufacturers in Europe. Knowledge of Africa began with the know-how needed to survive the climate.

Closer to our present understanding of the term *hygiene,* keeping clean was a problem that constantly preoccupied Europeans. Most agreed that in Africa, cleanliness was above all a matter of maintaining discipline in the absence of the usual social pressures and amenities of civilization. Such discipline was all the more important because self-control was generally understood as a prerequisite for the control of others. Demonstrating bodily vigor and concealing weakness were among the means of maintaining authority in leading a caravan and dealing with the people encountered en route. It is, therefore, not surprising that travelers made the chores of knowledge production—taking regular observations and measurements, collecting zoological, botanical, and geological specimens and ethnographic objects, drawing maps, gathering information, and keeping logs and diaries—a form of hygiene and often a matter of survival. This is how Wissmann describes an explorer's daily routine.

> All my time was taken up with entering sketches made on the road into my map, reading instruments for measuring altitude, maintaining instruments and guns in a good state, and making regular visits in the villages of the natives. Wherever this was possible, I took a refreshing bath in the evening and on days of rest I did some hunting. In the evening when, after dinner, we had finished talking about the experiences of the day or our expectations, the diary had to be kept and, if possible, astronomical observations made. In Africa we never had to complain about not sleeping well, for spirit and body really needed rest after such efforts. (1889, 159)

Some authors, notably Becker and Thomson, go to great lengths arguing that walking rather than being carried or using riding animals was the only way to maintain well-being during travel. This is how Becker puts it: "In my opinion it is healthy to react against [the danger of] sunstroke with regular walking, thus maintaining an equilibrium between internal heat and external temperature. The determined pedestrian that I am, I covered the toughest stretches on foot, and if I kept a little donkey at Tabora, it was only out of a sense of decorum" (1887, 2:380). There was something obsessive about his theory of equilibrium. Becker assures us that he owed his survival to the fact that he always, no matter how hot it was, wore a flannel sash (124; see also 314 on the importance of protective clothing).

Of course, our sources would not be what they are if statements to the contrary could not also be found: riding oxen, donkeys, and hammocks "will save us from many a fever," says Büttner, adding, "I always think that physical strain and lack of caution caused Lt. Schulze's death. He did not want to use either the pith helmet or the parasol" (*MAGD* 4, no. 5 [1885]: 315).

"THAT TERRIBLE AFRICAN FEVER"

> The malaria began to work out of me, and reduced me
> terribly. It can hardly be conceived how dreadful it was

> to pull myself over mile after mile of country, feeling
> that it must be done if I would live at all. At Poki-
> rambo I was delirious during the night, and full of the
> strangest fancies. I supposed that all the men were
> making preparations again to desert me *en masse*, and
> that this time every man would go and not come back.
> In an agony of fear I dragged myself out of the tent at
> midnight, and called on Chuma not to forsake me, and
> to try his influence with the men. What had I done that
> they should thus leave me? &c. All this I learned from
> Chuma in the morning, when I got over the delirium,
> and walked nearly ten miles. Each day I usually con-
> trived to pull myself together for the march; but I was
> just like a machine, wound up to go a certain time, and
> then collapse utterly. I began to think that after all the
> natives were not so far wrong in their belief that dis-
> ease was caused by devils getting into one. (1:279)

The state of medical knowledge in the nineteenth century caused these explorers to connect climate and other physical features of the environment directly with illness in ways that were decidedly premodern. When they spoke from experience of the dangers of "bad" water, they noted its foul smell or dirty appearance; they knew that the tsetse fly was noxious to animals and that mosquito bites were dangerous, but they generally still subscribed to a miasmic theory of fever caused, they thought, by insalubrious air and the exudations of swamps owing to the toxic effects of decomposing matter during the humid season. Parasites, except certain easily visible kinds, such as worms and sand fleas, were as yet ill understood. Against such a background, we begin to understand why and how FEVER (often capitalized in the sources), far from being regarded as just a medical condition and a reaction of the immune system to multiple causes, became essentialized as the ecstatic counterstate to ascetic hygiene. Fever was an ideology, a myth needed to make sense of the mortal dangers of exploration, a metaphor giving meaning to what would otherwise have remained brutal facts.[3]

Fever was the "sacrifice" every traveler must bring to the black continent. A kind of fever (the Germans call it *Reisefieber*) was what made many of the explorers embark on their travels. On the voyage out, even before he arrived, the traveler suffered, as Becker says, from "the fever of impatience" (1887, 1:6). Such expressions were meant more literally than we would take them today; all authors were convinced that fever could be brought about, not only by psychosomatic states such as fatigue caused by overexertion, but also by overexcitement and excessive

anger and aggravation. In a report to the German association, Büttner
made one of the most detailed statements to this effect when he reflected
on his experiences in the lower Congo and on the west coast. He, too,
observed the periodical occurrence of attacks. Yet in the absence of reliable statistics, he was unable to identify any other pattern.

> I found fevers at sea, on the coast, on the river, deep in the interior, in low-
> lying regions and places located at high altitude; fevers attacked natives and
> Europeans of the most different nations, those who had just arrived, those
> who returned, and those who had lived on the coast for a long time, mer-
> chants, missionaries, civil servants, and travelers; teetotalers, modest and
> heavy drinkers, single and married persons, individuals on arsenic or quinine
> prophylaxis or on none at all—no one escaped the illness, though I must ad-
> mit that some experienced coast people suffered remarkably little from it.
>   On myself I experienced that the intensive effects of the sun, overexertion,
> colds, passing through marshy regions, anger, and excitement brought about
> fevers, but they could also occur without such occasions and I am of the opin-
> ion that he who avoids those factors whenever possible and who has brought
> along a healthy body, knows how to live sensibly and modestly (but not
> badly), and has the occasion to treat his fevers properly may expect, but can
> never be certain, to resist the climate on the lower *Congo* for a while, espe-
> cially when the right moment for a short recuperative vacation in northern
> latitudes is not missed. (*MAGD* 5, no. 3 [1889]: 201–2)

Attempts to discern causes, occasions, and circumstances and to classify fevers according to length and seriousness of attacks or accompanying symptoms (there were "typhoid," "bilious," and "uremic" varieties
or stages) became more frequent in the course of the period covered here;
they did little to change its mythical, totalizing conceptualization as the
most formidable threat to the scientific enterprise of exploration, a threat
to be met with hygiene as a regime of body and mind. No wonder that authors given to philosophical and lyrical reflections would resort to a kind
of poetics of fever. Becker recalls his first encounter as a bad love affair.

> My first night on the African continent goes by with mortal anxieties…one
> attack of nausea follows the other…. Finally, toward dawn, the crisis eases,
> only to make room for fever, that terrible African fever to which I am the first
> to pay tribute. Yet the encounter is harmless. After three days of painful ca-
> resses, the evil visitor gets tired of her latest favorite and hurries toward other
> embraces. Farewell, Mademoiselle, and may your breakup with me be defin-
> itive, *n'est-ce pas?* I declare myself unworthy of your tedious faithfulness.
> (1887, 1:44–45)

He was wrong, of course. Once, after marching through the African
night, he exclaims,

> But what did poetry, nature, indeed the world, matter to me? I had the fever,
> that African fever which, in less than an hour, fells the most tried and tested
> man, undermines all his springiness and energy, makes him insufferable to his
> dearest friends, inspires him with ideas of suicide and, in the end, has led so
> many Europeans to their grave. (131)

And there are moments when fever pushes this usually up-beat writer
into darkest despair about the continent he came to explore. When he
hears some particularly gruesome news about a local ruler, he reacts to
horror with apathy: "What a dark wasp's nest this Africa is, always at
war, always hungry for murder and looting, and where man's ferocity
goes to battle with the hostility of the soil and the climate! I feel so sick
that this news doesn't even affect me. Everything becomes indifferent to
one who embraces the *Omma*" (160–61). That, paradoxically, fever may
also be experienced as exhilarating is reported by other authors but it is
again Becker who gives us this moving vignette from the last days of one
of his colleagues, Popelin, who had taken excessive doses of quinine
without avail (326): "Delirium had come, carrying our friend back into
the midst of joyful scenes of civilized life. Painfully moved, I heard him
speak at crazy parties with invisible friends and break out in cheerful
laughter" (367).

OTHER ILLNESSES AND MEDICINES

Fever was not the only illness from which travelers suffered. Others they
mentioned include rheumatic pains, pulmonary afflictions, bronchitis,
tropical ulcers, and skin diseases (especially the dreaded *roter Hund*
[prickly heat]). Some explorers accomplished heroic feats of suffering.
Pogge, on his second trip with Wissmann, had to have several teeth pulled,
after which his jaw got infected. A delay of four months in Malange did
not help much, but he insisted on pushing on after more teeth had been
pulled (Wissmann 1889, 14, 23, 25). Blisters and sores, sunstroke and
ordinary colds were constant companions. Travelers suffered from depression (or, in contemporary terms, "melancholy"); a few cracked and
had nervous breakdowns. For most of the sources these inferences rely
on allusions and hunches; reports of mental afflictions may have been
subject to censure except in generic descriptions such as this one.

> The life in the woods, which is generally miserable enough, becomes aggra-
> vated in all its worst features as the traveler plunges deeper into this great
> continent. The huge obstacles and constant privations not merely weaken his
> body, but at the end of some months' marching they produce a state of irri-

tability, and nervous excitement closely allied to derangement. An extraordinary change in individual character soon becomes apparent. The extravagance of gesture, precipitating of every act, abruptness in issuing orders, baseless fears, and a desire to rush along the road, as though pursued by some phantom, all are evidence of the change that is being wrought, and are symptoms of the malady known as African spleen. (Capelo and Ivens 1882, 2:100–101)

Capelo and Ivens have more to say about a "half-sleeping, half-waking condition" in which they found themselves during times of "spleen." "Did these strange vagaries," they ask, "these fixed prepossessions portend the dawn of madness?" They have a "feeling of pity and compassion for the suffering mortals... as though for men who were other than ourselves!" (102)—an allusion to fever's dissociative effects. Earlier they described an occasion when "both of us experienced a sensation so extraordinary that we cannot refrain from putting it on record" (1:374). Neither can I.

> During the time we were under the influence of the fever, and particularly when it was at its greatest height, it seemed to as if our individuality was composed of two distinct entities. We imagined another person was lying with us on the same bed, and we were taking note of the progress of the malady in each of these separate beings, so that our lips, echoing our thought would murmur, "How that fellow on the right is sweating!" or, as the case might be, "I think our friend on the left is a good deal worse!" It could not be considered a complete hallucination of mind, because, on collecting our ideas (though with difficulty), we found ourselves on various occasions muttering,—"Come, decidedly I must begin to *undouble myself*." Be it observed, however, that this species of dualism was subjective, inasmuch as, with relation to external objects, we never fancied any such *undoubling* to be necessary. (374–75; original emphasis)

They speculated on the causes and suspected "cerebral anaemia," but in the end they gave up trying to explain the phenomenon "under the apprehension that we should be doubling and undoubling when we were in our right senses" (375).

As far as other diseases are concerned, I suspect (but cannot demonstrate the point without an extraordinary effort of rechecking the sources), the most formidable killer of European travelers was dysentery rather than malaria, a term that was just gaining currency. The point is not moot. Fever's effects on the travelers' mind, and thereby on their work of knowledge production, were rather indirect and perhaps not very considerable. But they must have preoccupied our authors, if only as the foremost object of hygiene. In the case of remedies taken to fight or prevent dysentery and other illnesses, the effects were more direct.

All expeditions carried medical supplies intended for the Europeans rather than their African personnel. It would take an expert to gauge from available information the composition of these pharmacies, dosages recommended and actually taken, or the extent to which travelers spent their days more or less drugged. The three or four substances mentioned most often were the ominous arsenic, quinine, and opium, the latter either as laudanum (an opium and alcohol tincture) or as morphine. Morphine was injected. Wissmann mentions injections (see the next section) and in an appendix Coquilhat quotes Lt. Avaert as having been saved once by such injections, administered by the famous Congo missionary William Holman Bentley (1888, 488). Other medicines were zinc oxide (308), ipecac (to induce vomiting [Becker 1887, 2:315]), and the following list of supplies found by Becker when he took over from Dr. Theodore van den Heuvel, a physician who had kept the IAA post at Tabora.

> lead sulfate and quinine, tannin [an astringent], emetics, cantharidin [an alkaloid], *chloridine,* citric acid, Epsom salts, aloe, benzine, drops of senna [a purgative], rhubarb, kermesite [an expectorant], and so on. Left were also five bottles of Warburg elixir, frequently used, Arabian elixir, also called Missionary's elixir, invented by the abbé Loyet, mustard plaster, *charpie* [shredded cotton dressing] plus a display of poisons I will take care not to touch. (21–22)

Almost always the travelers had to practice self-medication. I found only one brief note of treatment that included a prescription. Dr. Willy Wolff, a German physician and member of the German Congo Expedition (not to be confused with Dr. Ludwig Wolf, Wissmann's companion), reports.

> Lt. Schulze just died, at 11 A.M., not having regained consciousness for ten days. When I arrived I already found him seriously ill. Chin. sulf. in tablets as well as 3.0 grams Chin. in a solution of acid. tart. had absolutely no effect on the temperature curve; opium and other medication inducing constipation also helped little against constant diarrhea. (*MAGD* 4, no. 5 [1885]: 313)

Quinine was recognized as a specific against fever and widely used, though there was apparently no agreement on dosage and much disagreement on whether to use it prophylactically or only to treat attacks of fever. Becker describes something that many anthropologists who did work in Africa a century later may still have witnessed. He sketches daily life among the European residents of Zanzibar, praises their food, and then mentions that the bottle of quinine "enthroned in a sinister way in the midst of spices, pickles, and English sauces, reminds us to use moderation in this land of fever and dysentery" (1887, 1:12). Coquilhat, from the other side of the continent, draws a similar tableau: "A curious detail as regards the table of Europeans: as a rule there is quinine and arsenic, much like pepper and salt. Before the soup, there were always several diners busy absorbing a dose of these medicines" (1888, 99n. 1).

An unexpected connection between medication and a traveler's capacity to meet his tasks shows up in an observation Schütt makes on his companion Gierow.

> Gierow, who usually did everything I told him to and who was willing to take on any kind of work, had until then taken no interest in the external matters [of the expedition], such as the how and where of our trip. Of course, this may have been due to the fact that, as a result of taking large quantities of quinine, he had suddenly become quite hard of hearing. He still had not been able to decide to learn Portuguese, or rather he made do with a few words from which, when listening to conversations, he drew general conclusions, something that often created comical misunderstandings. (1881, 63)

Some travelers must have realized the dangers of self-medication. After he had become an experienced Africa hand, Becker recommended moderation. In a disquisition on the traveler's pharmacy, he pleaded for minimal doses and for letting nature take its course, even in cases of serious illness. About himself he says: "Apart from quinine, Warburg elixir, iodine (for external use!), laudanum, common purgatives, zinc sulfate, *sel de Saturne,* ammonia, silver nitrate, and some caustic substances whose effects everyone knows, I touched nothing at all" (1887, 2:315). But he too took laudanum, and that brings us to the role of opiates in African exploration—and back to our traveler "out of his mind."

OPIATES AND ALCOHOL

> At night, thinking that the place looked unusually
> peaceable, I resolved that I would try to get a really
> good night's sleep—a luxury I had been deprived of for
> several days. To allay the feverish excitement of my
> brain I took a good dose of laudanum, and turned into
> my tent. (2:161)

After having studied the sources, I no longer think opiates alone could carry the story of ecstasis in exploration. Myriads of causes made travelers lose control, if that is the point of searching for ecstatic elements in the production of knowledge. As such evidence accumulates, drugs—a problematic term under any circumstances—lose some of their fascination. Still, we are entitled to imagine our explorers "drugged," most of them some of the time, and perhaps some of them most of the time. The obligatory presence of opiates in the medicine chests of expeditions is attested to; the extent of actual use can be inferred, for instance, from the endemic nature of dysentery, obviously a constant companion of travel in Africa and one that required frequent recourse to laudanum. Which does not mean that less radical treatments were not also applied; see Becker's recommendation in cases of diarrhea "to take care not to consume anything but broth or the water from boiling rice" (1887, 1:111).

Perhaps we are being too cautious when we base our estimate of drug-induced states on the medicinal uses of laudanum. More likely than not there was nonspecific taking of laudanum (as a soporific and sedative), excessive use of arsenic and quinine (see above) and alcohol (see below). And in assessing the effect of opiates on what our sources learned and wrote about Africa, we must be careful not to project into the nineteenth century the social stigmatization and criminalization of opiates that started at the very end of the period we cover. Millions of ordinary people in Europe and North America were more or less heavy users of sleeping drafts, and countless patent medicines that contained opium were available in pharmacies or drugstores, at peasant markets and fairs. Famous writers, poets, and composers, but also physicians and scientists, used opiates and praised their effects. So did famous explorers, such as the incomparable Richard Burton. In the unlikely event that our authors brought along "a habit" to their work in Africa, they might not have considered every case or incident of opium use worth reporting. Perhaps more on travel and tripping would come to light if we had more information about travelers whom our authors usually dismissed as adventurers. Torday observed the case of an Austrian named Rabinek, who must have operated in the Kasai and was eventually sentenced for smuggling: "The poor man was a morphino-maniac and suffered agonies when he found himself suddenly deprived of his usual drug. I gave him the little I possessed, so did everybody else; but he could not get enough for his craving" (1925, 29). So Torday also "carried."

To some of the instances of the use of opiates already cited we can add the following report by Wissmann. It shows (as does Thomson's comment at the beginning of this section) that yet another affliction frequently reported, insomnia, must have tempted travelers to dip into their medicine chests. This is what he tells of his efforts to give medical care to Pogge: "Following his own instructions I treated [Pogge] for dysentery and fever and repeatedly gave him morphia, because he could not sleep in spite of being quite weak" (1889, 25). Presumably, morphia, rather than morphine, was taken orally and therefore easier to use.

During his second trip, Wissmann again acted as a physician when he treated his Belgian colleague Paul Le Marinel (of later fame in the occupation of Katanga). The passage is worth quoting at length because it illustrates the problems of administering drugs in a certain form or using combinations of drugs.

> Since he was not at all able to keep down quinine, I gave him injections under circumstances made very awkward because of difficulties caused by the lack of appropriate medicines. I had only quinine on a basis of sulfuric acid which, for the purpose of injecting, I dissolved in acetic acid. As a result, the injections caused large and deep wounds. Nevertheless the quinine had its effect, and because the extreme excitation [it caused] was removed by injections of morphine, I was quite pleased to see him, after two days of sleep so deep that it was interrupted only very briefly by the painful injections of quinine, free of fever. After that, a so-called cocktail, a drink prepared with cognac, sugar, eggs, bitters, and nutmeg, had an excellent effect. It took a long time before this badly shaken, but otherwise strong, young officer fully regained his health. ([1890], 103)

Wissmann's "cocktail" is a cue to another topic that pervades our sources, alcohol. Its role seems to have been in many ways more important, and more complex, than that of opiates because alcohol was felt to affect not only health but also morale and morals. As we shall see, alcohol helped ease the encounters between explorers and their hosts. Under the heading of moderation, it certainly was subject to the regime of tropical hygiene. As a matter of "protecting the natives," control of alcohol became an issue when that philanthropic phrase came to mean the protection of a (potential) African labor force.[4] Alcoholism among Europeans was the principal concern during the period of exploration.

All expeditions to central Africa had among their supplies varying quantities and qualities of alcohol. Its uses for medication or celebration or gift exchange were sometimes hard to tell apart. Travelers appreciated cognac and rum, Bordeaux and champagne for their alleged or real medicinal properties, as relief in situations of physical or mental stress, as obligatory ingredients of festive meals, and, of course, as sources of pleasure and as rewards they accorded themselves when they had overcome hardship. All these applications were encompassed by hygiene, that is, by whatever it took to keep a European explorer in control of his body and soul. As a gift or means of exchange, alcohol could take on a political significance. It seldom became a mere commodity to buy, or be exchanged for, other goods.

Most negotiations for favors, contracts, and concessions, successful or not, called for social drinking. In its role of promoting conviviality—hence interaction and communication relatively free of the exercise of power and control—alcohol became a significant ecstatic element during encounters between Europeans and Africans, including those that produced ethnographic knowledge. And unlike the drugs and substances that served as medicines in a more narrow sense and were usually reserved for the travelers (if only because their supply was limited), alcohol encouraged the crossing of cultural boundaries. African rulers appreciated cognac, and many explorers became connoisseurs of *pombe* in East Africa or of *malafu* (palm wine) in western and central Africa.

Surprisingly, it is the "exceedingly teutonic" Frobenius who gives us the following glimpses at spirited ethnography.[5] In an episode reported from the beginning of his trip he tells of a visit to Galala village, where he is received with palm wine. Afterward, obviously mellow on *malafu,* he takes a walk through the village "arm in arm" with chief Galala, takes notes, buys some objects, and makes an inventory of household goods. He then returns to the European station, kills another two bottles with M. Mignon, the local agent, and is in bed at 9:30 P.M. (1907, 21–22). Later he is visited by Bayanzi "King" Bungu, and when he returns the visit at the ruler's residence he exchanges gifts and buys objects, and the two of them have a good time: "We chat and drink together" (27).[6] On his return trip Frobenius notes: "At the headman's village of Kibabo a short *malafu* rest and acquisition of two different Bolokos (grooving tools). With joyful singing we go home. Mr. Lemme [his companion who had been ill] is practically cured" (28). The drinking tour continues on a trip with the Belgian agent to some Bayaka villages where again a lot of palm wine is consumed with general merriment while Frobenius keeps looking out for, and buying, objects (29–30). Later, taking a rest after another day of collecting, he notes, "then gourds with the splendid *malafu* appear" (41). Of course, he did not disdain the European variety, either; at the end of another working day he celebrates with champagne: *malafu ya mputu,* the palm wine of the Europeans.

Frobenius's enthusiasm for *malafu* is echoed by Becker's praise of local brews—for their hygienic properties: "*Pombe* is a good substitute for the whitish and brackish water whose use leads to fever and dysentery. Then there is also mead, whose composition is the same as in Europe and which, because it contains little alcohol, is excellent from a hygienic point of view" (1887, 1:76). The easy availability of *pombe* must have been a consolation to him since he reports, with obvious anguish: "Our portable cellar [of Bordeaux] is modestly composed of 150 bottles, to be divided, during three years, among four drinkers" (66). Later in his account, when he is a seasoned traveler, he lets us know that there is more to *pombe* than hygiene: "I have become perfectly accustomed to *Pombe*, which is a pleasant drink, refreshing and easy to digest. Certain travelers are wrong when they attribute to it a flat and repugnant taste" (2:23).

Understandably, travelers who imbibed did not dwell in their accounts on inebriation. The travelogues tell of celebrations—New Year's, the monarch's birthday, or another national holiday—where everyone was in high spirits. Wissmann cites this laconic entry from the diary of Dr. Wolf, one of his companions during his 1883 expedition: "March 22 [year not given; the date marks the kaiser's birthday] is inscribed in Wolf's diary like this: 'Good palm wine, hail to the kaiser!' " ([1890], 44).

Unlike later colonial agents (and missionaries), most of our travelers did not stay in Africa long enough to turn alcoholic as a way of coping with the stress and the madness of colonial life. Only Torday, a long-term resident of the Congo before he turned explorer, gave us a sketch of life, and drinking, among expatriates who were stationary—surely a dreaded prospect for many explorers. He once spent six months at Kinshasa, soon to become, as Léopoldville, the most important colonial post on the lower Congo. Here is what he remembers: "Some of us founded a (manuscript) newspaper called *Le Petit Léopoldvillain;* the subscription was a case (forty-eight bottles) of beer per annum; this was drunk by the editorial staff. I really think we were a miserable lot, and even our gaiety had a bitter taste" (1913, 21). His travelogue is otherwise exceptional with regard to the topic of alcohol. Drinking among Africans is mentioned only a few times; alcohol consumption as part of exploratory travel, never. The latter also goes for Thomson and Capelo and Ivens (who are almost obsessed with African drunkenness).

On the topic of alcoholism among Europeans, Dr. Wolff of the German Congo Expedition refers to an observation apparently made by Stanley, namely, "that the climate is healthy and that most of the people who get sick on the Congo and die are themselves to be faulted because of their excessive consumption of alcohol" (*MAGD* 4, no. 6 [1885]: 365). His colleague Kund also cites Stanley's statement but offers as counterevidence the fact that mortality among American Baptists, all of them "teetotalers," and English Baptist missionaries, most of them abstainers, was the same as that quoted in an IAA statistic—25 percent each year (375)! Of course, this does not obviate the observation, authoritatively articulated by Stanley, that alcoholism was rampant in the Congo Free State and an object of concern and fear.

FOOD AND MEALS

Drink leads us to food, another topic that took on the characteristics of a regime for explorers: what they ate was not only to sustain them but to contribute to hygiene. In the preceding chapter we mentioned the logistics of planning and carrying food supplies. Being dependent on local sources put explorers "in place"; they had to stop to get acquainted with certain regions they would otherwise have hurried through. To a large extent a caravan geared its composition and loads toward procuring food during the march. Hence the trade goods it carried were not really for trade, but for barter against food (though Pogge and others did trade textiles for ivory). Food was a necessity; sufficient and good food made the porters and soldiers of a caravan docile. When a successful hunt enabled Becker to add game to the usual fare, he states: "We literally lead them by the stomach—and if we'd always had so much game to give them, we'd have been spared many a disagreeable situation" (1887, 1:253).

Logistical problems with food were only part of what made the topic so important in the mind and daily life of our travelers. Expeditions differed widely when it came to deciding how much they would rely on the canned meat and vegetables, biscuits, bottled sauces and condiments, spices, coffee, tea, and sugar that outfitters in Europe or Africa provided. Travelers who had been less well supplied or had used up or lost their provisions through theft or accidents came to rely on, and even grew to like, local staples. But everyone dreaded running out of sugar or tea. These items and perhaps preserved food in general had, apart from their pragmatic use, a symbolic function. Showing the travelers to be independent of local sources, they increased the Europeans' authority over their African auxiliaries. The advice Becker has to give about canned foods reflects the traveler's concern about control of his environment. Notice the religious symbolism, complete with taboos and prohibitions.

> It is, by the way, very useful slowly to adapt to the food of the regions one crosses. This very special suppleness of the stomach is an integral part of the qualities an explorer must by all means have, be it by vocation, necessity, or profession. Maize, sorghum, rice, beans, manioc tubers, edible mushrooms

constitute food that is quite healthy and perfectly adapted to the hot climate.... Nevertheless, there are a few essential refinements it would be too cruel to do without. A special trunk, fitted with compartments, is the tabernacle where, in daily portions, these precious foodstuffs are kept: coffee, tea, salt, pepper, mustard, oil, vinegar, and so forth. Oil and vinegar are practically indispensable on the road and the same goes for English sauces and above all for curry powder, which activates digestion and whips up the blood.... You add to this particular viaticum, but only for the case of famine, some select cans of precious preserved food to be used sparsely. Needless to say, the tabernacle is locked so as to discourage illicit tastings. (1887, 1:196)

Becker goes on for another page to list culinary necessities, including their brand names, until he realizes the effect this may have on his readers: "I beg the reader to excuse me if I enter such utterly prosaic detail. But in matters regarding travel no euphemism will do. The smallest disturbance can in fact become a question of life or death" (197).

Occasionally we get "scientific" statements and reflections on nutrition and health; more often our authors express awareness of the profoundly cultural and social significance of eating. They indulge in nostalgia, recalling favorite dishes and memorable meals. These memories or fantasies undoubtedly contributed to their sense of identity. When Becker finally manages to get some butter he exclaims (in French, freely translated): "You should see the slices of bread I spread it on! And how much more tender my sautéed vegetables seem to grow, my ragouts and pastries. Take his butter away from a Flamand and he will be unhappier than some of Moses' companions who longed for the onions of Egypt" (2:260).

CONVIVIALITY AND FRIENDSHIP

These preliminaries over, we had the supreme pleasure of a good wash after our hard day's work. Then in the cool evening air, under the grateful shade of the tree, we had our dinner amid all the romantic conditions of African travelling, and over our cups of coffee we congratulated ourselves for the successful start we had made. (1:90–91)

In December 1880, after a march of four months, the Belgian third expedition arrived at Karema on Lake Tanganyika, then the outpost of the IAA farthest from the east coast. Ramaeckers, Popelin, and Becker were honored by a formal meal in the course of which Ernest Cambier, the station's founder, handed the command over to Ramaeckers. Becker's enthusiastic description of this event, apart from being interesting from a

culinary point of view, documents—to use a common African metaphor—
that on such occasions Europeans "ate their power."

> Dinner is served around 6 P.M. What a delight to eat on a well-laundered table-
> cloth, from china instead of the metal plates, darkened and scratched, which
> began to spoil our appetite! In our honor, the chef excels. *Potage jardinière,*
> boiled meat we find delicious, roast leg of goat with sweet potatoes.... A
> chicken curry completes the menu, together with English preserves and can-
> dies.... Two bottles of champagne were opened for the occasion. Extrava-
> gance! We won't see champagne again on our table for a long time. But we
> must toast the king and the International African Association. Which is what
> Captain Cambier does after having been asked, by acclamation, to keep the
> chair of the meeting. He recalls and praises the initiative taken by our sover-
> eign, eager to get his country interested in the great movement of modern sci-
> ence, and our patriotic hurrahs resound with the clinking of glasses. Then we
> enthusiastically raise them again to the success of the Work [of exploration]....
> We will see to it that we do not stay behind as far as devotion to the common
> cause of humanity and progress is concerned. Meanwhile it is getting darker
> and we go out to take our coffee on the porch, in the dim light of a single can-
> dle. The cigars are lit. Squatting on his heels, in the native fashion, M. Cam-
> bier tells us some episodes from his stay in Africa. (1887, 1:272, 275)

Such scenes turn up occasionally in almost all the travel accounts. Explorers staged festive meals in the midst of Africa as occasions to celebrate, and remember, their European identity. Here is one of Wissmann's
recollections from his second expedition, noted after he and his Belgian
companion had traveled through a stretch without food: "On the road,
Le Marinel and I often indulged in memories of the Café Riche in Brussels. At home Le Marinel was a particular connoisseur of the most exquisite preparation of culinary delights. Often his descriptions made my
mouth water. Usually the conversation ended with belt tightening...and
hope for better times" ([1890], 162).

Not surprisingly Belgians, rather than most of the Germans or the single Scotsman or the two Portuguese on our list of authors, excelled in
haute cuisine.[7] The famed colonial hospitality, still enjoyed or sometimes
suffered by us latter-day travelers, was a common practice (especially in
the centers on the coasts) before most colonies were established. A
heightened sense of belonging, the relaxing of everyday controls, a freer
exchange of insights and opinions (and occasionally, blows)—all this fueled by a good meal and drink—puts colonial conviviality high on our
list of ecstatic elements in the exploration of Africa.

Conviviality, helped by alcohol and drugs, music and dance, kept a
caravan going during the hardships of marching; it built one of the few

bridges between the participants in these early and fateful encounters of future colonizers with the colonized. Reichard and Böhm of the German expedition aptly introduce this important topic. The two were on their way to visit Becker at Karema when they stopped at the residence of chief Rugogo (who had recently become a blood brother of their colleague Kaiser).

> Rugogo received us surrounded by his *waniapara* [headmen], most of them, like him, older men. The old *mtemi* [chief], with his kind face and gray beard, made a very *gemütlich* impression.... When we wanted to take our leave after talking with him for quite a while, he invited us first to have a glass of water (*maji kunua*). A vessel made of grass was brought, filled with the contents of a colossal container of *pombe* hidden in a corner. The drink was then passed around. We thought we were in a medieval pub, in the company of *gemütlich*, beer-drinking burghers [*Philister*]. Only Reichard's *el Globo* cigars that everyone smoked did not fit the picture. (*MAGD* 3, no. 3 [1882]: 200)

In this instance spontaneous hospitality is offered and accepted; other examples of relaxed conviviality with Africans are dispersed throughout the sources. But here the narrative transforms immediate presence into a tableau we can observe from a distance. Its author conveys emotion by using and reusing the adjective *gemütlich,* one of those terms with rich cultural connotations that are so difficult to pin down as to be nearly untranslatable. Here the best paraphrase is "something that makes you feel at home." Because that is clearly the dominant mood of the scene, it would be wrong to render *Philister* simply as philistines. It expresses good-humored self-mocking, not condescension. The traveler clearly enjoys himself and opts for a predominantly visual description. He frames and thereby contains his experience as a genre picture (or two, adding the portrait of the chief and his cronies).

In other words, there were occasions when Africans and European explorers enjoyed drinking together and within these, we may guess, even moments of truth, an unguarded meeting of minds. But ordinarily the participants kept to their distinct regimes of knowledge and power (or science and magic, as we rename them later), which saw to it that such moments remained rare and short. One passage from Coquilhat says it all. He tells of Africans often coming to visit him just to kill time: "These dear friends felt the need to pour their hearts out to me, especially when abundant libations had made them mellow. Sometimes, pressed within the circle of their oiled bodies, shining and redolent, I experienced an hour of astonishing questions and expressions of friendship that were difficult to stop before they became too familiar" (1888, 204).

To think the African hosts were always without guile or ulterior motives when they feasted with Europeans would be naive. Yet evidence—even filtered through European accounts—shows them to be more eager and culturally better equipped than their guests to give these encounters a form that would qualify as ecstatic. Hygiene put brakes on any inclinations some explorers may have had to indulge in uncontrolled relations. More often than not, their obligations to science caused them to make their conviviality into a method. Hygiene and method allowed them to create distance, to deny or avoid immediacy when they wrote about their experiences. That Europeans considered denial a condition of producing knowledge is clear when we consider the many reported instances where their travelogues instrumentalize conviviality and, indeed, friendship.

It is again Coquilhat, in this case every inch the classical colonial ethnographer working from his veranda, who gives us one of the most vivid descriptions.

> For a few months I have been organizing receptions where sugarcane beer is served.... My guests like them and for me they are quite useful.... Everybody and their wives settles down in my dining room around the beer pot.... I use these meetings to obtain the occasional geographic information... [while his guests drink and talk, he smokes his pipe and does his accounting]. Little by little, tongues loosen. People stop addressing me. In fact, I try to make them forget I'm there. They get to questions currently debated among the Bangala. And, almost imperceptibly, the conversation gets to be so interesting that I keep leafing through my copybook, pretending I'm not listening. It is incredible how many facts, projects, and current ideas I learn in this manner. (1888, 329)

MEMENTO MORI: DEATH AND GRAVES

> I shook Dr. Kirk's [the British consul's] hand and bade
> him farewell with a quivering lip, yet with heart full of
> great hopes and expectations. It was a moment when a
> little shrinking was pardonable as the dread uncer-
> tainty of the future rose before us. We were entering
> the valley of the shadow of death into which many
> have passed and from which few have returned. (1:88)

Those who volunteered for exploration and travel in central Africa knew that the odds for returning alive were about even.[8] A text by Dr. Wolff of the German Congo Expedition contains an oblique yet revealing statement about the explorers' attitudes to the prospect of dying in Africa.

He ends his report with practical advice on equipment with the recommendation to keep hunting dogs. He responds to three objections: they lose their sense of smell (all dogs do when the weather is dry and hot), they get too easily used to the blacks (of course they will if you don't feed and exercise them yourself), and they die: "We too," he concludes. "Many of the people who came to the west coast at about the same time as I did are already buried" (*MAGD* 4, no. 6 [1885]: 367).

Not all the travelers were as casual as Wolff when they saw their companions dying and contemplated their own prospects. Some recorded their thoughts about the sense of embarking on journeys that were likely to end with death. When Becker hears of Cambier being close to dying he exclaims: "Such self-denial, such stoical resignation in the face of a demise that is perhaps imminent! Death! It watches us everywhere; in these murderous regions it hovers above everyone" (1887, 1:241). Later he blames Kaiser's death on his imprudence but admires his perseverance: "Like faith, science has its martyrs" (2:383). Becker praises Reichard and Böhm for their determination to continue after Kaiser's death and is moved to the following reflection:

> "To the end." This motto, which used to be Captain Popelin's, guides most of the travelers, who resist the African climate during the first months. Contempt for death more than anything else drives such enterprises. Deep down, such contempt is maybe nothing but blind trust in the future. It matters little that you have seen the most seasoned champions drop all around you. Even during the red-hot attacks of fever you do not want to think of passing away. You always flatter yourself for having escaped dangers though at every step they touched you, embraced you, with their menacing horror. What does it matter that such optimistic presumptuousness—which, I confess, I nourish to a high degree—produces the same results as the fatalism of the Orientals? (1887, 2:389)

Few authors wanted to, or could, express their feelings as openly as Becker. But death as the ultimate danger was always in these explorers' thoughts (we will take up other dangers later). Death entered their feelings and actions, and the necessity to overcome dread by leaps of hope that had no rational justification must be counted among the ecstatic elements in their encounter with Africa.

An urge to externalize this fear, to give meaning to seemingly senseless dying, I believe, lies at the bottom of a recurrent theme in these travelogues: the preoccupation with leaving memorials and monuments to their dead, inscribing them on the material of this lethal continent. There is mention of tombs for Pogge and Schulze (the latter as a budget item when the German association dissolved) (*MAGD* 5, no. 3 [1889]: 134); cemeteries of explorers and pioneer missionaries existed in Zanzibar and Tabora. Becker was traveling and visiting with the German East Africa expedition when he learned that Jules Ramaeckers, his much admired superior, had died of fever and dysentery at Karema—making him the sole survivor of the Belgian third expedition (1887, 2:191). He hurries back to Karema, which he had helped build. Now he is in charge of the station but "the memory of [Captain] Ramaeckers never leaves me and, at any moment, I forget reality and expect to see him again" (203). The day after his return he retraces the route to the mountains along which Ramaeckers had himself carried during his last days. From there he had a view north, "casting his weakened gaze toward his faraway fatherland." He was buried nearby under a tree but Becker resolves: "Soon I will see to it that a modest mausoleum will tell future travelers the story of the career, full of merit, and the sad end of this hero of Civilization and Progress" (204). Later he describes this "humble monument" and tells us that the tombstone has an inlaid photographic portrait of the deceased. Its inscription includes, apart from his name, rank, and date of death (February 25, 1882), the sentence "Europe and Africa will honor his memory" (223).

I found in my notes only one report of a grave being marked as a monument for an African member of the caravan. After a strenuous voyage on Lake Tanganyika Wissmann reached the Belgian post at Mpala (then already occupied by the White Fathers), when one of the women who had accompanied him from the Lulua fell ill and died: "We were unable to detect the cause of death and had to assume that she had died from accumulated exhaustion due to seasickness. We dug a grave for poor Galula and marked the place by placing a number of large stones on it in the form of a cross. The loss of our friend Galula, always in a good mood and busy, was painful to all of us" ([1890], 204–5).

Monuments to the dead kept European explorers' presence in the history of Africa. How many of them noticed that this gesture somehow responded to one of the ways in which the history of the landscape they traversed, recent and remote, presented itself to them? Most sources mention skeletal remains and cadavers lining the routes of caravans or the sites of recent hostilities. According to widespread custom, African chiefs and other prominent persons such as great hunters and sorcerers of renown were buried near roads (especially at crossroads). In the travel accounts these memorials are often reported because they usually contained "fetishes"—objects of desire for the scientific traveler—or became occasions for ethnographic inquiries.

FOUR

Drives, Emotions, and Moods

Explorers traveled in a demanding, often dangerous environment. Its necessities constrained their lives, and a regime of tropical hygiene imposed rules and gave directives for most of the typical situations and tasks. Hygiene was a matter of discipline, and discipline was the quality most likely to ensure the success of scientific work under difficult circumstances. We have already touched on the links explorers perceived between bodily afflictions ("that terrible African fever") and their mental causes and effects. Tropical hygiene included maintenance of sanity and, indeed, of composure in social and political relations with Africans. Especially in later phases of European penetration, tropical hygiene was one of the most explicit means by which colonial powers exercised their regime, controlling colonizers as well as colonized.

Inevitably, rules of hygiene applied to the explorers' sentimental and emotional inner life as well. But it was easier to hold forth on sensible clothing, sanitary housing, and healthy food than on measures designed to promote psychological equilibrium and a clear mind. What our sources have to tell us about emotional (self-)control comes in bits and pieces. Their statements are often veiled and oblique. For this reason we must assemble the chapter on which we are embarking as a collage of seemingly disparate observations. Their relevance to the argument of this study derives from the depth and subtlety they give to notions and practices of control that form the context of exploration as a rational enterprise.

SEX AND EROTIC TENSION

> Now if there is one thing on this earth I abhor it is a
> dance by almost nude savages. One can sit through a
> good ballet with wonderful equanimity; and the whole,
> as seen on the stage, has such an air of unreality about
> it, that we are composed, and do not remark on the
> predominance of legs and the scantiness of skirts. But
> in savage Africa it is different. There is an air of intense
> reality in the entire performance, and reality of such a
> low type as makes one shudder. There are no skin-
> tights or glittering dresses, and everything speaks of a
> condition but little removed from the brutish. Quite
> unaware of the sensitiveness of my feelings, these dark
> damsels surrounded me, and commenced their dreadful
> bacchanalian exhibition. (1:245)

Not surprisingly, the element of erotic tension occasionally unsettles encounters between Africans and European explorers. It figures among the
ecstatic elements of knowledge production (and, perhaps, adds a new
twist to the biblical connotations of knowing).[1] In Thomson's account
and elsewhere, the explorers' reports leave little doubt that sexual energy and erotic tension were among the forces driving their authors to
extraordinary feats and also providing material for regimes of hygiene.
But what complicates our assessment of the role of sex and erotic tension is the array of conventions these Victorian travelogues observed.
The conventions permitted travelogues to be prurient—if at all—only by
allusion and implication and now and then through illustrations baring
parts of the human body that civilized people kept covered. Fortunately,
even these Victorian accounts offer more than just conjectures and extrapolations we could make about healthy young males spending long
periods of time away from the legal or sentimental unions they may have
enjoyed while living in Europe.

Let me begin with a *trouvaille* apt to illustrate the multiple encod-
ings that were to hide the unspeakable. The second volume of Becker's
La vie en Afrique displays the portrait of a young African woman (Figure 1) with the caption RISIKI, MA FEMME DE CHARGE (Risiki, my housekeeper). In the one-volume abbreviated edition of the work, titled *La
troisième expédition belge au pays Noir*, Risiki's portrait appears again,
except that now the caption reads LA SULTANE DE KONKO (the chief of
Konko; see Becker 1889, 78). Little is known about that second edition
or the rationale for what was cut from the original. The case of the

FIGURE 1. Risiki as Becker's housekeeper (Becker
1887, 2:49) and—misidentified—as chief of Konko
(Becker 1889, 78).

transformed Risiki suggests that Becker, who may have used "housekeeper" as an intentionally equivocal expression, did not change the
caption.[2]

Risiki came to Becker as a present from his friend Tipo Tip when he
stayed at Tabora (1887, 2:48). She keeps his "bachelor's" household and
he extols her qualities, the excellent "hygienic" meals she prepares, and
her cleanliness (to the point that she begins to manufacture her own soap
[77]). She meets Becker's gourmet standards when she cooks the festive
New Year's dinner for 1882, which he celebrates together with his German colleague Reichard (100). Later it turns out that Tipo Tip's present
included another slave girl, Madenngué, and that a third woman completed Becker's domestic staff (Snati, Popelin's former housekeeper; also
portrayed [229]). With the death of Ramaeckers a fourth woman, Dodo,
becomes free but she decides to accompany her soldier lover back to the
coast (225). When Becker leaves Karema at the end of his term he takes
Risiki and Madenngué along to Tabora. He sets them up there with a
little house and a piece of land and even takes part in their wedding with

two farmworkers (400). In the end we are left guessing just how close Becker was to these women. But doubtless they taught him much about Africa, in domestic and intimate ways and in situations that differed from the explorers' usual encounters with African men.

Incidentally, the editors or censors who made Risiki Konko's chief could not have read *La vie en Afrique* very carefully or they would have known that the true (female) chief of Konko—who had nothing what-soever to do with Risiki—and her *demoiselles* had moved Becker to one of a few relatively direct statements about amorous relations. Selika was her name (Figure 2). She was a stately matron by the time the IAA Third Expedition visited her residence, but "Selika is perfect. If she were twenty years younger I would have fallen in love with her" (1887, 1:167). Becker continues, pushing equivocation to its limits when he recalls this episode with obvious delight,

> We also have the privilege to receive [the chief's] *demoiselles d'honneur.* I am not going to report the amazing conversations that take place in the course of these intimate meetings. Impossible to recount them! These *demoiselles* want to know the why and how of things and ask us the silliest questions about our Western morals.... Above all, they are amazed that we are travel-ing single and—may God forgive me!—would not hesitate charitably to fill that void left by our long voyage. (167)

He adds more about the young ladies of Selika's retinue—to tease the reader?[3]

> Sergère, Ramaeckers and Baron von Schöler excel in the art of amusing them, whereas our friend de Leu absolutely cannot *smell* them. The butter, more or less rancid, with which they are coated makes him sick. Naturally, you must submit to all their whims with good humor and never show fatigue or bore-dom. Such a role is not easy to keep up and not everybody's cup of tea. As far as I am concerned, I am much amused by this and shall take back the fond-est recollections of my friends from Konko. (167–68)

In the second volume of his work, Becker returns one more time to this episode, now adding a very important piece of information regarding male-female relations: "Our joyful and frequent exchanges with the *dames d'honneur* of the chief of Konko, our increasingly intimate rela-tions with the natives, our conversations with the men of our escort, and our studies, assisted by the immediate help we had from our personal servants, appointed language teachers, made me amazingly competent in the Swahili dialect. Already [around September 1881] I no longer need an interpreter" (2:51). The transition from erotic banter to serious lan-guage study that Becker describes puts "sex" into a perspective of close

FIGURE 2. The chief of Konko and her *demoiselle d'honneur* (Becker 1887, 1:169).

social relations that were vital to the enterprise of exploration. The intimate and relatively lasting relations some of the explorers seem to have had with African women were not necessarily limited to the satisfaction of sexual needs. They were part of daily life, of days filled with travel and domestic chores that had to be planned and discussed with companions, male and female. In central Africa it gets dark around 6 P.M. and explorers had ample time to chat with their women, listen to stories, and gather information about the country and its people—before they sought, if they did, the comforts of a shared bed.

Becker, a gifted and candid writer, offers the most quotable passages on the subjects that interest us, including the topic of sex and erotic tension. But his observations are by no means idiosyncratic or atypical, as two examples from other sources will show. Coquilhat once met a chief's invitation to avail himself of the females of his household by declaring "that one of our woman servants was my wife" (1888, 202). Later he named one of them, speaking of her as his—not our—servant. Her name, we learn, was N'Doumba (218). Even if it is, coincidentally, a homonym in a local language, Coquilhat must have known that *ndumba* (often badly translated as "prostitute") meant "unattached woman" in Swahili, the language of his Zanzibari soldiers. They would have called *ndumba* the kind of woman who was a European's temporary companion. One statement of Wissmann's is equivocal but—if he wants us to read between the lines—might be a direct admission of sexual relations: "He [the Congo Arab Djuma] was content that his women/wives often brought me fruit, milk, and fine pastry, consorting [*verkehren*] with me" (*Verkehr* can mean "intercourse" [1891, 183]).

Other travelogues contain similar reports on male-female relations beyond those of sexual intercourse. They tell of numerous instances of gender- or sex-related incidents between African members of a caravan and local people, which may have involved Europeans. But acts of sexual violence by European explorers against African women—or tales of sexual prowess from the masculine world of African travel—have no place among the accusations travelers sometimes leveled at each other. And yet the reports leave little doubt that erotic tension between abandon and control existed. Travelers dealt with it differently, as we observe in two encounters with female African rulers, one reported by Pogge, the other by Reichard.

For several months in 1875–76 when Pogge was staying at the Lunda ruler's residence, Musumba, he repeatedly had visits from the Lukokesha, an officeholder in the Lunda state. The first time she arrived with her entourage with due pomp and circumstance but then sought a tête-à-tête with the explorer in his hut. The conversation was animated and, Pogge tells us, "after a while, she began to touch me again and again." Things heated up a little when the Lukokesha (who was in her early twenties) returned for a second visit together with her younger sister, both riding on the shoulders of slaves. "When they arrived in front of my hut, the porters who carried the sweet burden bent down a little so

that the riders got to stand on their feet and could leave their seats"
(1880, 138). The phrase "the sweet burden" shows the ever-cool Pogge
betraying his feelings. But there was more. The two ladies were invited
inside, sat down on the explorer's metal case, and chatted with him for
more than an hour. "I must confess," Pogge says, "that the kind and gra-
cious demeanor of the two ladies made quite a pleasant impression on
me. I had to show them in detail my hair, my arms, and my feet. They
gaped at them admiringly and touched them" (139). Why "confess," unless he suggests the sentiments were mutual?

The plot thickens with a visit of the Lukokesha's sister, who "seemed,
however, a little tipsy. She also begged shamelessly and was inordinately
amiable. She took the pipe from my mouth and smoked. Then she expressed regrets to my interpreter that the door remained open and that
so many curious people were crowding outside my hut. While she made
these reflections, she did not stop giving me longing looks" (139). This
promising scene ends with Pogge sending her away with some presents.
He then continues his report with ethnographic remarks on the function
of this lady (she was her sister's personal physician [*Leibmedicus*]).

There were more meetings with the Lukokesha. Several times, Pogge
was invited to visit her and assist at some of her state functions. During one
of these another aspect of corporal knowledge is revealed: "On the Lukokesha's request... I had to show my arm, then my chest, and so on. Then the
eminent lady wanted me to get undressed, a wish that met with energetic
protest from my interpreters. As a reason for my refusal they pointed out
that undressing was against the customs of the whites. After an hour's chat-
ting we shook the hands of the entire company and left" (156).

My placing this particular episode in the context of erotic tension may
reflect a gender bias. Other (male) African rulers asked explorers to exhibit their white skin—parts of the body that were not usually exposed
to the sun—to satisfy their curiosity about the visitors' otherness (Thomson reports several such occasions; once, he notes, a chief kept him on
"exhibition of four days" [1881, 192]). Therefore, this particular request
by the Lukokesha for public exhibition of the naked body may have been
a display of power. Such an interpretation would fit the event's context.
On this occasion, the Lukokesha danced in public in a customary performance of chiefly power. This being said, we may of course still want
to ponder connections between the curious, the exotic, and the erotic in
a play of power between an African ruler and her European visitor.

The erotic does come back in another, private, scene in Pogge's hut,
where the Lukokesha insisted on performing a "labor of love" (*Liebes-*

dienst). She wanted to help him into a shirt she had given him as a present (157). Pogge tells us, distancing himself by the choice of words: "Today the person made me an outright declaration of love, which made me
quite uncomfortable. I should visit her and stay with her, and so forth"
(160). In German, applied to a woman, *Person* often expresses moral or
social disapproval. As if he needed to be sure of his feelings, Pogge adds
that the "real" purpose of this visit was just to extort another present.
He keeps his self-control here in an all too familiar way, by rejecting and
demeaning the other.

About five years later and more than a thousand miles to the north-
east, the German East African Expedition had dealings with another
female chief, Disha of Ugunda. These, too, involved frequent visits and
return visits. Compared to Becker's cherished memories of the chief of
Konko and her *demoiselles d'honneur*, Reichard's reports seem to be absolutely straight, bare of erotic overtones. Only tiny cracks in his ano-
dyne story let us guess at the tensions it holds under control. When he
described Disha's physiognomy he discovered a lascivious trait (*lüstern*)
(*MAGD* 3, no. 3 [1882]: 159) and may have hinted at some uncomfortable incident when he noted that she made her frequent visits "always in the company of her jealous husband" (164).

Sexual-erotic tensions and anxieties, rather than puritanical morals,
of which most of our protagonists cannot be accused, must also explain
the tirades against "native obscenity" directed, for example, by Büttner
of the German Congo Expedition. He holds forth on "'Medicines' that
are taken as aphrodisiacs, all sorts of fetish rubbish—often in the form
of a phallus—of which one expects the same effect; innumerable an-
thropomorphic fetishes with sexual organs rendered out of proportion,
and the obscene dances, which in the most explicit manner present the
story of courtship and marriage—in the end, such circumstances hardly
allow one to come to a flattering conclusion with regard to the morals
of the natives." Perhaps he realizes he has gone overboard with such
wholesale condemnation. Immediately following the quoted statement
he tries to balance it with a compliment, managing, however, to give a
racist twist to his opinion, subtle but all the more insidious: "Incidentally, it is well worth mentioning, that the natives, although they must
be called immoral, nevertheless do not indulge in unnatural vices,
though, in some cases, they are led to them by representatives of the Latin
race" (*MAGD* 5, no. 3 [1889]: 188).

Finally, we should note that even the liberal and candid Torday was
equivocal and evasive on the subject of sex. Consider the following re-

mark from his later book. In a chapter on courtship and marriage among
the Luba he speaks effusively about romantic love, trying to counter the
prejudice that natives have no such feelings. But he seems to get prudish
as soon as his own person is concerned: "The chief led me to a hut and
told me that as his guest the whole of his enclosure was at my disposal;
he paid homage to my ignorance and innocence by going into details
which I will spare my readers" (1925, 52). More than once in this account Torday announces that what he reports has been "slightly altered
to suit the taste of my chaste readers" (97). Did he anticipate censorship,
or did he play the theme so coyly because this left all the more to the
imagination? And what are we to make of the following remark in his earlier book? During a disquisition on love and love affairs among the natives he confides, "I trust my readers will not be shocked when I mention
that I got engaged to more than a dozen of them [little girls]; but if, when
I return, I find that they have got tired of waiting for the lover who wooed
and rode away, I will not be too hard on them, though by native law I
alone am entitled to release them from their engagement" (1913, 266).

To sum up, information on sexual and amorous relations is scant in
our travelogues;[4] it is seldom direct and often dispersed in clues here and
there. All the quoted statements are guarded; some are humorous and
appealingly human, others rather contemptible, racist, and chauvinist.
Either way they confirm impressions we form of an author's character
in the course of reading his account. In all cases, the writers show restraint and it is easy to see the encompassing regime of tropical hygiene
at work. I end the material on sexual and erotic tension as elements of
knowledge production by capping my own argument with Frobenius's
reflections on the availability of pleasure *and* on the need of keeping one's
distance:[5] "The economy of pleasures, which the journey offered [Wiss-
mann], life in countries where palm wine flows and the women are not
everywhere ugly, life among a race that is amiable and, at first, submis-
sive, albeit always indolent and irresolute, but one that immediately becomes impudent as soon as one gets carried away and becomes too familiar—this is what Hermann Wissmann had to learn from Paul Pogge"
(1907, 4).

OF LIONS AND LICE:
DANGERS, NUISANCES, AND ACCIDENTS

> We had come prepared for all this; indeed, we should
> almost have felt disappointed if our route had proved

easy and pleasant. Ridiculous as it may seem, we
thought ourselves entirely unworthy of the honourable
title of African travelers until we should have under-
gone such an apprenticeship of endurance and physical
discipline. (1:115)

The image of the explorer as a hero calls up dangers that loom and obstacles that must be overcome. All the travelogues recount perilous situations; the drama and adventure that kept readers entertained would
be difficult to convey if they only told stories of interminable treks, daily
chores and routines, and predictable annoyances. At times, we wonder
whether these danger tales do not reflect generic demands rather than
individual experiences. The travelogue's literary form requires them and
warns us not to take them all literally; as Becker once put it, there are
"poetic dangers" (1887, 2:352). We shall return to this question when
we look at genre in chapter 10; at this point we want to consider how
danger and other threats affected the explorers' minds and whether they
are among the uncontrolled and uncontrollable elements in the production of knowledge.

First a remark on the reasons for placing this and the following section on moods and feelings here rather than, say, in the chapter on travel.
Much like illness, conviviality, and sexual desire, dangers interest us as
subjective experiences—experiences with little statistical bearing on an
expedition's outcome. Moreover, we want to understand experiences of
danger and hardship as they befell or overcame explorers, much as
moods and feelings did. The two kinds of experience differ in that, unlike moods and feelings, dangers were as a rule not thought to be con-
trollable, hence not subject to the regime of tropical hygiene. The qualification is needed in order to accommodate exceptional statements about
danger stemming from lack of self-control, such as Becker's "Nothing
here is more dangerous than getting carried away and resorting to brutality" (1:98).

Our sources contain surprisingly few stories of getting waylaid, attacked, and robbed, the classic dangers of travel in foreign parts. Most
caravans were large enough and sufficiently protected by armed soldiers
to make such incidents unlikely. Even in the east, where organized banditry existed as part of a larger situation of endemic violence and war,
the accounts do not give the impression that travelers spent their days
or nights fearing attacks. As Becker put it, "We look our precarious situation squarely in the eye, and it does not cause us undue concern. We
begin to be blasé about our emotions. When one is always on guard, one

loses the sense of danger, or rather the heart gets used to it and feels driven to action" (164). The image of a "heart that acquires a tan," as the French original should perhaps be translated, aptly describes a psychological condition of insensitivity, acquired in situations of danger, which some of our authors regarded as a prerequisite of travel in Africa. It did not seem to trouble them that such a training might well dull their alertness as scientific observers. Real or not, the perceived dangers of violent attacks on life and property accounted at least in part for the martial outlook and organization of even the earliest expeditions (only Pogge's first trip and Torday's had no military escorts). The space such precautions took in a caravan's economy of goods and time could only limit the scope and intensity of scientific inquiry. A cursory survey of the travelers' accounts shows use of the term *attack* more often in the context of illness (fevers were almost always "attacks") than with reference to assaults from hostile Africans.

And what of attacks by wild animals, another classic among the dangers of travel in the wild? The few reports I found mostly served to embellish hunting stories. Images of a dangerous wilderness that belong to the myth of intrepid travel do not fit the prosaic realities encountered by our explorers. Apart from large rivers where hippopotamus and crocodiles were the targets of trigger-happy Europeans, game, even birds, had become so rare in the west that it took weeks or months for some travelers to spot their first wild animal, and it was unlikely to be a dangerous beast. In the interior parts of the east, game and its predators still seem to have been plentiful enough to warrant hiring some members of expeditions as hunters, who made a significant contribution to the provisions of a caravan. Profitable elephant hunting (for ivory) had become the monopoly of organized bands of specialists who dealt directly with local rulers or Swahili merchants.

As to attacks from wild animals that are not part of hunting stories, Becker conveys horror rather than heroism when he tells of a series of incidents that occurred when the caravan traversed the region of Ugogo. Local custom prohibited burying a porter, a stranger to the region, who had died of dysentery. During the night a pack of hyenas devoured the body. This horrible event was topped by the story of one of the caravan's soldiers, who "under a virulent attack from fever" took to the bush and was eaten alive, presumably also by hyenas. Here again, Becker seems to need to assure the reader, his motive for reporting the incident is not sensationalism: "Might one not say that this is a lugubrious story, born from the somber imagination of a [E. T. A.] Hoffmann, an Edgar [Allan]

Poe, or a Jules Verne? And yet what I am recording here is the exact truth, although I omit detail that may be too terrifying. Africa is a tough school and to get to know its mysteries one must have, as Horace says, a heart clad in triple armor" (172).

Later Becker tells a decidedly unheroic story of one of his rare encounters with savage beasts. Suffering from an attack of fever—the kind, he says, that gives one "ideas of suicide"—he commanded the small rear guard of the caravan. Exhausted, he collapsed against the trunk of a tree, when he saw a lioness with her young pass at a distance of about a hundred meters. He reached for his gun but was restrained by his servants, who feared he might miss the animal, which would then attack them. Instead, the Africans resorted to the customary tactic of gesticulating wildly and making a lot of noise, whereupon the "queen of the *Pori* [bush]" beat a dignified retreat (131, 132–33). If this story makes a point, it is to show the mastery of danger by Africans keeping their nerves, not the traveler's heroics. Toward the end of his account, he reports that two lions appeared at Karema station. They were shot and killed from the safety of the ramparts (2:364–65).

Stories about danger from wild animals are easily outnumbered by reports of being attacked by insects. Prosaic as these events may have been, the accounts often have a sense of drama and much military imagery. Bedbugs, spiders, fleas, lice, bees, mosquitoes, and above all ants appear as so many armies out to conquer the traveler's abode; compared to them, rats, bats, snakes, and other vermin are minor nuisances, with the exception of the sand flea, which buries itself in the wanderer's feet and whose extraction calls for special expertise (possibly the most frequent occasion to report dependence on, and bodily contact between, explorers and their auxiliaries). Pogge, who was not given to hyperbole, recalled a nocturnal attack by "some bedbug-like insects," which "stung such that I woke up sick to death and had to spend the rest of the night outside, fainting repeatedly" (1880, 42). He goes on to tell us that his bedding and clothes proved to be infested and had to be treated with *Insectenpulver* (insecticide), thus adding another item to our lists of medicines and poisons used by African explorers.

That insects carried dangerous parasites was not foremost on the mind of our travelers (during most of the period the causes of malaria were only vaguely known). Almost without exception, they decry the loss of badly needed sleep, already endangered by worries and the din of night-long dances. That this belongs to an inquiry of what drove travelers out of their minds is best illustrated by one of the most vivid descriptions in our corpus. Büttner, of the German Congo Expedition, recalls "truly horrible nights."

> What makes these creatures so annoying is not only the fact that they bite but rather the determination with which they keep on buzzing at night around a tired person. Though we are sometimes plagued by mosquitoes at home, one cannot imagine the agitation, nervousness, and despair they cause here.... Of course, there are noticeably fewer bloodsuckers around during the dry season because of the lack of stagnant water to favor their development, but sometimes a single little beast is more than enough to drive a human being to despair. (*MAGD* 5, no. 3 [1889]: 222)

This is just a brief excerpt from a six-page treatise on the topic of insects (220–25) in the course of which Büttner also mentions (giving us a glimpse into the minds of some explorers) "unavoidable contact [*Berührung*] with the indigenous population and spending the night in their huts" (224) as an aggravating problem of hygiene in Africa.

Among the tribulations that befell travelers were spells of hunger and thirst. Lack of drinkable water was a chronic problem that could become life-threatening when a caravan had to move through arid regions. Describing the effects of starvation, Capelo and Ivens report that, at one point, things had got so bad that they "were no longer capable of thinking, that is to say, in a regular and consecutive manner; we let matters simply drift, and saw with perfect indifference things which at a later period would have evoked our anger, our compassion, or our active interference" (1882, 2:140). Most sources make it clear that something other than uncontrollable environmental conditions often made them run out of food. Lack of foresight and planning was to blame, or logistical problems (foodstuffs could not be got to the place where they were needed). Often, bad relations with local populations made it impossible to buy provisions. Authors do not dwell on hunger, but occasional remarks remind us that it was real enough. Coquilhat, for instance, recalls a trip up the Congo with the illustrious Stanley during which they are unable to buy provisions. "We smoke," he says, "enormous quantities of native tobacco, very strong and acrid, in order to deceive our stomachs" (1888, 119, see also 128).

Pogge suffered from hunger and, as a result, from fever during his first trip when he reached the Kasai River. To add to his troubles—and bringing us to the topic of accidents—he was attacked by his one remaining riding ox, suffering two broken ribs (1880, 214, 215). In his diary he noted observations on Africans being killed by snakebites, crocodiles, and lightning (*MAGD* 4, no. 4 [1885]: 253–54). On the whole, however, it is remarkable how little European travelers were plagued by serious accidents. Our sources contain only two catastrophic events. One is reported by Böhm in a letter dated August 1882. Near Gonda (the German station near Tabora) the German expedition had constructed a hunting lodge, called Waidmannsheil. It was used to store provisions, arms, and ammunition as well as the "archive with the originals of our reports and correspondence, ledgers and copybooks." On August 16 the building caught fire when some employees, against explicit instructions, burned the grass nearby. Everything was lost in the flames. Here is Böhm's personal inventory, which incidentally gives us a glimpse at how seriously he had taken his scientific tasks.

> Burned was not only my entire personal equipment, not only the entire scientific literature I had taken along and almost all the material needed for collecting, preparing, and conserving, but all my written notes, summaries on the fauna of West and East Africa that I had prepared in Europe, excerpts, memos, collections of illustrations, and so on, all my diaries save a small, carbonized remnant that I tore from a burning trunk, all my zoological journals, botanical notes and catalogues of collections, all my watercolor sketches, more than fifty of them, the zoological collections assembled since the last one was sent away in May of this year, and the zoological papers I had just completed, there being only one whose broad outlines I can reproduce from memory. (*MAGD* 2, no. 4 [1883]: 285)

The loss was all the more grave because Böhm was just preparing to enter what he considered truly unexplored country and, he now realized, "without working material, work itself becomes impossible for the zoologist" (285). How much of a catastrophe this accident was is confirmed by Becker, who laments the loss of the collections stored at Waidmannsheil, which "housed, apart from numerous samples of natural history and ethnography, a magnificent album of sketches and watercolors" (1887, 2:390).

The same Böhm later got wounded during a punitive expedition organized by the Belgian expedition from Karema station. Shortly before this incident one of his companions, Kaiser, had died of fever and possibly quinine poisoning (*MAGD* 4, no. 2 [1884]: 95, 97–99). Böhm put the fire, lethal illness, and his own wound down to "constant bad luck" following this expedition (99)—but is getting shot at during a punitive expedition "bad luck"?

Capelo and Ivens had celebrated a national holiday on July 24, 1879, when a fire, also started accidentally, destroyed their encampment (1882, 2:173–77). They vividly describe the conflagration, their rushing about amidst exploding ammunition to save their instruments and records and then sifting through the ashes for pieces of paper and remnants of their belongings. Apparently not everything was destroyed, as in the case of the German hunting lodge. But their text does not tell us how much and what exactly was saved, for instance, of their diaries, or hint at how the losses affected the writing of their travelogue.

MOODS AND FEELINGS

> But now, with only thirty good men and true, I seemed
> to have no anxieties or cares. So light of heart did this
> feeling make me, that I was tempted sometimes to exe-
> cute a good Scotch [sic] dance for the benefit of the na-
> tives, in order to reduce the effervescence of my spirits.
> (2:20)

Even if Böhm wanted to hide his feelings behind a matter-of-fact account of the catastrophe, a closer look at his breathless, repetitive enumeration of items lost betrays his emotions. Moods and feelings overcame all travelers. That almost all of them chose to consign them to their diaries and report them in their travelogues does not surprise us now. As we have seen from one angle after another—trying to identify the conditions of knowledge production that are significant in the history of modern ethnography—reason and unreason, heroism and baseness *together* describe the nature of exploration. What explorers felt in, about, and for Africa and, above all, what they were moved to communicate of their feelings belong without question to an inquiry into the conditions of experiencing and knowing.

Depending on their character, intelligence, and integrity, travelers protected themselves with ironclad prejudice or countered what they perceived as threats with hatred and contempt. For others (most of them, I think), travel out to Africa became travel into their selves. Not many would have dared to state this as clearly as Becker does toward the conclusion of his work. Against the *statisticiens de la science*—as he calls those who are interested in results alone, not in the persons and actions that produced them—he declares: "Everything is matter for personal exploration on this mysterious Continent" (1887, 2:495).

Let me begin the presentation of relevant texts with a suggestion that may be surprising. The conviction that knowledge begins with, or at least cannot do without, sensory perception and that sight is, as Locke put it, the noblest of the senses has deep roots in Western tradition. Accordingly, we would expect that the sights of Africa affected, or assaulted, explorers more than other impressions and therefore caused the strongest emotional response and the most urgent need to counteract or control this form of exteriority. Yet our sources contain statements showing that the sounds and something we may call commotion—caused by the travelers' need to keep themselves and the apparatus of exploration in motion—became the greatest challenge, and threat, to the scientific enterprise. The authors express it in recurrent complaints about a lack of calm and a struggle for self-composure.

One evening when Pogge stayed at the Lunda capital, he decided to take a quiet walk with his interpreter Germano and to offer some *Magenbitter* (bitters) as medicine to the Lukokesha, the female ruler. When they come to the central public square they find an agitated and noisy scene. Some two hundred warriors back from a raid are performing a war dance he tries to describe; after all, this is a splendid occasion to do some ethnography. He ends the entry in his diary: "A large crowd of people, mainly women, formed the spectators. Mwata Jamwo and the Lukokesha donated palm wine to the dancers, which duly contributed to the general mood of gaiety. However, the latter, especially that of the ladies, became too animated for my taste such that, after a while, I preferred to enjoy the mild beautiful night, calmly and in tranquillity in front of my hut" (1880, 164). Buchner expresses a similar feeling, though less graciously. On his trip to the Lunda but still in Portuguese territory he makes this observation: "I, for one thing, want to work as much as I can. For this Malange is an excellent place, deserted and so calm that you actually only hear the buzzing in your own ears, totally different from Dondo, where you are disturbed day and night by the disgusting squabbling and racket made by the black riffraff" (*MAGD*, no. 3 [1879]: 157).

Some of the most explicit and poetic statements on moods and feelings we owe to Becker. Once he recalls how he had suffered through a long, futile palaver with chief Simba, who got drunk and stayed drunk during their negotiations. But instead of the usual acerbic observations travelers would make on such occasions, Becker refrains from comments and goes on to describe how he felt later when his caravan set up camp somewhere in the bush: "In the shade of my tent, the thermometer is at 34 degrees centigrade. I feel unspeakably content to camp in the middle of the bush, a long way from so-called hospitable villages where the only thing people worry about is how to rob you blind. Surrounded as I am by soldiers and porters who squat at crackling fires, tired but undefeated by a long stretch of marching, I sit and smoke my pipe with serene delight" (1887, 1:392).

When circumstances were right, travelers had moments of bliss wherever they happened to be. But one kind of experience seems to have moved these men more than others. European travelers, after all, were urban people, used to working and living indoors, in their own studies or in barracks. It is not surprising, therefore, that they were often overwhelmed by "great African nature." Here is how Becker put it.

> You experience an infinite and indefinable well-being when, in the evening, you rest on a soft bed of herbs and leaves as the bright constellations of the southern hemisphere scintillate in the heavenly canopy. Thought, as if it had slipped the shackles of terrestrial life, glides unfettered through the immensity. Then, waiting for sleep to take hold of you, you observe with curiosity the lively crowd of soldiers while from everywhere come the rustling sounds of animal life laboring to give birth. And when the night advances and man and beast are lying down, overcome by the day's fatigue, and you hear only the sigh of a gentle breeze and the plaintive cry of some savage animal, then you are in total communion with the great African nature whose secrets you came to catch, having grown tired of the marvels of the old world. (107)

As a translator I am no match for Becker's poetic effusions, but I found some consolation in a remark he noted a little later, when he tried to convey the impression travel through a desert region made on him. Of the experience of nature "even the most puffed-up descriptions could give our etiolated urbanites no more than a weak notion. That is why I did not even try to start drawing an image that is untranslatable" (126).

Our predecessors appear farthest removed from modern sensibilities when they express pride or elation. Almost always in similar terms, these feelings reflect patriotism—sentimental at best, chauvinistic at worst—or their consciousness of serving humanity through the *oeuvre civilisatrice*. Here is how Becker goes overboard after his long trek from the coast when he sees Karema station on Lake Tanganyika for the first time.

> The breeze blowing from the lake makes the banner of the International African Association, blue with a golden star, flutter in the wind! Should I admit that, at that moment, I had tears of joy and pride in my eyes? If there is a sacred and legitimate emotion, it certainly is the one caused by the sight of the Flag, emblem of Civilization and the Fatherland, for which you have suffered, which you have sworn to hold high and firm in victory as well as in danger, and to which you have pledged all the vital strength of your being, all your ardor of devotion and faith! (267)

Bliss and despair, elation and depression often were close companions, a fact Becker pondered toward the end of the first volume of his work, where he came to a conclusion that takes him back into the fold of discipline and self-control: "Like the weather, the human soul has its gray phases and others that are full of light. We have overcome fever, why should we be weaker when we face discouragement? After all, we did not come here to amuse ourselves" (346).

At the end of his exploration of the Lulongo River, Wissmann's companion von François speaks, in one of a handful of reflective notes in an otherwise impersonal account, of a feeling that must have also inspired many of his colleagues: "This day had given me exceptional satisfaction and filled me with suspense, looking forward to the days to come when I would travel on the Tshuapa River" (von François 1888, 93).

To conclude this section, here is a text illustrating one more time how quick travelers were to identify moods and feelings as threats to their health and self-control. The writer is Wissmann. On his first trip across Africa he had reached Lake Tanganyika, and during an excursion along its shore his thoughts turned back to his family and his friend Pogge, whom he had to leave behind.

> In this savage country such thoughts in a soft mood are rare. During the day, you must worry, work, and struggle; the evening keeps the mind busy with the prospects for the next day until sleep claims its due. It is just as well not to have time for brooding; a soft mood makes you less able to exert yourself and, in my experience, favors malarial fever. For me, constant stimulation of the nerves, combined with success, has always been the best remedy for fever. Idleness, grief, or gloom cuts your resistance to the climate. (1889, 223–24)

HUMOR AND LAUGHTER

> While collecting the plants I was the subject of innumerable jokes. My guides could not understand all this work, and made themselves very merry at my expense. However, as I did not understand them, I let them laugh. (1:57)

Envy and stubbornness, dejection and sadness are sentiments our authors express during the enterprise of exploration (or contempt, rage, and fear, of even more relevance to the topics of power and authority we will discuss in chapter 6). Among them, sadness has been an ingredient of anthropology ever since its beginnings as a science of disappearing cultures. In more recent times, sadness became accepted as a predicament of ethnography after the publication of Lévi-Strauss's *Tristes tropiques* (1955)—whose opening sentence was "I hate travels and explorers." Perhaps anthropologists and many other readers of his book were prepared to indulge in *tristesse* because they were still susceptible to an unbroken myth of the traveler as hero;[6] invocations of tragedy, together with a good measure of *Kulturpessimismus,* let the hero's accomplishments shine in a brighter light. One thing is certain: fun and humor have not been among the strengths of ethnographic writing, and that is an impression we also take along from our sources.

Still, if the experience of mirth and the urge to laugh somehow affect the production of knowledge, humor and laughter should have our attention in this exploration of the explorers' minds. So much seemed clear to me—until I went about compiling texts and references. Humor and laughter are notoriously difficult subjects, philosophically, psychologically, and culturally. Looking for a pattern in the cases and references, I settled on five kinds of evidence. First, there are travelers' simple reports on humor and laughter they observed among Africans. Second, travelers occasionally recorded what they found amusing as they watched Africans. Third, some authors offered reflections on humor as a measure of hygiene. Fourth, travelers gave examples of the effects and usefulness of humor and laughter in communicating with Africans. Fifth, they present their findings through irony, parody, and caricature. Only the first three, I decided, have their place in the present context concerned with understanding exploration as it was lived. Laughter as a response to objects and performances will be taken up in the next chapter.

First, then, about humor observed among Africans. A remark by Pogge ideally suits our purposes; it contains ethnographic information and at least a hint at how such information impressed the explorer's mind (as we shall see later on, often this meant literally what it *re*minded him of). It also typifies the backhanded compliments many of our authors paid to Africans whenever they could not avoid doing so. Here is what he says: "I am always delighted by the humor of my people. They laugh and joke about everything." So far, so good. Then he recommends: "A bad theatrical comedian should travel to Africa. Here, his act would be a great success" (1880, 83). The offhand pairing of compliment with insult, of recognition with denial is a figure of speech in these accounts. Its very effortlessness counts as a sign of the observer's humor. Wit feeds on the incongruous, found or created.

Pogge's statement was a generalization. We may compare it to a passage of a more descriptive nature. While the explorer was living in the Lunda capital he was the object of curiosity and attracted many visitors even before the Mwant Yav made his first official appearance. When a son of the ruler and his wife called on him, he noted: "There was not much of a conversation. Every time he looked at me, the Mwant Yav's son could not refrain from laughing, which I returned copiously, while the princess, as if petrified, gave me a fixed and silent stare" (1880, 130). Pogge drops the incident and leaves us at a loss. What was so funny as to make the visitor laugh? And why did Pogge laugh? Did he, in a flash of intuition, realize how bizarre a European explorer must have looked to an African? (Some travelers do report noticing how ridiculous they looked when they emerged from months in the bush and faced their well-kept colleagues at a station.) If so, why did the princess not seem to get the joke? Perhaps the two men were just hiding their embarrassment because they could not talk to each other? It is easy to get lost in conjectures when we try to fathom such deceptively simple incidents. I am sure an ethologist could be found who sees in this scene only two primates baring their teeth to show aggression.

African ethnography has taught us what these travelers could perhaps not have known. What counts as funny or, conversely, what laughter indicates, is profoundly cultural and therefore most difficult to understand and share. Incidentally, even though there are some hints here and there, our sources did not as yet conceptualize or dwell on "joking relationships" (kinship and other relations calling for obligatory banter and exchange of insults) that became one of the most frequently visited topoi of anthropological writing. On the road, it would have been difficult to observe such relationships or, observing them, to recognize them as cultural practices.

Explorers, as infectious as African laughter may have been, seldom caught the joke and limited themselves to generalizations about cheerful natives. I found one striking exception to this rule (remarkable also for the author's exceptional capacity to empathize) in an observation Torday made on laughter as response to a story well told: "The men laughed quietly, with the quaint gurgling sound which is the only polite way of showing glee when a story is told. It has survived amongst the civilized people; if you want to hear it you must surprise a mother laughing to a tiny baby when she thinks herself unobserved. It is the gentlest sound of merriment in the world" (1925, 249).

Pogge gives us more food for thought when, two pages after the remark we quoted earlier, he describes his official reception by the Lunda ruler. After the ceremony of greeting, the Mwant Yav asks him to take off his hat, a request that at first is not understood linguistically and has to be expressed by means of a "pantomime": "When I finally took off my hat, general cheering erupted. Muata Yamwo laughed and it seemed that he made remarks about my hair, while his entourage clapped their hands and whistled on their fingers" (1880, 132). One of the lessons Europeans, especially missionaries, had to learn about African laughter was that what they often took for derision was in fact applause and recognition, for instance, for a phrase well turned. Torday's observation and this text confirm this. By the way, Pogge's comment shows too that he did not recognize one of the most common expressions of joy in these parts of Africa. In all likelihood, the sound he identified as whistling was ululating, a high-pitched cry the spectators emitted while rapidly touching their lips with their fingertips. Women especially express cheer and delight in this manner.

Becker reports the following incident without a comment but presumably with a purpose. Soldiers of the caravan had joined the local population in a harvest festival. Some of them were about to express their joy by firing their rifles, which had been prohibited by the leaders of the expedition. The first soldier who was caught trying was given a *bastonnade,* a caning. But "this act of severity only adds to the enjoyment of the escort. With a lot of laughter they greet their unfortunate comrade's contortions, caused by shame more than by pain" (1887, 1:98). Other travelers also observed Africans laughing at the misfortune or misery of others. They were quick to interpret such behavior as morally reprehensible, if not as generally expressive of African savagery. In sum, when explorers observed African laughter, they were often left at a loss, occasionally outraged, and seldom moved to join in it.

As regards the next point on our checklist—things that travelers laughed at—we face again reports that are anything but straightforward. Europeans often found African performances, such as dances, greeting ceremonies, rituals, and demonstrations of stateliness, comical. The more thoughtful among the observers sometimes felt they had to suppress their reaction. Becker gives an example when he describes the scene of a *grand chauri* (from Swahili *shauri:* consultation, deliberation), a solemn palaver. On an earlier occasion he had reported that his colleague Popelin simply left such a meeting in disgust because he found it ridiculous. Now he observes Emile Storms, his successor at Karema station: "Warned by the amazing pipe [that circulates at the *shauri*] my successor, more patient than Captain Popelin, manages to keep a straight face. As far as I am concerned, I became armored against laughing long ago" (2:376).

Few bothered to reflect on what their laughing at Africans may have done to their ethnographic understanding of the events they witnessed—framing it with a European observer's mirth. For instance, travelers invariably thought that Africans who began to adopt European manners, habits of speech, or fashions of dress were ridiculous. When examples were noted, the authors assumed a sort of complicity with their readers: only they saw the funny side of this. As yet, they did not suspect Africans of being able to wield those powerful "weapons of the weak" that mimesis and parody can be. To Gierow, treated as the most humble among the explorers who were given a voice in *MAGD*, we owe one of the rare reports that manage to record mimetic behavior without condescending derision.

> In the morning, a young Kioko [Tshokwe] came to the camp who, after having seen whites yesterday for the first time in his life, tried to make himself similar to them; he had framed his face with a beard fashioned from fiber, came up to our tent and sat down. All the porters stood around him and did not stop laughing aloud, but there was nothing that could make him lose his composure; for hours he suffered the mockery of those around him and only after all of them had had their fill of laughter, did he make a dignified exit. (*MAGD* 3, no. 2 [1882]: 114)

More typical of white humor are stories such as the one Buchner tells in the following excerpt. He was at Malange, on his way to the Lunda, when he was asked to be the godfather at the baptism, followed by an oath of loyalty to the governor, of a local chief, a very old and frail man. Other whites were also present at this mise-en-scène of Portugal's crumbling colonial regime (the officiating Catholic priest and his acolytes, incidentally, were from Goa). The text is a monument to lack of sensitivity and comprehension.

> Like everything that happens with this race of negroes, the religious ceremony that now followed lacked dignity.... The whole event was more comical than serious. When you looked at the person to be baptized, as he knelt with embarrassing awkwardness, his hands folded rigidly and his lips trembling, it was almost impossible to resist laughing. The whites who were standing around made bad jokes, and the *Soba's* [chief's] entire entourage responded with giggling as if they were watching an unusually funny spectacle. (*MAGD*, nos. 4–5 [1879]: 241)

It was this sort of "humorous" observation, devoid of empathy and understanding and combining embarrassed defensiveness with contempt, that I first found in Frobenius's work. It made me angry enough to write an essay on "White Humor" (Fabian 1992). At that point I did not recognize that the ethnographer's insufferable attitude was but one of many tokens of madness in exploration. In a chapter titled "Among the Conquistadors of the Kasai," Frobenius describes the operations of one of the most notorious villains in the drama of the Free State, the Belgian rubber company (Compagnie du Kasai). With his usual thoroughness, he assembles an impressive dossier of cases of brutality against Africans, of mismanagement, incompetence, alcoholism, and slave trading by agents of the company. In a vain attempt to remain objective and see some sense in this madness, he tries to explain violent oppression by invoking the colonial situation. European agents, most of them of a low class and ill prepared for their work, must use force: "Furthermore, there is the fact that, on the one hand, the lassitude of the negro and, on the other, the nervous transformation which the psyche of the European undergoes due to fever and climatic influences unfortunately too often lead to a more severe treatment of the native. All this is obvious" (1907, 293).

The callousness of Frobenius's explanations is nothing compared to the semiotic metamessage his chapter encodes. Before its heading and interspersed in its text are thirteen caricatures by the expedition's artist whose captions all start with the formula "Exercises in the humoristic contemplation of the negro." We will return to these images in chapter 10 when we discuss the illustration of travelogues. In the present context, they document an aspect that falls under our fifth category, humor as a means of presentation. But the passage immediately after the excerpt just quoted will make it clear why I took this detour to reach the third category on our list, humor as a means of hygiene.

> But there is one means to protect the European against the effusions of choleric fits—that is humor.... It is not without reason that I illustrate this tragic chapter with gay little pictures from the life of the Boys. These are sketches, conceived by the expedition's draftsman after humorous experiences in daily life. The fact is, you cannot do enough in Africa when it comes to self-control and, above all, self-education. He who begins to get bitter and to cultivate his bitter mood is on a crooked path. Since the beginning, therefore, I have endeavored always to see the comical in a situation, always the humor, and to emphasize the humoristic side. In the course of doing simple daily chores, you find occasions, from early morning to late night, to get terribly angry with your servants and porters. In Europe, you would laugh about similar actions and the same situations. I always took recourse to comparison and so we actually always had fun.... Every day you repeat the same thing ten times, and twenty times it is done wrong. Get used to laughing about their bizarre getup, their fantastic nature, their vanity, and you will be ahead in the game. That is how it goes with the Boy, that is how it goes with the porter, the worker, and the Kapita [foreman]. (1907, 294)

Humor helps us through adversity—that is how it goes with us, being the kind of people we are. That being the kind of people *they* are is an adversity humor helps *us* bear—this is a strange proposition for a student of Africans to assert. "To laugh means to gloat [lit., to enjoy another person's misfortune], but in good conscience," Nietzsche says in *Die fröhliche Wissenschaft*. He understood why Africans laugh at the misfortune of others. Perhaps this aphorism illuminates what explorers observed about African laughter, but it is difficult to see "good conscience" in their laughter at Africans. On the whole, explorers were too much concerned with maintaining distance and decorum to give themselves over to the joys of shared laughter. European humor is safe behind an enclosure that marks resistance to the pull that Africa exercised on the minds of explorers—the thousand ways to absorb its sounds, sights, smells, and tastes, the countless temptations to join in feasts and conversations. These are the topics that will occupy us in the two chapters that follow.

FIVE

Things, Sounds, and Spectacles

IMPRESSIVE OBJECTS

> Our examination of Debaize's stores revealed some
> strange things. There were twelve boxes of rockets and
> fireworks, which would require about forty-eight men
> to carry them, several boxes of dynamite (for what
> conceivable use no one knows), two large barrels of
> gunpowder, innumerable revolvers and guns, two coats
> of armour, several boxes of brandy, two loads of penny
> pop-guns, a load of small bells, large quantities of
> botanical paper, insect bottles and tubes smashed, sur-
> gical instruments, boxes of medicines without labels,
> photographic apparatus, every conceivable appliance
> for geographical research—though he was perfectly ig-
> norant of the working of even the most simple instru-
> ments. He brought with him also a hurdy-gurdy, val-
> ued at 12,000 francs. (2:96)

Among the "strange things" that drew explorers outside the safe confines of rationally controlled inquiry were certain objects and performances (the reason for naming the two in one breath will become clear
presently). The communicative relations researchers depend on in gathering ethnographic knowledge hardly ever fit simple models of a transfer of information by means of a code of signs. In addition to theoretical and practical models—language and speaking—we must pay

attention to nonlinguistic forms of communication explorers had to rely on in their early encounters. The project of transcribing African languages, reducing them to lexica, grammars, and manuals, was still at its beginning. And the idea (an illusion at all times) that languages could serve as readily available instruments or simple tools of ethnography would prove difficult to maintain.

Human beings communicate by means of language, signs, and symbols but also by their ways with space and time, with things and events; by sensory perceptions of sound, touch, and smell; by habits of gaze and bodily movement—all of which vary greatly as regards the extent to which they can be made subject to conscious control and methodical scientific investigation. Realizing this adds an important dimension to our search for ecstatic aspects in the exploration of Africa.

Among the oddities that make us wonder about the explorers' minds is their duplicity when it came to appreciating the role of things, or objects, in producing and representing knowledge. For instance, our authors shared the premise that African religious and philosophical beliefs had their quintessential form and expression in "fetishism." They were convinced that Africans not only made certain objects their fetishes but perceived all things that were somehow remarkable, new, or strange to them as fetishes too. Since travelers usually surrounded themselves with such things, they imagined themselves endowed with a magical aura. Projecting their power, they set out to impress Africans with the help of striking objects. Let us look at a few examples.

Pogge, less prejudiced in these matters than most of his colleagues, tells of several days during which the Lunda ruler is unavailable because he is busy "preparing fetishes." Presumably for that purpose he sends someone to Pogge to ask for a mirror. This is what the explorer recommends: "On this occasion I advise all travelers to take the necessary precautions at Musumba and to take account of the fact, for instance when experimenting with instruments, that the current Mwant Yav is quite superstitious and distrustful" (1880, 162).

Wissmann's scientific instruments once earned him an accusation of sorcery: "Barometer and thermometer were looked at with the greatest distrust. When a man suffering from a lung disease died during the night, it was evident to all of them, that only the instruments had to be blamed for his death, all the more since the day before a number of sorcerers had passed the hemp test" (1891, 301).[1] Wissmann knew that some Africans did not show the expected reaction but simply asked questions about the purpose of things that were new to them, as he observes here.

> The Bakuba are very superstitious. All things unfamiliar to them they call magic and fear they may bring misfortune. Thus, what with all my possessions, I was regarded as the most dangerous sorcerer they had ever seen and whose presence in their country boded nothing good. When I pulled out my watch or compass, this caused general excitement. Unlike the Baluba, they did not ask for an explanation of things unknown to them. They rejected them with hostility and demanded they be removed at once. (232)

In other words, there were travelers who may have shared the usual assumptions about fetishism but recognized that Africans related to objects also in ways that were neither exotic nor magical. Side by side, ideological projection and realistic experience come out in two episodes reported by von François. Here is, first, the expected story about the magical power of unfamiliar objects: "My meter was a simple measuring cord that, when extended, could be made to disappear in its casing by pushing [a button]. A visible quiver went through the limbs of the strongest warriors when the long, snakelike cord disappeared with a jerk in its container. Where was the snake? There must be some evil magic behind this" (1888, 108).

So much for the predictable. A little later, in another observation on how Africans relate to objects, in this case familiar objects, von François surprises us with one of the most touching passages I encountered in our sources. In the company of George Grenfell, the famous missionary and explorer, he was traveling on a small steamer, exploring the lower Tshuapa River. The people along the shore were hostile and attacked the boat several times with their bows and arrows. The explorers' guide and interpreter, a native from a place called Lukolela, was so scared that he never left the engine room. This angered Grenfell and especially his boatman, a certain Joaquim, and led to the following incident.

> Joaquim reprimanded the man from Lukolela. But when nothing worked to give him more courage, Joaquim yanked the man's pipe from his mouth and, as a sign of thorough contempt, threw it into the water. Now the guide cried like a child; his favorite pipe was lost, his pipe that he had cared for like the apple of his eye, his pipe that was a present from his wife and that reminded him of the time of his first love. The whole day we heard his sobbing from some corner; he was thoroughly broken. (110)

Thus, some explorers took care to note that Africans, besides being fetishists, were able to think logically and practically about objects and (as we just saw) form strong sentimental attachments to them. But even these observers assumed that the Africans' attitude to certain objects and practices was distinctive, curious, and typical, hence deserving of special attention in scientific investigation. In practice—we could say, methodologically—the explorers matched this assumption by collecting African ethnographic objects, especially "fetishes," in a manner that ranged from the dutiful (after all, collecting was among the assignments given to expeditions) to the obsessive: the premise of African fetishism had its counterpart in the explorers' accumulating "curios," a preoccupation that in some cases did become "fetishistic" in its obsessiveness.

Another topos in our travelogues is the use of objects by Europeans in order to *épater les indigènes*—to impress, shock, and occasionally scare the natives: the explorer as a sideshow operator. An astounding array of commodities and items from what we called earlier the European expeditions' material culture helped travelers achieve this effect. It probably did not occur to most of these explorers who collected for museums that their own caravans were veritable museums for the Africans they met: exhibits of European clothes, arms, foods, implements, and instruments that must have been all the more curious because they were displayed "out of context," and at odd moments. Of course, to inform Africans about Europe was not foremost in the minds of explorers. On the contrary, their goal-directed scientific (and political) mission demanded that they control and, whenever this was to their advantage, manipulate African curiosity.

Here is a telling incident as reported by Pogge on his trip to the Lunda. At Tshikapa village he notes the curiosity caused by white travelers. People congregate and watch him as they would do "in Europe with a wild animal in a cage." He suffers them for a while "until I dropped the curtain in the form of a door made of straw, whereupon the audience went away, one after the other, somewhat as in Europe after a theatrical performance" (1880, 66).

Aside from a few prominent persons such as Mirambo or Tipo Tip, travelers seldom credited Africans with any sort of sustained or systematic interest in things European. Reports of Africans' curiosity traced its cause to fear or greed, or both. Take Pogge again, who by now had made it to the capital of the Lunda. From there he wanted to continue north to reach the true center of Africa, that is, countries not directly controlled by populations eager to protect their trade with the coast. He tried to pass himself off as a simple hunter in search of big game, appreciative of Lunda hospitality but eager to move on. Instead he was kept waiting for months by a seemingly never-ending series of visits (remember his dealings with the Lukokesha), elaborately staged exchanges, and partial negotiations. Clearly, the Lunda court had decided to take a long look at this European visitor and learn as much as possible from him without giving much away (in the end it refused Pogge permission to travel north).

If only because questioning the European through an interpreter was too cumbersome, the court's attention fell on the objects Pogge carried. Hence the explorer took precautions when the Mwant Yav finally deigned to visit him at his home. He reports, "Everything was taken out of sight so as to make it possible to receive the noble lord in a dignified manner and not direct his attention and curiosity [*Wissbegierde:* lit., 'desire for knowledge'] to objects for which I had better use than he" (135). With his usual candidness Pogge adds a fine touch to the asymmetrical image of the invisible observer and the visible observed when he notes how useful a bright red coat he had given to the Mwant Yav turned out to be. He now was able to tell from far away whether the ruler was among the crowds of Lunda that would come almost daily to visit him (143).

Wishing to control, or play with, African desire for knowledge, explorers sometimes staged exhibits of European objects. As we might expect, they frequently were asked to demonstrate the working of their superior modern arms and did so with relish. But other implements would also be used for effect. Becker recounts a visit by chief Siranda, whom he describes as an intelligent, considerate person, sympathetic to the work of the Europeans. He is shown "physical instruments, perfected weapons, and other European curiosities.... Siranda does not fully understand our practical demonstrations though he listens carefully. All this seems to him a bit of a miracle. Above all, it is the electrical machine that intrigues him" (1887, 1:313). That same *petite machine électrique* had been used earlier by Ramaeckers, then Becker's superior, to impress another chief who visited Karema station. The chief's reaction was as expected: "The whites can do everything" (1:291). On such occasions natural science impressed and entertained, as it does today in technical museums.

More notorious in the history of exploration of central Africa than the Belgian electrical machine were Torday's famous toy elephants. Their display fits with our earlier comments on projecting fetishism. Here is how his companion, Hilton-Simpson, recalls one episode: "Before leaving the Kwilu we gave an exhibition to a large number of Bambala of one of the clockwork elephants which we had recently received from London." The contraption, he notes, impressed the Africans as a "most potent fetish" (1911, 261). While marching through Bambunda country they show the toy occasionally (263) and at Bondo village among the Bapindji, the explorers stage an appearance of the clockwork elephant when they meet the chief. He wants to buy it and Torday, hopeful of getting some unknown fetish in return, begins negotiations. The chief ends them by offering ivory and slaves in return for the elephant (270–71). That the chief takes a purely commercial approach (and refuses to barter one fetish against another) does not cause Hilton-Simpson to revise his ideas of how the African perceived this object.

The story continues. A clockwork elephant is promised to the Pende chief Dilonda on the condition that he help the expedition reach the Kasai River (286). Later, the toys also serve in the Bakongo villages of Bwabwa (300) and Kanenenke where they—because they move?—are said to have been interpreted as instruments of divination (312). According to Hilton-Simpson, Torday indulges these expectations and predicts a great future for the chief's grandchild. We are also told that Torday teaches children how to suck eggs, suggesting to them that the empty shells become fetishes that must be removed before the Europeans' departure (315). After they get to Kenge, one of the two local chiefs declares war on the expedition. They expect an attack and when it does not come after the second night, Torday decides to put the clockwork elephant "to the test, and to exhibit some little black dolls which we had received from London" (320). He is convinced that this works and that the objects have their desired "magical" effect. When some of their chickens are stolen the travelers try the elephant on the other chief in the darkness of the tent. The chickens are returned to them and the explorers take this as proof of the efficiency of their fetish (321–23). In the end, they stay a few extra days at Kenge "employing our time to take photographs, for the natives were much too frightened of our elephant to object to our wandering freely about, and using our cameras as much as we liked" (323). Hilton-Simpson has some second thoughts about using the elephant—it *does* mean taking advantage of ignorance and superstition—but he finds the trick justified because it prevents bloodshed.

In his own account of that trip (published later when he was an acknowledged ethnographer), Torday gives a much shorter version of the episode at Kenge. He does not mention at all the other occasions recorded by Hilton-Simpson and refrains from fetishistic interpretations (1925, 257). Was his caution a reaction to responses the story had re-

ceived? Torday gives us one of only a handful of hints at the effects of
editing on these travelogues when he notes the following (without further identifying the person): "The charming young lady who claims the
right of criticizing my manuscript tells me that the book was just beginning to get interesting, when I spoiled everything with that silly old elephant" (265). Incidentally, the book has a photograph of the explorer
standing at a table on which he demonstrates his toy elephant to some
suitably warriorlike Africans who seem, if anything, amused (illustration facing 272). The caption reads: "A WONDERFUL TOY. This little elephant played an important part at Kenge when the author was in a tight
corner."

Arms, scientific instruments, and mechanical contraptions do not ex-
haust the list of marvelous objects that served the explorers to impress,
or lure, Africans.[2] Again it is Torday who recalls how he once overcame
African fears (or diffidence): "I had recourse to a sovereign remedy in
such cases—curiosity." He showed them an old number of the *Graphic*
(an illustrated journal or magazine), noting that this trick was taught to
him by H.H. Johnston, who "had pointed out...how useful it was for
the traveller among uncivilized nations to have a stock of pictures by
him" (1913, 165). The toy elephant and the magazine pictures alike become means to forward the explorer's ends. Torday does not seem to realize that uses of objects in communicating with Africans may be deceptive—he could have been deceiving himself by deceiving Africans.
When explorers methodologized African curiosity (and African friendship as well, as we shall see), they closed off precious sources of ethnographic knowledge.

But let us suspend for a moment our distaste for cheap tricks and agree
with the travelers that we can uncover interesting things by watching
how Africans react to "European curios." A closer look at the cited cases
(and many others much like them) shows that such experiments were intrusive and often aggressive. Rather than knowledge gained, African ignorance demonstrated seems to have caused the pleasure Europeans obviously derived from these exhibitions. Also, we should not forget that
the objects destined to stun the natives met criteria and expectations
preestablished in the lore of scientific travel. Travelers bought them in
Europe and took them along as part of the equipment of an expedition,
much like scientific instruments or photographic apparatus. And yet—
our sources report—these European curios hardly ever triggered productive exchanges.

There was, however, one class of European objects picked with the same kind of forethought that does not quite fit the pattern. These were musical instruments and, later during our period, the phonograph. Why are they different? The objects of marvel described so far were available to view, touch, and perhaps smell. Some also rang, exploded, or were machines that made noises. But musical instruments, in the hands of more or less competent players, lend themselves neither to selective exhibition nor to detached contemplation. Sound reaches and envelops everyone in hearing distance. Music, modulated and rhythmic sound, reveals what the exhibition of objects may hide: its production is a performance demanding a sharing of time, based on the co-presence of participants in an event. As such, music effectively subverts the controlled distance and hierarchical relations that constitute the politics of scientific observation (and exhibition). Even in its most reduced forms, music induces passion and the kind of ecstasis whose role we try to document and understand in this study of European encounters with Africa.

By now, these scattered observations on sound have taken on an importance that requires separate treatment in a later section. Here I limit myself to documenting some of the more remarkable, and entertaining, uses of musical instruments to *épater les indigènes*. Let us start with a mechanical instrument, a music box Pogge took along (apparently on both trips). In a report to the German association from the Kasai region he described the impression this device made on Kalamba (a Luba chief and charismatic leader we will meet again). This was the situation: Pogge was ready to depart on the next leg of his trip, together with Kalamba, when the latter asked him to stay for another day. He needed time to construct a "small fetish hut" in which to keep two of Pogge's presents, a brass necklace and the music box. Pogge comments,

> Biserra, my interpreter, had convinced him that the sounds [of the music box] were the voice of Fidi-Muculo [*vidye mukulo*], the God of the Kasselange. Therefore he now listens reverently to the sounds of the clock. The other day I had it played for him and, when it began to turn more and more slowly because it needed oiling, I showed my courage by simply closing the lid. He jumped to his feet and harangued at length the crowd that was pressing around us, telling them that if the clock did not want to play properly, it was because of the noise they were making, "for the voice of Fidi-Muculo demands respect." (*MAGD* 3, no. 3 [1882]: 221)

What are we to make of this? Travelers' reports published in *MAGD* usually were rather dry and bare pieces; why did Pogge embellish his letter (dated November 27, 1881) with this episode? Was it to document "fetishistic" interpretation of European objects? Pogge's talking of his own courage seems to suggest this; he demonstrates he is free of fear. But from his own description, the audience does not exactly look awe-stricken. Pogge knew enough about Luba beliefs to cite the name of their supreme spirit or divinity, and that association would make of the "box with a voice" a divinatory rather than a power object. Power comes into play when Kalamba harangues his people. As a person who had a keen sense for innovations, he may have wanted to make sure that the box would serve him later, when the Europeans had left. Be that as it may, the music box was a standard item among objects brought to Africa. Buchner carried one (see below); Capelo and Ivens mention one among the presents offered to a chief (1882, 1:184). An inventory list at the beginning of their book has "2 music boxes" and "1 small portable organ" (xlix).

This inventory brings up another musical machine, the barrel organ or hurdy-gurdy (*orgue de barbarie*)—the very same object Thomson mentions in the list of Debaize's "strange things." Cambier, of the first Belgian expedition, inherited the instrument from our French abbé, who had made himself quite a reputation with his ways of impressing Africans.[3] Becker, who called himself an amusical person, made the first of several notes on this marvel when the caravan of the IAA Second Expedition reached Karema station: "It is to the sound of this instrument, so much ridiculed in Europe, that we enter our new home. An African servant turns the crank with delight and, believe it or not, we are as enchanted as he is of this music carrying us back into the midst of civilization" (1887, 1:267). I cannot think of a better, more concise illustration of our reflections on musical instruments as distinct from other European curiosities. In one sentence, Becker demonstrates what we said about the impossibility of controlling music's effects, of keeping them unidirectional; he records its capacity to create shared experiences and (a theme to be addressed later) call up situations stored in our memory.

Buchner apparently had a similar experience. At the farthest point of his trip to the Lunda—in one of his last reports to the German association before he lost contact—he writes: "The music box [brought along as a present for the Mwant Yav], an instrument I cannot stand in Europe, had to play for me for two days, giving me much pleasure, from which one can see that I am getting dangerously close to negrodom" (*MAGD*, nos. 4–5 [1879]: 242). The last part of the remark is the kind of racist slur we have come to expect from this author. Yet the fear it expresses confirms more strongly than any direct testimony what we have said about the power of music to subvert barriers and distances.

Becker, sensitive as he may have been, did of course share the scientific perspective of his colleagues. He too was an observer who calculated the effects musical instruments had on Africans and expressed his findings in quasi-musicological terms. In his second note on the same barrel organ he tells us it does regular service at the station, providing holiday entertainment for the crew (on Fridays, following Islamic custom).

> For them I let the barrel organ be played. They squat around it, with the ecstatic expression of Javanese listening to the harmonies of the gamelan. The devotees of the hurdy-gurdy each take their turn cranking the instrument, which showers them with dreamy or stirring melodies.... But their hearing doesn't seem to be made for our diatonic scale. Only a few among them are able to hum some shreds of [melodic] phrases; they pick up the rhythm more easily. (1887, 2:235)

Debaize's *orgue de barbarie* returns two more times in Becker's account: once when he reports its use to embellish the marriage rite he invented for his station personnel (286) and then again at the very end of his stay. His successor, Storms, breaks out in laughter over this instrument—Storms reacts like a newcomer, Becker informs the reader—until he too succumbs to its charms (355, 356).

With Coquilhat we come to a popular musical instrument in the strict sense of the word, the accordion. Already during his sea voyage to the Congo he had noticed that on the Kalabar coast African seamen would exchange "gaudily decorated accordions, empty bottles, tin whistles against woven mats, parrots, monkeys, leopard and civet cat skins, and so forth, to be resold in England" (1888, 19). Later he has two reports, one from Equateur station, the other from his time further up the Congo among the Bangala. Taken together, they confirm our observations on the two-way effect of musical instruments and the methodologization of European objects. Coquilhat had been away from the station and his return called for a celebration, complete with musical entertainment: "Amelot [one of the Belgians stationed at the post] owns an accordion and plays it quite well. Our ears, deprived of European music for a long time, are enchanted. On the road, our virtuoso had composed a *Hymn of the Equator,* a happy mixture of somber and gay motifs that we intone in chorus" (180).

Amelot makes another appearance when Coquilhat mentions his playing among the "methods to be employed in these parts" Europeans

would find ridiculous. During difficult negotiations with a local chief
and his entourage, the Africans, having noticed the accordion, "their first
reaction to the full sound, totally unknown to these poor devils, was stu-
por. Then they were in the throngs of a crazy, general, irresistible laughter: they mutually grabbed and clapped their hands with vigor. They
danced, bent over, and writhed about. This formidable expression of joy
lasted a good five minutes" (180).

Wissmann also reports African reactions to European tunes played
on an accordion (or a concertina). The situation was quite similar to the
one Coquilhat describes. But, we notice, now the laughter comes entirely
from the European side.

> The sounds of Müller's accordion had a peculiar effect on these people. At
> first, they seemed to be overcome by deep sadness, which expressed itself in
> their faces and gestures, then apparently to be replaced by a feeling of great
> bodily pain. Making terrible faces, they pulled their knees up to their bodies
> and seemed ready to cry at any moment. While they were doing this they kept
> trying to protect themselves and motioning to make Müller stop playing. The
> whole thing made such a comical impression that none of us could refrain
> from breaking out in loud laughter. (1891, 382)

Another traveler to reflect and report on the use of musical instruments was Frobenius. His companion Lemme, the expedition's artist,
had brought along a guitar, which he played masterfully. Frobenius notes:
"In the evening Hans Lemme plays his guitar for the negroes. But this
art is too refined for the people around here" (1907, 32). The people
may not have appreciated that particular performance but, as we are told
only a page later, they were definitely interested in the instrument: "Then
many negroes visit, offering me beautiful things at very high prices. At
noon Bungu [a local chief] shows up, among others. He listens atten-
tively to the master playing the guitar. Then he closely, and with a certain understanding, inspects the instrument and finally declares that he
wants to buy it. He offered two, even three, goats" (33). The exchange
did not take place. From one of Frobenius's typically effusive statements
we learn that the ethnologist saw the European instrument and the music performed on it as endowed with a mission. His view fits the one-
way perspective on communication through objects and performances
we encountered earlier. The context is a stay at a place called Zongo
among the Badinga, whom he depicts as "dark and gloomy" like the forest they inhabit: "I could detect nothing friendly, never any sort of cultural wealth among these Badinga, these true forest people. The only
thing was perhaps the friendly mood caused by the playing of the guitar

that one could sense among the inhabitants of Zongo. Otherwise they are true 'savages,' diffident, work-shy fellows of black color." Frobenius goes on about their indiscriminate cannibalism and the display they make of human and animal skulls before he ends with this challenge: "But look out, you savage grumbling bears! Today culture rests in this place.... And, to spite all your savagery, today we are going to hear Lemme's songs, and the sound of Beethoven and Bach ennobles even your savage nature, your savage spirits. Was high, Nordic culture ever proclaimed in these parts before—or ever since?" (133).

With Frobenius and Torday we reach the era of the phonograph. Torday's came in the mail from Europe (in 1906). Without explaining his reasoning (the point must have been evident to him), he states: "I advise any of my readers who is planning a trip among primitive peoples on no account to omit to take one of these instruments" (1913, 266). It is not clear from the text whether he could use his machine to make recordings. At any rate, he played it to Africans and it triggered the expected reactions, as reported by Hilton-Simpson: "As usual our phonograph created a great impression. After we had given a concert, at which the entire village attended, someone asked us, 'What do you call that? Witchcraft?' 'Oh, no' modestly replied Torday, 'that is only our cleverness.' 'That is witchcraft,' said the native; 'cleverness stops short of that'" (1911, 51).

Frobenius's phonograph apparently was the hand-cranked Edison machine working with wax cylinders that many ethnographers used until portable wire- and tape recorders became available. Much like the devices used fifty years later, it recorded or played back voice and music. Frobenius had already done what many of us would do when we filled tapes with recordings of our favorite music that could be played in the heart of Africa until the tapes were used for field recordings.[4] He found a justification for such unscientific use of a scientific instrument. When he was staying in the Kasai region, he received a phonograph and cylinders in the mail. On some of them there were recordings of music and of his wife's voice. Never one to miss an opportunity for lecturing, this moved Frobenius to make the following recommendation: "This is one use of the phonograph to which I attach great importance. One does not need to use it all the time for the purpose of making scientific recordings. I think it has a certain cultural mission when our officers, civil servants, businessmen, and so on who leave for the protectorates [i.e., the colonies] see to it that, from time to time, they are sent from home spoken, not just written, words" (1907, 445).

Frobenius also used the phonograph as part of a performance to impress Africans (31). Incidentally, that performance included his putting on a "Japanese mask" to scare his audience—strange objects being used to impress strangers. The phonograph returns one more time at the end of his book, this time as part of a mise-en-scène of his departure from Sankuru region. Frobenius had paid off his people and a steamer was waiting to take him back down the river. "To mark my departure I had a small fireworks go up and my phonograph play the beautiful melodies from Wagner's operas. It was a beautiful and dignified evening, just the right mood to say farewell to the interior of Africa" (451).

I cannot help but think of similarities between this scene and others in two film classics: Francis Ford Coppola's helicopter pilot playing Wagner during a mission in Vietnam (in *Apocalypse Now*) and Werner Herzog's crazy opera lover listening to Italian arias on the deck of a steamer gliding through the Amazon jungle (in *Fitzcaraldo*). As the three scenes evoke (and invoke) quintessential European culture, their gestures look more than slightly mad. All three of them use art to inflate power. In Frobenius's case we come to suspect that "beautiful" and "dignified" art is to compensate for the rather ugly and undignified uses of science to justify imperial designs and the tottering-around that counted as African exploration. Now and then travel writers, like filmmakers, give us vignettes, small but revealing images. It is difficult to translate their condensed meaning into an argument without diluting their message.

FROM NOISE TO SOUND:
EXPLORATION AND AFRICAN MUSIC

> Though such orgies are awful to the civilized ear when
> in the immediate vicinity, yet I must own that during
> the night, when about a mile off, I felt a certain pi-
> quant enjoyment in lying listening to the wild tumult of
> sound. The weird thrilling scream of the women, and
> the wild clangour of the drums could not but affect a
> lively imagination. (1:108)

The longer I worked with the sources for this study, the more important I found certain topics of little interest to me when I began my readings. In fact, I see certain parallels between this process and developments in my own life as an ethnographer. I am reminded of the many years it took me to appreciate African music and, more generally, African performance in various cultural practices that were the objects of my research. Barrel organs, accordions, guitars, and phonographs prepared us for the topic of music, and timing now makes me ask how our explorers experienced African music. Letting themselves be affected by African music was, I believe, one of the qualities that distinguished explorers who were able to give themselves over to experiences from others who could and would not get ecstatic about Africa—in the epistemological sense we gave to the term.

But let us start at the beginning of the argument. Among the conditions of knowledge production that travelers could not control, such as heat and cold, the state of roads, illness, and local politics, there was noise. Explorers could close their eyes; they could not shut their ears. Often they were unable to sleep or concentrate on their scientific work because of noise; the din of quarrels and conversations kept them awake, but most of all they felt assaulted by the sound made by drums and other musical instruments. We owe one of many telling examples to Böhm, of the German East African Expedition, recorded when he traveled through chief Mirambo's country (in 1882).

> Because of the many mosquitoes I had been unable to sleep the night before. I was very tired and had retired when, right in front of my tent, an infernal *goma* (dance) began, accompanied by the enraged beating of three big drums, rattling of bells, and call-and-response singing by women which went on, without interruption, till the morning so that I could not close an eye. When I prepared to leave, haggard from lack of sleep, I was approached for a present to the dancers, who were still busy, with the remark that the *goma* had been put on in my honor. (*MAGD* 3, no. 3 [1882]: 227)

Böhm took the request as adding insult to injury and never bothered to make sense of the performance.

Even those travelers who do not give the impression that all things African made them suffer to some degree suffered acoustic experiences. It is all the more fascinating to watch in some of them a process of change that is crucial to all ethnography: the transformation of noise to meaningful sound. Rather than try to document it from as many sources as possible, I follow the theme as it develops and grows in Pogge's experiences with African music. Later there will be occasion to complete the picture with a few texts by other authors.

Pogge begins his book with a sort of catalogue of ethnographic subjects, among them music and dance (1880, 6). Even for the amateur he was, music was an obligatory topic of research before he started his inquiries. When he actually encounters African music he feels the need to force the unfamiliar into familiar categories (most of them blatantly irrelevant by later musicological standards). Because what he hears does not sound like the kind of music he probably knew best, Prussian marches, he declares that African music comes in a "three-time" (*Drei-takt*) rhythm. Apparently he based that rather doubtful generalization on a dance he witnessed early on his trip among his porters who were hired on the coast: "Although I am not a dancer, I would like to maintain that the Batuk dance is a kind of *française*. In Loanda it is prohibited by the police because of its indecency" (8n.). Later he notes that his coastal porters always adapted to local ways and customs, with one exception: "But my people never let go of their Batuk dance" (14). We know from Capelo and Ivens that *batuque* dancing was a popular form of entertainment through much of the area they (and Pogge) traveled. Without mentioning the term, they describe such a dance as monotonous, gross, and obscene (1882, 1:70).

Early in his trip Pogge was quick to generalize, as beginners do, and came up with this indictment: "Music is very popular among negroes, although one must say that they have no [musical] ear whatsoever" (12). Dutifully, he goes on to describe some instruments and observes that many people carry an instrument when they travel. He begins to discern styles of singing, noting repetitiveness as an outstanding feature and as something he obviously dislikes. But only two pages later he shows the first signs of appreciation when he recalls the people of his caravan, women among them, singing in the repetitive call-and-response pattern characteristic of much African music (and speech). He admits, "Such singing sounds good and has always made a peculiar impression on me" (14).

Pogge's attitude begins to change when he leaves the Portuguese sphere and routine settles on the caravan. African music has become a familiar sound. Inserted in his account, without visible connection to the passage that precedes it, I found this observation: "We lead a very monotonous life. Nothing new on August 30 and 31 and during September 1–4. Every evening the people dance at the fire to the sounds of the drum, because the nights are no longer chilly" (57). Still in the vein of "monotony," he reports that "during rainless nights there always rises the monotonous sound of the drum, as a rule accompanied by the choral singing of the local population" (72–73). This remark also shows that music created links between the locals and the strangers passing through with the caravan and sometimes the two actually got together: "At night there was a big dance my porters had arranged with the girls of [the village of] Kalungo Zenga" (109).

When the caravan neared its destination of Musumba, the Lunda capital, Pogge's porters celebrated with a "Batuk dance and all of them seemed to be delighted" (123). Singing, they enter the outskirts of the town (127). After much preliminary ceremonial back and forth between Pogge and members of the Mwant Yav's court, the ruler himself appears. Eight men carry him on a portable chair, and two drummers and two marimba (xylophone) players—the royal band—follow him (129). As it turns out, Pogge has to settle down in Musumba because the ruler wants to keep him from traveling north. Also the ruler has just recently been installed in his office and is obviously busy with all kinds of ritual and political machinations to set up his reign. Perhaps because the traveler is annoyed, his attitude changes again. Once more, Pogge feels assaulted by African music (notice his stress, "from all sides"): "As soon as it does not rain at night you can hear from all sides the sound of the drum to which the Kalunda almost always sing. This racket can be perceived from all sides and goes on till midnight or longer" (132–33). The sound of African music is still strange to him but he takes an important step toward ethnographic understanding when he says (as in a remark quoted earlier) that song accompanies the drumming, not the other way around, as we would expect from a European.

One of the ruler's delaying tactics was to let the explorer wait for weeks before he made his ceremonial return visit to Pogge's house. Forced inactivity may have helped Pogge cross the line, as far as African music is concerned: "In the evening I passed the time making music because I had tuned a thumb piano a little and was able to produce, with some effort, a few melodies" (137–38). This was the lamellophone, known in the Congo as *shanza, likembe, mbira,* and so forth. Pogge comes back to this instrument in the ethnographic appendix to his book: "Everybody plays this instrument. In Musumba, when they are not busy and just hanging around, men and women often carry the thumb piano in both hands and play on it. Poor people and children make their own instruments" (241). Casual as his playing the *likembe* may have been, it shows Pogge's willingness to "join the crowd" and to share an ingredient of African daily life most other explorers would have kept at a distance as an object of observation. Not much later, it seems, he actually began to enjoy African music.

Tonight again a band played in front of my *Fundo* [his house]. It consisted of musicians mentioned earlier.[5] These people had got used to coming here because I always saw to it that they were given a small present for their accomplishments. Among the natives of Musumba the music is, by the way, not bad. Either all three instruments are worked at once, or there will be a solo that the other instruments then join. Also, the musicians know the difference between forte and piano; only the melody is weak. (161)

Meanwhile, the Lunda ruler remained friendly but adamant; Pogge was not allowed to continue his trip beyond Lunda territory toward Luba country in the north. By then the explorer was exasperated: he had seen enough of the ceremonious Lunda court and, as it appears, his flirt with African music also came to an end. Politics had spoiled the pleasure, and frustration made him respond with violence: "In the morning the royal band played in front of my hut. Cheered by my porters, I slapped the band leader in the face, rather forcefully. He had got up and would not stop begging. After this *rencontre* with their master the artists left the camp never to be seen again. Never again could I savor this musical pleasure in front of my hut" (175).

Still, Pogge kept an open mind. Before leaving he had one more chance to hear the musicians perform at a dance in the presence of the Mwant Yav. He describes movements of the dancers and avoids the prejudice about the obscenity of African dancing we meet in many other sources: "Although the dance looked wild, one could not say that it was ugly or obscene; on the contrary, the young men swinging green branches showed a good deal of grace. Maybe many a European dance teacher could learn some nice new steps from the negroes at Musumba" (196).

Other travelers went through similar changes from rejecting to appreciating African music. In the end, all of them dutifully listed and collected musical instruments among ethnographic objects, yet most remained guarded and ambivalent toward musical performances. As in their reactions to other expressions of African culture, explorers wavered between dismissal based on unmitigated prejudice and reluctant surrender inspired by insights and emotions. Most often they settled somewhere between the extremes and did not cross the line that separates observation—or even a measure of passive enjoyment—from active participation in African music and dance. Taken in a context of incidental but in the end impressive evidence for similar refusal of ecstatic experiences, the Europeans' refusal to join the dance can be seen as a form of abstinence based on the rules of hygiene and scientific method.

The struggle between observation and participation is illustrated in a report by Kaiser and Reichard from the German East African Expedition on the installation of a female chief, Disha. During the ceremonies the explorers took ethnographic notes. Among them, they recorded the text of a brief war song they reproduced in Nyamwezi, Swahili, and a German translation. But they had trouble transcribing the tune: "Because, unfortunately, we are not musical and the 'Ne plus ultra Accordion' we had at our disposal lacked half-tones, we must forgo transcribing the most pe-

culiar negro melody. We ourselves participated in the dancing and singing
and were led home dancing" (*MAGD* 3, no. 4 [1883]: 271). The dancing was remarkable; the scientific-sounding observation probably is nonsense. As far as my own limited knowledge goes, an instrument equipped
to play European scales would include half-tones.

Kaiser and Reichard show themselves to be careful observers when
they go on to report a curious and complex ritual, also part of the installation ceremonies. They note the use of a "magical drum," made for
the occasion: "Then, while the funnel-shaped drum is beaten, at first
forcefully, later with slowly decreasing force, its pointed end is held first
to Disha's right, then to her left ear. The procedure is repeated with the
dignitaries so as to drum reason into them. But this is not to be taken
symbolically; 'reason comes out of the drum' " (273).

By today's standards, this observation was a minor triumph of ethnography: it must have been through questioning the performers, or from
bystanders' knowledgeable comments that the travelers came to note
the difference between semiotic and pragmatic (or metaphoric and
metonymic) interpretation of rhythmic sound. At least, this is what I take
them to mean when they insist that the beating of the drum was not symbolic. "Unmusical" explorers may have caught in this case a profound
characteristic of African musical experience and sensibility because they
took the trouble to follow their observations with questioning.[6]

I am inclined to give similar weight to another casual observation, this
one by Coquilhat. For two reasons it is of special interest: it takes us
back to our point of departure—African noise suffered by European explorers—and the event that set it off was almost certainly a possession
rite, an ecstatic event par excellence: "One day, I had to laugh a lot when,
attracted by a sudden din, I came to the hut of a young man who was in
an extreme state of agitation. People were working on him with song
and dance and the deafening beating of the drum. 'In Belgium,' I told
myself, 'one would spread straw in the streets to muffle the noise. Here
it is the contrary.' The funniest thing is that the young man got well"
(1888, 290). Coquilhat packs a lot into these few lines: laughter as a reaction to something strange; a remarkable expression in the original,
danses chantées, literally "sung dances," expressing an accurate perception of a characteristic of African music; an oblique reflection on cultural differences in attitudes toward noise; and, finally, a reluctant acknowledgment of the efficacy of African music.

Becker gives us a last example in this series of texts. His account contains many observations on African music, including an entire section,

a sort of brief monograph, in the second volume of his book (1887, 2:236–39). Apart from a summary of the subject, he gives the transcription of a song (text and musical score) and then analyzes it, offering some general thoughts on European perceptions of African music. Here and elsewhere he shows himself aware of close connections between music and movement, dance as well as work. An observation on the latter produces a flash of insight into African musical sensibility we would not have expected from someone who considered himself amusical (1:35). At the end of his term Becker spent some time in Zanzibar, observing local customs and taking in the smells and sounds of the town. He recalls how, walking away from the sounds of a smithy, he entered a new soundscape. Intriguing noises moved him to come up with this poetic yet precise description.

> What kind of mysterious work is going on in the secrecy of a private home, playing a carillon that fills with muted vibrations this new island of sound from one end to the other? Quite simple—it is the act of pounding coffee in cast-iron mortars. Of lifting the pestle in time and striking the metal wall. The muffled sound, crushing the beans that first had been roasted in large basins, represents the useful; the vibration that is added, the pleasant. And this combination transforms a rather insipid chore into an intimate concert. So much is it savored by these virtuosos that there is nothing in the world that could make them pound their coffee without accompaniment. (1887, 2:475)

To me, this is a striking instance of ethnography that comes from an act of surrender to the experience. Imagine the sensory impression: it makes Becker's prose vibrate and allows him, if only for a moment, to reach the highest goal of our work, fashioning representations of other cultures that do not erase their immediacy and presence. There is much to ponder in this passage. It is part of sketches of Zanzibar that are cast in a style Said (1978) would identify as decidedly "orientalist"—except that Becker's excursion into orientalist discourse was triggered by sound (and, in others instances, by smell) rather than predominantly by vision, a difference that is central to Said's critique. In his *tableau vivant* of the Swahili town, the emphasis is on *vivant,* on representation inspired by lived experience.

PERFORMANCES AND RITUALS

> We entered this important place with all the barbaric
> pomp and circumstance attainable in an African cara-
> van. A new English flag replaced for the time being the
> torn and tattered Union Jack which had led us from

> Dar-es-Salam. The men donned their best, while in
> front I myself marched, surrounded by a brilliantly-
> dressed bodyguard of head men, each carrying a hand-
> some spear in his hand, and a gun slung on his back. In
> the centre of this assemblage of dazzling colours and
> imposing turbans, I presented a considerable contrast
> in my sober, free-and-easy suit of Tweeds and pith hat.
> I had only a stick in my hand, and I carried my az-
> imuth compass at my side, instead of guns and re-
> volvers. (2:11–12)

Politics, timing, conviviality, objects, music. All converge on one topic that is as prominent in our sources as it is central in our attempts to understand what happened—or did not happen—in the exploration of central Africa. Performance, in the sense of a broadly understood theatricality, characterized encounters between Europeans and Africans. As a rule, the explorers ascribed theatricality to Africans; more often than not they resented it as an imposition, ridiculed it as incongruous and lacking dignity, and barely suffered its more exuberant and raucous forms. Yet the same men who saw their scientific mission endangered by African pomp and circumstance were in Africa as agents of an enterprise that was sold to the European public through pompous campaigns of propaganda, through exhibits and shows, and through the drama and tragedy reported in travelogues and in the press. The drama had its heroes and villains and a grand plot called the *oeuvre civilisatrice*. Countless readers avidly followed the progress of explorers who often engaged in veritable races with one another and among the nations they represented. Imperialism was a theatrical enterprise.

Imperialist theatricality shows up, however obliquely, in a policy statement by the German association. That organization had initially favored an approach to central Africa from the west. Later it termed the approach "a mistake, stemming from a lack of experience with this region [the Loango coast] and leading to a *staging* of operations that was too grand and therefore too cumbersome" (*MAGD* 2, no. 5 [1881]: 221; emphasis added). The German term *Inszenierung* (equivalent to French *mise-en-scène*) points to the world of theater but is, much like the English *staging,* also part of military language (which has its "theater of war"). Military theatricality was as much a part of the colonial enterprise as it was of many forms of African response and resistance.

Once more, a pattern of incongruities and contradictions emerges from the sources (I use the term *pattern* deliberately: our aim is to find out what got explorers into contradictions, regularly and predictably, not to note random or accidental occurrences). No European expedition did without flags, uniforms, parades, and exhibits of weaponry and goods. Becker, describing the contents of a special trunk carried by his caravan, tells us, with a theatrical reference, that it included "the indispensable scientific instruments, such as the sextant, the *Knowledge of Time* by the Greenwich observatory, the *Artificial Horizon,* and so on. Added to these is, as in the popular comedies of [Eugène] Scribe, every necessity for writing, not forgetting the precious travel journal, where in the evening you enter the day's facts and impressions" (1887, 1:83). Later Becker remarks on the same subject: "Like traveling comedians we had made up a detailed list of the contents of all our trunks" (102–3). Taken together, the two references to comedy in these texts show that Becker was conscious of there being something theatrical about their travel. When he compared an expedition's equipment to the props needed for a theatrical performance he expressed his awareness of the spectacle that caravans made for the local population.

That Europeans were a spectacle to watch comes out too in an observation by von François, noted when their steamer arrived at a village: "Full of anticipation, the entire population stood on the shore. They really were like the audience in a theater; nothing but suspense. How they stretched their necks to see the steamer more closely; how they kept pointing things out and calling them to somebody else's attention!" (1888, 108).

Becker was among those who realized that theatricality was not only in single events. The whole enterprise of exploration was a spectacle. And, he thought, the travelogues should reflect their drama: theatricality in narration should match theatricality in action. He refers to the point in the preface to his book where he has some critical remarks about Stanley but then acknowledges that the Englishman's works had "the pace and the interest of a drama splendidly acted" (1887, 1:xvi).

Why were explorers—some of them able to make ironic comments about their own theatricality—so annoyed when African rulers, major and minor, met them with shows of power? Take the afterthought Buchner notes in his diary about his reception by the Lunda paramount chief. The ruler had arranged for the explorer to witness the arrival at the court of a dignitary, surrounded by numerous wives, and a war party: "Only later it became clear to me that this whole scene, in itself highly interesting, was nothing but a spectacle, mounted only for my benefit, by means of which the Mwant Yav tried to impress me. The prince in question [leading the war party] actually lived at Musumba and had not left it for a long time. The number of his wives did in reality hardly exceed three or four, and the soldiers had been put under his command only for this fake tribute [to the chief]" (*MAGD* 3, no. 2 [1882]: 94–95). For Buchner, African theatricality was just another token of African mendaciousness that thwarted his scientific work. Undoubtedly also, he and others were defensive in such situations because they felt threatened by the power that was demonstrated in performances. But this could not have been the only reason that made explorers resent African theatricality. Why, the following example leads us to ask, would they have felt the need to take their distance from performances whose actors were not powerful?

When he was commanding Equateur station, Coquilhat was visited by two explorers and missionary pioneers, George Grenfell and Thomas Comber. They talked about their latest findings among the natives of the region and claimed to have seen "proof of a certain dramatic art. They [the missionaries] then tell of a 'presentation' which, they declare, was quite pleasant and lasted for several hours" (1888, 156). Here, according to Coquilhat, is how the missionaries described the event.

> The spectacle began with some agile dances followed by an act evocative of the Greek style; the "chorus" was graciously represented by small girls between eight and twelve years. Four men carried a strange-looking stretcher on their shoulders. On it was, hidden under a red flannel blanket, a corpse or some invisible object. A little girl sat quietly at one end of the bier, looking serious and sad. This stretcher, which was made of bamboo, was put down on the ground and the chorus placed itself around it. A woman took her position alongside the litter and sang a plaintive tune. We did not understand much of what she said but caught an often repeated refrain: *Kawa-Ka* (he is not dead). After a certain time, the incantation was considered to have had its effect, and the red cover began to undulate. It was removed and revealed a young girl shaking all over as if she were in the midst of an epileptic seizure. Two persons approached, took the girl by her arms, and put her on her feet. This representation [the missionaries explained to him] had been made to please the whites. (156)

So far so good. But then Coquilhat adds a remark that made me pick this text: "I'm a bit tempted to believe that, in this case, the natives simply imitated one of their numerous superstitious ceremonies" (157). Event classified and put aside. What happened? The missionary explorers reported on what they experienced as a theatrical performance. They guessed at the intention behind it: what they saw was a self-presentation of this culture, put on to "please" them—to make them feel welcome, to entertain, and perhaps enlighten them. When they compared what they saw to Greek tragedy, they built a bridge to their own culture. In a single sentence Coquilhat manages to block it and shore up cultural distance. He labels the event superstitious *and* denies the Africans any creativity when he calls their performance merely imitative. Coming from a person who elsewhere demonstrated much ethnographic sophistication, the dismissive remark is surprising. Does he react in this way because an African performance that interests or entertains others somehow threatens to move him?

When the same Coquilhat, in the company of Alphonse Vangele, a fellow officer, later witnesses the "drama" (169) of a human sacrifice among the funerary rites for a deceased chief, he keeps a cool, clinical distance. He describes the victim, the apparatus and method of decapitation (with an illustration on 173), the behavior of other spectators, the music, and additional rites. Though he says he and his companion felt pity for "these savages" (170), a pragmatic relativism deflects the impact of this deadly performance. They discuss the matter and decide in the end to watch the ritual killing because any use of the expedition's weapons and manpower to prevent it might end up antagonizing the local population and cutting their own supply lines.

In Coquilhat's ethnographic reaction to the missionaries' story there may have been yet another element to consider here (when he "classified" the event). This is the notion that theatricality, especially if it comes with rites and ceremonies, does not go with modernity. When Becker meets chief Mirambo, whom he depicts as quite modern and open to European ideas, the ruler fits his image: he appears without the usual pomp and circumstance. There is no music or spectacle, just sitting down to a conversation (1887, 2:159).[7] Of course, the same logic that opposes modernity to tradition may have operated to value a performance's expression of traditional culture. Becker, for example, has detailed comments on the performer's skills he found in a Swahili storyteller in his entourage, MASKAM L'IMPROVISATEUR (243, caption to an illustration).[8] Either move, classifying theatricality as primitive or valuing it as traditional, could serve as yet another strategy of hygiene protecting the explorer from the power of performances, especially those that threatened his work.

Though their general attitude toward African performances may have been dismissive or defensive, travelers did know the difference between an artful show and ordinary deception. Sometimes they actually played along in events they appreciated. Probably it was his experience with military theatricality rather than his ethnographic sensitivity that made

Lieutenant Wissmann tell a festive assembly of the Geographical Society in Berlin about his ways of breaking through, as he calls it, the "*Kalunda*sperre," the barrier between the coast and the center of the continent set up by the Lunda and Tshokwe in order to protect their trade monopoly.

> These *Kioque* [Tshokwe] get the ivory, almost the only one that still reaches Loanda, from the *Tushilange* [Bashilange: Luba in the interior]. Because they fear we might spoil this very lucrative trade for them, we constantly had to open our way through presents and hostile demonstrations. Such a demonstration consists of giving out ammunition in response to the enemy's assembling, blowing, and drumming, threatening and jeering, whereupon the porters also intone war songs, shoot in the air, and shout. (*MAGD* 4, no. 1 [1883]: 39)

In his later travelogue—on a visit to a stronghold of *rugaruga* (armed bandits)—Wissmann describes such a scene where he counters the theatricality of African possession induced by wild dancing with a demonstration of European shooting and military drill (1889, 279).

Wissmann also thought that dealing with performances as performances was a matter of experience. Here is his commentary on an incident reported by von François that the latter took as proof of hostility on the part of some Kanyok people.

> What this gentleman, who was then a neophyte in matters African, experienced was probably the same that happened to many others: he took the noisy reception, the raging, restless, and wild behavior of these people for a sign of hostility whereas it was probably excitement, caused by surprise and joy. When I interrogated the people who were with Mr. von François so as to punish the chiefs who might have misbehaved, they also thought that the chiefs, maybe a little wildly, had competed among each other to have the white man stay with them and that the traveler had interpreted the means they employed to have their wish as hostility and that they, the porters, had not been worried at all. ([1890], 83)

In this context of performance and power let us return to communicative behavior we encountered already several times as a reaction to striking objects—laughter. Wissmann, more than others, decided that derision was a useful instrument when it came to maintaining authority. From him we have the recollection of a scene to illustrate the aggressiveness of that strategy. He and his companion, the Belgian Le Marinel, had experienced some hostility from a Songye chief. The two travelers on horseback were consulting and turned their exchange into a performance: "My arrogant manner of speaking and, above all, the repeated

laughter to which I resorted in my conversation with Le Marinel may
have been an indication for the natives that I did not really think they
were dangerous. During the conversation, I kept my gun in the saddle
before me, its muzzle aimed at the chief and my finger on the trigger, so
that at the first sign of anyone using a weapon the man who stood before me would have fallen" (137).

It was an incident among the same Kioque, or Tshokwe, whom Wissmann had observed twenty years earlier, that inspired Frobenius to make
the following observations, adding yet another variant to forms of European disdain for African performances. His rejection has a decidedly
modern, ethnological character; the issue is no longer the truthfulness
but the authenticity of cultural performances. The commodification of
folklore causes Frobenius to reject what he observes, although it is clear
from his own account and from many of the other sources that paid performances by dancers and musicians were part of what he would have
recognized as authentically African. Here is what Frobenius tells us:
"Then the women of the village came—another business trick—and
danced, actually dancing the artist of the expedition into a state of excitement, such that he picked up paper and pen to record some of the
admittedly very lovely scenes." And there is more to come on the same
page: "[a group of] gay, masked Bakishi came from the neighboring village, because there the season of circumcision was on. The masked
dances of the Bakishi used to be rather solemn ceremonies, but here their
voice sounded lovely, vibrating in the highest falsetto: *Matabishi,
matabishi* [a tip, gratuity]! Among the Tshokwe, everything leads to business, presents, revenue" (1907, 327).

This, I believe, is what we learned from looking at things, sounds, and
performances: explorers traveled in Africa with the goods needed to feed
and pay their auxiliaries and to buy their way into the interior. Most of
these goods were to be had from local traders who specialized in outfit-
ting caravans. All expeditions also brought things along from Europe:
foodstuff, clothes, camping and photographic equipment, arms, scientific instruments, and books and writing gear. But there were also objects, few but quite important, that did not fit at all or fit badly into the
categories of commodities and equipment: playthings, from children's
toys to scientific gadgets, musical instruments, and phonographs. We can
only imagine what made the travelers choose these items over others.
Guitars and accordions accompanied competent players who most likely
just did not want to miss their musical hobby. But why a barrel organ
and music boxes, toy elephants and dolls (a whole supply of them!) and

"electrical machines"? The question may sound as silly as the things mentioned. Who did not know, at the time, that travelers used cheap trinkets, beads, and bangles to trick the natives? We used reports on such objects, on the intentions they served, and the reactions they are said to have caused because they open a view on elements in the exploration of Africa that fit into what we call its ecstatic dimension.

Quickly and inevitably, "strange things" led us to consider how they drew explorers to beliefs and practices such as "fetishism" but also to African music and dance and, finally, to dramatic and theatrical performances. They all had something in common: as subjects of scientific study (or of ideological projection) they made demands on participation; they annoyed and enchanted, intrigued and seduced European ethnographers and put before them the alternative to surrender and indulge or to control and engage in "hygienic" restraint. Travelers differed in the ways they put these experiences to productive use or let them bring out insurmountable prejudices, more often than not the latter. The point is not that these explorers seldom if ever sang, danced, or played along but that their ideas of science and their rules of hygiene made them reject singing, dancing, and playing as sources of ethnographic knowledge. Taken together, things, sounds, and spectacles provide the complex background for the theme of communication we take up next.

SIX

Communicating and Commanding

SPEAKING

LANGUAGES AND ETHNOGRAPHIC KNOWLEDGE

> It is almost impossible to exaggerate the advantage to
> the traveler of a personal knowledge of this language
> [Swahili]. If he has even a rough acquaintance with it
> he can speak to his men directly, and ask questions
> which a native translator would almost certainly bun-
> gle; and what is of quite as much consequence, he can
> draw closer the bond of sympathy between himself and
> his followers by having a kindly chat with them. If he is
> ignorant of their speech, he is of course practically sep-
> arated from them. (1:30)

By now we have worked our way through multiple layers that made up
the enterprise of African travel. We looked at the planning and organization of expeditions and at the movement of caravans. We examined
exploration as a way of life and showed some of the means and methods travelers employed to keep control of their bodies, drives, and feelings. Finally, we recognized the role played by objects and performances
in making contact with African populations. We come now to practices
that, according to our present views of ethnography, made up, or should
have made up, the core of exploration: communicating with the people.
Our sources contain copious information on the subject, ranging from
reports on events and incidents in which communication is a theme to

theoretical reflections and methodological recommendations regarding the importance of language. Most explorers would have subscribed to Coquilhat's summary of his experiences, formulated in the concluding pages of his work.

> In order to know what a country has to offer, it is not enough to have visited it during a few months, even as an attentive observer. You must have taken part in work and efforts that make you struggle with necessity. Necessity is the best tutor as well as the most demanding teacher. I also believe that, in order to know what you can get from a native tribe, more than anything else, knowledge of its language is the foremost means. All interpreters exploit and deceive us. By being able to communicate directly with the populations, you grasp the spirit of their customs and manners; you understand their character and their needs; you obtain the most valuable information about them; finally, you inspire them with the kind of confidence without which you will not succeed in making them take part in your projects. (1888, 471–72)

The ability to converse with Africans directly without the help of interpreters was, if not absolutely required, a great advantage in the work of exploration. Modern anthropologists agree on this linguistic imperative, as we could call this rule, and they still profess it as a tenet, as something that needs no critical discussion. However, much like the equally reasonable methodological principle of participant observation, the linguistic imperative may by its very assertiveness hide unresolved questions, even oddities and contradictions. Some of these emerged already during the early period that occupies us here but were probably difficult to recognize. Today we know that calls for language-centered ethnography may cover fundamental distinctions linguists have tried to catch analytically by opposing *langue* to *parole,* language to speaking, syntax to semantics, semiotics to pragmatics, and so forth. Because of the many meanings and aspects of language, knowledge of a native language is anything but easy to acquire.

Our sources are particularly interesting in this respect because they show how issues in field linguistics, few of them formulated theoretically, first came to be experienced practically, existentially, as well as politically. One is the very idea, again apparently quite reasonable, that language is a tool of scientific research: somewhat like a claw hammer for pulling out nails, a native language serves to collect information. But learning a language and acquiring the competence to converse in it in culturally appropriate ways, especially without language manuals, grammars, and dictionaries, bear little resemblance to picking up a hammer from the toolbox. Significantly, Coquilhat brings up language under the heading of necessity. Surrender to a way of speaking rather than its control characterizes (successful) language learning, especially when the aim is to live that language, that is, to make it the medium of daily relations and negotiations.[1]

Practical language learning needs time. Its pace may depend on many factors, such as the intensity and diversity of contacts and communicative situations (and, of course, the often-invoked talent for languages). Above all, practical language learning demands humility, a willingness to risk shame and ridicule for mistakes and lapses in competence. It hardly needs pointing out that all this fits neither the typical scientist conducting research nor the typical explorer commanding a caravan, both of whom, in different but related ways, need to be in control of situations at all times. No wonder that the accounts of language's role in producing ethnographic knowledge show us practices ridden with tensions and contradictions.

INTERPRETERS

> I spoke in English to Chuma. He translated it into Kiswahili to our interpreter, who recited it in the language of the Mahenge to the chief's son, my brother, according to the rite we had passed through in Ukhutu. (1:182–83)

Most of our explorers came to their task without linguistic preparation. Some of the Germans even had little, if any, knowledge of Portuguese, a necessity for those taking the western approach. Schütt admits that he was still learning the language when he got to Malange (1881, 16); and when Capelo and Ivens met von Mechow, who was on his way to Malange and the Kwango River, they "soon discovered that our language was not very familiar to him; still by dint of patience and pauses in between we managed to comprehend each other" (1882, 2:223). Similar scenes must have occurred between Belgians and Germans, who usually resorted to English, making it their work idiom in the sphere of the Congo Free State. As far as I can see, our sources mention only one traveler, Böhm, who had prepared himself for his work before he left Germany by learning Arabic and "principles of Swahili." Since language manuals in other African languages of wider communication did not become available until the end of our era, we may safely assume that all our travelers acquired their linguistic competences after periods of varying length during which they communicated with most Africans through

interpreters.[2] This made for an intriguing situation. All interpreters ex-
ploit and deceive us, says Coquilhat, expressing the consensus among
our authors. Yet all travelers had to work with interpreters, and most
never could do without them.

The problem was perhaps less severe in the east, where Swahili, a language considered easy to learn, was already established as an intercultural medium and as the language of caravans. From Becker's account
and from reports by members of the German East African Expedition it
appears that these travelers soon got on mostly without interpreters. They
had become sufficiently competent in Swahili, which served them from
the coast to the upper Congo. In the west, the situation was more complicated. After centuries of colonization Portuguese had a certain currency, but it alone was not sufficient for travel to the interior. The German expeditions that approached central Africa through Portuguese
territory all relied on interpreters. During his first trip Pogge employed at
least three, Germano, Ebo, and Elunga (see 1880, 58, 73). All of them
acted also as servants, assistants, and intermediaries. Of Germano, who
served again in the Pogge-Wissmann expedition, Pogge remarks that he
was a "negro who takes a job only on the condition that he be treated by
the whites like one of their own" (*MAGD,* nos. 4–5 [1879]: 174). Pogge
disliked his thieving ways but considered him one of the most intelligent
interpreters in the colony (*MAGD* 3, no. 1 [1881]: 79–80). Germano
eventually had the task of starting construction on the German station of
Luluaburg (*MAGD* 4, no. 1 [1883]: 44, 68). Later, when Pogge occupied
that station, he put Germano in charge of a caravan getting supplies from
Portuguese traders at Malange (*MAGD* 4, no. 4 [1885]: 232).[3]

In some cases, these African middlemen, especially the young boys
who served as guides and interpreters, got attached to their employers.
Pogge made this reflection on Elunga: "I regret not having brought him
along to Europe, to show him European manners and have him learn
the German language; he might have been of great value to a new German expedition as an interpreter and advisor" (1880, 73).

Wissmann mentions that a certain "Sankurru who has now, in 1888,
been with me for six years and has participated in all my travel, went
with me to Germany twice. He speaks, writes, and reads German, speaks
Portuguese, some English, Swahili and many negro languages. He is a
good cook and interpreter and now accompanies my friend Dr. Wolf to
German Togoland" (1889, 187n. 1).

But these cases were exceptional, not only because relations of trust
were rare, but because, contrary to what Europeans often thought of their

servants, Africans did not always personalize their dealings with their employers. To be a "trusted servant" was a job. Like the outfitter's and guide's, the interpreter's function was institutionalized by the time modern exploration got under way. Expeditions taking the eastern route employed experienced specialists, and those coming from the west profited from professionals whom the German travelers called *Lingster*(s). According to Büttner, "*Lingster*s are natives who are used by white traders to arrange deals with their compatriots" (1890, 106n.). Wolff adds another touch when he speaks of "*Lingster*s, that is, negroes who speak a European language and arrange, for a commission, the trade between uninformed bush negroes and the whites" (1889, 115). In West Africa these terms (appearing in the literature also as "linguists" or "linguisters") designated the spokesman of a ruler (often this was a formal office). That making this connection is not far-fetched is suggested by the fact that one of the German expeditions (led by Schulze) hired several *Accra-Leute* (people from Accra), among them the interpreter David Kornelius, who spoke excellent German and English (*MAGD* 4, no. 4 [1885]: 290; see Büttner's comment on him in chapter 2). Explorers tended to think of interpreters as personal aides—much as modern-day ethnographers do—and judge their work accordingly. They rarely acknowledged that the roles of interpreting and guiding put those who held them under constraints to behave in certain prescribed ways toward the parties they served.

As to the linguistic media of communication available to expeditions starting from the west, next to Portuguese and an unnamed variety of Afro-Portuguese, one other vehicular language is mentioned. This was (Ki)mbundu, the *língua dos ambaquistas,* that is, the language of Christianized Africans from Ambaca (Buchner in *MAGD* 2, no. 1 [1880]: 49).[4] Along the Congo, the emergence of common vehicular languages such as Lingala and Fiote accompanied European penetration, probably more as its result rather than as a precondition.[5] Travelers who were beginning to turn into colonial agents did not yet have the power to impose reduced, pidginized forms of vehicular languages on the people with whom they dealt and, conversely, African expectations regarding the linguistic competences of Europeans were probably higher than in later colonial times.

At any rate, collecting information was more important to explorers than making themselves understood. As can be imagined, failure to communicate and, even more so, inability to control and verify what was communicated to interpreters, were sources of constant irritation. What is not so easy to understand is that such irritation sometimes took the form of moral and racist aspersions cast on interpreters. True, persons who offered their services for this function were often of mixed cultural background (Afro-Arab, Afro-Portuguese), well traveled, and worldwise; not exactly the type of the faithful servant.[6] It is also likely that their experiences with white patrons or the heritage from a long history of trade and travel made many of them ruthless and self-serving; or perhaps they simply decided to "manage" the information at their disposal (in both directions of the exchange) for reasons that may have been political as well as mercenary. There can be no doubt, as we shall see later, that misinformation was a form of resistance. It is safe to assume that its practice began long before the explorers appeared on the scene as the forerunners of modern colonization. Still, there is something decidedly irrational and mad (in the sense of angry) about the image of morally inferior, lying scoundrels that European travelers projected on their interpreters (and, we should add, sometimes on entire populations in the perceived role of intermediaries).

When they engaged in such projections travelers may have been compensating for their frustrations. Few were willing to reflect on their situation and ascribe its problems to their own shortcomings and to the demands of possibly ill conceived scientific methods of gathering information. They certainly were not willing to abandon claims to a superior position vis-à-vis the objects of their research and expose themselves to the strain and pain of effective intercultural communication by reaching beyond an exchange of stereotypes and "useful phrases," most of them commands.

GRAMMARS AND TEXTS

> One marked characteristic of the Swahili language is its peculiar defining prefixes. This same feature distinguishes all the tribal dialects in Africa, south of the fifth degree of north latitude. Indeed it is one of the principal links connecting various parts of the great Bantu race of negroes comprised within that area. (1:29)

Behind the careful devotion to describing language—without the immediacy, the hesitations and vagaries, of conversation—we may glimpse a traveler's need to compensate for feelings of powerlessness. But he probably justified the reduction of language to writing as a kind of ascetic exercise, a withdrawal in the service of higher aims. What else, to cite an example, explains the *Manuel du voyageur*'s recommendations to collect vocabularies of native languages as a measure of tropical hygiene?[7] Heeding such instructions, even explorers who had little or no linguistic training began to abstract the system from practice, language from speaking. They soon went beyond humble collecting of word lists and busied themselves as grammarians, turning description into prescription.

We find an example of this urge to "rule" a language an individual does not speak and thereby to escape the messiness of communication in a report by Buchner, a scientifically minded physician with little patience. He had got tired of his interpreter Pedro, whom he despised anyway as a "negro in pants" [*Hosenneger*], an "Ambakist," that is, a Christianized African, belonging to an "insufferable race," and speaking a "Portuguese gibberish" (*MAGD* 2, no. 1 [1880]: 45). Buchner had decided to learn the Lunda language from Pedro but found him lacking in intelligence for that task. So he extricated himself from that situation by studying his interpreter's "native language, *Mbundu,* which is to serve as a bridge, being probably as closely related to Lunda as Dutch to German." The examples he gives of his teacher's obtuseness are classical instances of mutual misunderstanding between ethnographers and their informants. They show the difficulties researchers have keeping their interlocutors in communicative frames construed to elicit strictly linguistic information. Here is an example: "Often, when Pedro, translating for me, really gets going and I ask, for instance, [the translation of] 'today I want to go to Kimbundu,' he suddenly leaves his role and answers: 'But you did not want to go to Kimbundu.' That is usually the end of the language lesson and I close my notebook with a sigh." Undaunted, Buchner finds solace in his role as the linguist: "Incidentally, the necessity to establish every rule and exception through all sorts of tricks and ruses sometimes has a certain charm and, in the end, it gives me much pleasure to find my rules confirmed when I overhear conversations among my people. If only I had more time and were not so dead tired when I have the time. My travel apparatus absorbs too much of my capacity to work" (49).

Some explorers who dabbled in linguistics may eventually have produced pioneering work. But often the travelogues' reports of their efforts look like Becker's folly, if we may so label his posturing as a grammarian and pronouncements about the poverty of Swahili that his own communicative practices refute.[8] Capelo and Ivens too appear to approach the topic of language with trepidation. "Turning now to the question of language we must admit at the very outset that it is so vague and obscure that we hardly know how to tackle it" (1882, 2:248). And they immediately embark on several pages of listing languages. They voice some truly "imaginative" opinions on tones and other prosodic features reflecting the shapes of the physical environment in which a language is spoken and go on to discuss genetic relationships between different languages, numerals and counting, ideas of time and distance, and basics of noun-class prefixes (248–54). Lack of well-founded knowledge about any of the above, which they admit, does not prevent them from making obscure general pronouncements such as this: "The African languages are generally poor, imperfect, complicated by most varied signs, which of themselves complete a phrase through the nonexistence of correlative ideas." They blame difficulties with, and poverty of, communication with Africans on their languages. Capelo and Ivens observe that the languages they got to know do not mark gender and must do with circumlocutions when gender distinctions are important. They conclude with a remark that speaks volumes about language and exploration: "From this peculiarity sprang those long-winded speeches which tried our patience so severely, and the unconscionable delay in replying to the simplest question" (251).

An analog of abstracting language from speech was to extract texts from communicative events. In the travelogues we occasionally get fragments of reported dialogue that look like protocols of actual exchanges made during visits or negotiations. But methods of documentation were still at their beginning and classed most texts, like objects, as ethnographic only if they fit into recognized genres, such as proverbs, song lyrics, and folktales. What actually made it into the travel accounts varied between short phrases in an African language—pathetic little snippets meant to demonstrate authentic lore—and extensive transcripts of texts. The use of native terms to lard prose in European languages would become an anthropological habit (documented and analyzed in Fabian 1985); the transcripts ranged from short texts such as the trilingual example of a song reproduced by Kaiser and Reichard (*MAGD* 3, no. 4 [1883]: 226–27) to Frobenius's *Dichtkunst der Kassaiden* (1928), based on a collection of Luba texts.[9] Interesting as these early examples are, most of them show little more than that Africans had begun to provide the oral content for literary representations through which European authors demonstrated their knowledge and ethnographic authority.

LANGUAGE, POLITICS, AND RHETORIC

> I tried threats, but they only laughed....They saw they
> had me quite in their power, and as I felt it was useless
> to struggle against a united band, I was *nolens volens*
> compelled to give in. (1:179)

The misplaced linguistic zeal we find among some of our authors may of course also express political motives. Our sources indicate that explorers were already under pressure to identify languages that could serve as ethnic labels and, by extension, as the territorial and political divisions needed to establish colonial rule. Slightly later, this service was to become a specialty of missionaries, and some carried it out for the colonial regime on a contractual basis.[10]

Where power is at stake we can expect power plays. By the 1880s the distinction of African languages and their appropriation (through description) became a contested field. An odd but interesting example of this comes from Coquilhat. Already during his sea voyage to the Congo in 1882, he noticed how his fellow passengers, all of them traders, commercial agents, and missionaries, observed one another. He sensed "a hidden current of commercial rivalry." To his surprise he also detected such feelings among some English members of the Baptist Congo Mission: "They, too, fear competition. Imagine, they lent me a dictionary of the language of the lower Congo only after carefully having removed the name of the publisher. I discovered it, nevertheless" (1888, 13).

Even more than the anecdote, the fact that Coquilhat thought it worth reporting shows that knowledge of African languages was of political importance in more than one sense. First, the identification of languages and of boundaries between them was as important in the exploration of central Africa as geographical features. Second, even in this early phase of colonization, language communication was a political factor in establishing the Europeans' relations with African populations and their rulers. Therefore, to puzzle out the role of language in ethnographic inquiries we must look once again at the explorers' communication through interpreters and language learning, this time paying attention to pragmatic and rhetorical aspects, in short, to language and power. Our authors did have interesting things to say about this subject and, as we have come to expect, often contradicted one another. The same Coquilhat who gave us his devastating opinion about African interpreters has this report about linguistic efforts undertaken at Equateur station: "We have a very decent interpreter in the person of one of our negroes recruited in Zanzibar although he is a native of Nyangwe on the upper Congo. This man has studied Kibangi at Bolobo and, with the help of this dialect, he quickly learns that of Equateur, Kilolo. As for us, we are making progress in the Swahili language and beginning to master the first elements of Kibangi and Kilolo" (147).

No matter how negative explorers were about their interpreters, they needed them and used them. As they reported on various difficult exchanges, they gave little thought to the possibility that their intermediaries may have had pragmatic and rhetorical rather than linguistic or moral reasons for acting as they did. Failure to appreciate these—instances of language as action—caused them to treat interpreters as servants who did not need to know about the travelers' backgrounds, current tasks, and future projects. How could these intermediaries replace or represent their employers in conversations, negotiations, and interrogations? Conversely, how could travelers—knowing little or nothing about their interpreters—give them meaningful questions and answers to translate? How could explorers who lacked linguistic as well as communicative competences expect to use languages and linguistic intermediaries as effective and accurate instruments if they formulated their questions in a cultural void? It would not be fair to ask these questions—after all, a beginning had to be made somewhere if a common ground was to be found or established—if we did not have the example of some explorers who made the necessary efforts to get along without interpreters. Some of them did, because they understood that language and communication do not work purely instrumentally. The contradictions they faced were all the more severe because their enculturation into African ways of speaking conflicted with the demands their mission imposed, to maintain distance and superiority.

Becker was among these exceptions. Because we have already heard so much of him here and elsewhere, Torday now deserves our attention. He held interesting, and interestingly contradictory, views on the subject and he, too, makes a general statement about interpreters. It sounds much like Coquilhat's: "It is quite impossible to travel in security if, for your communications with the blacks, you have to rely upon the untrustworthy intervention of an interpreter. There is no situation, however difficult, out of which you cannot escape unscathed if you only know how to speak to the people" (1925, 240). To reinforce the point, Torday recollects a peace mission he undertook in the Kwilu region.

> As I speak Kimbala fluently I had not much difficulty in bending them to my views. I addressed them very differently from the way in which I should have addressed a European audience. It is no use appealing directly to their reason with arguments based on the relative advantages of the various courses: the native mind is accustomed to allegories, and to argue successfully with a native audience it is necessary to draw one's illustrations from their daily life. (161)

In other words, Torday knew that explorers with some competence in an African language still had to fit it to the rhetorical rules and conventions of their audience. Comparing him to others, we give him credit for his ethnographic finesse even though his point seems fairly obvious: all natural communication needs contexts and employs figures of speech and culturally appropriate images—in Africa as well as in Europe or anywhere in the world. That he thought a native audience was more context- and culture-bound, more caught up in images and allegories than a European audience, was one of those unexamined, thoroughly unreasonable a priori notions we found crowding the minds of explorers. Generally, such stereotypes may express evolutionist and positivist ideas. This particular one reflects plain ignorance of the working of language and its author's alienation from ordinary speech because of his training. The first limitation no longer applies to recent language-centered ethnography; the second will continue to haunt us as long as we think of scientific discourse and its practices as intrinsically superior to ordinary life.

But back to Torday. What he tells us is that once a European has become competent in one or several African languages, his attitudes toward interpreters may become more realistic, along with his views of African languages as instruments of inquiry. Competence in a language does not by itself guarantee communication. In a situation where he was able to converse with people in a common language he had this experience: "Communication between us was carried on in Kimbala, and as soon as I trenched on ethnographical questions they forgot their Kimbala or had a pressing engagement elsewhere" (129).

The less he depends on a translator's referential exactness, the more the traveler can appreciate his rhetorical services. Torday's exceptional sensitivity to these problems comes out in several remarks on his eight-year-old "boy" Buya, whom he did not rate high as an interpreter but admired as a rhetoric genius.[11] He was an effective intermediary in many difficult situations, among them the crossing of a pocket of resistance to white rule between the Kasai and Loange Rivers. When Buya scolded culprits, we are told, he was more effective than his employer (see 1913, 243–44); he defused tight situations simply with his laughter (254). At one confrontation with some tough Bakongo negotiators, Torday pays him this compliment: "The Bakongo were poor performers; all they could say never rose above strictly parliamentary language; not so Buya. That boy was remarkable for his eloquence and for his power of invective" (257).

It must have been the same person, under another name, about whom Torday notes in his second travelogue:[12]

> His value to me in my ethnographical investigations it is impossible to over-estimate. The native often refuses information and in such cases I always ex-plained to Meyey the point at issue, and left him to get at the facts. He often said nothing to me about it for days, but carried on his inquiries systematically till he was able to give me the information required. When I brought up the questions before the natives in order to verify the information thus obtained, I found that he had never failed to get to the bottom of them. (1925, 104)

Ethnography out of the mouth of babes? That he should have thought so much of his boy, in this case literally a child, remains intriguing. Several authors shared the opinion Torday expresses here: "The brightest period of the intellectual life of the negro is between the ages of ten and twelve; after that age he falls into a slough of sensuality" (1925, 241). We have mentioned the practice of employing children before;[13] that Europeans recognized above all their value as "communicators" has something to do with language and power. Boy servants were "unattached" former slaves or otherwise separated from their families. Yet none of the reports we have credits them with submissiveness. It must have been their ability to maintain (relatively) power-free, playful relations with both sides that made them so useful to explorers.

A relationship of (relative) equality may also have been the reason why certain adult interpreters managed to gain the respect of their employers. Wissmann, for example, describes the interpreter he and Pogge hired. He calls Kashawalla a black "Falstaff" and adds that he was often in a "state that among us in the army is called, from the rank of corporal downward, drunkenness." But Kashawalla was a great linguist, very funny "and, since he spoke Portuguese well, quite entertaining company" (1889, 44). In a report to the German association, Pogge expressed his appreciation of Kashawalla even more strongly: "Wissmann and I had the advantage ... of traveling with a reliable and intelligent interpreter, a man from Ambaqua by the name of Johannes Bizerra Correia Pinto, called *Kaschawalla* by the natives, the only negro known to me who I attest is a *homem honrado* [honorable man]. Thanks to him I am tolerably well informed about the local ethnic situation" (*MAGD* 4, no. 2 [1884]: 202).[14] Intriguingly, the traveler who rarely passes up a chance to draw general conclusions and recommendations from his experiences is strangely silent on the subject of interpreters: Frobenius mentions learning Luba (which?) and Kuba, which he eventually claims to have used without an interpreter (1907, 225).

Understanding what Africans say, either directly or through interpreters, is one thing; presenting the contents of a conversation or story to European readers is another. In the following passage Torday, still reflecting on communicating with his servants, lets us take a closer look at problems of translation, anticipating some of the epistemological problems that now litter debates on the relative merits of scientific and literary conventions of representation in ethnographic writing.

> I always spoke the native languages with my boys, and when I report their remarks I simply translate them into English, though I am well aware that a more amusing effect would be produced if I made use of pidgin English. But it is my endeavour to show the native as he is, and no report of a conversation in pidgin English could give anything like a true expression. For a work like the present, which does not aspire to be a serious contribution to science except in a very small way, it seems better to give a straightforward translation of a conversation. I need hardly say that I regard the use of pidgin English or pidgin French in scientific works with the utmost contempt. As a means by which to acquire anthropological information of value it is simply unworthy of notice. An anthropologist should of all people seek to reflect the mind of the people whom he describes, but pidgin English is a distorted mirror which metamorphoses the image it reflects. (1925, 119–20)

His arguments must have appealed to at least some of his colleagues, who also decided on straightforward translation, though they did not discuss the issue in their accounts.

Finally, I cannot refrain from quoting Torday once more, this time to show him aware of the need for cultural knowledge in interpreting the nonverbal means that are integral to all communication. He compiled a list of gestures for which I did not find a parallel in any of our sources.

> Negation. Shrug of shoulders.
>
> Affirmation. Raising the eyebrows.
>
> Affirmation for a girl. Shutting the eyes after looking sternly at her (= I only have eyes for you).
>
> Pointing. Is done not with the fingers but with the lips.
>
> Calling a person. Back of the hand uppermost, draw the half-bent fingers inward.
>
> Astonishment. One hand before the mouth, shake the head from side to side.
>
> Very great astonishment. Arms at full length by the sides, snap the fingers, and say "My Mother." (240)

Here is one legacy the exploration of central Africa bestowed on ethnography: explorers cannot just observe but must converse; they need com-

petence in local languages; and the services of interpreters may pose as
many problems as they solve. Even in those times of first and early contact, our authors knew, they could not simply instrumentalize language
and language learning. Languages made demands and caused fears. Travelers reacted by taking refuge in attempts at linguistic description. Or
they found relief in moral indignation, using it to offset their own shortcomings. This is not to cast indistinct blame on our authors (though some
deserve blame for their racism and bigotry). Only a rather naive view of
communication as a mode of ethnographic knowledge production can
overlook the fact that, like all human relations, communicating occurs
in contexts of power that range from rhetoric to violence. All our travelers experienced a tension Pogge expressed when he stated, "The traveler must not talk much, he must act resolutely" (1880, 21). Which
brings us to the next topic.

LEADING AND COMMANDING

LEADERSHIP AND AUTHORITY

> Then I became apologetic and appealed to them to re-
> member I was but a boy, wholly inexperienced, and
> therefore liable to make mistakes. They should be fa-
> thers to me, and tell me quietly and gently when I went
> wrong, so that I might be put right.... This harangue
> took immediate effect, and they became so enthusiastic
> in my favor, that they at once commenced a dance of
> universal good-will. (1:196)

The theme of control has already shadowed our discussion of the organization of expeditions, the movement of caravans, and health and living conditions. It appeared in doctrines of hygiene that articulated the
links between self-control and empire. Now we can give our inquiries
another focus by looking more closely at what our sources have to say
about leadership and authority. In a wealth of quotable texts, descriptive as well as reflexive, they bear out our argument: even at its beginnings, the ethnographic exploration of central Africa had to deal with
conflicts and tensions over power and communication. Travel in caravans required leadership, a complex blend of self-control and control of
others. Many situations reported in our sources show how easily the conflicting demands for control could cause scientific inquiry to self-destruct.

To begin the commentaries, Becker puts communication in the context of authority as he weighs the problems of leading and directing

Africans who are not used to military discipline. He summarizes his recommendations.

> Infinite time, and miracles of sangfroid, energy, and impassive firmness will
> be needed to dominate our men. Even then we will not succeed except after
> a complete study of their language. Too often, because we cannot make our-
> selves understood, we are inclined to exact with rudeness what we would get
> more easily with the gentleness of persuasion. Nothing is accomplished by of-
> fending and mistreating the negroes. It is much better to amuse and seduce
> them, to enchant them; only then can we lead them as we see fit. They are big
> children we must study and get to know. (1887, 1:85)

This plea for seduction instead of force speaks well for Becker's humane
outlook.[15] But notice the statements framing it, ones that were to become classical topoi of (Belgian) colonial discourse: the expectation that
civilizing Africans by controlling them needs a lot of time and that they
are big children who need paternal guidance.

This programmatic statement leads to a portrait of the good explorer
who is also a good leader. Contrary to European prejudices, Becker tells
us, Africans are perfectly capable of recognizing the qualities of legitimate authority, among them common sense and frankness. Ambitious
individuals who lack self-control should stay at home: "He who only
dreams of his return and accepts the present only for the advantages it
will bring him later in Europe—who does not open-mindedly live in surroundings that call on all his abilities and powers, all his ingenuity, and
his complete self-abnegation—will not produce a single lasting and serious result. Excellent, perhaps, in theory, but in practice if such a person has the misfortune of getting involved, [the experience] will simply
make him a sacrificial lamb offered on the altar of ambition" (86–87).
Becker's profound insight is to state that the explorer must work in "the
present" as he finds it. I don't know of an anthropological text that more
concisely or compellingly puts the idea of a researcher's active presence
as an epistemological condition of ethnographic inquiry. Presence for
him was fresh, unshaped by scientific methodology. It had not yet become "participant observation."

But back to leadership. Authority proves itself in two ways: in seeing
to it that the daily chores get done and in keeping control during moments or times of crisis.[16] Routine, by definition not an exciting subject,
barely enters the travelogues; narration tends to move from event to
event. Exceptionally, Becker and Coquilhat each devote much of a chapter (vol. 2, ch. 31; and ch. 8) to daily life at Karema and Equateur stations, extolling the joys of power unchallenged. As Coquilhat puts it,

> It is a delicious experience to feel that you are the absolute master of your actions, totally responsible for their results, and invested with a well-defined mission that is beautiful because it has a lofty goal and is ripe with benefits for progress if it succeeds. That is the stimulant for our activities, the reason we pay no attention to the absence of comfort, and one cause for our good health under adverse conditions of hygiene. (1888, 139)

I first came on the passage as a quotation in a manual for travelers and residents in the Congo.[17] Coquilhat's contemporaries judged it a classic. Oddly, they too paid no attention to what it hides: his clear-eyed view of life around the station. He goes on,

> No sense in fooling ourselves: our situation is full of obscurity. We know neither the real importance of chief Ikenge—with whom, by the way, there is only a verbal accord—nor the authority of neighboring rulers. What is the location and the size of their villages? What are their political relations? What does the region produce? So many question marks. And who has the answers at this point? We don't know the dialect of the country and we don't have an interpreter. (139–40)

Commanding a station had its problems, but they were nothing compared to the troubles explorers had maintaining their authority during travel. Desertion, insubordination, and sometimes outright revolt loomed for all expeditions.[18] Here are two texts by Becker; the first a general assessment of the situation, the second a piece of advice for the traveler in Africa who faces uncooperative personnel (another facet to the topic of performance and power). Few of the European travelers shared the views Becker expresses here and none would have been as outspoken as he was.

> The times are gone when the Arabs went from the coast to Ujiji [on Lake Tanganyika] carrying nothing but a stick, or when the Muzungu [white] was taken for a supernatural being and, by his mere presence in a caravan, inspired fear and respect. The black demons have discovered our vulnerable points. They have seen us suffer, as they do, from hunger, thirst, and fever in spite of all *our riches,* unable to make our soldiers obey us and, abandoned by our porters, reduced, finally, to beg for the support of petty native tyrants who exact tribute according to their whims and greed. Today, most of the negroes who settle along the road know that we are weak mortals, less resistant than they to the surprises of the climate, and that the only advantages we have are our industrial products and the superiority of our firearms. (1887, 1:312)

Here is the background, says Becker, for the challenges to a white explorer's authority. The challenges weighed hardest on the inexperienced newcomer (a recurrent theme in the sources), who, as we have seen, commanded a personnel that had much experience in the caravan business.

Becker knew from experience that the later success of an expedition depended on how the leader came out of the first confrontations with his
auxiliaries. His advice is frank.

> Never meet their unwillingness with recrimination and, above all, never re-
> sort to violent means. Impassiveness succeeds best. The porters, who are far
> from devoted to the travelers, would desert as soon as the first one among
> them is punished. Among their established practices, by the way, is a little
> comedy that will quickly show you how matters stand. At the beginning of a
> trip the best porters feel an urge—rather, an obsession—to *measure* the leader
> of the caravan, white or Arab. They call this *Kou-pima Msafiri* [Swahili: to
> try the traveler]. To do that they put him, without scruples, to a test, playing
> at resistance, even insubordination and revolt. Unlucky the traveler who, be-
> cause he lacks self-control, loses in this sly struggle a single one of his ad-
> vantages. He opens himself to never-ending snubs. Under all circumstances,
> he should marshal all his calm and sangfroid, without giving the impression
> that he must make an effort to control himself. Throwing a tantrum with the
> negroes lowers him to their level. The Arabs never get angry, they never raise
> their voice and this is how they keep their prestige. (2:197–98)

No less a challenge to the leader's authority came from situations
where the personnel of the caravan fought among themselves or with the
local population. In his address to the Geographical Society quoted earlier, Wissmann has this to say: "Moments such as this are very dangerous for the European, because it has often happened that senseless rage
turned against the caravan's leaders and resulted in the murder of the
whites" (*MAGD* 4, no. 1 [1883]: 42).

Frobenius reflects at length on conflicts within a caravan and with local populations (most of them relating to theft or relations with women).
Knowing that conflicts can ruin expeditions and trying to deal with them,
the European is at a disadvantage; he knows neither the customs nor the
language well enough to adjudicate them. To avoid constant appeals for
a decision, he sets up a rota of foremen. They hear palavers and decide;
he confirms (1907, 436–37). Indirect rule, as colonial regimes were to
find out, had its advantages. But was setting up protective screens and
barriers to direct access a good strategy for an ethnographer?

PHYSICAL FORCE AND VIOLENCE

> Seeing the position of affairs I unbuckled my belt, and
> without a word of warning I let fall such a whack on
> the bare skin of one of the sleepers as made him jump
> up with a yell. Fairly at it, I felt like a slaver, and

> sprang from one to another, dealing right and left with-
> out the slightest compunction. In a few moments every
> hut was cleared. I spoke not a word. I was in too great
> a rage for that. (2:104–5)

The use of violence Becker warned against was not a hypothetical situation. The record in our sources is uneven, to say the least. Some travelers resorted to violent acts and described them with relish. Others presumably used force without reporting it in their travelogues. And not all of them were brutal. The differences in behavior may have reflected personal character; they also had much to do with social class and professional habits. After all, the physical punishment of subalterns and the physical settlement of differences were more or less accepted practices in nineteenth-century Europe, certainly in the military from which most explorers were recruited. But our focus here is on acts of violence caused by states of excitement and rage that are possible instances of ecstatic behavior.

Presumably, most of the violence the travelers justified after the fact was not rationally calculated. Sometimes, accounts of these acts give off an eerie impression of detachment from reality. The acts were blind outbreaks of frustration or exasperation whose relation to the circumstances at hand is hard to figure out. Those who now and then gave themselves over to rage and force lost self-control and, for a while, control of their scientific and political missions. With persons like Torday, who was not above slapping and kicking Africans (or, probably, insubordinate Europeans), we get the feeling that such behavior made him more human in the eyes of his people and, in the end, improved his rapport.

Still, given the professed aims of exploration, acts of violence are also indications of travelers being "out of their minds." How, given their own vulnerability and often total dependence on the goodwill of Africans, could they dare to behave in such a way? One relevant factor is the performative aspect of violence. Travelers almost always meted out physical punishment in public, preferably in the presence of spectators, often with a mise-en-scène of the event. It is also likely that travelers got drawn into an existing culture of violence and, in their eagerness to assert their authority, assumed prerogatives of chiefly status by arrogating to themselves the right to punish as well as the privilege of demonstrating power by physical force.

The same Becker who is on record for his condemnation of violence and who thought that "nothing here is more dangerous than getting car-

ried away and resorting to brutality" reports, approvingly (and in the
same passage), how one soldier receives a *bastonnade* for insubordination (1887, 1:98). More than that, once when he caught a looter who
injured a woman while trying to remove a bracelet from her ankle, he
himself took action: "Without fooling around with negotiations I use my
revolver to crack the miserable fellow's skull and, after a temporary
dressing of her wounds, put the unfortunate woman into the hands of
my retinue" (2:373). This statement is so offhand that we barely register the fact that it may be the only report in our sources of an explorer
killing an African other than in combat, in self-defense, or by execution
after a trial—if our translation is accurate.[19]

Not every demonstration of physical violence came to such a dramatic
end. Most were of the kind reported, for instance, by Wissmann when
he faced his first porters' strike at Malange: "I managed to remove [the
leader] from the rostrum with a resounding slap in the face. This happened so fast that I had the people laughing and on my side" (1889,
19).[20] Buchner mentions intimidating Africans by deliberately loading a
gun, using a whip, and threatening to take recourse to a measure already
tried and tested by Galton—riding his ox into a crowd of rebellious
porters.[21] A similar scene faced von François (a member of Wissmann's
Kasai expedition). It was one of many hostile situations he got into
among the Kanyok: "I was riding at the head [of the caravan], but now
I immediately turned my ox, drew my revolver, called for the interpreter,
and galloped into the throng. The Kanjoka could not take the onslaught.
The way I looked, and the ox thundering right at them, threw them in
such panic that they abandoned the fight and fled back to the village"
(Wissmann et al. 1891, 276).

This was bullying in the literal sense of the word. The incident (while
he charges, he calls for his interpreter) also shows the tangle of coercion
and communication that occupies us in this chapter. On another occasion the same von François resorted to stronger means. He was one of
the few explorers to admit, albeit in veiled terms, that he actually shot
at Africans: "Unable to help myself in any other way, I made serious use
of my gun, with success. [As regards life] among the savages...security
will always be tied to the superiority of our arms" (1888, 143–44).

No sharp line separated exploration from military action. As we assess the role of force and violence, in the case of Reichard we can watch
the one turning into the other. He had no military mission. Yet if his reports are to be believed, Reichard conducted part of his travel as a hostile campaign—exhibiting considerable signs of madness. Here is the

background: the German East African Expedition had experienced great difficulties. From their station near Tabora they planned to move west and eventually reach central Africa beyond Lake Tanganyika. Kaiser, their astronomer and topographer, had died of fever on Lake Rikwa in November 1882.[22] The two survivors straggled into the Belgian station at Karema. There, Lieutenant Storms (Becker's successor as head of station) had planned a punitive military expedition for March 1883 against the village of Katakwa, which had robbed and killed couriers of the IAA. Böhm offered to go along because Reichard was down with "a strong, intermittent fever causing delirious states." In combat, while storming the fortified village, Böhm sustained a bullet wound in his right leg; the wound got infected because they had forgotten to bring along the medicine chest. Böhm's recovery dragged on for months (*MAGD* 4, no. 2 [1884]: 96, 97, 98, 99). His letters during this period describe excruciating pain and suffering (1888, 143–44).

To kill time until Böhm got well enough for the trip west, Reichard decided to undertake exploratory trips across the lake. His report starts conventionally with an account of troubles with native chiefs on land and on the lake. Then he tells of a request by chief Kapampa to join him in a war expedition against his enemy Kalimba. According to Reichard, such requests are expected by "custom" (161). They travel to the Marungu mountains on the western shore of Lake Tanganyika, where Kalimba has his residence. It turns out that the expedition is in revenge for Kalimba's killing Kapampa's own brother a few years earlier (163–64). When they arrive at Kalimba's village, the tone of Reichard's story shifts. He now refers to Africans as *Wilde*, savages. They are not just generically *savages*—people we would now call "non-Western." To Reichard they are literally "wild," or feral. Without seeming to feel the slightest compunction (and, obviously, with the approval of *MAGD*'s editors), Reichard regales his readers with an account of the looting and killing binge on which he now embarks. In the end, he offers this justification for his behavior: "I want to state explicitly that we, in contrast to other travelers, realized that the only correct procedure is to respond immediately to hostilities on the side of the natives, because all ill-timed leniency, also as regards the manner of waging war, will be interpreted as weakness or fear so that the situation really gets dangerous" (166–67).

Throughout the rest of the trip the terrorized natives do not live up to Reichard's projection of European savagery on his African opponents. They simply flee and leave messages to the marauders, telling them just to take what they want. Removing possible doubt about the significance of such action to our topic, Reichard adds: "We made the most ample use of this concession and I myself collected a pile of ethnographic objects, especially beautiful carvings" (167). To top off the pleasures of this trip, Reichard went out (four times) to hunt *soko*, chimpanzees, "but I only once saw a capital specimen without being able to get a shot at it" (169).

The German expedition completed its mission when it eventually reached the Lualaba (the upper Congo) and found itself on territory ruled by Chief Msiri in what was to become the Katanga province of the Congo. A cable Reichard sent to the German association in December 1884 from Mpala station contained mixed news: "Böhm dead. Lake Upemba, Lufira [River], copper mines Katanga discovered" (*MAGD* 4, no. 5 [1885]: 303). Going on the report of his trip through Katanga, which covered the time before and after Böhm's death, Reichard followed his stated policy and acted with force and violence whenever he had the upper hand. In the end, however, he had to beat a hasty retreat that took him past *Kunde Irunde* (presumably the Kundelungu mountains) across the Lufira River and once again through the Marungu mountains to the IAA station of Mpala on Lake Tanganyika (305–7). When, in one confrontation, circumstances did not permit him to attack he was forced "to throw away and burn 3 loads of beautiful ethnographic collections, a lot of drums, 3 loads of war trophies, lead, trunks, and clothes, so as to reduce the porters' burden and have them carry foodstuffs" (305). There are no traces of regret or doubt in this account of a rather murderous trip, except this apology at the very end: "Please excuse the hasty writing because right now I have no patience for good composition" (308).

This source does not represent the entire period or all the explorers we have studied. Yet its weight is beyond question. True, Reichard's status as a scientific explorer was at first somewhat doubtful. He had joined the German expedition as a young volunteer, paying his own way. At the beginning of his five-year stint, he helped his two learned colleagues (Böhm had got his doctorate under the famous evolutionist Ernst Haeckel!) with their work. His practical and commercial talents apparently stretched to ivory trading. But his success as a traveler later made him an authority on East Africa, an important colonial agent, and a rather prolific writer.[23]

Reichard's excesses occurred during the final years before the establishment of colonial rule after the Berlin Conference of 1884–85. At that time—when Europeans could tell themselves they were in Africa for humanitarian or scientific reasons, not for conquest—punitive military expeditions were conducted from Belgian stations in the east (see above) and in the west. Coquilhat, for instance, reports an incident where two soldiers of a unit at Equateur station had been killed by the people of a local chief and Boulanger, the resident, had one of the *provocateurs* killed in retaliation. Obviously not happy with this, Coquilhat describes the basic dilemma of exploration on the verge of occupation: if provoked you must respond with force, but you cannot really use force because you have ulterior goals. Nevertheless, the bottom line, as we would label it today, was "to keep your dignity" (1888, 124).

We might suppose European travelers did not have to worry about keeping their dignity intact after colonial rule was established. They could leave punishment and enforcement of laws to the colonial authorities. But such was not the case. Frobenius denounced the brutality of many colonials, especially the European employees of the rubber company, the Compagnie du Kasai (1907, 281–92). He himself, however, was not above slapping or manhandling Africans (267, 275), and at least once he describes a hostile confrontation in the Kwilu area as a regular military action, complete with a map of the battlefield (170–75).[24] Almost casually he tells how he stopped the enemy from advancing: "So I put the Görz-telescope on my heavy rifle and then the one among those fellows who came closest...said good-bye to the world" (172).

Killing Africans was not the rule; intimidating and beating them was. Once more Frobenius gives us examples of rather violent ethnography. Talking to a crowd of "nervous Bapende" (as he calls them in a chapter heading [259]), he announced his intentions to deal with any silliness (*Dummheiten*) on their part as one would do with children: "lay them across [my knee] and spank them" (268).[25] The threat may have been an appeal to their sense of humor, as he says. But Frobenius was not joking when he put the threat of force "in realistic terms" and treated the same audience to a disquisition on "the significance/importance of a rifle holding eight rounds" (269). And at length he profited, much as Reichard did, from his display of military superiority. The Bapende overwhelmed him with friendliness, which added "to the growth of my ethnological knowledge and of our collections. Now I could, with a little nudging, acquire legends and little stories, and also the first masks and all sorts of beautiful carved statues, and so on" (271).

Perhaps this episode with the eight-shooter should count as just a bit of bragging before the natives few travelers could resist, or an anecdote fitting the tough world of the Free State with its heavily armed Europeans strutting through Africa like the heroes through a Western? Not in its context. Frobenius did not stick to his role as explorer and man of science. He got himself involved in local and colonial power games. His account contains long passages devoted to his efforts as a peacemaker between hostile groups. It is not clear whether he was asked to intervene or simply decided to do so on his own. At any rate, time and again Frobenius got himself into hostile situations. His report on one of them (in a passage introducing his harangue to the Bapende quoted above) is the cue for our next chapter, on a remarkable episode in the exploration of central Africa.

Here is the relevant part of his speech, coming immediately after he meets the "impudence" of a Pende man with a hefty slap behind his ears. He tells the crowd that he had not come to make war and appeals to old loyalties.

> They, the Bapende, knew quite well, that I was not at all a Moena Bula Matari (son of the state, or state agent), nor a Moena na Ndundu (son of the rubber buyer) but a Moena Kabassu Babu [the name given to Wissmann]. Now, I told them, they knew perfectly well from the olden times that the Bena Kabassu were the friends of the blacks and that they came to the country only to see what they could learn from them about how to do good things for the blacks. But they would be wrong to imagine that I was doing them any good by putting up with just anything. (268)

Frobenius probably got the idea of identifying himself as the son of Kabassu Babu from "a strange sort of meeting" he had with a wizened little old man who turned out to be the great Tshokwe chief Mwila. Twenty years earlier, this "tiny, prattling forest ghost" had met Kabassu Babu and Kasongo—Wissmann and Pogge—and was now eager to treat one of their "offspring" to his memories of the times. Among other events, he fondly recalled a beating by Pogge. But then Mwila got himself entangled in a complicated political story that, with apologies to his readers, Frobenius cuts off just when it gets interesting (151–52). The wizened companion of earlier explorers often makes an appearance in the travelogues, and the topos still shows up in ethnographic accounts from time to time. Mwila's recollections sounded familiar to Frobenius because he carried with him the books of the men in whose tracks he was now traveling (257). How Pogge and Wissmann got their African names is part of one of the most curious, moving, and in the end tragic stories that the exploration of central Africa holds.

SEVEN

Charisma, Cannabis, and Crossing Africa

Explorers in the Land of Friendship

A country called El Dorado fired the imagination of Spaniards invading the New World. European travelers to Africa had their driving myths in King Solomon's mines, the Christian kingdom of Prester John, and the realm of Monomotapa with the mysterious ruins of Zimbabwe. A proverbial hopeless quest since antiquity, finding the Nile's sources, became a consuming obsession for generations of travelers. This quest ended as our period opened (as did one for the course of the Niger in West Africa). Another river and its sources, the Congo, became the great riddle that occupied geographic societies and made them send expeditions to central Africa. Their discoveries entertained European readers, fed the greed for power and wealth of many nations, and made explorers famous.

Our sources report one discovery that was absent from ancient myths and contemporary projects of exploration. It apparently never captured scientific or popular imagination. Though its story could have been the stuff for novels such as Rider Haggard's, it lingers now as one of those historical anecdotes even experts have been permitted to ignore. And yet the celebrated first European crossing of the continent from west to east by Pogge and Wissmann (in the end by Wissmann alone) and the founding of what became a strategic post for the Congo Free State—Lulu-aburg—hinged on the discovery of the *bene diamba*, "the children of hemp," who lived in the land of *lubuku*, "friendship," or *moyo*, "life."[1]

THE CHILDREN OF HEMP: FIRST REPORTS

Let me begin by recalling the scene: the expeditions to central Africa
sponsored by the German association took their approach from the west
coast. Their assignment was to get through the zones that resisted European penetration for political and economic reasons.[2] Throughout the
period that interests us, Bangala, Tshokwe, and other populations attempted to safeguard their intermediary position in the trade (with slaves,
later above all with ivory and rubber) between the interior and the coast.
Their strategy was to set up and expand relations with populations in
the interior of the Congo Basin and to discourage Afro-Portuguese entrepreneurs from attempts to bypass the chain of intermediaries. When
the first European caravans appeared on the scene, they were understood
(correctly) as trying to do just that. Our reports and travelogues are filled
with stories of African resistance, subterfuge, dishonesty, and endemic
violence. Explorers invariably experienced the complex local political
situation as a frustrating obstacle to the scientific exploration of central
Africa because it did not fit political categories the Europeans brought
along to their enterprise. Only the "Lunda empire," which they imagined as a central state administrated with the help of a system of vassals
and tributaries—as a central bureaucracy headed by one ruler, the
Mwant Yav, who, they knew, controlled access to the regions north of
his territory—seemed to represent a political partner European powers
could treat with.

On Pogge's first trip to the Lunda capital, Musumba, he spent four
months there (December 1875–April 1876) but accomplished little more
than prove that expeditions could get there and back. And he confirmed
that the regions to the north were important enough for the Lunda ruler
to bar access to them. One of the newly constituted German society's
first acts was to sponsor an expedition that would try again for access.
Its leader was Otto H. Schütt, who had worked as a topographer in the
Ottoman empire. Schütt departed in 1878, accompanied by one Paul
Gierow and later by Pogge's former interpreters and guides, Germano
and Bizerra. He mostly followed Pogge's route but turned aside to meet
a Luba chief by the name of Mai, who ruled a territory north of the
Lunda sphere.

When Schütt came to the Tshikapa River, he managed to have a traveling Tshokwe carry a letter back to Kimbundu, from where it reached
the coast and Europe. In this brief undated document he announced his
further plans: "I want to cross the *Cassaï* and the *Lulua* to get to the

mythical people of the *Cashilanga*, who are supposed to inhabit a region bordered by the *Lualaba* (*Zaire* means sea). There, they tell, is a huge lake which no bird can cross flying" (*MAGD*, no. 3 [1879]: 111). Intentionally or not, he gives his report the flavor of ancient travel tales, a fitting preparation for the first appearance the Bene Diamba make in the *MAGD* reports under one of their ethnic names, and as we spell it here, *Bashilange*.[3] As it turned out, Schütt was forced to return to Europe before he saw them. Not only that, he was cited before a committee of the German association (meeting in Berlin on October 12, 1879) and reprimanded for improper financial conduct. He had overspent his allowance, partly to pay for Gierow, whom he had taken along without authorization. Because an expert attested to the excellent quality of Schütt's topographic work and to the fact that he could not have done it without the help of a companion, he was exonerated (*MAGD*, nos. 4–5 [1879]: 171).

MAGD published his long report of a trip from Malange to the Luba chief Mai and back, July 1878–May 1879, complete with a map (nos. 4–5 [1879]: 173–207). In spite of being robbed by Bangala, deserted by most of their porters, and plagued by fever, Schütt and Gierow reached the country of chief Kimbundu. It was there that he heard stories of the Luba and after long negotiations with the chief decided to visit them. Their guide was to be a certain Caxavalla—the Kashawalla we met earlier[4]—an Afro-Portuguese, "who, three years ago, had traveled north with a band of *Quioquo* [Tshokwe]. He had been presumed missing but had luckily returned not long ago after having got as far as to Muquenge, a chief of the Luba tribe of the *Tuchilangue* [Bashilange]" (180).

Kashawalla's story was encouraging enough, though he too pointed out that the Lunda would try to prevent contact with the Luba. Schütt hired Kashawalla and left Kimbundu, accompanied by several African traders and a Portuguese deserter who had "gone native" (he describes him as *vernegert*—"gone bush," I believe, was the phrase used in English). After crossing the Tshikapa with the help of a Tshokwe chief, Mona Hongolo, and his nephew and heir, Camba N'Guchi, he reports: "Here, with this chief, I had for the first time since I traveled among negroes the comfortable feeling of being among kind, I am almost tempted to say, among good people" (181).

Then Schütt tells what he learned from Camba N'Guchi about the Luba, especially the *Cachilangue* (Bashilange), a tribe allegedly still practicing cannibalism. He heard a somewhat confused story of their dealings with the Tshokwe and of a group of twenty members of that tribe

who had come to Tshokwe country searching for fabrics and guns (182).
The Tshokwe chief encouraged Schütt to travel north and take these men
back to their chief Mukenge. More stories, now directly from those people, follow; the huge mythical lake appears again, this time identified by
the explorer as Cameron's *Sancorra* (probably Sankuru, a large river).
He now declares it "the real center of the Congo Basin." Pygmies are
mentioned, with attributes that seem to have come straight out of ancient monster tales (183).

Somewhere at this point the report becomes fictional: after two days
at Camba N'Guchi's—it states—Schütt and Gierow moved on and came
to their first Luba villages; eight days later they entered the residence of
chief Mai, who offered a pact of blood brotherhood and expressed his
desire to get baptized. But then, the tale goes on, because of protest from
his own people and instructions by chief Musevo, a vassal of the Lunda
ruler, Mai informed Schütt that the travelers would not be allowed to
continue. A mock attack in the middle of the night failed to scare Schütt
(he tells us); he undertook further negotiations and even predicted a so-
lar eclipse, expecting that this would make him appear to be endowed
with magical force. However, the Lunda envoy remained adamant and
the caravan had to turn around and head back toward Malange, where
Schütt, to his surprise, found Dr. Buchner, whom the German association had sent out on another expedition to the Mwant Yav. Schütt gave
Buchner a map of his trajectory and urged him to seek a direct route to
chief Mukenge in the north without bothering to get permission from
the Lunda.

The rest of Schütt's report is a rubricated compilation of notes on geography, climate, fauna, and so forth. Toward the end of a section titled
"Ethnographic Remarks" we find a summary of information about chief
Mukenge and his Tuchilangue, including the first mention of hemp:
"Their religion, their only fetish, is hemp, *liamba;* they broke their poi-
soned arrows and no longer keep idols; everyone who wants to belong
to the tribe must smoke Liamba, and if he doesn't want to, he is expelled"
(206).

Pogge and Wissmann later confirmed this statement and other observations Schütt made in the same passages. We try to present relevant
facts in as much detail as is feasible. But our goal is to understand the
circumstances, conditions, and practices of our authors' reports on
ethnographic material—how they found out what they reported as well
has how they reported on what they found. And it is precisely at this
point in Schütt's search for the mythical children of hemp that he puts

us on the trail of what must be one of the strangest twists in the strange story of the exploration of central Africa.

After his first report, *MAGD* published a list of Schütt's collection of birds, prepared by an ornithologist (*MAGD*, nos. 4–5 [1879]: 207–12), and his measurements of altitude in places east of Malange, with a positive comment by one of the journal's editors, Dr. Richard Kiepert (*MAGD* 2, no. 1 [1880]: 11–17). Then nothing is heard of Schütt except a brief announcement, made when the committee met on June 9, 1881, saying that a Herr Lindenberg plans to come out with a book on Schütt's travels at Dietrich Reimer Verlag in Görlitz (*MAGD* 2, no. 5 [1881]: 219). With the help of this editor, who worked from his diary, Schütt had been quick to get his travelogue to the avid public (it appeared in 1881).[5] Early in 1882, the editors of *MAGD* duly cite this book in a note justifying their decision to publish extracts from the diary of Gierow, Schütt's once unwanted companion. Here they make what must have been a rather sensational revelation at the time: these excerpts offer "nothing essentially new from a scientific point of view" but the editors put them in "because, unfortunately, the work by Schütt-Lindenberg turns out not to be entirely reliable. Several sections of the route, as they are represented on the maps and in the text, are fictitious, especially the final leg...to chief Mai, where the expedition actually never arrived. Schütt's original diaries, which are in the possession of the African Society, leave no doubt about this" (*MAGD* 3, no. 2 [1882]: 95–96).

Having stated this in no uncertain terms, the editors end with an attempt to salvage most of Schütt's report. The faked parts—with their fantastic elements such as the mock attack and Schütt's prediction of an eclipse—become "additions": "Numerous as these additions may be, they fortunately do not cover much territory. They are outweighed by the undoubtedly genuine part of the route. It would therefore be unjustified (albeit understandable after such a regrettable incident!) if distrust, once awakened, were extended to all the results of Schütt's expedition, important as they are for the special topography of the region traversed" (96). That is all. No comment on what led Schütt not just to imagine but elaborately fake (with maps and all) a part of his trip that would have been his most important contribution if it had taken place. No comment on the value of the information reported from this fictive visit to chief Mai. Obvious questions—why Schütt dared to fake part of it; how the German association came into possession of material incriminating Schütt—are not raised. Nor did it occur to the embarrassed sponsors that the analogy between topography (where some parts can be demonstrably correct, others invented) and ethnography (whose validity is always based on trust in an author's truthfulness and only occasionally on independent confirmation or refutation) does not hold.

In the travelogue Schütt's account of his trip—including the fictive leg undertaken to meet with chief Mai—is essentially the same as in his report to *MAGD*. One difference I noticed is that the Bashilange make a more gradual appearance, first as *Tuchilange,* later *Cachilange* or *Caxilanga* (1881, 32, 42, 145). The name of their chief Mukenge occurs several times (as *Muquenge* [42, 140, 156]), and toward the end of the book Mukenge's rival Tshingenge makes a brief appearance (as *Quingengue* [164]). The Bashilange are said to be cannibals (96, 138) and *Luboco* is a mocking epithet for them (*ein Spottwort* [96, 150]). A summary of the hemp cult Kashawalla gave him has many of the essential traits we later get to know from Pogge and Wissmann (145–46), except that Schütt plays down the role of hemp when he speaks of Diamba as "a sort of tobacco" (146).

But back to our story. We gave as much space to the Schütt affair as we did only because it seemed appropriate to show that the smokers of hemp entered the ethnographic scene in a sphere of myths, partial truths, and outright fabrications. And without evidence of Schütt's fake, would the editors have published Gierow's diary? It is an important document, unpretentious and informative. It confirms what Schütt said about the Bashilange, including the story of a group who planned to travel with the expedition back to their home country in the north. That the caravan never reached chief Mai's territory is clearly stated; the residence of a chief by the name of Kiluata was as far as they got. There they were informed by the Mwant Yav's envoy, Musevo, that they had no permission to travel north: "We were no longer free and had to obey him." The caravan had to turn around and leave the Bashilange behind, says Gierow, adding that "at Kiluata's we had been received by an envoy of Mukenge, ruler of the Bashilange. The news of our trip had already reached him" (123). Here is the first indication of the Bashilange actively seeking contact with European travelers.

REACHING THE BASHILANGE

Meanwhile—as Schütt and Gierow made their way toward the Bashilange—Buchner was on his trip to the Lunda empire and had his first meeting with the Mwant Yav on December 11, 1879. Like Pogge before him, he was denied access to the coveted regions in the north. Undeterred, the German society then sent out another expedition led by Pogge, whose first trip had made him a famous and respected explorer. He was accompanied by Hermann Wissmann, an army lieutenant on leave who had never been to Africa. Buchner, on his way back from the Lunda, and Pogge-Wissmann, on their way out, met, in Malange, to exchange information (on February 8, 1881).[6]

Of the Pogge-Wissmann expedition we have a voluminous account, both in Wissmann's travelogue (1889) and in reports, letters, and excerpts from diaries by Pogge and Wissmann published in *MAGD*. This expedition was to break through the cordon of belligerent trading populations who had kept earlier caravans from the west coast out of the center of the Congo Basin. The children of hemp whom Pogge and Wissmann finally met there made it possible for Wissmann to cross the continent to the east coast. More important, on the eve of colonial rule, the Bashilange presented them, as ethnographers, with a most intriguing case, a chance to break through that other cordon of preconceived images of savage Africa. Another chance, as I begin to see it, would not come around again until the 1960s, after the colonial regime's end. To think what Pogge and Wissmann could have made of that chance and see what they did make of it may be one of the most important lessons we take from this study.

Let me stop for a moment to review without giving away too much of the story that is to follow. We have seen in detail and from many different angles that the success of expeditions depended on qualified personnel, sufficient funds, good logistics, and luck. But what counted, probably more than any of these, was politics: even before the era of treaties and concessions, European explorers had to be able to identify and deal with power structures and officeholders. Yet scientifically minded travelers—skilled at describing the physical features of the regions they traversed and taking notes of the appearance and customs of the peoples they met—were not prepared when it came to politics. They filled this blank space with concepts such as emperors, kings, rulers, and chiefs. If they could match the officeholders with named tribes and bordered territories, the terms were of practical use. There was room in the picture for exceptional figures, rulers of ancient empires, such as the Mwant Yav of the Lunda, and recent usurpers, such as Mirambo, the "Napoleon" of East Africa. That Portuguese colonial rule, long-distance trade, and Arab penetration had brought considerable change in political institutions and relations could hardly remain hidden even from casual observers. On the whole, however, our authors still saw the typical

African chief as someone who held an ancient office, drew his power from fetishism, and ruled a closed little world, sometimes wisely, most often with force, greed, and corruption. They interpreted armed conflicts as local tribal warfare. Political powers in this mosaic of ethnic units added up to a void—one canceling out another—that European imperialism claimed it was destined to fill.

Presumably, Pogge and Wissmann more or less shared these images and expectations. But what if they encountered African political leaders with a vision of the future and the strength to break with custom and tradition, undertake daring social experiments, and welcome the outside world as an ally in bringing about peaceful change in a situation characterized by endemic violence ranging from human sacrifice to slave raids? Our sources give factual answers to this hypothetical-sounding question.

From the beginning, the Pogge-Wissmann expedition, though probably better prepared than any of the preceding ones, suffered from problems. The worst of them began in Malange, where Pogge suffered from a toothache that turned into an infection of the jaw, caused a delay of four months, and later made him travel under indescribable pain. Heroically, he overcame an affliction that often threatened to drive him out of his mind. It eventually got the better of him. Wissmann treated his superior with deep respect and sympathy but inevitably emerged as the leader. When, after reaching the Lulua River, Pogge's condition did not permit further travel, Wissmann was the one who completed the crossing of the continent.

Another problem that plagued the caravan until it reached Luba country was what Wissmann refers to in German as *Striken* (striking)—constant insubordination and insurrection among the personnel. As further background of deep hostility and context for the contrast the travelers would encounter among the Bashilange, here is an episode Wissmann reported. It documents another kind of threat to European authority we have not yet mentioned, an ecstatic form of conduct that can be qualified as collective hysteria. When the caravan reached Pende country, confrontations with local populations came to a climax. Under the influence of palm wine, the cooks and porters erupted into a brawl. While Wissmann was trying to get the guns away from the fighting parties, he was attacked. Those who were immediately involved were separated but others went into a frenzy.

> Many cried and shouted in rage, lying around in cramps; they pulled their hair, clawed the ground, and made, again and again, for the guns that, again and again, were taken away from them.... Eventually the crisis seemed to be

over. I began to pour water on several persons who were still raving with senseless rage, with much cooling success.... On a similar occasion two years ago, two Portuguese were murdered and all their merchandise stolen. (Wissmann 1889, 77)

By that time, the expedition had already met the Bashilange chief Tshingenge, a relative and rival of the famous Mukenge. Tshingenge arrived in a grand procession, with drummers and dancers. Altogether his entourage counted about one hundred people, some of them armed. The encounter reached its climax in the evening with the first *Riamba-Fest* of many Pogge and Wissmann were to witness. The sources have two descriptions of this event. I quote from both because the differences offer a rare glimpse of the options ethnographers had in representing their experiences. The first one, from Wissmann's travelogue, has the flavor of immediacy—most likely as he noted it in his diary: "Soon the curious group was enveloped in a cover of sweetly malodorous smoke from which there came the sounds of convulsive coughing and snorting and protestations of friendship with the white man inspired by the narcotizing effect of hemp" (Wissmann 1889, 71). He goes on to describe the drumming and dancing and then notes: "To us, this curious orgy was exciting and new, the ear was deafened by the half-melodic hellish din that spoke of the narcotic effect, the eye enthralled by their fixed stare and the contortions of their limbs, the sense of smell offended by the repugnant vapor" (71–72). Wissmann figured out what this orgy was all about. The Bashilange were celebrating the end of the monopoly that the Bangala and Tshokwe, by controlling regions between this country and the Atlantic coast, had held on contacts with Europeans (see also Frobenius 1907, 3).

The second description of a hemp feast was part of Wissmann's lecture before the Geographical Society in Berlin. The *Fest* has now become a generic event; it is no longer "exciting and new" and there is no reference to a specific, political occasion.

A *riamba* feast makes an extraordinary impression. Imagine a large number of naked negroes, their bodies covered with tattoos, their heads shaved, lying down in a circle; some of them taking long drags from huge gourd pipes, others caught in spasms of coughing, howling and shouting and uttering words of divination inspired by *riamba;* those who are already intoxicated are singing, their arms raised, fingers spread, swaying back and forth; letting their eyes, staring and glassy from intoxication, wander far away; and with this shouting, the mighty *goma* (drums), rattles and ratchets, all of this half shrouded in the yellow-gray clouds of sweetly malodorous *riamba,* and you have a picture of hell better than any you may be able to imagine. (*MAGD* 4, no. 1 [1883]: 41–42)

The event is now condensed to an image, an ethnographic tableau that may have impressed the audience but, as we shall see, in its negative connotations, contradicted the essence of Pogge and Wissmann's relations with the children of hemp.

IN THE LAND OF FRIENDSHIP

Who were these Bashilange, sometimes simply called Luba, and what was hidden, literally and metaphorically, behind the ominous clouds of hemp smoke? Though information comes in bits and pieces, our sources are full of answers to these questions, often recording minute detail. We cannot, and need not, try to reduce this confusion of observation, hearsay, and speculation to a coherent picture.[7] I struggled with this problem more than with any other I encountered in my readings and decided in the end on a minimal structure. First comes a capsular account of the most important (reported) facts, supported by a few passages in which the travelers themselves offer brief summaries. Next is an assessment of what this encounter with the children of hemp meant for the Pogge-Wissmann and later expeditions. A final section sketches how, in the years just before the formal establishment of colonial rule, this unique phenomenon of "friendship" mutated into one of domination and ethnicization with consequences up to this day.

"Residence of *kalamba* Mukenge, November 27, 1881. I have the honor of informing the honorable board that we have arrived in *Kasselange*" (*MAGD* 3, no. 3 [1882]: 216). Here is the announcement, solemn and laconic, that begins Pogge's letter to the German association. It is immediately obvious that the expedition will not be able to deal with the desired single ruler, at least not right away, and the caravan splits: Wissmann goes to Tshigenge (or Kingenge) on the eastern shore of the Kasai River; this chief's claims to supremacy must have been convincing. Pogge crosses the Kasai and travels to the residence of Mukenge, who was soon to become the central figure. Unlike the Lunda, the Luba-speaking populations in the Kasai region had no recent statelike political organization prior to the arrival of the Arabs some time after the middle of the century.[8] However, by the time the European explorers arrived, several larger political formations had begun to emerge, one of them led by Mukenge. It appears that these processes hinged on one invention (apart, of course, from economic and demographic conditions): an ideology with symbols and practices that legitimized centralized authority, created identity, *and* endorsed a certain anomie, a break with existing customs that made it possible to undertake innovative action. Possession of guns was among these symbols, but military capability based on firearms can, at that stage, be discounted as a significant factor.

Kalamba Mukenge had held a traditional office before he became a textbook case of a charismatic leader.[9] The movement he headed started in the generation before him, probably as one of many periodical anti-sorcery revivals that have swept parts of the area up to the recent past.[10] A new element here was the stroke of genius that made the founders adopt cannabis in a multitude of functions. A sketch of hemp's use in a wider context will help us appreciate its special significance for the Bene Diamba.

According to our authors, the Arabs from the east coast introduced the smoking of hemp, and it spread, though unevenly, all the way to the lower Congo. Several references to "wild hemp" suggest that the variety in use was not (or not always) *cannabis sativa* but a weaker sort, which would explain the huge quantities smokers inhaled in order to produce the intoxicating effect. Yet Capelo and Ivens speak of the "fumes of *cannabis sativa*" when they draw a typical image of an African chief (1882, 1:334). Later, when they meet the practice among the Lunda, they describe the Mwant Yav's entourage as "smoking tobacco out of long pipes or inhaling *liamba* from *a-topas*" (393). The Luba term and the special pipe would indicate either that the habit of the children of hemp had spread beyond their region or that it had been around before they made it the core of their movement. Capelo and Ivens later mention the "fatal *liamba* (*Cannabis sativa*)" and describe a smoking scene much like those reported by Wissmann (2:27–28; see illustration on 29).

One thing is certain: by the beginning of our period, caravan soldiers and porters commonly smoked hemp and caravans carried it among their provisions for trade. Travelers also observed hemp smoking in local populations. According to Pogge (reporting from his first voyage): "Tobacco and hemp are smoked in Mussumba [the Lunda capital] and the smokers habitually swallow the smoke. Smoking hemp has an intoxicating effect" (1880, 240).[11] In a report from the German East African Expedition we find this comment on a group of local Nyamwezi: "The smoke is inhaled through the lungs, a habit, also applied to the custom of smoking hemp, which causes vehement coughing; when the smoker gets intoxicated he accompanies this with an animal-like roar and shouting in falsetto" (*MAGD* 3, no. 1 [1881]: 11). The tone of distance, if not disapproval, contrasts with a voluble description we owe to Becker, showing once more his gift for empathy and imagination.

We marvel at them, seated around their fires, as they pass huge pipes containing the smoke of vile hemp whose acrid emanations they inhale with an expression of bliss and pure delight. Every inhalation makes the smoke go down deep into their throats and it is quite enjoyable to see them savor their suffering as immeasurable delight. Violent nausea is followed by formidable sneezing that lasts for a long time, all this prolonged by sharp little cries, savage and senseless, that announce every drag. Yet this troublesome pipe, inevitably disgusting, gives them one of their most cherished pleasures. Once again, let us not laugh but remember the painful apprenticeship we have to go through before we can, without wincing, take a few good puffs from cigars and cigarettes. (1887, 1:67)

Our sources also have reports of chiefs who smoke. Writing from a village near Mpala on the western shore of Lake Tanganyika, Böhm recalls the visit "of the *mtemi* [chief], a gaunt old man, half-blind, whom hemp smoking had made shaky and stupid.... Again and again the beloved *banki* [Swahili *banghi:* hemp] water pipe was filled for him by a member of his entourage, who each time after he had handed it to the chief knelt down, his face averted, and clapped his hands. That pipe obviously occupied the chief much more than the matters we needed to discuss with him" (*MAGD* 4, no. 3 [1884]: 175–76).

In this variation on the topic of drunken chiefs, Böhm expresses his rejection of the drug by assigning it destructive properties. Others took a more practical and positive view of the matter, accepting it as a fact of life and one of the necessities a caravan (or, as it turns out, a station) had to satisfy. Becker apparently tolerated smoking at Karema and mentions hemp among the provisions he bought for his trip back to the coast (1887, 2:398). As far as I was able to detect, he never noticed (or noted) hemp smoking among his higher-placed Arab-Swahili friends and acquaintances, whose lavish hospitality he often enjoyed and sometimes described. It also seems remarkable that Europeans who grew to love palm wine and maize beer did not develop a taste for African hemp (I found only two or three reports of Europeans actually joining a smoke; more about that later).

Whereas our texts offer only a diffuse picture of hemp smoking as something neither Africans nor Europeans got terribly excited about, the weed in all its imaginable forms—grown in kitchen gardens or large fields, smoked, ingested, applied in salves, drunk in potions, its seeds mixed with food, even dried, and its green branches carried or waved around—pervaded the life of the Bene Diamba. Probably, ceremonial smoking (among men; the texts are vague about women's participation) was one of the social rites of the original cult and had to do with the celebration of fire as symbol of life. Mukenge built on habits and rites when he made hemp a cultural and political symbol capable of creating a sense of identity among his followers and of obligating or pacifying other chiefs and officeholders in a fairly large area. His message and program drew their effectiveness—and this is another classic textbook trait—from sharing charismatic authority with his sister, Sangula Meta (or Meta Sangula; both occur in the sources). He was the leader and chief arbitrator; she was the principal ideologist and ritual specialist: there was no noticeable hierarchy to come between the leaders and their followers. Mukenge and Meta were able to get acceptance for many radical reforms that appear to reflect a deep anthropological knowledge of this society—they had reflected on it and made conscious decisions about cultural experiments that were truly daring. In fact, if anything, this movement can count as an "invented tradition" (Hobsbawm and Ranger 1983) that came into being well before fully developed colonization. Here is a brief summary of the measures and reforms the chief and his sister introduced, or developed, among the Bashilange.

The children of hemp had a distinctive greeting, *moyo* (Luba: life; sometimes they were referred to as *bena moyo*), and a name for their country, which they called *lubuku* ([land of] friendship).[12] This usage superseded designations by clan; it projected the principle of kinship onto a higher level and all members of the movement called each other brother and sister. But, whereas almost a century later Mobutu pushed similar symbolic reforms as a "recourse to authenticity," that is, to a cultural heritage experienced as endangered, if not lost, by colonization, the leaders of the Bene Diamba took the opposite direction. "Friendship," most radically expressed by a prohibition on shedding blood, even that of animals, opposed a tradition of endemic warfare, executions, and (alleged) human sacrifice and cannibalism. In place of the poison ordeal, an often lethal test administered to persons accused of sorcery and destructive magic, the leaders used the forced smoking of hemp, continued until the culprit confessed or lost consciousness. They meted out similar punishment (sometimes also rubbing capsicum juice into the accused's eyes) in cases of theft, adultery, and manslaughter or murder. Prohibitions on killing animals made radical changes in Luba ritual life. As sacrificial animals, goats and especially chickens had had a central place in Luba culture as well as in their everyday life and their lore.[13] A more thorough daily reminder of obligations to the movement is hard to imagine, unless it is the use of hemp instead of traditional herbal medicines or the prohibition of palm wine in a region famous for this drink—European travelers too enjoyed it wherever it was available. This last measure was intended to symbolize the break with old habits rather than a fight against alcoholism; Mukenge did allow the brewing and drinking of millet beer. Finally, we should also mention (ritual) nudity, one more practice that makes the Bene Diamba comparable to other ecstatic cults or movements.

The movement inscribed itself on its followers' bodies (sons of hemp shaved their heads, beards, and body hair), in the layout of villages (each had a large central plaza, called *tshiota,* for gatherings and communal hemp smoking; shade trees were removed), and in the architecture of dwellings (Bene Diamba villages had square, saddle-roofed dwellings). Finally, it found expression in material culture. It removed traditional weapons and ritual statuary ("fetishes") and made gourd pipes dangling from sticks emblems of the movement (some of these pipes were huge, about 1 m in diameter). The sons of hemp shouldered these pipes wherever they went. A small number of men carried guns, traded from the Tshokwe mainly, it appears, as symbols of modernity. At the same time, these weapons were proof of extraordinary devotion to the movement as they could be procured only at great risk, sometimes by selling relatives as slaves or undertaking a veritable quest into Tshokwe or Lunda lands that often involved (temporary) servitude.

As an arbitrator and political leader, Kalamba Mukenge had to steer a difficult course between demonstrations of mildness toward culprits and enemies and accusations of weakness from rivals. One means to assert his authority was a sort of cleansing ritual (involving hemp, of course) that visitors, other chiefs included, had to undergo before they were admitted to the court. Finally *lubuku,* friendship, and the self-designation as Bene Diamba as concepts of identity were matched by a term for outsiders and nonmembers, *tshipulumba,* which was applied not only to other Luba populations who had not joined the movement, but also to members of the followers' own descent group and—this is hard to believe but is asserted repeatedly—even to immediate kin. As could be expected, resistance to radical changes came often from older persons who were ostracized when they refused to smoke hemp. This earned the children of hemp the reputation of chasing away their elders, a heinous crime in the eyes of outsiders. Incidentally, if chasing away old people was a "law," as Wissmann seems to say (1889, 94), the leaders were exempt from the rule. Pogge who, unlike most of his colleagues, was not a young man, describes Mukenge as an "old gentleman" (*MAGD* 3, no. 3 [1882]: 221). His sister, Sangula Meta, was also elderly.

ENCOUNTERS AND INCORPORATIONS

Can we begin to dismantle the myth of modernity's march into central African savagery? Expeditions, at once symbolizing and enacting the march, did not proceed from open civilization through mixed regions toward closed savagery. In their wish to participate in what we would later call the world system, some African populations—among them most of those the explorers met—were just about as far removed from savagery and modernity as the European nations the explorers represented. The Africans had started forming political structures capable of accommodating economic activities that could be linked to a world market for commodities. If there was savagery, it existed in the endemic violence characterizing the intermediate zone of trade monopolies and, ultimately, in European military conquest based on technological superiority. Dichotomous colonial ideology opposed primitive savagery to modern civilization; that was a smoke screen to hide imperialist expansion. When anthropology reflects on its modern beginnings, it must face its part in setting up the myth. Our discipline's role was to construe the primitive as an object (rather than subject) of history and as a target of colonization. Actual political complicity pales beside the epistemic work anthropology performed when it fostered such images. But rather than moralize in sweeping statements or admit our guilt and wallow in regrets, we must struggle to understand what went on and what went wrong in the fateful early encounters.

Admittedly, the meeting of the Pogge-Wissmann expedition and the children of hemp is an extraordinary example of these encounters. From the outset it puzzled the European observers. In his first letter to the association (quoted above), Pogge gives few signs of recognizing the role the Bashilange were to play in the exploration and colonization of this part of central Africa. He tells of a friendly reception by Mukenge but seems more interested in reaching the mythical lake of which Schütt had dreamed (after all, if it existed, it would have to count as a sensational discovery). Mukenge calls it Mucamba and claims that it is on his territory. Untroubled by the implications of this claim—how big an inland sea could there be on the territory of one chief?—Pogge decided to make the trip. He thought he could do it in about ten days. He would return to Mukenge's residence, which he had found much more suited for establishing a station than the Lunda capital as envisaged in his original assignment. Wissmann would then try to reach Zanzibar via Nyangwe on the upper Congo. Pogge mentions that the Tusselange, as he calls them, are proficient agriculturalists and only has this offhand remark on their most striking feature: "The Tusselange also cultivate some tobacco and, being passionate hemp smokers, a lot of hemp" (*MAGD* 3, no. 3 [1882]: 219). He then gives descriptions of the landscape, fauna, flora, climate.[14] Pogge's notions concerning the political situation were still vague.

> As yet I don't know the borders of the *Kasselange*. Mukenge claims his em-pire reaches to the lake in the east, after which [that of] the *Tukettes* begins. Many big chiefs rule in Kasselange land, such as *kalamba* Mukenge, Kin-genge, and so on. To these the smaller chiefs owe tribute, much as in Lunda country. Every village, or several together, form, so to speak, a family; the in-habitants consider themselves, as it were, related and stick together through thick and thin. If you come to a village and ask for its name, then it will sim-ply be, for instance, *Bena Katschia,* meaning "They are Katschia people," or *Bacua Calembue,* "They belong to the Calembues," or they belong to the Calembue family. *Bena* and *bacua* are synonyms. The people living at Mukenge's residence belong to the *Bena Katschia.* (220–21)

As we know from later research in the area, Pogge's letter—tentative and vague—gives a realistic picture of the political and ethnic situation in the Kasai. A large area was united by closely related languages, founding myths, ritual, and legal institutions; it had chiefs who, because so much of the culture was shared, could easily expand or shift their spheres of influence when they found the economic or military means to do so. The most important social unit was not the "tribe" but what Pogge describes as family and we would now call clan. These were groups, if that term can cover large parts of a population, that claimed common descent and often shared territories but were not completely defined by either.

The absence of clear territorial boundaries and central authority was not the only thing that bothered Pogge and Wissmann. They also re-ported some of Mukenge's legal innovations as nuisances: "At the mo-ment, the laws imposed by Mukenge cause some minor discomfort to the traveler. He forbade his subjects to keep goats and chickens or to cul-tivate bananas and pineapples. Therefore it takes an effort to procure the necessary provisions. However, the chief promised me to have this law abrogated and to see to it that, after my return, plenty of goats, ba-nanas, and so forth would be available" (221). Wissmann, talking about this problem, also mentions pigs among the forbidden animals but says that this was "a prohibition we abolished immediately" (*MAGD* 4, no. 1 [1883]: 43).

In exploration, the logistics of travel, especially food for the caravan, came first; before the explorers could figure out what was behind

Mukenge's prohibitions, they tried to get them lifted. Later they did learn much more, and perhaps we should balance this report from the beginning of Pogge and Wissmann's relations with the Bashilange against their later awareness. But it is a small token of what may have been one of the most encompassing and troubling contradictions that beset the whole enterprise of exploration. It parallels the perennial problem of ethnography: how to observe a site but not disturb it. Pogge's reaction to Bashilange taboos shows us the gap between ideals of science and a practice of travel. Taken together with other instances, it throws an element of irrationality into the explorers' rational hierarchy of political and economic purposes.

To move on with our story, Pogge then entertains his sponsors with the music box episode we quoted earlier and briefly mentions a "festive dance where Mukenge treated people to millet beer" (222; no hint at hemp, which such an occasion called for). Before he ends his letter, he expresses what we now recognize as a topos of early ethnography: when Europeans meet a population that is new to them they will almost always find reasons to state that they have come too late. Here is Pogge's version: "It is a pity that the Tusselange in these regions have lost many of their own original customs due to interacting with the Kioko and Bangala" (222). What is the basis for this complaint? From his own observations, he mentions only one example of lost traditions: younger people no longer have their bodies covered with intricate tattoos. Having just got there, he lacks well-founded prior knowledge. And his views do not echo Mukenge's; the chief's lifework was to bring about changes. As for an opposing, conservative faction among the Bashilange, it had gone underground or out of action. Could Pogge have been repeating what he heard from his knowledgeable interpreter? If so, why would he, a trader interested in new opportunities among the Bashilange, express regret about changes that worked in his favor? The answer, as I suggested in earlier theoretical reflections (Fabian 1983, 1991, ch. 10), is that the "disappearing native" is one of the topoi of European discourse that have a way of imposing themselves; they are in place before inquiries are made or interpretations worked out. In this specific case, Pogge has regrets for a vanishing past that was not his. Recognizing the Bashilange was predicated on rejecting the presence or contemporaneity of their culture. More will be said about this in later chapters.

Two years later Wissmann, who, like Pogge, was not a trained ethnographer, presumably gave his scientific best when he formulated the results of their expedition in his address to the Geographical Society in

Berlin. Their accomplishment had been to break through the "notorious Lunda barrier" (*MAGD* 4, no. 1 [1883]: 39) and reach the country of the Bashilange. There they had overcome the problem of having to deal with two authorities. "For us, the animosity between the two heads makes no difference" he says (35). Both welcomed them.

When Wissmann gets to describing the population of the region, he performs for his audience one of the founding acts of both ethnography and colonization: he distinguishes kinds of natives:[15] "[The Bashilange] are a large and important part of populations that still call themselves *Baluba*. They are divided among the western or, as Pogge and I called them, the thieving *Tushilange* who form small republics and are already spoiled by trading *Kioque* and *Bangala;* the central or *Bena Riamba,* the sons of wild hemp, and the eastern groups, who call themselves *Bashilange* and whom we call savages" (41).

The explorers put the Bashilange in the places and slots their discourse provided for them. So, it seems, did the children of hemp when it came to locating the Europeans within their universe. Taking a comparative stance, this is how Wissmann explains what happened.

> A fable, observed among many savage peoples in all parts of the world, also developed here among this central African people of thinkers, in a manner that was attractive and, for us, quite agreeable. Some years ago, two rulers, Kasongo munene, elder brother of Mukenge, and Kabassu Babu, predecessor of Dshingenge, had traveled to the coast where they perished. The two of them (because I cannot say "the souls of the two")[16] had descended into *maji kalunga,* the water of the spirits (the sea, about which they had heard stories from the *Kioque*), had gone through a metamorphosis, and now appeared, returning as whites, to visit their former principalities, Pogge as Kasongo munene, myself as Kabassu Babu a mokamba, names which we also kept. (43)

Probably local peoples gave most explorers African names that ranged from unflattering epithets to honorific titles. Whether the labels served as terms of address or not, they made it possible to tell their carriers apart, talk about them in everyday situations, and incorporate them into stories told around the fire. But incorporation went farther with Pogge and Wissmann. How literally or naively the Bashilange took the story of the returning chiefs we will never know. We can assume that they, like the explorers, could tell a story from real life and that the leaders made use of this piece of lore as consciously as of the hemp rituals and food taboos they introduced. At the same time, the arrival of the travelers did much to invigorate the movement, and the myth made it possible to take them "for real." One day, Wissmann tells us, Kabassu Babu's—and therefore, his—mother and some of his cousins presented themselves and were going to reinvest him with his namegiver's "30–40 wives and some ivory" (43).

CROSSING AFRICA—AND SETTLING IN

Pogge and Wissmann were thrilled by the open-armed reception they found among the Bashilange. Just how closely the latter integrated them into the hemp cult is not clear. That neither Pogge nor Wissmann mentioned Mukenge's sister, Sangula Meta, in their first official reports may indicate that they feared to confuse their sponsors with too much detail of their involvement with the children of hemp. They are less reticent in other documents, such as Pogge's diary and Wissmann's reports from this and a later expedition to which we turn in the final section.

In his diary Pogge explains how Meta got her other name, incidentally adding an important piece of information on the precariousness of Mukenge's leadership. In 1876 or 1878 (both dates appear) there was an uprising against Kalamba Mukenge, going back to a witchcraft accusation. His younger brother Dibue Tukela and his sister, Meta, were subjected to an ordeal and had to smoke hemp until they were unconscious. They would have been killed then and Mukenge himself attacked if it had not been for an outsider, a Bangala who happened to be in the village and intervened: "Kalamba's sister, Meta, escaped death by being left for dead. When she came to, she sought refuge with the neighboring Bangela [Bangala] chief Kineme. Because of these circumstances, she got the name *sangula*, for someone who is deadly ill but gets well again in an unexpected manner is called *ku sangula*" (*MAGD* 4, no. 5 [1885]: 243). Of course, this also sounds much like the classic death-and-resurrection story that launched the careers of countless prophets. If so, it adds another touch to the picture of a prophetic-charismatic movement.

By now the reader must be wondering: did Pogge and Wissmann too join in the delights of smoking hemp? I found no evidence of it, direct or implied. Their integration into the movement by a mythical reincarnation did not require them to go through the usual initiation that required smoking. Both, incidentally, were heavy tobacco smokers, and at one point Wissmann suffered from "nicotine poisoning" after smoking native tobacco because he had run out of his own supplies (1889, 213). But the spectacular effects of hemp inhaled must have scared them and other Europeans off "social smoking" (though Europeans took eagerly to palm wine and even millet beer).[17] Hemp would be hard to adopt as a private vice, or consolation, as the odor would betray a user to his companions. Finally, going on impressions I had when I lived in Zaire, hemp smoking may already then have been socially beneath the Europeans and modern Africans who were outside the cult. In the 1960s the down-and-out, too poor to afford even a bottle of beer, used hemp as their last resort.

Much as Mukenge's visitors enjoyed his hospitality, troubled only by his occasional greediness, Pogge and Wissmann had to move on. With Mukenge they crossed the Lulua and reached the region of the lake. This is what Wissmann told his audience in Berlin: "There, on December 20, 1881, it lay before us, the fabled lake, the greatest geographical puzzle of western central Africa, and, woe on the land of lies, it was so insignificant, half pond, half lake, that I could walk around it in five hours" (*MAGD* 4, no. 1 [1883]: 44).

Now that the fable had evaporated, the expedition had to complete its task. Pogge had already announced in his letter that this region, rather than the Lunda capital, would be ideally suited for an IAA station; he would devote his remaining energies to building it. But Wissmann decided to expand their original assignment and push on eastward until he reached Zanzibar—to make the first European crossing of central Africa from west to east. Pogge, still suffering from the infection of his jaw, joined his colleague for the first leg, which took them to Nyangwe, then a flourishing Swahili colonial town on the Lualaba, the upper Congo.

There a serious problem faced them. Sedition, desertion, and shortage of supplies and trade goods had plagued the expedition all the way from the west coast. As they got closer to the Bashilange, they had less and less control of the African auxiliaries and porters they had recruited in Portuguese territory. When they finally made it to the land of friendship, not much was left of their caravan. They were stuck in the heart of the continent. And the Bashilange came to their rescue: "They made it possible to advance far enough east to reach the Arabs, where we found help for continuing the enterprise" (Wissmann 1889, 113).[18] A large party of Bashilange, led by Kalamba Mukenge and Sangula Meta, escorted them through Luba country until they reached Nyangwe.

Grim determination kept the explorers going, but the children of hemp had fun. As Wissmann recounts a meeting of their caravan with a crowd of dangerous-looking Luba warriors, "Many of our Bashilange only carried staffs because, aside from guns, the Bena Riamba are forbidden to carry weapons. These people of our escort made a curious picture among the savagely painted, armed crowds. Chattering and laughing, shouldering a stick from which the mighty *riamba* pipe dangled, they continued their carefree march" (1889, 136–37).

By the time they reached Songye country, the Bashilange were tired but continued out of loyalty to their friends. Eventually, however, a brawl erupted between Mukenge's people and the remaining porters of the caravan. Sangula Meta broke it up, single-handedly: "First she tried it with her magical wand, a bunch of dried *riamba,* then she started, with the fortitude of an amazon, to wield a hefty stick, beating people without respect for their persons" (154).

Despite such incidents the caravan safely reached country controlled by Arabs and was given a hospitable reception in Nyangwe. After some rest, the time came to part. On May 4, 1881, after a solemn farewell Pogge (though his health had improved), the Bene Diamba, and a few porters of the original caravan returned to Lubuku. Wissmann stayed on to organize his trip to the coast. During the trek he had memorable encounters with Tipo Tip and Mirambo and also visited Tabora and the station of the German East African Expedition. Observations on hemp smoking among Mirambo's people caused him to formulate this conclusion.

> The Waniamwesi are in many respects on a much higher level than any population of the interior, perhaps with the exception of the Bashilange, though quite amazingly they are, like the Bashilange, more addicted to hemp smoking than any other tribes known to me. I am convinced that hemp has a domesticating effect on the negro, that the narcotic weed mitigates their restless savagery, the pervasive inclination of staying away from external influence. It makes the negro more approachable and more useful for culture and civilization, without denying a certain harmfulness to their physical constitution, a fact that is probably exaggerated but nevertheless must be admitted. The Bashilange, who used to be the most savage tribes, living in constant feud among each other, proved to us what kind of change had happened with them since the introduction of the hemp cult. Similar observations apply here [among the Nyamwezi], with the only difference that the former first achieved progress through Europeans, the latter through longer exposure to the Arabs. (254)

But back to Pogge. Even with the usual problems of logistics and local hostilities, he and the Bashilange had a safe trip back to Mukenge's residence. Before their departure for Nyangwe, Pogge had ordered their chief interpreter, Germano, to stay behind with some of the personnel to begin with the construction of a station. Now he found it almost completed; his report of the trip back is dated "German Station *Mukenge* on the *Lulua,* September 20, 1882" (*MAGD* 4, no. 1 [1883]: 56). He settled down and, after learning more about the children of hemp, offers an atypical general observation. He praises them as ideally suited to sustain a station. They have their faults, a certain "impudence and immorality" and an "obsession with trading"—they will even sell their wives and children to make a profit, he says—"but they have a certain ambition to improve themselves, to attain a higher level; and those whom I knew better often asked me religious questions which actually showed traces of imagination. The local Tusselange are a people created for the successful work of a missionary" (70). A prophetic remark, as the later history of the Luba and the Catholic mission in the Kasai region would show. But the report also marks a watershed between exploration and settling in, reflected in the establishment of a station.

While Wissmann returned from the east coast to Europe and participated in the German society's deliberations about future plans (including the ominous resolution to meet African resistance with more force [70]), Pogge led a peaceful life among the children of hemp. An entry in his diary at the end of 1882 says: "My life here is so beautiful, so pretty, so quiet, so calm; friendly, splendid people, what else do I want; this is the monotony I love!" (*MAGD* 4, no. 4 [1885]: 230). Dutifully, he submitted an extensive report to the society (*MAGD* 4, no. 1 [1883]: 179–205), recording progress in completing the ethnography of the Bashilange and in strengthening Mukenge's and, therefore, the Europeans' political position. Mukenge, incidentally, had built himself "a new, and larger, house in the Nyangwe style, a veritable caricature of a house, a camera obscura in the true sense of the word" (181–82). The chief's attempts to get his clan, the *bene katshia,* settled in one place and found another Nyangwe, however, had failed so far.

By mid-1883 Pogge's mood had changed. He noted in his diary, "Now I am all the time quite unwell—bad food, no tomatoes, always only chicken boiled in water; I have become sick of manioc flour boiled in water, bad, bitter salt, no clothes! It is an almost hopeless situation" (*MAGD* 4, no. 4 [1885]: 230). He awaited the successful return of a relief expedition (on July 10, 1883) he had sent to Malange under the direction of Germano. An editor of the diary comments: "Among the things brought by Germano were gin, coffee, cigars, but these pleasures he was not used to excited Pogge so much that once more he had trouble sleeping and had to take quinine" (232).

Between August 18 and 20, Pogge nonetheless accompanied Sangula Meta on one of her ritual-political missions, but his health did not improve. He left Mukenge station for Malange on November 9, 1883 (235). In the evening of November 25 he started coughing blood. He kept on noting observations on the country and the people but lost his last riding ox on December 16. The diary stops on the following day or soon after, before he reached Malange. There he was reunited with Wissmann, who was on his way east with his new expedition (in February 1884). He found Pogge "well, but in a quite irritable, nervous state." Lieutenant Müller too reported on his nervous state (*MAGD* 4, no. 4 [1885]: 207). Pogge made it to Loanda on the coast, where he died less than a month later (on March 17, 1884). The circumstances of his death are unclear; he had been well enough the day before to accept a dinner invitation. On his deathbed he made the intriguing request to have his diary destroyed. We will come back to this in a later chapter.

I devoted so much space to Pogge's return from Lubuku to the coast because his story conveys a sense of tragedy, a fall from high hopes to dark despair. True, he had suffered from a serious physical affliction since the trip began. His decline, however, apparently came after a period of good health. Quite likely, a tropical disease we could name today was the immediate cause of his death, but he had also come to the end of his mental energies. According to his contemporaries, he had more common sense and practical intelligence, more sensitivity, more sympathy and kindness toward Africans than most of his colleagues. But why did he ask that his precious records be destroyed? Did he lose control of his mind?

We must now find our way out of this already long chapter on exploration and the children of hemp. Remember that Wissmann, not plagued by dark thoughts, had reached the east coast and returned to Berlin. The Berlin Conference was approaching. Perhaps a last effort by German interest groups to keep a foot in the Congo led this German officer to serve Leopold II of Belgium and participate in preparations for setting up the Free State. The German society had lost contact with Pogge, and Wissmann was to find him. But his principal assignment was to explore the Kasai region. Apparently Crown Prince Friedrich Wilhelm advised Wissmann to accept the commission. It was agreed that the expedition could fly the German flag (hence the title of its published account) and that ethnographic and other collections would go to the royal museums in Berlin. *MAGD* only published a brief notice of this expedition and some fragmentary information from Wissmann's letters.

On November 16, 1883—at about the same time Pogge left Mukenge on his trip to the coast—Wissmann's expedition set out from Hamburg; it included seven other Germans. As already mentioned, Wissmann and Pogge met one last time in Malange. Before the expedition continued to-

ward the Kasai, it rehired several of the old guides and interpreters, some
going back to Pogge's first trip almost ten years earlier. Eventually the
caravan split up into separate undertakings. There was some back-and-
forth trekking, and meetings with other expeditions became frequent. In
September 1885 Wissmann left the expedition for reasons of health. Dr.
Wolf took the command and later wrote most of the travelogue (Wissmann et al. 1891).

As the main caravan entered Luba country, more and more signs of
the hemp cult were noted and when they reached Mukenge, thousands
welcomed them. The Germans put their people into uniforms, flew their
flags, and fired their guns. Mukenge, Sangula Meta, and Tshingenge arrived in solemn procession to meet them: "Sangula, a bunch of fresh
hemp in her hand, concluded the procession, together with fifteen girls
who sang while they carried baskets and gourds filled with manioc flour,
millet beer, and corn" (152). This time, the friendship between Wissmann and the children of hemp was to be sealed with a pact of blood
brotherhood. The need to do that, it appears, had not occurred to Pogge
and Wissmann during their first visit to Lubuku. But since then the situation had changed in favor of Kalamba Mukenge (Tshingenge had to
give up his opposition to the chief), and Wissmann was now on a primarily political mission. Spontaneous sympathies were welcome but
friendship now required legal foundations in view of preparing the territory for the Free State. Perhaps the pact was Wissmann's idea. It put
the Bene Diamba in an embarrassing situation. In order to accommodate their beloved Kabassu Babu, they introduced a change in the ceremony, which Kalamba Muana, Mukenge's son and designated successor, explained as follows (revealing, incidentally, some of the movement's
central tenets).

"When, according to an old custom, we drink each other's blood, the people
will say that we are no longer sons of Riamba, that we have become blood-
thirsty. Fire is the highest power on earth, and Riamba (hemp) the only means
to secure health and life! When we now drink Kishila from fire lit with hemp,
then this is a pact that cannot be broken. Whoever then dares to break his
word will be consumed by fire, no fire will burn for him or give him light and
he will no longer be helped by Riamba. Without fire no one can work iron,
without iron no one can cultivate his fields or build a house, without Riamba
no one can live on earth, therefore everyone must take care not to make fire
and Riamba angry by breaking his word!" We accepted this proposition, as
did Kalamba and Sangula. The latter, as priestess of Riamba, then dropped a
few grains of hemp into boiling cognac and we all shared it with the highest
chiefs who were present. Kalamba's fate was now tied to ours. He himself,

his sister Sangula, as well as Tshingenge and several chiefs wanted to accompany us on our further travels with a large following so that we could look calmly toward the immediate future. (153)

A more ingenious extension of the meaning of fire, a more striking mixing, symbolic as well as actual, of two intoxicating substances, a European favorite and that of the Bashilange, could not have been devised.

Apart from the description of this ceremony, the travelogue has a report by another member of the expedition, Hans Müller, who had led a detachment of the caravan on a trip through the territory of Muata Kumbana, a Lunda chief (September 24–November 13, 1884). This is how they were received when they reached Mukenge's residence: "In the *Kiota,* the marketplace, I was greeted by Sangula Meta, Kalamba's sister, and Kalamba Muana, heir to the throne. The former is the priestess of hemp. To welcome me she anointed my forehead and hands with a hemp salve and made a line on my coat with white clay, called *Pemba.* Then she led me to the house where Pogge had lived, the great explorer who was a shining example for all of us" (120). Later that day, Müller has a reunion with his brother Franz, whom he has not seen for eight weeks. They have much to tell each other but incorporation into the hemp cult takes precedence.

> Our conversation was somewhat disturbed by Kassongo, the son of a brother of Kalamba's by the same name. He appeared with nine of his wives in festive attire to greet me as Dibue Toselle, an uncle of his who had been murdered, and to assure me of his friendship with a big hemp smoke. The young girls, some of them quite pretty, brought the big pipe. It circulated and everyone had to take a few drags. My brother and I also were compelled to participate in this, although it was not exactly a pleasure to share the pipe with this whole black gang. (120)

Settling down once again, the Wissmann expedition decided to move Pogge's station some distance from the town, to a place where they could more easily ward off the expected attacks from the Bangala and Tshokwe. This then became Luluaburg, a station of the German society (151). By now it was clear that the explorers were in a new, and different, game. In it, their friend Mukenge would be a pawn. He was to be a colonial agent; his demonstrated ability to unite separate populations and chiefs would serve to make the Kasai region a stronghold of colonial rule soon to be established. Mukenge fell into these plans when he asked Wissmann to honor their pact and accompany him on a campaign against an enemy, chief Katende.

The party traveled in the usual somewhat chaotic manner of the Bene Diamba, who carried their unwieldy pipes and smoked hemp, looking more like a band of musicians than a war party. Sangula Meta herself beat the drum. Wissmann tried to get some order into the bunch by a measure that must have been one of the first uses in this region of what was later to become a dreaded institution, the *mukanda,* a term covering all sorts of identity cards and traveling permits without which no Congolese could move in the colony. So that the whites would be able to distinguish friendly troops from the enemy, "a notebook was sacrificed and every warrior put a piece of white paper in his hair or on his forehead. These badges were called *Mikanda* (letter, message)" (179). The party accomplished its task: chief Katende was captured and brought to Mukenge's residence.

There the members of the expedition met the prisoner in order to get information about his territories. They found him "disfigured beyond recognition. Hair and beard had been cut off according to the custom of the Bena Riamba. He was so confused and listless as a result of the disgrace he had suffered and the quick hard blows fate had dealt him that we could get no precise information out of him" (184).[19]

While the main caravan was busy building the new station, Wolf and von François carried out separate reconnaissance missions among the Kuba and the Kanyok.[20] Wissmann then set out for the main target, the Kasai River, once more accompanied by the Bene Diamba. At that time, his friend Mukenge must have had premonitions of a change in their relationship. Wolf reports: "During the night Kalamba had a disquieting dream which he immediately communicated to his people in a *Moio* [speech]. He had seen himself being beaten and mistreated by the whites. In the town of the whites he was kept in chains. But that cannot be true because he [Wissmann] is our friend and blood brother. His dream must have lied! Incidentally, he only calmed down after Wissmann had smoked hemp with him" (318–19). So something that never happened during the ecstatic phase of encounter (or, more precisely, never showed up in the reports) happens now that Wissmann has redefined the relationship on his terms: hemp smoking is now a political expedient.

After making contact with many other populations, always with a view of "preparing" them for future colonization, sometimes by the tried and tested means of incorporation into the hemp cult, the explorers and the Bashilange traveled down the Kasai and the Congo until they reached Kinshasa station. There the explorers met several colleagues and competitors such as Büttner and Captain Massari, while Savorgnan de Brazza (who was to secure the right bank of the Congo for France) camped across the river. The Bene Diamba were too exhausted to return to their home by the land route. So the Germans applied to the general administrator of the Congo state, Francis de Winton, for passage on a steamer, which they got. Too ill to go on, Wissmann (who had "a nervous asthmatic affliction") sailed for Madeira, where he underwent an "arsenic cure." Müller left a week later, sick with a pernicious fever (411), and Wolf led the expedition back to the interior (October 5, 1885).

Wissmann still had one year of service left on his contract with Leopold II. He tried to get out of it, offering his services to the German colonies. Given the choice of either serving as governor of the "inner" Free State or carrying on his earlier work, he chose the latter. The instructions he received for his expedition no longer held out any pretense at scientific investigation. We could ignore this trip, except that it brought back the Bene Diamba for a final appearance on the stage of African exploration. When Wissmann passed through the lower Congo and Kinshasa station, he heard that many Bene Diamba had died from pneumonia before they were taken back by the steamer. He himself followed the river route and at length met Wolf, who had founded another station at Luebo, called Wolfshafen, on April 12, 1886. In Luluaburg, he says, he was greeted by "my friend Kalamba and the worthy Sangula" ([1890], 50). This was an occasion to reiterate his debt to these people and to describe once again one of the overwhelming receptions the children of hemp gave their Kabassu Babu.[21] A throng of five thousand had gathered, and when Kalamba Mukenge, taller than anyone else, approached with Sangula, Wissmann confesses,

> I don't have to be ashamed of the emotion which took hold of me when I cordially received them and shook the hands of my two friends, often tried and tested, to whom I owed so much. There were questions without end and the cheering around us was deafening. I mounted my horse to be more visible and, with a *Bantue* shouted at the top of my voice, asked for silence and soon calmed the din. Then I gave a *Moiio* [speech] in which I said that the sea had given me back my health and that I had followed my heart's desire and had come to my friends here. ([1890], 55)

So much for feelings. But business is business, and Wissmann soon set about it. Apart from some geographical and political reconnaissance trips, he saw his major tasks in the transfer of the two German stations to agents of the Free State (incidentally, he left his "small cannon, a present from Friedrich Krupp," to the fort at Luebo [47]) and what he referred to as "putting order into political relations" (68). He now admits that originally his tactic had been to play the two opposed parties, Mukenge and Tshingenge, against each other so as to keep his options open. But he decided that Mukenge and his successors were to be the paramount chiefs of the country, as the "point... from which the Congo state would have to undertake the further exploration and civilization of its southern countries" (69). To implement his strategy, he summoned about fifty chiefs, or heads of clans, most of whom complied after some persuasion or coercion. They received new insignia and flags with the star of the Congo and had to pay a nominal tribute to acknowledge their submission to Mukenge.

At one point in Wissmann's report he comments: the reader may be surprised that the author did all this with a troop of only twenty-five or thirty men, all of them tried auxiliaries picked during his earlier travels. "After all, my strongest support was the trust which the Bashilange had put in me after four years of acquaintance, a trust that must appear miraculous even to someone who knows the negro and which can be explained only by their abnormal intellectual genius" (71). A mind-boggling statement. Perhaps from a boggled mind. It is one thing to make use of the trust the children of hemp had put in him in order to subject them to colonial rule. But to ascribe their willingness to be used for such a purpose to their extraordinary intellectual gifts is not only callous but very odd.

Be that as it may, in November 1886 Wissmann left Luluaburg to complete his second crossing of the continent. He commanded a huge caravan of almost one thousand men and women, among them six hundred Bene Diamba led by Sangula, Kalamba Muana, and Tshingenge (108). By the time they reached Arab-controlled territories, the caravan was weakened and down to nine hundred people. The children of hemp proved nearly useless in situations that more and more often led to armed hostilities. Lack of food became a major problem, but the Bene Diamba kept going and Wissmann repeated what he concluded about his first crossing: "This trip could never have been made with anyone except my Bashilange" (167). Then smallpox hit the caravan. The expedition got embroiled in conflicts between the Arabs and the Free State, and Wissmann at times hid the Congo flag that he had been flying next to the German flag. The reception in Nyangwe was cool, to say the least. Wissmann, as he had done on his earlier trip, sent the Bashilange home. He noted that he had passed on his friendship with them to his Belgian companion Le Marinel, but he recorded only one short sentence about their farewell: "The Bashilange also felt that I was left behind in a difficult situation" (179).

Wissmann managed to leave Nyangwe, reached the Belgian station Mpala on Lake Tanganyika, and continued to Lake Nyasa. By that time he was sick with fever, rheumatism, and nervous asthma; his caravan was down to one German companion, eight West African porters ("Angolans") and three of their wives, a man from Zanzibar, one guide, two boys who served him, and two dogs (228). He reached the coast at Quelimane and finally got to Zanzibar, "without a premonition that I would soon have the privilege to lead the deadly thrust against the plague that ruins the African continent, Arabhood" (226).

End of story. Almost unnoticed, the Bene Diamba leave the stage. As individuals, they had already been fading from the account. Wissmann turned his mind toward reaching the coast and referred to his friends collectively, and possessively, as "my Bashilange." Chiefs were nameless, and (inter)actions went unnoted. Wissmann gave us much of what we know of this remarkable movement that was to play a crucial role in the exploration of central Africa. His protestations of friendship and gratitude to the children of hemp make us wonder what went on in the mind of a man who paid his debts to the Bene Diamba with what history can only regard as betrayal.[22]

The long-term effects of Pogge's and Wissmann's association with the Bashilange have been fateful. In short, they set up one of the most conflict-ridden ethnic categorizations and divisions in colonial and postcolonial times: between the Lulua—the name Mukenge's people gradually adopted toward the end of the century—and the Baluba Kasai, populations who, under pressure from Arab slave raids, migrated to the region of Luluabourg at about the same time. Mukenge's enthusiasm for the Europeans did not last long after Wissmann's departure. The Belgian colonial administration then put their bets on the Baluba, creating chiefships that ignored older territorial rights. In the 1930s the Lulua began to express their opposition to colonial rule and the Baluba, in whom they saw its servants. They organized themselves shortly before independence and the conflict exploded in a massacre of Baluba in 1959. Most of them left the region and founded a new town in Mbuji-Mayi, the largest urban center to be created after independence.[23]

EIGHT

Making Knowledge

The Senses and Cognition

What happened in the land of friendship took us to the center of Africa and to the core of this endeavor to map the field of tensions and contradictions in which we seek the beginnings of African ethnography. It put the broader account of exploratory travel we are building up—the caravans, the explorers, and the ways they communicated with the people they studied—in one developing context of events. Now we turn to more systematic inquiry into the production of knowledge about Africa—always with an awareness that search for a system in the history of European exploration will be in vain. As we did in the first chapters, we will consider the rationality of the enterprise, but now by concentrating on what our sources tell us about methods of investigation and about the meaning explorers gave to their findings. What, we will ask, do our travelers report about how they made knowledge out of experiences, and what kind of knowledge were they after?

EXPERIENCE AND OBSERVATION

> It is seldom, however, that the geographical explorer
> can form just conceptions of the manners or customs of
> a native tribe, or of their moral character, travelling as
> he generally does straight through the country, and
> meeting the natives but a short time when under influ-
> ence of fear or suspicion of the great men. It can only

> be by a prolonged residence in the district and a thor-
> ough command of the language that a person is entitled
> to speak with confidence of certain knowledge. The
> Central Africans have not had this justice done to
> them, and till such justice is done, we have little right
> to draw very definite conclusions about the negro
> mind. To me it seems that most travellers under the in-
> fluence of fevers and the thousand troubles attendant
> on African travelling, have much maligned and unjustly
> abused the natives, and that few people have studied
> them with unprejudiced and unbiassed minds. (1:238)

No matter how much they differed in national origin, professional training, and personal inclinations, the explorers of central Africa shared a conception of science as natural history. That idea itself had a long history
and was, at about the time when exploration got under way, undergoing
changes that caused its eventual demise.[1] Based on what our sources reveal, the main tenets of natural history are as follows: Scientific knowledge is produced by observing nature. Knowledge of peoples, of their culture and social organization, is scientific when it is produced and presented
following the rules that govern the observation of nature. The possibility
of a natural science of society rests on assumptions such as those formulated in the positivist principles we discussed in the first chapter.

Whether natural history reflected the orientation of the explorers'
sponsors and employers (mainly geographical societies and governments
who claimed that their imperialist designs were scientifically grounded)
or whether the kind of person who was attracted by, and recruited for,
exploration was likely to be someone with an engineering, medical, or
natural-scientific background does not make much of a difference. The
point is that alternative conceptions of knowledge—historical or aesthetic—were, if not ignored, assigned a low status.

True, "artists" were in some cases recruited as members of expeditions or employed when travelogues were published. We touch on their
role in the presentation of knowledge when we discuss the topic of illustrations. But it is hard to keep the production and presentation of
knowledge apart as separate phases. The history of scientific investigation and artistic representation of nature came together in the illustrated
travel account.[2]

If we want to understand how natural history worked in exploration
and emerging ethnography, we should give some thought to its use as a
myth not unlike that of exploratory travel. Its ideology was ridden with

contradictions and incongruities, much like other presuppositions and assumptions held by the explorers, their contemporary readers, and those of us who succeeded them in the history of anthropology. For the institutions and their vast personnel, science counted as a "universal" and common human enterprise. Yet the ideal agent was the individual scientist who faced nature in two ways: through actively observing and through submitting to, in fact, suffering, nature. A vignette that von François noted down while traveling on a river illustrates this double bind:

> We are kept in constant suspense by a continual feeling of running into enemies, expecting, at every instant, that invisible hands will shoot arrows at us from the thick brush along the shore. We keep a keen watch on every suspicious spot on the banks, our eyes are everywhere and we observe, as soon as we have passed another promontory, the vegetation on the shore through the telescope as far as we can see. In spite of this mood of elation, increased by the fact that we are all the time traveling into the unknown, forced to absorb everything that is geographically significant, the sun takes its effect. Covered with sweat and hungry, because food has become scarce, we decide at noon to buy provisions at the next settlement. (1888, 142–43)

Observing is, above all, seeing. As an activity, vision requires taking and changing positions, hence movement in space. Paradoxical demands come together in exploration when the need to keep moving—and the attendant problems of getting on the road—results in cutting short time spent on observing. Our authors often worry about losing time and having to fill "empty" time during idle periods with writing, labeling, mapping. We quoted some of their comments when we talked about time and timing; here are a few more complaints voiced by Böhm of the German East African Expedition. "When a larger expedition is marching—and ours consists of about 300 people, counting all—there is very little time left for observing and collecting" (1888, 25). Six or seven months after the expedition's arrival from Europe he writes to his sister: "Up to now circumstances have unfortunately been such that they did not afford me the free time and opportunity to do what I had come to Africa for, collecting and preserving specimens" (34). A month later, desperate about the time he had to spend in Tabora taking care of expedition affairs, he tells his brother: "Meanwhile I was bored in this place to the point of losing my mind, while the thought of the precious time that had to be killed in such a ghastly manner almost broke my heart" (39).

As a servant of science in the wilds of Africa, the explorer was alone and lonely. His suffering also made him a hero in the face of adversity.

Whenever he did scientific work—struggling for control over nature—
he needed to achieve self-control. Rather than simply pull an intellectual
kit called natural history from his ample baggage, he faced problems
with his ideals of science even before he took up the practical problems
of meeting assignments.

In the shared frame of natural history, emerging ethnography had its
place together with more established disciplines such as biology (including highly specialized fields such as ornithology), geology, topography, and astronomy, all of them represented in our sample of authors.[3]
When they studied people, travelers rarely questioned the assumption
(or injunction) that observation was their principal source of knowledge.
Having adopted a natural-science orientation, scientific explorers were
expected and obliged to approach African societies and cultures as natural objects. And yet during the first encounters they had no frame for
their relations. There was no colonial regime, no colony to simulate a
laboratory, a place where objects held still and variables could be controlled. Inevitably, explorers who subscribed to ideals of ethnographic
knowledge of other peoples based on meeting them as human subjects
and tried to follow positivist rules of observing Africans as objects of
natural history faced contradictions and, indeed, existential tensions and
anxieties. The very choice of an episteme that must have appeared to explorers as natural, hence rational, contained the seeds of madness.

We can begin to make these general reflections more concrete with
the help of an example that already had our attention in a preceding
chapter. There we documented differences in the ways explorers experienced African culture in one of its most powerful expressions: music. We
saw how Pogge went through a learning process. Perhaps naively, but
also without pretensions, he noted observations on the singing, drumming, and dancing he witnessed almost daily. Noises and movements, in
the beginning suffered as strange and annoying, eventually turned into
sounds and performances he began to appreciate as meaningful and, at
least occasionally, as pleasant. He achieved an understanding of African
music because he was affected by it.[4]

Becker, who declared that he had no sense for music, dutifully observed and reported his findings. In a passage that amounts to a brief
monograph on African music he made remarks, much more sophisti-
cated than Pogge's, on instruments, songs (including a musical and linguistic transcription of an example), choreography, and call-and-
response patterns in musical performance (1887, 2:325–29). Yet in the
end, the knowledge he conveys is of something that did not affect him

and did not make him try to understand what he reports from within, on its own terms. The concepts he uses are his own, little more than a spattering of "musicological" terms he probably remembered from his general education. In the passage we referred to, significantly, his observations focus on the analysis of a song text. By reducing the song to writing, he extracts himself from the immediacy of experiencing this piece of African music. He does this with a few predictable comments apt to establish his position above the observed instance of cultural expression and its creators. He finds in the boatmen's song "a strange poetry. The text is, by the way, most curious. It celebrates the blessings of Arab and European science: 'Ink! Ink!' sing the naive children of Africa. 'Where there is ink and paper, there is wealth!' Indeed, in their eyes, the tiniest piece of writing takes on an almost magical importance" (1887, 2:327). Taking another step away from experience, he ends with this speculative, or prophetic, pronouncement: "We should have no doubts that, when the time comes, education [he means literacy, of course] will find in this repudiated branch of the race of Cham a soil marvelously prepared" (328).

The racial reference in this remark is an occasion for us to note the sparse "anthropological observations" in the narrow sense of physical anthropology (body measurements, determinations of skin color and hair type, collection of crania and other skeletal remains, photographs). Combinations of racism and evolutionary theory were as yet tentative and diffuse, and a clear research agenda supporting such views had not yet emerged.

One traveler who, as a physician, did some physical anthropology and more consciously and fervently embraced ideals of natural-scientific objectivity was Buchner. More vividly than others, his case shows us the seeds of madness within scientific exploration. An eerie picture emerges from his reports to *MAGD:* here is an observer whose unshakable faith in science leads him to limit his search for knowledge and truth to the land and environment that can be observed with instruments, recorded in measurements, or collected in samples. For Buchner, all information about Africa gathered through communication was not only inaccurate by scientific standards, but outright deceptive. For this scientist, Africa offered a marvelous field of investigation—except for its lying, cheating, dishonest, lazy, dirty, noisy, greedy, disloyal, stupid inhabitants. All these epithets show up in Buchner's prose (though more evenly spread through his writings). He was still on his way to the Lunda and in excellent health but losing control of his porters, hence of conditions permitting him to do his scientific work, when he resorted to a kind of therapy that kept him in touch with objects and figures. He began to record in writing "almost every yard of fabric and every shot of powder I spend....I take this rather horrible work upon myself, not so much because I am concerned about conserving my means, but rather because of a purely emotional need not constantly to be lied to and robbed" (*MAGD* 2, no. 1 [1880]: 44).

From the last reports he submitted before the unsuccessful end of his trip we get a distinct impression of insanity, of raving and ranting paranoia. If this reflects his actual condition, we have not only a literal, clinical case of an explorer "out of his mind," but also one of scientific truth and investigation detached from the pragmatics of the research situation—and alive only in his mind.

That our interpretation is not merely speculative is apparent from an editorial note to Buchner's reports in *MAGD*. Obviously, the gentlemen in Berlin were concerned about his state of mind. As might be expected, however, their words are more cautious: "In the letters that follow the traveler, under the immediate impression of his long separation from everything that counts as culture, understandably emphasizes the dark sides of his semi-captivity. We empathize with him...but also have reasons to be pleased with his extended stay in the capital of the Lunda empire." The note speculates: "the stern self-critique of his activities that is contained in his letters probably was written in a moment of ill humor and is definitely too harsh" (*MAGD* 2, no. 4 [1881]: 158). In fact Buchner does not engage in self-critique; he blames everything that goes wrong on Africa and Africans.[5]

But back to observation and to some of the contradictions that lurk behind this deceptively simple concept. We may assume that observation acquired its weight as part of a philosophical position of empiricism or, in positivist terms, phenomenalism: nothing enters (or should be permitted to enter) the mind that was not first perceived by the senses. So far so good; our explorers would have approved. But their reports show that the senses never get equal play in the game of observation. Vision ranks highest; touch, hearing, smell, and taste (not necessarily in that order) come off as less reliable and productive. Yet there is much in our sources suggesting that the travelers were profoundly touched by sensory perceptions other than vision. Few among them had the literary skills to report such experiences and to reflect on their significance.

The difference between vision and the other senses grows particularly noticeable in reports of negative experiences. All the travelers document

unusual, abhorrent sights; they often link nondramatic everyday mean-
ness and contrariety to the "passive" senses of hearing (they suffer noise),
smell, taste, or touch (they have to endure stench and filth and cannnot
avoid breathing noxious fumes that cause fever; taking in poisonous and
indigestible substances comes with life in the wilds; burns, itches, and
soreness are a traveler's constant companions).

As a source of knowledge as well, vision outclasses other senses. Visual experiences are easier to express through description and proposi-
tional statements (ones containing "truth"). This common assumption,
too, is a cultural, ideological notion, not a natural property of vision.
The superiority of the objective gaze, a cultural ideal, was for the explorers a value other sense experiences undercut. As vision guided scientific observers, hearing, smell, taste, and even touch made them vulnerable. Here, I believe, is the reason the explorers never aimed their
monkish rules of hygiene at vision; they had no prescriptions for dealing with visual overload, no remedies for the roaming eye. In fact, from
some authors we get the impression that visual observation of nature
was a relief, a vacation from the strain of travel and its human problems.

Our traveling observers knew that they, too, were being observed. If
the explorers' gaze expressed their superiority, how did they react whenever the observed directed their gaze at the observers? I think they experienced African curiosity as a steady presence and, above all, as an in-
vasion of their privacy. Circumstances often made it impossible to retreat;
inside his hut or tent the European was still audible and it is safe to assume that his whereabouts were always known, even when he took solitary walks. Travelers accepted inquisitive natives with resignation. What
never gave them pause to think (at least, no statements to this effect come
to mind) was that their own presence and gaze invaded the lives of
Africans. Africans, they assumed as a matter of course, had no notion
of privacy; this was one of the most common stereotypes. It had the advantage of freeing explorers from worries about their own intrusion with
scientific observations. It helped cover up contradictions between an idealized, ideologized concept of scientific observation and the necessities
of interaction and communication that observers of people must face.

MEASURING AND COLLECTING

> We had here a visit from an *Mganga*, or medicine man,
> fantastically dressed. He had with him an obscene im-
> age of a woman, clothed with beads, and looking like

> an absurd toy. Though he did not appear to have much
> respect for this goddess, if such we might call it, yet he
> would not sell it under an exorbitant price. (1:117)

When explorers spoke of scientific work to be conducted during expeditions they had, above all, two activities in mind: measuring, in the larger sense of operating instruments to produce readings they could enter in logs and tables; and collecting, obtaining specimens of whatever domain of nature they were directed to observe for later analysis in the metropolitan country. Many of our authors were natural scientists (zoologists, botanists, geologists, topographers, astronomers, physicians) or had acquired basic scientific skills as part of their military training. Did their background equip them to carry out scientific work as a rational, organized enterprise?

To put it bluntly, it did not. In fact, the picture that emerges from the sources is rather dismal. They mention scientific instruments or list them as part of a caravan's equipment but rarely describe them in any detail. Often these implements served purposes, such as impressing Africans, that can hardly count as scientific. Some instruments could be operated discreetly (chronometers, barometers, thermometers, microscopes); others (telescopes, sextants, photographic equipment) only outside, in public view, and that could cause problems. Pogge warned travelers to take precautions when operating instruments in the presence of the Lunda ruler: the current Mwant Yav, he said, was superstitious. Others showed less delicacy, and Buchner may have had Pogge's caution in mind when he bragged,

> I never caused offense with my instruments, everywhere I set them up undisturbed and made my observations with them as if this was a natural thing to do. With 100 men and 20 guns, there is no danger in the part of Africa I got to know....If I had with me an army of 3 or 4 whites, I would not even take notice of the Muata Yamvo [the Mwant Yav]....As it is, I must accommodate the moods of His Dwarf Majesty. (*MAGD* 2, no. 4 [1881]: 160–61)

Tempting as it may be to ponder the deeper implications of Buchner's remarkable leap from scientific method to military might, the statement fits our argument: in pronouncing one of the most powerful African rulers of the time a dwarf (*Liliputmajestät*), Buchner shows us he has lost his mind, or at least his sense of reality.

By far the most frequent comments about instruments are expressions of regret (not having better ones; not being able to make better use of them; losing or breaking them) or complaint (about the climate making

them malfunction or fail; about their not being available when needed).
I found a long passage, too long to be quoted here, in a report by Reichard from the German East African Expedition where he describes how
just about everything went wrong with his chronometer, aneroid (barometer), and hypsometer (instrument to determine elevation) (*MAGD* 5,
no. 2 [1887]: 76–77). Wissmann also had difficulties with his instruments ([1890], 115) and Coquilhat at one point complained that he, like
the other Belgian officers of his expedition, never received any "instruments of observation" and had to determine his course with the help of
a pocket compass (1888, 284). Of course, by then he probably had few
illusions regarding the scientific purpose of his travel. When he voiced
his complaint, Belgian pacification and occupation of the Congo were in
full sway.

What can we say about measuring in the pursuit of anthropological
knowledge? During the early part of our period, at most two or three of
the travelers had anthropological interests in the more narrow sense of
the term (now usually called physical anthropology). While strolling
through the market at Tabora, Becker did make *observations anthro-
pologiques* and drop a few evolutionist terms (rarely elsewhere [1887,
2:28]). Though a tape measure and scales, perhaps a pair of calipers,
were all the explorers needed by way of instruments, I found little on
taking, say, cranial measurements—later a must for anthropological expeditions. The single exception is Wolf (Wissmann's companion and later
leader of the 1886 expedition), who took such measurements and was
concerned with distinguishing cranial types and races (the latter according to types of hair). Among distinctive features of the skeleton of
Africans he claimed to have observed "the more horizontal position of
the pelvis," which, predictably, he takes to indicate "an approximation
to the form of animals" (*MAGD* 4, no. 6 [1885]: 365). His observation
came after a visit to the chief Mwene Putu Kasongo. In the travelogue
he coauthored with Wissmann, Wolf also tells of his unsuccessful attempts among the Kuba: "It was absolutely impossible to make anthropological measurements with my instruments. A measuring tape was
enough to cause panic, and I even had plaster of Paris with me to make
facial casts! I was deeply disappointed" (1891, 232).[6]

Wolf apparently also made anthropological measurements on the
mixed population at Kinshasa station. Coquilhat refers to these in his
book at the beginning of some general remarks on the ethnography of
the Bangala. He notes a few physical racial characteristics (using measurements made by Carl Mense and Ludwig Wolff [*sic*] in Léopoldville)

but warns against easy conclusions from physical or cultural "analogies" and gives examples of what he considers absurd and false analogies (1888, 359–61). Later Hilton-Simpson, Torday's companion, mentions that they measured and photographed "types" (mostly soldiers ordered to submit to the procedure) in Léopoldville, that is, before their expedition reached the interior (1911, 13–14). Presumably, the idea was that an urban location would offer the greatest variety of types—as if measurement needed no place. How could they know *what* they were measuring? What did they expect to find?

If measuring and quantification were the hard core of scientific inquiry—as we have good reasons to assume sponsoring agencies, explorers, and their readers all asserted—actual accomplishments were meager, to say the least. Only some tabulated data that looked scientific (latitudes, meteorologic values) actually involved calculations; most entries were just readings taken from instruments of questionable reliability by people who had questionable qualifications to use them. This goes for strictly natural scientific investigations. Even less came out of the domain of social research. Many reports had lists of prices for commodities and trade goods, but their compilers hardly thought of them as scientific social data. Yet I did find one of those surprising exceptions that we have come to expect in this story of exploration. Frobenius, of all people, the ethnographer and theoretician who would later formulate one of the most "qualitative" and aestheticist theories of culture (his famed *Kulturmorphologie*), was the only one who tried to meet one of his assignments—to investigate economic conditions—by a piece of research that had all the trappings of a scientific experiment. He reported on it in a remarkable chapter titled "Experiments with Workers" (1907, 97–111).

Circumstances had immobilized Frobenius in the Kwilu region. Without ammunition for his arsenal of pistols, rifles, and shotguns (something had gone wrong with a shipment from Antwerp), he did not dare to travel on his own and, because of a bumper crop of rubber, the steamers of the Compagnie du Kasai had no room for passengers. Immobility forced him to adopt a new modus operandi. His ethnographic work became stationary. From his veranda, as it were, he interviewed visitors from various tribes and hired some "talented and willing natives," whom he sent out to villages in the region to "reconnoiter, summon [prospective informants], and collect [objects]." Meanwhile the expedition's artist made drawings of "human types and various activities" (100). All this was not enough to occupy Frobenius's boundless energy, and he decided to make a thorough study of the ways Africans worked. In the beginning, he had problems recruiting persons to observe, and he took the occasion to indulge in some moralist and racist pontificating about Africans' aversion to work. That people who had to endure the atrocities of the rubber company (he mentions them [101]) would not be eager to work for a European did not cause him to have second thoughts. He finally made agreements with two work gangs from different ethnic groups, one from the Dinga, a people considered backward and savage, the other from the Yaka, known to be outgoing and independent-minded. Frobenius gave both gangs the task of building a typical native dwelling. To ensure an element of control and comparison, Frobenius picked two different modes of remuneration. The Dinga got free lodging and weekly wages for eight hours of work each day; the Yaka had a weekly portion of salt and would get a bonus, to be set and paid after completion of the work. They were free to come and go as they pleased.

Frobenius observed the workers from a window of his house, visiting the site now and then. He kept time (to the second) of each sequence of operations and tabulated the results (104). In the end, he calculated hours and cost and came to the conclusion that "the product of voluntary labor [was] three and a quarter times more expensive than the equivalent of contract-bound labor" (106). And while he was at it, he treated his readers to generalizations about the psychology of the negro, including his thoughts about slaves and women as the most promising subjects of education. It is on their situation of dependent and regulated labor that "you can observe all those symptoms that lead to a higher form of culture work, and among the women who were brought up in this manner for who knows how many generations you can discern what must be the most beautiful flowering of a cultured form of work, the *sense of duty*" (108).

So much for measuring and exploration. Collecting was the other method of scientific inquiry practiced by almost all the travelers on our list. Explorers were expected to gather what Becker called *échantillons d'histoire naturelle et d'ethnographie* (samples of natural history and ethnography [1887, 2:389]).[7] So as not to get lost in a topic that may appear relatively simple and straightforward but quickly turns out to be quite complex and easily confusing, we must begin with a few conceptual distinctions regarding both the activity and purpose of collecting and the objects at issue.

As our authors gathered up objects to take back to Europe, the activity gathered momentum. It went from being one of those things travelers do (like keeping a diary) to being a main purpose and, therefore, a major problem for the logistics of travel. Some of the earlier explorers seem to have been content to pick up what they found interesting or curious; by the time we get to Torday and Frobenius, collecting had become more ambitious though not necessarily more planned and systematic. Its purpose was to amass material knowledge for institutions that either (co-)sponsored travel in the first place or could be counted on to acquire the objects brought back from Africa. Perhaps more clearly and directly than any other aspect of exploration, this trend reflects the professionalization of ethnography. It parallels the emergence of a category of things contemporary sources already called "ethnographic objects." Like the object of anthropology in general (see Fabian 1983), ethnographic objects were not found; they had to be construed.[8] And thus ethnographic collecting must be part of our inquiry into the production of knowledge about Africa.

It would be wrong, however, to suggest that the course of this process ran from simple beginnings to intricate methodologies. Explorers brought along to Africa ideas and habits that owed as much to a long history of collecting curiosities as to the then modern techniques of natural history. Their ideas of what was collectible ranged from curiosity to discovery, from objects that were odd, striking, and unique or rare to others that were destined to confirm expectations and hypotheses, fill taxonomic pigeonholes, and document nature according to scientific rubrics and disciplinary divisions. Somehow they had to accommodate the wildly exotic fetish and the inconspicuous mineral or zoological specimen within a common frame of scientific investigation as "natural" objects. Classification became, and remained, an intractable problem of ethnographic collecting.

A piece of rock, a plant to be pressed and dried, a lizard to be preserved in alcohol came from the bush; a spear or mask came from human hands. Ethnographic collecting involved entering social, commercial, and political relations; the injunctions of natural history made explorers define that activity as scientific, hence natural, and could only exacerbate the problems of intrusive, often aggressive, exploration. Therefore, the story of ethnographic collecting we piece together from our sources—telling of a shift from incidental gathering to systematic collecting—is anything but a tale of rational improvement. Its protagonists often exhibit odd behavior and its plot moves through episodes of incomprehension, deceit, and violence that strain the idea of scientific investigation.

When we now turn to our sources for concrete illustrations, we should first note some general points. Aside from Frobenius, who offered extensive opinions and advice on collecting what he called "ethnographic stuff [*Kram*]" (1907, 355 and elsewhere), our authors were remarkably casual in their reports on the topic. Belgian explorers give the impression that collecting was at best incidental (a remarkable idea in view of huge treasures of African objects that eventually found their way into the Royal Museum at Tervuren, near Brussels). Coquilhat even appears to have been one of the exceptions mentioned earlier—a traveler who did not collect. One brief remark at the very end of his book shows that he was aware of collecting as an established practice. The context is an observation on African attitudes toward "fetishes": "In any case, the negro is practical. If he is not satisfied with a fetish, he gets rid of it or sells it to a white collector" (1888, 500).

Becker expresses admiration for the "magnificent ethnographic collection" assembled by Reichard of the German East African Expedition (1887, 1:397; more will be said about Reichard later). About his own efforts he has only a few brief remarks. The first one he notes in Tabora: "My little ethnographic collection was augmented by a shield from Uganda, some lances, bows and arrows, and native textiles. I also bought from my two disciples some musical instruments from their country" (2:63). The two disciples were young men, "subjects of King Mutesa," whom he taught Swahili.

> [They] brought from their country some curiosities which I acquired. For two *dotis* [measures] of cotton fabric they let me have a harp from Uganda with almost Moorish contours, and some pieces of bark cloth of a yellowish-brown color, dry and spongy like tinder. I also bought from one of Tipo Tip's *akidas* [captains] a receptacle of carved ivory which once belonged to an ancient chief from the Maniema region. It is a curious piece of work, embellished all over with crocodiles, engraved and naively dotted with a burin. (71)

Though Becker was fascinated with these objects, he acquired them as a hobby, without pretensions to systematic scientific collecting. At the end of his mission, before his departure from Zanzibar, he picked up a few more items and tells us: "Thus, little by little, my small African museum takes shape, but, again, owing more to my friends [in this case Sewa, the Indian trader] than to my own particular acquisitions" (451).

Even if we leave aside Frobenius and Torday, two travelers who represent the professionalization of collecting toward the end of our period, a different picture emerges from reports by German explorers. On his first trip Pogge gathered natural historical samples but had little interest in ethnographic objects. His interest picked up during the second expedition when Wissmann joined him, yet the reports remain scanty. The first remark on collecting comes near the middle of Wissmann's travelogue and is an expression of regret. They simply did not have the means to acquire what was offered, otherwise they would have made "splendid ethnographic collections" (1889, 135). Their illustrations of weapons and other implements—presented like museum displays—are evidence of successful efforts.[9] Wissmann notes that Pogge, despite his illness, keeps on collecting butterflies and other insects; he admits that he himself gave it up because he could not protect his collections from rot and insects (159). He closes the subject with this resigned observation: "During long trips, collecting is by no means small work and the manner in which what is brought back is treated at home often does not compare to the efforts made" (159–60).

On his second expedition, though, Wissmann seems to have increased his efforts, and by the end of the first year (December 1, 1884) we find the following aside in a letter published in *MAGD*: "I have as yet been unable to collect anything useful for Professor Bastian; the north [meaning Kuba country] will, I hope, offer rich compensation" (*MAGD* 4, no. 5 [1885]: 321). The pressure to get objects must have been great enough to make him adopt a rather odd method of collecting. In the travelogue (Wissmann [1890]), he describes a difficult situation among the "savage" Bassongo Meno (in the Kasai region). He recalls earlier clashes with these hostile people, who now flee from his caravan. He organizes several excursions to abandoned villages and resorts to what ethnologists would have called silent barter: "On one of these expeditions I could not resist the temptation of taking some new and interesting weapons and tools from such a deserted village. In place of them I put some bright-coloured handkerchiefs and beads, which amply made up for the value of the things annexed" (quoted—for the verb "annexed"—from the English translation: 1891, 24).

Wolf, his companion on this expedition, seems to have been more systematic as a collector. On one occasion Wissmann mentions: "With Ilunga, chief of the Lussambo, Wolf struck up a friendship and bought a number of valuable collectible items which I was able to complete later at the same place. The tribe can be considered distinguished by their wood carving industry" ([1890], 40; some of the items appear in an illustration facing that page). Later, among the Kanyoka people, the trade got more brisk: "Within an hour I bought 125 very beautiful hatchets, which I paid for with one colorful handkerchief each. Already a year ago Tenda [the chief] had sent, almost every month, some hoes and hatchets to Luluaburg [the German station]" (84). In other regions Wissmann had no success at all: "Here nothing could be acquired for ethnological collections. For these tribes had just entered the stage when the first guns and the first European fabrics spoil the pleasure they took in their own industry" (116). Wissmann's explanation sounds plausible but he most likely described a situation that showed the effects of antifetish campaigns conducted by the children of hemp. Later, Wolf will confirm this interpretation. To him we also owe several observations on the precarious nature of ethnographic objects. We will take a look at two of them, but in order to appreciate what he has to say we must first briefly return to our discussion of the theoretical and conceptual aspects of collecting.

Trying to meet demands from metropolitan museums and collectors, African travelers construed the ethnographic object. A composite picture emerges from the statements of what they collected and what they valued in the collectible objects. Attributes and adjectives suggest above all the uncertain scientific status of cultural artifacts. Items interested them, we learn, because they were curious, tempting, interesting, valuable, beautiful. As we shall see presently, this list came to include attributes such as old, authentic, and rare. Some—perhaps most—of the properties expressed in these adjectives may also reflect what naturalists felt about their samples. But the visually striking, the economically valuable, and the aesthetically pleasing in collected rocks, beetles, and ferns did not constitute their status as samples of nature. Even if they were in every respect unremarkable, they had assured places in taxonomies that would go to support scientific theories and explanations. To claim such a status for cultural artifacts—and make ethnographic collecting serve natural history—required, if not acts of faith, then a projection of values onto things that was analogous to, and often identical with, the constitution of objects as commodities.

Where there are commodities, there is a market. Exchange relations were among the elements or conditions of exploration we counted as ecstatic because they were, more or less, out of control. So were the weather, some could object, the state of roads and river passages, and, for that matter, the mood and attitudes of populations encountered. The difference, or the point, about ecstasis in the production of knowledge is that it demands an active engagement. The search does not pursue us; we pursue it. That in a given situation the ecstatic or the merely uncontrolled elements may be hard to tell apart does not invalidate the point. Ethnographic collecting—on the surface, a matter of rational routine—asked for abandon: giving in to whims and fits of desire for specific objects, yielding to circumstances and people in order to get the objects or, as we shall see, using force when obstacles loomed.

Before we get to the use of force we should mention an interesting observation based on von François's travelogue. It suggests that the mode of travel, in this case river travel, affected practices of collecting. Von François could buy only what he noticed or others offered during brief stops the steamer made for taking on fuel and provisions. Most of these items were weapons, household implements, and musical instruments. Riverain collecting resembled surface archeology: gathering objects without contextual information. Unwittingly, von François also gave us a beautiful illustration of differences between European and African attitudes toward these objects.

> My collection was augmented by several bows, arrows, and spears. A beautiful ivory horn, 1.5 m long, extended by a two-foot wooden tube, excited my desire to buy [*Kauflust*] but the owner was not to be separated from his horn; instead, he blew it for us with much perseverance and was then presented with a spoon. Immediately, another person appeared who also wanted to earn a spoon and produced from the horn a similarly beautiful, deep, and drawn-out sound. (1888, 138)

In the end, von François did obtain the horn—otherwise it would not have appeared among the illustrations[10]—though he does not tell us how. Given the general picture that emerges from his account, he probably got it without using force. Reichard, however, did use force and documented it in his reports to *MAGD* (we commented on them in chapter 6). There he also bragged to his sponsors how he profited from the panic spread by the expedition to collect a "pile of ethnographic objects, especially beautiful carvings."

Few travelers resorted to Reichard's methods (though some came close: see Wissmann's silent barter above and Wolf's quasi-extortion below). The more thoughtful among them were aware of the precariousness of ethnographic objects and hence of ethnographic collecting. The difficulties they experienced and reported were caused not only by natives refusing to part with their possessions, nor by lack of funds and problems of logistics—each load of curios demanded a porter who would consume food bought with commodities the expedition carried—but by the very nature of the objects the explorers marked for collection. These ethnographic objects refused, as it were, to stick to their original function and context, at least while exploration and ethnographic investigation went on. Which brings us back to Wolf. Here first is what he observed among the Kuba.

> The Bakuba are a surprising phenomenon. Intermediate trade did not suc-
> ceed in destroying their autochthonous culture, but the first personal ac-
> quaintance with the white man was enough to give their taste a different di-
> rection. Already during my presence they began embellishing their woven
> fabrics with applications of European material I had presented them with. By
> accident I was able to lay hands on a sample of this first transition from an
> indigenous to a foreign culture and it is now in the Royal Museum of Eth-
> nology in Berlin. (Wissmann et al. 1891, 256)

In other words, some objects changed because of external influences during the process of collection.[11] Others all but disappeared because of
changes instituted by the society concerned, which is what Wolf experienced when he tried to still his appetite for ethnographic objects in regions influenced by the children of hemp.

> Because Kalamba Mukenge...had sworn to destroy all fetishes and tradi-
> tional weapons and led a reckless campaign of destruction that was to make
> room for the Riamba cult, I counted myself lucky when I managed to save
> for science a few pieces which still had the stamp of authenticity and origi-
> nality from the cultural heritage [*Völkerleben:* lit., the life of peoples] of the
> Baluba who are ethnologically interesting. Kalamba has all fetishes burned
> in public and their owners are severely punished. Only a few Baluba chiefs
> who live as far as possible away from Mukenge and have put special confi-
> dence in the power of their fetishes dare to keep them. They, as well as their
> subjects, keep that a secret and will part only in extreme cases with their
> trusted protectors. Under normal circumstances I could have sacrificed what
> I wanted but would not have got the *Makabu Buange* [fetish], which now
> found its home in the Royal Museum of Ethnology in Berlin. (Wissmann et
> al. 1891, 266–67)

The passages just quoted put Wolf among the more thoughtful traveler-
collectors. But even he was not squeamish when it came to taking possession of a desired object. At least in one case he used force when he
requisitioned the collectible object as a punishment for having earlier
been cheated by its owner, a chief (265–66). Incidentally, Wolf also "collected" a skull he found displayed on a stake (as a trophy?) in chief Tshigenge's residence. We are told that it "is to be found with other skulls in
the collection of the Museum of Anatomy in Berlin" (178). On this
macabre topic, Büttner has a story from Yaka country about the bodies
of numerous ritual victims being exposed to rot on a hillside near the
capital. From there "my porters brought me many skulls during the
night. Unfortunately these were almost always torn apart and damaged
by the pigs, who liked human flesh. Nevertheless, I was able to bring
some that were in a good state back to Germany" (1890, 150).

All in all, as reported in the travelogues, the realities of gathering artifacts for the purpose of taking them back to Europe make it difficult to
see early ethnographic collecting as the kind of disciplined activity it
should have been as part of scientific investigation following the methods of natural history. As far as we can tell, many collections never
amounted to much. Some that may have been important never reached
Europe.[12] There were two notable exceptions: Torday's Kuba statues, fabrics, and other objects became a classic collection at the British Museum
(the expedition's sponsor).[13] The material assembled by Frobenius, the
most methodical and prolific of all collectors, was dispersed in several institutions; there was certainly enough to go around. Toward the end of
his stay, he tells us, he faced the problem of getting four hundred loads,
each requiring two porters (roughly 24,000 lbs.), to a point where they
could be transported further down the Kasai River on their way to the
coast (1907, 435). Frobenius was so much preoccupied with the problem
of transporting ethnographic objects that he took it as an occasion for
one of his general disquisitions on the logistics of caravan travel (435–40).

Such a manifestly chaotic aspect of exploration deserves so much
space here because documenting the chaotic is one of our aims. But there
is more to it. Gathering ethnographic material according to whim or desire—acquiring ill-defined and ill-understood objects by methods that
ranged from buying what was offered to extorting and looting what a
traveler desired—became the database (to use an anachronistic expression) on which anthropology first built its reputation as an academic and
scientific discipline. Ethnographic objects stored in museums were a capital without which anthropology would not have been institutionalized
and professionalized under the paradigms of evolutionism and diffu-
sionism. Central Africa had the cultural resources, and the expeditions
we have been studying contributed to amassing the wealth of objects
that, when they are not on exhibit or circulating on the art markets of
the world, are still securely stored in magazines and vaults.

ORDERING, INSCRIBING, AND MAPPING

> I asked our guide the chief's name, and jotted it down in
> my note-book in his presence. He seemed to be much in-
> terested in the book and the writing. Thinking that this
> arose from his thirst of knowledge, I politely handed it
> to him for examination. The moment he had got hold of
> it he set up a wild halloo, and began shouting out that I
> was using witchcraft, and intended to bewitch him by

putting down his name. In answer to his shouts the people crowded round with threatening gestures, and again
we found ourselves in a critical situation. Fortunately
Kisa arrived, and took our side, telling how we always
had taken the chiefs' names beside those of streams and
villages, and explaining that no harm had come from it,
but that it was simply to refresh my memory. (2:144)

Could labeling, sorting, and classifying samples of natural history and
ethnographic objects not wait until the collections had reached the metropolitan country where experts would do the work? The image of travelers as mere gatherers of data is part of the myth of exploration and not
a minor one, either. It embodied one of the most lasting misconceptions
to affect anthropology (and other disciplines), the notion that field research, analysis, and writing are distinctly separate phases in the production of knowledge. It is likely that most of our travelers saw themselves in the role of pioneering collectors, but they soon found out that
they needed to know what to collect for which kind of knowledge. At
the least, when packing things for transport by caravan or shipment to
Europe, they had to label cases and their contents. Assign names (or at
least numbers) to objects, make decisions about what to include and
what not to include, what to place in one case rather than in another,
and compile inventory lists. In short, packing (not to forget frequent unpacking and repacking) involved travelers in classification, a cognitive
yet also sensory and physical activity.

Now and then, we all engage in such cultural classification when we
pack our suitcases for a trip. We follow a logic that is part of tacit knowledge (though not always a matter of general agreement, as painful pre-
travel disputes with companions have taught us). We saw such a logic of
classification operating when we considered the material culture of
African travel (chapter 2) and found that it was a complex combination
of necessities and amenities, of choices made on the basis of practical experience and of wild guesses. As to the logic of ordering material to be
brought back, the situation was even more complex. Most travelers had
some expertise, self-taught or from prior training, in observing and sam-
pling nature. But what about the observation of peoples, their culture,
society, and everyday activities? Our sources show that no explorer came
to this task empty-minded. Before travelers began to gather ethnographic
data they already had knowledge, set down in instructions, manuals, and
questionnaires, derived from general reading or simply from popular
conceptions and stereotypes. But ethnography based on actual encounter

with strange peoples could not rest on certainties brought along; it demanded leaps of imagination, acts of identification, choosing sides in disputes, and whatever else is required if communication is to occur in
situations where participants cannot simply follow their habits and routines. I don't think it is exaggerated to qualify such acts as moments of
ecstasis. As reported in our sources, they ranged from intense pleasure
caused by discovery to mad projections pronounced to cover confusion
and the discomfort, indeed the pain, of incomprehension.

Many examples of all this can be found in the texts already quoted.
Speaking of texts, they remind us that one cognitive aspect of travel and
exploration is easy to overlook. All the basic cognitive operations such
as naming (or eliciting names), distinguishing and lumping, and representing ordered arrangements somehow acquire significance only when
we put them in writing. Travelers began producing knowledge by writing down lists, terminologies, and vocabularies (often before they
reached their destination they had to learn terms for commodities, foodstuffs, and household items). Conversely, when they gave accounts of
what they had learned, one of the most effective means of displaying authoritative knowledge, aside from lists and tables, was to lard their prose
with native terms. In my study of Becker's travelogue, compared with an
account of the first expeditions conducted by the White Fathers, I have
tried to show what this involved and how much there is to learn from
such writing practices about language and communication in early colonial encounters (Fabian 1984). Most often writers use a given native term
or phrase, together with a gloss in a European language, once or a few
times. Some terms may occur, without translation, repeatedly throughout the book; these are usually introduced in such a way that the reader
learns them as he proceeds through the account. But there are extreme
cases such as Capelo and Ivens, who do all the above but also employ
scores of African terms without glosses in the text.[14] Native words may
function purely as indexes; in print they become material traces or emblems of ethnographic authority and (an aspect easy to overlook) of pre-
tentiousness. Only a few readers had then and have now the competence
to judge the linguistic prowess displayed by writers of travelogues.

Naming often involved acts of imposition. This was literally the case
when explorers gave salient geographical features the names of European explorers or rulers. "Nobody contests the right of discoverers,"
says Torday, "to name lakes and mountains, rivers and dales after themselves or after one whom they desire to honour" (1925, 39). Topographic
names also served to commemorate persons or events. In this respect,

practices of naming places resembled those of erecting monuments. Both were modes of inscribing European presence as a way of creating an instant historical past, one that would eventually serve to legitimize colonial presence. Frobenius has a long argument for naming a waterfall—Pogge and Wissmann each reported a native word for it: Kangombe and Lulomba—after one of the prominent directors of the German society, Ferdinand von Richthofen (1907, 396–97). He noted the African practice of naming a river, and changing its name, to commemorate a person who had found his death in its waters. But, he continues: "We have no reason to name this place which is distinguished as a geographical feature and as a landscape after just any native" (397).[15] Reichard, to quote just one instance, reports: "We camped on a small bay [of Lake Tanganyika] which Storms, to commemorate our trip, named 'International Bay'" (*MAGD* 4, no. 2 [1884]: 101).

Two instances highlight the travelers' regard for commemorating exploration by literal inscription. The first one comes from Wissmann, who on one of his trips passed the place where two other German explorers, Richard Kund and Hans Tappenbeck, had camped. He inscribed their expedition by cutting a large K into a tree that marked the site ([1890], 24–25). For Becker, a similar gesture became an occasion to express fears and doubts about his mission. On the trip from the coast to Karema, the travelers had climbed a hill to get a view of the landscape: "Before we descended to the camp we cut our initials into the bark of a tree trunk.... A gesture of childish bravado! Who can be sure of the future? Maybe it will be the only trace I leave on this formidable continent!" (1887, 1:115–16).

Enough has been said in the literature about such imperial gestures, much less about practices that began to establish what I called the habits of our discipline. Naming was one of the chores and routines of travel. Compiling vocabularies was a task perhaps even more important than collecting objects. Not only was this a first step in the description of languages and a way of assembling practical guides of use for future travelers and linguists; the activity of establishing lists of terms and phrases also counted among the means of hygiene, that is, of maintaining mental and physical health.[16] Most travelers spent much time and energy asking for, and noting down, the names of things that could be pointed to; of villages, chiefs, and tribes; of rivers, mountains, and other features of landscape. Some explorers tell us of techniques they devised to extract terms and labels from people who were fearful of Europeans or simply were not interested in vocabularies. "For every word the Batua told me,"

Wissmann says, "I gave them a bead; when I handed it over I had to take care not to touch the people's hands. For they shied away whenever I got too close" ([1890], 130). Torday used a similar procedure to overcome diffidence or lack of interest among his informants.

> My first care in the Bayaka country was to collect a vocabulary. As I was near the Bambala frontier most people understood, more or less, Kimbala; and if one of my informants made a mistake, the others were always ready to correct him. In order to stimulate public interest I provided myself with a packet of sewing-needles; and when I asked in Kimbala the Bayaka name of some object, the first man to give it received a needle; if, however, he told me a wrong word, he had to surrender one of those previously earned, and the reward went to the man who corrected him. Thus I accumulated my vocabulary at a cost of about twopence. (1913, 145)[17]

A nice trick, but it leaves us wondering whether the explorers appreciated how much indulgence such language games required of their informants. (But then even the most modern methods of eliciting lexical items ask respondents to suspend their communicative and rhetorical competences and behave as if language were but a collection of words.) Sometimes travelers compensated for their own ignorance of the intricacies of signification with outbursts of rage and racist invective. After days of trying to establish a genealogy of Lunda rulers that would have met his naturalist's standards, Buchner exclaims: "Apart from ignorance and intellectual laziness [*Denkfaulheit*], a multitude of current epithets is to blame for this confusion and also, as regards geographical concepts, there are several different nomenclatures" (*MAGD* 2, no. 4 [1881]: 166). Polysemy and synonyms, not to speak of metaphors and other tropes, were more than he and others were prepared to deal with.

Collecting names and terms, of course, is but a first step. Labels become significant in the production of knowledge when they serve to classify, to distinguish, and to generalize. For the domains of botany and zoology, specialists usually prepared or edited lists and classifications of collected specimens before their publication. No such help was available for ethnic and cultural labels and terminologies. In these domains, even the best scientific intentions could not produce results that were up to the standards of natural history. Though we cannot elaborate the point in adequate detail here, our authors apparently used the concept of race to bridge the gap between natural and social knowledge (and ensure a place for both within the paradigm of natural history). The lack of valid criteria involved all the travelers in confused and corrupt practices of shoring up uncertain ethnic (that is, cultural and political) distinctions with racial classification. A fault line runs through our sources: on one side are domains where collected specimens fit into the rubrics and taxonomic pigeonholes of biology and geology; on the other are inquiries into society and culture where specimens—bits of information—are lodged only in linguistic contexts whose pragmatic and political dimensions explorers were unable to control, no matter how hard they tried.

A most interesting case illustrating this dividing line is Büttner's lengthy report on the German Congo Expedition. He combines his own botanical and zoological collections with lists of identifications (with Linnaean nomenclature) compiled by various experts in Europe (*MAGD* 5, no. 3 [1889]: 206–66). In the brief section of his report on ethnographic matters (182–93) he links tentative and fragmentary information to judgmental stereotypes of peoples, institutions, and customs, masking them as classification. The next section on the country, its climate, hygienic conditions, and its products (193–206) again shows Büttner as a critical scientist, cautious when it comes to generalizing yet capable of descriptions that are remarkably dynamic, even processual (*naturgeschichtlich*). At one point, introducing his observations on rainfall, he voices a warning he obviously saw no need to express, or heed, when he reported on ethnography: "With a word of caution against arbitrary generalizing from singular observations—the only kind available to the traveler who, fraught with worries and work, takes a quick tour of countries that are little or altogether unknown—I offer my own, convinced that they could become useful in certain cases" (196).

Aside from collecting specimens and terms, one of principal tasks of explorers was the mapping of routes and territories crossed. It demanded much time and energy. Determining positions and directions with the help of astronomic observations, measuring (or, most often, calculating and estimating) distances, entering these observations in sketches for use later in drawing maps—all this observation of nature would seem to be among the most detached, objective modes of knowledge production imaginable. In other words, we would expect geographical, especially topographical, knowledge to be on the other side of the line between ethnography and natural history. Nothing could be further from the truth. That goes for metropolitan imperial expectations and colonial designs, but also for the explorers in the field. While they rushed (or crept) through the wilds, geographers and geographical societies in Europe were engaged in a race to publish the latest, most up-to-date maps of travel routes and newly discovered regions of central Africa.

For many travelers maps became a matter of deep personal concern. Maps were a means of showing an individual's value to exploration by correcting or improving those of predecessors or competitors; they were the most palpable proof of having completed assigned trajectories. This brings us back to one of the more dubious figures in our story, Schütt, leader of an expedition to the Lunda and a trained topographer with previous experience of service in the Ottoman empire. Perhaps something in the nature of maps drives their makers to fill gaps with guesses and conjectures. At any rate, as we saw in a previous chapter, Schütt was caught actually faking part of his trajectory—and may have hoped the maps he brought back from his expedition would justify the lapse into imagination. In *MAGD* we found several comments on his work to show how much he got away with. When his German sponsor, the African Society, had to reprimand him for financial irregularities, the gentlemen of the committee apparently deferred to metropolitan authorities who thought highly of his cartographic work, though we get a first inkling of his later troubles when we read: "But he is ordered to mark in his further work distinctions on the maps between that which results from actual readings and observations and that which is based on inquiries and hypothesis" (*MAGD*, nos. 4–5 [1879]: 171). *MAGD* nevertheless published Schütt's final report. In the passages that cover the part of the trip that later turned out to have been fabricated, Schütt gives an example of the slightly delirious quality geographical naming occasionally took on. He has Zaire, or N'Zaire, take on different meanings in different contexts, ranging from a generic designation of a large body of water (such as a lake), to the term for river, and to the name of a particular river.[18] Of course, what may outweigh the geographer's confusion is the ethnographer's gain. Taking the Kongo generic term for river, *nzadi*, for the name of the river to which the European explorer happened to be pointing (and mispronouncing it *Zaire*) goes back to the discovery of the Congo by the Portuguese.[19] The example of Schütt's place-names is extreme but not unique. We can easily imagine the notation of similar partial understandings—which became misunderstandings only when they were misinterpreted—when Schütt questioned his informants.

On the topic of questioning natives about the names of rivers, von François has an interesting observation. It not only illustrates the problem with eliciting generic versus specific terms but also documents the surprise Africans felt at Europeans having to ask such matters at all: "To our questioning them about the name of the river they responded: 'You ought to know more about that than we do, you are the children of the water, we are the children of the land.' The river is water and water cannot have another name" (von François 1888, 133). "Children of the water" was a current term for Europeans we already encountered in earlier chapters.[20]

Returning to Schütt and his ways with scientific knowledge, slightly later in the same issue *MAGD* published a remark by Buchner, who may have known of the doubts the association had begun to have about Schütt. He had met Schütt—who was returning from the interior—in Malange and received information, including cartographic material. In a statement typical of his frame of mind he praises Schütt's accomplishments: "I cannot adequately express how much Schütt obliged me by letting me have his map, which at once transported me from a sultry profusion of lies into most agreeable clarity" (244).

Meanwhile *MAGD* continued to publish results from Schütt's expedition, such as his readings of altitude, with laudatory comments from an expert (2, no. 1 [1880]: 11–17), and announced his forthcoming travelogue (2, no. 5 [1881]: 219). Later acknowledging that the account was partially fictive (*fingirt*), the society declared most of Schütt's "special topography of the region he crossed" was "authentic" (3, no. 2 [1882]: 96). Maps—and here is our reason for giving this episode so much attention—had a special, especially precious, status as representations of space. Once drawn, they were not easily abandoned.[21]

A few years after the Schütt affair, *MAGD* published an extensive commentary on the late Dr. Kaiser's topography of the region between Tabora, Lake Tanganyika, and Lake Rikwa. The author was Dr. Richard Kiepert, the same Kiepert who had prepared the printed edition of Schütt's maps. He pays the highest compliments to Kaiser's accuracy and takes the review of his work as an occasion for trying to establish a sort of concordance between the maps and topographic data other travelers, among them Stanley, Cameron, Thomson, and Cambier, had left of this region. Kiepert comes to a devastating conclusion: "From a purely cartographic point of view their works are of little value" (*MAGD* 4, no. 2 [1884]: 110). W. Erman, another expert commenting on Pogge's and Wissmann's maps, was less severe but left no doubt that they were inaccurate (*MAGD* 4, no. 4 [1884]: 264–65). Later we read in a footnote that the two travelers had no accurate watches (and thus could not take exact positions) and were about three days off on the calendar (*MAGD* 4, no. 4 [1884]: 272n). Similar troubles affected the German East African Expedition after Kaiser's death. Reichard complains about broken and inaccurate instruments though he carefully describes his topographic and cartographic work (*MAGD* 5, no. 2 [1887]: 76–78). Again, an expert commentator praises his efforts but concludes that his measurements (in this case of elevation) showed only "values that are quite relative" (79).

QUESTIONS AND ANSWERS

> At Pakechewa, where I camped next, I determined not
> to wait for the chief's present, but to give mine first,
> which would be an immense saving to us. I accord-
> ingly sent off to him a small present. It was returned
> promptly with the remark that it was not the custom of
> the Mahenge to receive presents from their strangers,
> but that he would come in the evening and talk over it.
> He did arrive in the evening and proved to be a fat, in-
> telligent personage, from whom I received a good deal
> of information; but as I never got the same story from
> any two persons, I had learned by this time to put no
> faith in anything I was told. (1:194)

As activities of knowledge production, observing, collecting, measuring, naming, classifying, and mapping occupied the daily life and the minds of explorers. On balance, these methods gave our explorers the certainty that their work would make valuable contributions to the natural history of central Africa. Yet none really worked as expected, and the cumulative impression we get is of science untidily assembled in the service of imperial designs. If anything, the production of ethnographic knowledge was even more erratic.

Not so long ago, the historiography of anthropology and ethnography recovered a long history of the methodologization of travel, an *ars apodemica* that had its start in the philosophy of one sixteenth-century logician, Petrus Ramus, or Pierre de la Ramée. A growing number of travel instructions and manuals began to formulate questions and set the rubrics that would allow travelers to gain and present knowledge. Such knowledge was, of course, most useful to the rulers of states and their bureaucracies; hence we also find the origins of "statistics" (lit., knowledge of matters that concern the state), including questionnaire-surveys in this tradition.[22]

Since the time of discoveries and conquest, seafarers and other travelers had received instructions that often contained detailed lists of tasks to perform and of questions to ask. Toward the end of the eighteenth century and at the beginning of the nineteenth we get attempts by French au-

thors such as the comte de Volney and Constantin Degerando to transform the old art of travel into a scientific enterprise.[23] At just about the
time our authors began to draw up their agenda, a British committee,
headed by E. B. Tylor, one of the founders of our discipline, published the
famous *Notes and Queries* (1874), a manual that is usually credited with
an important role in defining object and research agenda of anthropology.

In view of all this, it is intriguing to discover that the explorers of central Africa seldom related the knowledge they reported to such manuals
and that hardly anyone admits using a questionnaire as a methodological tool. They were probably acquainted with Francis Galton's 1855 classic, *The Art of Travel; or, Shifts and Contrivances Available in Wild
Countries*. Becker mentions a *Manuel du voyageur* that circulated among
the members of the Belgian expeditions, but only Coquilhat actually tells
us that he organizes information according to a prepared questionnaire.[24]
Of Torday we know, though not from the works we have been quoting,
that he traveled with a French version of *Notes and Queries*.[25]

Though the travelogues appear to ignore other manuals and questionnaires, nearly all the authors interrupt their narrative to give detailed,
systematic advice and instructions to future travelers (see also the extensive appendices to Becker's work). Wissmann later published a hand-
book for colonial agents (1895), repeatedly quoted in the 1900 edition
of another work of this genre, the *Manuel du voyageur et du résident au
Congo* (1896), a collective effort by explorers and early administrators
in the service of the Free State.

In sum, there is little evidence that our authors used questionnaires,
and when they did it seems to have been for organizing the presentation
rather than the gathering of knowledge. Manuals and questionnaires
were then and, I would argue, are now primarily instructions for writing. In this sense, form precedes content, which brings me to a second
observation. The only way to gather ethnographic information is to question people; the travelers had a hard time going about it. Hilton-Simpson,
who was a keen observer of Torday's methods of research, touches on
the struggle to "obtain any great amount of information" in a particular region. "For we had to rely," he explains, "mainly upon our own observation, and therefore could glean nothing of the social organization,
&c., of the tribe" (1911, 138). Thomson sets out the problem in the preface to his work.

> My travelling experience has convincingly shown me that no one can hope
> to become genuinely acquainted with African society without a long residence
> among the people. The traveller passing through the country sees practically

very little. Many people will be astonished to learn, that during the fourteen
months I was in the interior, I never once saw an African marriage, or the
burial of a native, or the ceremonies on such occasions as the birth of a child.
My aim has been to describe *only what I myself saw*. Hence the comparative
scantiness of anthropological detail. (1881, viii–ix)

After this bit of prefatory rhetoric Thomson does note that he made "inquiries" whenever he saw dances and initiation rituals and other events.
But his words signal a conundrum all explorers faced. Few were as candid as Thomson. Lack of time and restricted linguistic competences were
the crucial limiting factors. Occasionally, as we saw in the second chapter, travel became stationary and narratives switched to "monographic"
passages on peoples and customs, but reports and reflections on ethnographic questioning are rare. One exception to this rule raises questions
of truth and meaning we need to address now (deferring others to the
following chapter).

At one point in his travelogue, Coquilhat interrupts his narrative to
offer general thoughts on the difficulty of "getting exact answers to
ethnographic and geographic questions." He makes his observations after having lived in this particular region for quite some time. Since he
had learned the language, the problem is not one of communication; it
is of a moral nature. "By instinct," he says of his informants, "they feel
the urge to deceive you" (1888, 244). He thinks, however, he can get by
this obstacle with the help of method: "I have come to the point where
I never interrogate directly," he says, and he goes on to develop this procedure in some detail. When he seeks information, he tells us,

I make, in an ordinary tone of voice, a remark indicating an arbitrary opinion on a point I want to clarify. Often I even affirm the contrary of what I
was told by a preceding interlocutor. If the native is caught unawares, that is,
if he thinks that I don't care, he will correct me with the exact answer and I
will be satisfied for the time being. I will then repeat my inquiry with another
individual on other days and in other circumstances and only after having
gathered, compared, and controlled a large number of responses, I will obtain more or less reliable results. Experience has revealed to me the grave errors I had committed before I adopted this method—a method which admittedly requires a long stay and knowledge of the native language. (244)

This is an impressive example of ethnomethodology *avant la lettre;* it
more than foreshadows "controlled comparison," an issue much debated
in my student days. But what I find truly remarkable about this reflection—given the perspective and intentions of this study—is something
else. It does not seem to have occurred to Coquilhat for a moment that

the natives' alleged mendaciousness is matched by the tricks and dissimulation he recommends as his own method.[26] Let us be clear on
this: in situations of chronic strife and political oppression Africans probably took on habits of deceit in dealing with uninvited and dangerous
strangers. And no one likes being lied to, as every ethnographer probably can confirm. But to project moral faults (or immoral intentions) on
informants and treat the problem of veracity by using contemptuously
manipulative methods and legitimizing them as scientific inquiry is to set
up a double standard. What kind of truth can we—and I use the first
person plural advisedly, because little has changed in this respect—hope
to unearth if the "exact" ethnographic response we extract forces us to
ignore the political and communicative conditions of our inquiries or,
worse, to conduct our interrogations from a position of assumed or real
power, at least as long as we can get away with it?

I am not indulging in a fit of righteousness or trying to get even with
Coquilhat and other ethnographers for the moral judgments they passed
on their informants. What counts is to perceive the distance supposedly
successful methods create or presuppose between researcher and re-
searched—a distance through which madness gapes—unless we find
ways to bridge the void with acts of intellectual empathy and imagination. Such acts require us to go beyond ourselves, beyond positions an
ill-understood rationality makes us take, and approach the ecstatic.

NINE

Making Sense

Knowledge and Understanding

A story makes its sense as it unfolds. The texts that make up our corpus are stories, at least much of the time. Their sense is in their plot: they tell of the progress of exploration. European travelers with their African, Afro-Portuguese, and Arab-Swahili auxiliaries enacted scenarios set down in metropolitan scripts. There were instructions from sponsors, the writings of earlier travelers, and the research agendas of many scientific disciplines. In Africa these scripts were rehearsed and (trans)formed in encounters with the people and the environment. Contrary to what its myths would have us believe, exploration, its activities and its findings, constantly had to be made sense of. Physically, travelers moved by walking or being carried. Mentally, their efforts were supported by sense and meaning. Far from being just collectors of knowledge, explorers needed to justify their presence on this continent, spell out what they understood, explain what they observed, give reasons for their interpretations. This process of making sense—as we now try to document it and probe it for evidence—will help us further revise our received images of exploration and of ethnography's origins in that enterprise.

MOTIVES AND IDEAS

> In the summer of 1878, just escaped from Edinburgh
> University, where I had been studying my favourite sci-

ence of geology, I was wandering somewhat listlessly
through the pleasant hills and dales of my native
county, Dumfriesshire. Like most young fellows emerging into manhood, I wondered what my lot in life
would be, and strove to set before myself some aim to
guide my actions. While in this mood of uncertainty, I
observed one day a simple paragraph in the newspapers, stating that the Royal Geographical Society were
about to despatch an exploring expedition to east-central
Africa, under the command of Mr. Keith Johnston.
That paragraph gave the "turn of the tide of my affairs," and determined my future action. Though I had
never for a moment thought of Africa as the possible
field of my future work, yet like a bright ray of inspira-
tion it immediately struck me that there was ample
scope for all my unused energy. Visions of adventure
in unexplored lands, and among strange tribes, rose
vividly before me. The geology of this great region was
also unknown. Might I not with my newly acquired
knowledge throw some light on this subject? (1:2–3)

Throughout this study we kept our focus on exploration as practice, as
concrete, localized, sensual activity. Imperialist ideologies, the dynamics
of expanding capitalism, and also the cultural topos of travel and the
ideals of scientific progress remained in the background. We called on
the growing literature that documents this background only as necessary
to account for the actions and opinions of our travelers. As much as possible, we again let the sources speak for themselves.

On the whole, the travelers are not much concerned with examining
the personal motives that had made them accept their missions. Direct
statements (in contrast to extrapolations from reflective passages here
and there) are rare. A notable exception comes from Becker, candidly
tracing his vocation's apparent contradictions in the preface to his work.
Like others, he looked up to his predecessors. Though he is critical of
Stanley's "march-or-die" style of travel, he admits being influenced by
his writings. Stanley's ability to give exploration the sense of drama filled
him with a "nostalgia for the unknown, first cause of my departure"
(1887, 1:xvi). Becker confesses (*j'avoue*) that the decision to leave Europe was a matter of passion, of giving in rather than making a deliber-
ate choice. Long before he gets to the hardships and dangers of travel,
he invokes the topos of fever to describe the explorer's calling. Then he
cites himself in this passage from the end of his travelogue.

Fed on numerous accounts which kindled our vocation, doubling in our imaginations the beauty of the sites our predecessors described, we generally expected to find concentrated in our own travels all the fairytales, all the poetic
dangers, all the extraordinary adventures spread through a hundred volumes.
Before we took to the road, we drew a program, much as young girls fashion for themselves an ideal of love long before they fall in love. It was all daz-
zling scenery, thrilling encounters, fantastic hunts, difficulties conquered,
heroic fights, inebriating triumphs. But in the face of austere reality, much of
this has to be written off. All these ingredients are rare spices in a rather un-
pleasant routine, few and far between. (2:350)

Becker means to dampen the enthusiasm that, he notes, got recruiters
for the Free State fifty times more applications than they could use; later
he sorts out motivations and aptitudes in his traveler's typology that had
our attention in chapter 2.

Coquilhat as well begins his book by quoting Stanley: "'It was a passion for the unknown and the novel which brought the young lieutenants
Vangele and Coquilhat to Africa.' This is how M. Stanley puts it in his book
Cinq années au Congo, and what he says is true" (1888, 1).[1] But he insists
on adding, "it was also enthusiasm for the great and useful humanitarian
work" of Leopold II. Like Becker, he needs to distance himself from anything that hints at romanticism. Addressing criticism of his group's motives,
he says of himself and his companions (all of them military men),

We were neither tired of humanity nor tired of the military profession. We
greatly enjoyed the benefits of civilization and were not inclined to melancholy. Rather, we believed we would find fresh sources of satisfaction and direction in a new kind of hard work and in the fight against difficulties and
the unforeseen; and we hoped to steel our characters. Finally, we wanted to
test our strength and find out whether we too could add a stone to the building. I must say this because others have raised questions: maybe we had exaggerated ideas of our capacity for resistance, but we didn't have too many
illusions about the living conditions waiting for us in Africa. (1888, 1–10)[2]

Other writers were less articulate (or less wordy), but Germans in particular mentioned one motive common to exploration and earlier (or
later) travel in Africa: big-game hunting or sports, as it was then called
in English. Pogge appears here as the leader of two expeditions, but on
the first he actually started out as one of Major Alexander von Homeyer's
three companions. When Homeyer and the two others (a botanist by the
name of Hermann Soyaux and an Austrian officer, Anton Lux) left Africa
for health reasons, leadership of the expedition fell to the person who
had not professed any scientific interests.

Pogge had traveled as a hunter in Natal and in the Cape (in 1865) and offered his services to the African Society as "an amateur of hunting and a collector." His application was accepted by Bastian (*MAGD* 4, no. 3 [1884]: 150) and he was permitted to join the party at his own expense. When he published his travelogue, he insisted it should be appreciated as the work of "a plain farmer and hunter" (1880, iv).

That the prospect of hunting for big game was one of the attractions of African travel is confirmed indirectly by a disparaging statement I found in Büttner's final account: "Someone who hoped to travel in these regions to test his courage and love of adventure in a struggle with rapacious, dangerous beasts would be quite disappointed. Even the traveler who wanted to do some hunting in order to feed, or help feed, his caravan would soon be taught by hunger and misery to discount this factor altogether and to regard every success at hunting, even the smallest, as a boon" (*MAGD* 5, no. 3 [1889]: 210).

Fascination with incongruity was not my only reason for putting nostalgia for the unknown alongside big-game hunting in the mix of motives that attracted these men to exploratory travel. Galton showed how intimately the two were connected around the middle of the century and they remained so at least to the end of our period. "Ever ready to help forward the efforts of the scientist and sportsman" (1911, vii) was Hilton-Simpson's telling phrase when he got word of his place in Torday's expedition. Seemingly contradictory motives and pursuits—scientist and sportsman, professional and amateur, scholar and adventurer—flamed in the imagination of future explorers and often in the daily practice of accomplished travelers. Not knowing what chance encounters will bring—and not trying to negate or control the strain this uncertainty causes—fuels a longing for the unknown. That, it seems to me, is one of the afflictions or strengths (for the less foolhardy) ethnography inherited from its beginnings in exploration.

THEORIES AND EXPLANATIONS

> The whole country seemed covered with colossal blocks. Some formed caps to pillars; some had almost reached the condition of rocking-stones, and everywhere they lay scattered in wild confusion, naturally making the unscientific mind conclude that there in this chaos is the evidence for some grand convulsion of nature, which has smashed the underlying rocks and hurled the fragments into the position they now oc-

> cupy. But this would be a mistake. A moment's reflec-
> tion shows that here we have only another instance of
> the "long results of time," the infinitely little working
> unceasingly in the falling rain, the changing tempera-
> ture, and the corroding influence of carbonic acid.
> (1:227)

When Becker, describing how he and others were eager to leave for Africa, spoke of "a program" they drafted, he more than hinted at connections between motives and explanations that take shape in projects before, and results after, the fact. Both give meaning to what the travelers undertook to do. It would be anachronistic to seek elaborate research designs behind the exploration of central Africa; the young men drew their shared expectations from a pervasive but rather vague paradigm of natural history. Also, their expeditions approached and in some cases crossed the watershed between exploration and occupation. No matter how deeply individual travelers or sponsoring institutions believed in their scientific mission, they saw their task above all as practical, as an assignment to carry out. But—we argue in this chapter—that does not mean travelers had no need for meaning or taste for theories and explanations. Hypotheses and plans helped them confront danger and violence, as Coquilhat explains after his initial contacts with the hostile Bangala: "The reader will appreciate the labor of imagination I carried out during the long months that preceded the realization of this mission. I will spare him the reflections made, the eventualities considered, the hypotheses envisaged, and the plans conceived by my mind, tormented by the fever of the enterprise" (1888, 185). Here is testimony, apt and telling, of the feverish, ecstatic state of the mind of a traveler faced with the task of exploration.

Most of our authors were eager to go beyond mere description and to make connections between phenomena or events they observed. In brief asides, sometimes in lengthy disquisitions, they interrupt their narratives to offer explanations and engage in theorizing. As we saw in the preceding chapter, they all brought along conceptions of natural history, of race and evolution, and used them to present information they had gathered in taxonomies and typologies.[3] Terms from the vocabulary of evolutionism and Darwinian phrases, always loosely applied, come easily to them but, on the whole, their arguments show a distinct lack of enthusiasm for systematic, encompassing, evolutionary reasoning. Throughout the sources they express their dislike of facile theorizing from a distance. Of course explorers' prejudices often clash with the facts they report and occasionally even with opinions they voice in other

places of the narrative. Yet again and again, faced with the living presence of the strange and the exotic, the authors refuse to settle for the generalizations or stereotypes that were current at the time.

To document this struggle for meaning against the temptations of received ideas, we look at three topoi of anthropological and sociological
discourse that challenged rational understanding and moral evaluation
at the time (and do so now): race, magic, and cannibalism.

RACE

Obvious as it may be as an example for scientific categories brought
along to Africa, "race" figures surprisingly little in our sources. Or rather
they make surprisingly few references to the Africans they encountered
as evidence for evolutionary theories, though Büttner does distinguish
"Bantu" from "negro" types (to be quoted below). But the overwhelming majority of our authors shared a tacit assumption of difference that
was racist in that it linked external appearances to intellectual and moral
qualities and, more specifically, dark skin color and certain facial features to *inferior* qualities. A firm belief in their racial superiority, a kind
of social Darwinism, constituted an unshakable a priori that influenced
the production of knowledge about Africans in every imaginable respect.

Here, in the context of race, the question of period- and context-
bound prejudices is inevitable. Was it possible for a nineteenth-century
European explorer of Africa not to be racist in the sense just described?
Limiting ourselves to our sources, we can answer this question positively,
albeit not simply. First, with Torday as an example in mind, we can point
to individuals whose cultural background and personal decency kept
them from speaking about and, presumably, treating Africans with racist
contempt. Second, a closer analysis of the texts would reveal that all travelers, even those who showed themselves most explicitly racist, occasionally made statements about Africans that contradicted the dominant
ideology. We have seen in earlier chapters and will note again the capacity of experiences to subvert racist certainties. But one explorer de-
viated dramatically from the expected pattern. Strangely enough, he is
on the margin of our group and was not an intellectual giant or even a
terribly serious person (his travelogue is perhaps the most casually composed of all). Dr. Willy Wolff was one of the few to leave the expedition
he was assigned to, simply because he thought he had seen and done
enough. Wolff was a physician (like Buchner and Wolf) and a member
of the German Congo Expedition under Lt. Schulze.

In the preface to his travelogue Wolff himself announces that his contribution to the knowledge of Africa will be rather different from what the reader may expect. Indeed, the second part of his programmatic statement is unmatched among our sources.

> The special purpose of this document is this: to initiate the reader in the difficulties with which the organization of such an expedition, particularly ours, had to struggle; furthermore, to bring the negroes, whom we mostly only know as savage, uncultivated, and uncultivatable populations, closer to us as human beings. The attempt is made to describe the doings and activities, even the thoughts of the negroes down to minute detail and to compare their life with that of the Europeans. Therefore, the reader who expects to find in such a travelogue only savages and cannibals will be greatly surprised to meet in Africa people who are as reasonable as they are in Europe. (1889, iv)

Later Wolff puts some of his insights together, for instance in the chapter titled "*Genus homo:* Why Are the Negroes Black?" He begins with a discussion of creationism versus evolutionism and opts for the latter: it "implies the unity of the human species under which the different races are classed as subspecies" (80). While he thus seems to accept his contemporaries' concept of race (a fairly neutral synonym for a population or ethnic group), he almost immediately argues that the differences separating the races as customarily distinguished are so insignificant that "it is clearly very difficult to posit a correct principle according to which humans could be divided into different races" (81). He goes on to show the arbitrariness of earlier attempts based on cranial structure or growth of hair, points to the effects of mixture or interbreeding, and concludes, "We are compelled to believe that physical traits can change" (85).

Finally he faces what must have been the most popular question about racial difference because it regards the most visible difference between Europeans and Africans: color. Should the dark color of Africans be seen as a racial trait or as an effect of the environment? Wolff brings several arguments on not regarding color as an essential trait of any race and then asks a question of those who think a dark skin is caused by the tropical sun, a question few of his contemporaries would have thought of: "How might the negroes imagine the origin of white color? Don't they perhaps also assume that it is the effect of the sun, that we are bleached by a cold sun?" (86).

The issue here is not whether Wolff was a more decent person than his colleagues. Our concern is epistemology, not morals. His case is remarkable because the scientific background he presumably shared with his contemporaries did not dull his imagination and courage or keep him

from taking positions others would never have expressed for fear of losing their precarious beliefs in European superiority. Sloppily put, they
were not crazy enough to do it.

But back to Wolff and race. In a later chapter he takes up the question of African savagery and backwardness. He qualifies others' reference to savages as "so-called," "because it takes all the European con-
ceit and arrogance to call these quiet, decent, and talented people
savages" (197). And yet he does not want to romanticize a noble savage
and argues, accomplishing a remarkable feat of "recognition" (more on
this below), that those who express a low opinion of Africans make a
fundamental mistake.

> When comparisons are made with other races, especially with the white race,
> the negroes usually are not matched with the majority of the other people,
> the rural population. Generally, most of the travelers and writers have in mind
> their own person and social class when they make comparisons. Also, usu-
> ally one does not distinguish the capacity for education from education and
> when critique is expressed one does not take sufficiently into consideration
> that a lower level of education or rather of what we call education may have
> many other reasons than a lack of capacity for training. (197–98)

With ideas available since the Enlightenment, Wolff takes a position on race
and formulates a point of departure for producing knowledge about
Africans that the founders of modern anthropology such as Franz Boas
adopted a generation later. At the same time, he is not among the most productive ethnographers in our sample (but the expedition was not well organized and he stayed only one year). In the end he left because he saw no
use in risking his life. The general situation did not permit work with
Africans based on mutual respect and confidence. Anyhow, the expedition
had accomplished its true aim: "The ring that separated the peoples who
lived further in the interior from [those on] the coast was broken; now it
was up to other members of the expedition to reap the fruits and to penetrate deeper into the interior with a larger, better equipped caravan" (235).

MAGIC AND RELIGION

Magic, embodied in objects called fetishes, intrigued the explorers. They
diagnosed it as evidence for the inherently backward, superstitious state
of the African mind locked in a state of savagery. Yet close attention to
the reported facts and events shows that magic as it was practiced in
daily life often subverted this stance.

Deconstruction of the stereotype of fetishism (often a synonym for magic or religion) began when travelers realized that magic was a complex set of practices ranging from what we would now call traditional medicine to personal and collective rites of protection and to aggressive actions identified as witchcraft and sorcery. The travelogues' ethnographic passages have instances of all the above and often add evaluative or explanatory remarks to them. Given the currency of evolutionism, some travelers showed remarkably little interest in seeking the underlying unity of these phenomena in a postulated stage of inferior mental development. Of course such a position would have closed the books on magic and kept African objects and practices from becoming a matter of concern for the observers—which is what happened in some cases.

When the explorers realized that these superstitious practices were about power, they fell in with them. Anything relating to power concerned them. Magic unsettled their own claims to superiority and, though the discourse of fetishism went a long way to resettle them, evolutionary classification of power objects and rituals created no safe distance.[4] Two concrete instances illustrate such an encounter with magic— one productive, the other not. To be precise, the first one is about divination, but the authors, Capelo and Ivens, would not quibble.

> My arrival caused a considerable sensation and the Sova [chief] declared that he would not allow me to pass on to the Cuanza without consulting the fetishes, as he feared that evil might otherwise come of it. I was compelled to submit to this absurd arrangement, and remain quiet while my future movements were being discussed and decided in secret councils. Fortunately, the oracle was favourable, and I was free to depart on the following day. (1882, 1:128)

The gain of knowledge from this confrontation was nil; it did nothing but confirm "fetishism" as a category a priori.

Matters were different in another case, one of the rare instances described as it originated and developed through time (or a space within the travelogue). Becker was in Karema, by then a formidable military fort not easily recognizable as the "hospitable and scientific" station it should have been according to the IAA charter. Explorers had settled in and the nearby population began to have second thoughts about the blessings of civilization. The power of the whites (to recruit labor, procure food supplies and building material without respecting local authorities) was challenged by a young chief who had recently taken up his office. At the same time, Becker met with defiance from an "old friend," a *nganga* (practitioner of magic; in this case also the keeper of a spirit shrine). What makes this episode especially interesting is that Becker obviously draws for its account on his diary and refrains from correcting earlier observations in the light of what he learned and understood later. Thus we find him groping for the predictable stereotypes before he realizes that the two forms of resistance, political and "magical," are connected.

The confrontation begins with a "magician" who demands the sacrifice of two oxen, to appease the Spirit of the Lake for the intrusion of the whites. Becker brushes off the *nganga*'s request: "I don't care to sacrifice two head of cattle to the greed of a clever old man exploiting popular superstitions" (1887, 2:291–92). Then he begins a discussion with Kanghérennghèrè.[5] In the course of the dialogue Becker turns the magician's argument around, taking his turn at exploiting popular superstition: the spirit is angry with his people, he tells him, because they refuse to cooperate with the whites. He has left his shrine on an island in the lake and now lives in the little house he, Becker, constructed for meteorologic observations. Obviously enjoying this turn, Becker goes on to claim that from now on he alone is entitled to offer sacrifices to, and speak for, the spirit who revealed to him that the *nganga* never was his legitimate spokesman. Then something he had not really expected happens.

> When I made a move to open the door of my observatory, the sorcerer drew back, terrified. He, the mendacious oracle of a force which he lets speak as he pleases, apparently believes in the Spirit of the Lake! Since then, the natives who come close to the station look with respectful terror at the hut where I placed the Mouzimou [*mzimu:* spirit] on my own, private authority. The day after, I was brought a goat and flour which I curtly refused, saying that I alone would be in charge of caring for the Spirit! As to Kanghérennghèrè, I thought it good to reassure him. Among sorcerers, each one owes the other consideration. He may not have got his oxen but, after a few days, I brought him assurance that Mousamouéra was no longer angry with him. (292–93)

All this comment sounds tongue-in-cheek and perhaps cynical, but in a long passage immediately following Becker shows that he did not remain altogether untouched by this confrontation. He takes time to reflect on Kanghérennghèrè as a person and representative of a powerful institution. He places him in the local constellation of power (a conflict between generations), describes his physical appearance and his practices in great detail, and begins to revise his image of him as simple fraud feeding on superstition. "In his sphere," he says, "he is a great politician, one who is conscious of his moral value" and he tells us that "Kanghérenn-ghèré, endowed with a firm and, I believe, sincere faith in the science he inherited, or based on his own experiments, never grows tired of recommending to me his recipes" (294). In the end, the sinister magician becomes his informant, as modern ethnographers would have called him: "Sometimes, I invite him to sit on the *barza* where I make him talk about the origins of his strange practices" (295).

Immediately after this, Becker moves his reflections up to a higher level with generalizations about the lack of ideas among Africans that could be called religious. Here he speaks as the evolutionary theoretician when he assumes that they simply lack the intellectual faculties for abstractions like the notion of a soul. But then, in one of his flashes of irony, he adds: "What a problem for these poor savages—one that we are unable to resolve except with the help of theories that are dogmatic rather than philosophical!" (296). More follows on dreaming, possession, ancestors and spirits of the deceased, and transformation into animals. Then he cranks up the machine of the comparative method and invokes the spirit of Auguste Comte.

> The peoples living on the shores of Lake Tanganyika appear to be advanced by several stages over the Wanyamwezi and Wagogo, who are in the grip of their backward and anti-deist beliefs in the living dead. Among the former, a vague tradition of a beginning, a creation, constitutes real progress on the course toward abstract ideas to which the negro's brain seems to be obstinately opposed. Nonetheless, these populations have not yet got beyond the second stage of religious evolution, that is, of fetishism. (299)

A few pages later (after making a surprisingly modern distinction between diviners and sorcerers), he takes up this thought by including in his taxonomy people from the Marungu region on the western shore of the lake, who "are already given to idolatry, the third stage of religious evolution," because they venerate their chiefs and the statues of important ancestors. Still further on he cites an origin myth (of the Wakwendi and Wanyamwezi) according to which the parents of mankind were made as we are, except that they were endowed with a "caudal appendix," a little tail. "O Darwin!" he exclaims, leaving us to guess whether he speaks admiringly or ironically (304). He continues to present information on religious beliefs until, in a summary, keeping his distance from lived reality, he qualifies these as "inveterate beliefs, ignorant negation of the higher conceptions of our religious systems" (309).

Becker's journey—from sheer prejudice to discovery of another conception of reality and then to a distancing scientific discourse requiring denial of that reality—has an uncanny resemblance to the history of an-thropological approaches to magic and religion. In the space of about twenty pages, it illustrates the "victory" of reason and theory over ex-perience and empirical knowledge that became the predicament of mod-ern anthropology. Yet all our authors did not take such a stance (and Becker did not maintain it in other parts of his travelogue). The ecstatic nature of travel and direct encounters with African realities saw to it that, in practice, the problem of magic and religion would not obey the dictates of current scientific notions. To make this point somewhat more concretely I want to end this section with another instance of con-frontation that did not end in closure.

During his stay at Musumba, the Lunda capital, Pogge found himself in a situation that sticks in my mind as the prime example of clashes between explorers and African holders of power. Reading his richly de-tailed description of visits and return visits, of presents offered and pres-ents received, and of a back-and-forth of royal personages and interme-diaries that preceded and followed his first encounter with the Mwant Yav, I had the distinct impression of a choreographed demonstration of power. While Pogge experienced most of this as a nuisance and as the delaying tactics of a potentate who wanted to make sure that he got as much as possible from this visitor, there are many indications that the other side was playing for time necessary to test and contain the Euro-pean's capacity to impinge on royal power.

Occasionally this subtler purpose comes to the surface, for instance when Pogge, returning from an excursion to nearby regions and ap-proaching the capital, witnesses the mourning for a deceased "princess." Perhaps sensing that death, as it does in most African societies, caused disturbances in relations of power, he notes this indirect message from the chief: "Mwant Yav is supposed to have declared that, as the ruler, he would not tolerate in Musumba any person who wished him ill and op-erated magic against him" (1880, 193). For a while, the Mwant Yav con-tinues his attempts to simplify his relations with the traveler by pressing on him the role of a trader out to buy ivory and slaves. Pogge refuses to play along. Just before he is finally allowed to leave the Lunda capital he reports, in a casual aside, first that the Mwant Yav "often dances by himself in the afternoon, around four o'clock"—a customary demon-stration of chiefly power that may or may not have been triggered by this specific situation—and then that the ruler thwarted another and, as it turns out, last attempt to meet him by letting Pogge know that he is busy "with the fabrication of fetishes" (196, 198). In other words, Pogge, like other Europeans, *knew* magic when he saw it in fetishes and rites because his prior knowledge had prepared him to recognize it there. Yet it apparently never occurred to him that he *experienced* Lunda magic every day, in all its cosmological and political complexity. Like most of his European colleagues, he saw the trees but missed the forest. And that, we may say with postmodern hindsight, may have been to his credit.

CANNIBALISM

Neither Becker's gusto for, nor Pogge's abstinence from, facile theorizing covers the possibilities that were open to our travelers. Even before Torday and Frobenius offered observations and interpretations that would still meet professional standards of acceptability, Coquilhat tried to deal with that pièce de résistance of ethnography—cannibalism. Two reasons made me decide to give his ideas some space in these pages. What he says anticipates contemporary discussions of the subject and, more important for our purposes, illustrates how far the colonial mind was able to reach in an encounter with realities of African experience.

But first we should assemble from other authors a few reports and opinions about cannibalism to show what serious ethnographers were up against. Cannibalism was a topos, definable as a sort of mark in discursive space to which writers of travelogues and proto-ethnographies of central Africa were inevitably drawn. Rather than a topic for exposition and perhaps argument, a topos is a space without place: it is everywhere and nowhere; it goes without saying and may therefore be (almost) without specifiable content. As long as, and to the extent that it remains a topos, cannibalism cannot become a topic or object of ethnographic research.

Much of this ubiquitously elusive material shows up in the travelogue by Torday's companion, Hilton-Simpson.[6] It begins with the title: *Land and Peoples of the Kasai: Being a Narrative of a Two Years' Journey Among the Cannibals of the Equatorial Forest and Other Savage Tribes of the South-Western Congo*. This, though printed in 1911, has the flavor of countless relations from earlier centuries in which cannibals were a synonym for Africans living in the interior of the continent. It does seem to contain an element of specificity and distinction: within the general realm of savagery, cannibalism's environment is the forest but, then, it could easily be shown that the forest (or the "jungle") itself has been a topos to which images and imaginations of savagery have been hitched through the ages. Perhaps we should not make too much of the wording of a title: Hilton-Simpson's publishers may have encouraged him to use it to sell more copies of his book. So we turn to the text, where we find statements like the following (the first part of which we quoted in another context in the preceding chapter).

> Nor could we obtain any great amount of information at Gamba, for we had to rely mainly upon our own observation, and therefore could glean nothing of the social organisation, &c., of the tribe. In the course of conversation, however, we learned that all the other Bankutu villages were in the habit of frequently eating human flesh, but were assured that the people of Gamba were far too virtuous to do anything so horrible. Curiously enough we heard a similar tale in other villages, the inhabitants of the place we happened to be in always claiming to be the only Bankutu who were not cannibals! (1911, 128)

How odd. And how odd that stories of practices everywhere an explorer and his informant *are not* do not lead the traveler to wonder if cannibalism is indeed a common practice like dancing or beer drinking. Nothing in Hilton-Simpson's report or those like it tells us how Africans talked about cannibalism. Did they have unequivocal terms or phrases? Did they use such terms in the register of plain referential speech or did the explorer's questions cause them to respond with metaphors and quotations from a repertoire of the fantastic? But, then, not to have to report exactly how questions were asked, and answers secured, has been a privilege claimed by most ethnographers.

What he cannot make plausible from observation or direct information Hilton-Simpson props up with images he must have felt were additional evidence for cannibalism. This is how he describes the Bankutu: "Small and very dirty in appearance, superstitious, timid, and treacherous, they appear to have been influenced by the oppressive atmosphere and almost ghostly gloom of their native forest."[7] As if this was not enough, the same page has another list of negative characterizations: "The Bankutu, on the other hand, are undersized and ugly, sullen and disagreeable in their manner, and, with the exception of the building of huts, the only art that has been developed...is the art of killing their fellow-men by stealth" (133). What these sweeping statements do show is that the Bankutu were hostile to outside intruders, unwilling to engage in trade relations the travelers could have exploited for their own purposes. Especially annoying was the absence of a visible political organization. Without chiefs to deal with, European exploration's games of power could not be played.

In fairness to Hilton-Simpson, we should note his attempts to bring some critical refinement to the theme, for instance, when he later elaborates on the term *cannibal*. It does not simply designate the occasional, ceremonial flesh-eater. The Bankutu, we are told, "actually stalk and shoot men for food" (148). His descriptions get more and more vivid but, throughout, come from unsubstantiated "information" (see 149). In the end he opens a perspective on cannibalism that gives us an inkling of its political function in colonial discourse: "Some day, no doubt, the forest around Kole may be as peaceful a district as any in Africa, but until the Bankutu have been completely brought into subjection there can never be peace in the land" (149).

Hilton-Simpson's observations and opinions invite comparison with those of his superior, Torday. In his first travelogue Torday too begins by citing rumors and stories until he comes to the Bambala, who—he is certain—practice cannibalism. But he fails to come up with firsthand evidence and does not engage in discussion or explanation except to note he has "never been able to trace any magical or religious basis [for cannibalism]." Unaware of the contradiction this entails, he proposes some applied anthropology (or social engineering) when he suggests: "To wean the Bambala and other tribes from cannibalism it is necessary to give them a *kissi* [a magical prohibition], which will prevent them from eating human flesh under penalty of death if they disobey" (1913, 84). In his later recollections (1925) Torday is even less specific but does reveal yet another twist of the explorer's mind. In the first chapter, somewhat obscurely titled "Coast Impressions—A Cannibal View," he notes observations he made in Kinshasa-Léopoldville before he reached the interior. Among others he describes his crew of Sango paddlers and praises them for their magnificent physique, adding almost admiringly that they turned out to be real cannibals, proven before a magistrate (1925, 21). At that time he was still a colonial agent rather than an ethnographer, which may explain the curious expression of regret at the end of this introductory chapter when he exclaims: "Real cannibals, real savages, real slavers; I was at the door of all of this and had never thought of having a look at it!" (27). For explorers, the cannibal was an object of fantasy—and of desire.

Matters are different with Coquilhat. When he addresses the theme of cannibalism among the Bangala he almost flaunts his carefulness. He begins by recording the usual stories told by others about the Bangala but keeps a skeptical distance: "With respect to this I had been given no proof whatsoever, but the reports made by strangers were unanimous" (1888, 203). Only a few weeks later (he notes the date, June 17 [1884]) he witnesses the return of a war party and the butchering of one of the killed enemies. The pieces were distributed and one of them, "nicely wrapped in a banana leaf," was carried past his camp: "My men were unable to refrain from screaming with horror. In the evening there was a big dance and feast. Our neighbors' cannibalism is proven. It would be neither efficacious nor opportune to try and get them away from this during the initial period [of colonization]" (217).

This first report might not hold up as proof in a court of law, but later Coquilhat has an eyewitness account. Dated October 15 [1884], it is a detailed and ghastly description. The victim was a slave suspected of approaching a local woman with adulterous intentions. Coquilhat observed at close quarters how chief Monganga killed the suspect, how the body was prepared by soaking it for a while in the river, how the flesh was cooked, together with goat meat, in palm oil and salt, and how a festive meal was organized, complete with twenty jars of beer. In the afternoon, the party decided to move the feast to another host who had a supply of beer. They went by canoe and Monganga tried to stop at Coquilhat's wharf. He prevented this, Coquilhat says, "expressing all the horror I have of his cannibalism" (270). The chief responded, "You are joking, aren't you?" In the face of such incomprehension Coquilhat writes again: "At this moment, to use force against cannibalism among the Bangala would be as inefficient and absurd as using it in the Equateur region and elsewhere against the practice of human sacrifice and everything that is deeply entrenched in the customs of the country.... Only a progressive method of education will overcome customs whose monstrosity does not occur to these peoples" (270–71).

In sum, Coquilhat is now convinced of the reality of cannibalism. He finds it abhorrent, and he is aware that its suppression must wait until Europeans have established power. Unlike others who base their indictments on stories and rumors, he does not stop with comments on immorality. He knows the practice exists and he must make sense of it. This makes him embark on an extraordinary theoretical discussion of possible explanations, extraordinary also because his inquiries included arguing with the Bangala.

He first questions the received opinion that cannibalism enacts superstitious ideas such as the belief that eating one's enemy makes one invincible in war. "I discovered nothing of the sort," he states, and points out that the Bangala also eat slaves and people who died from noninfectious diseases. They simply crave human flesh. "This is horrible, I told them one day. Not at all, with some salt it is delicious, was their response." Debating the matter with the Bangala, he resorts to philosophical argument and points to acknowledged differences between people and animals. People have intelligence, belong to the same species, have names, and can talk. His opponents reply: all this only "proves how distinguished it is to eat human flesh" (271). Even the economic argument that to eat a slave is to destroy property does not register. The superb pleasure is worth the loss of an asset (273). As Coquilhat recognizes, until the Bangala accept the fundamental premise of his argument—that the custom is "horrible"—his reasoning will get him nowhere.

After that, he returns to an academic discussion, taking up one of the current explanations of cannibalism as a survival from earlier periods when there was lack of food, especially during times before the current staples, such as manioc and maize, were introduced to Africa. Hunger, he concedes, may indeed have caused people to eat human flesh but cannot be the current cause of cannibalism. Today the Bangala have plenty of food. Fowl, sheep, and goats may be rare but the rivers are full of fish, and Africans will eat just about any animal, including insects. At any rate, he reasons quasi-statistically, based on his observations, the Bangala simply don't consume enough human flesh to allow the inference that need is the cause of their cannibalism. Also, neither women nor certain older people participate in the practice (274).

Having thus rejected the protein-deficiency theory hotly debated among modern anthropologists, he interrupts his reflections and continues the narrative, following his diary until a human sacrifice on the occasion of the death of a chief brings him back to theoretical questions, in this case to the theory of degenerationism. A certain Dr. Sims had cited the people of the upper Congo as evidence for this theory. Coquilhat points out that the present state of these populations is perfectly adapted to climate and environment and that there are no remains whatsoever of an alleged higher earlier stage of civilization. And did our own ancestors who lived at the stage of barbarism—that is, above savagery—not practice "cannibalism, human sacrifice, slavery, polygamy and most of the current customs of the savage negroes?" "In the absence of scientific evidence [to the contrary]," he says, "I prefer to believe that these disadvantaged people are, to say the least, on a neutral level, ready to be led upward" (277).

Taken together with his rebuttals of current explanations, such a statement implies a position of value relativism: cannibalism, though it may be abhorrent to Europeans, is a custom, a cultural choice. Because cannibalism is cultural rather than natural, it can be abandoned. It does not lock Africans into some lower stage of development or make them degenerates who have sunk from earlier levels of civilization.

Though Coquilhat mobilized what current scientific knowledge was available to him, it was not simple logic and common sense that enabled him to deal rationally with a phenomenon whose existence he had no reason to doubt. Unlike those who merely peddled stories and mindlessly reproduced preconceived ideas about cannibalism, he confronted a reality that was beyond his experience and imagination. This, I believe, required an ecstatic move toward its ambiguous challenge. Perhaps local circumstances helped Coquilhat find his unusual stance. Equally plausibly, he gained his knowledge and insights because he dared to leave the confines of received certainties, suspend his "normal" reactions, and talk with people about matters he found abhorrent. His insights still command our respect. Yet Coquilhat's case leaves us with a question. The answer to it must be deeply disturbing to the critic of colonialism (*and the critic of anthropology; the analogies are obvious*). Did his efforts at understanding, made with reason and passion, make Coquilhat ever doubt the colonial enterprise he served with his exploration of the cannibalistic Bangala? Even the fragments of his writing we quoted here and elsewhere in this study indicate that this was, on the whole, not the case. Unlike Becker, or even Wissmann and Frobenius, Coquilhat seldom permitted flashes of understanding to subvert faith in his colonial mission.

As I conclude this section, already quite long, I must point out that, apart from magic and cannibalism, the topic of slavery would have lent itself to documenting most of the principal points. Becker gives it extensive treatment. But slavery is a question we cannot take up without addressing the complex and ambiguous relations between the exploration of central Africa and what contemporaries called the "Arab question." Arabs-Swahili are omnipresent in accounts of approaches from the east and they appear in earlier chapters of our study. Zanzibari auxiliaries were also crucial before and during Free State occupation of the Congo as described, for instance, by Coquilhat. Furthermore, "Orientalism" (see Said 1978) loomed large in the colonial mind and, as was argued in chapter 2, much of the "opening up" of central Africa was but a race with Swahili colonization. I can only repeat what I stated there: slavery is a topic that would extend the scope of this study beyond its self-imposed limits.

KNOWLEDGE AND RECOGNITION

> We get a delightful view, which might well remind us of
> our own Scottish land, in its character of hill and dale,

> clear sparkling stream, open glade studded with stately
> trees, and cultivated field. Let us take a commanding
> position, and look about us. (1:146)

Preconceived ideas and prefabricated theories helped explorers make sense of strange beliefs and practices. The reactions to cannibalism we just read document the gap between sense and knowledge. The sense we make of things affirms and supports us; knowledge changes us. To find out how travelers dealt with concrete situations and experiences, we must leave the popular topic of Europeans' images and stereotypes projected on Africa and its people or the explorers' grand gestures of theorizing and generalizing. What can our sources tell us about the struggle with glaring contradictions between received theoretical or ideological certainties and their own unexpected, disturbing insights and understandings? When we watch this struggle, we realize how much the making of ethnographic knowledge owes to memory and aesthetic perception, faculties we do not readily associate with research in the social sciences.

As I worked through the sources, I grew more and more puzzled by problems travelers had—producing accomplishments as well as failures—with the intellectual capacity of recognition.[8] That I find this term useful and illuminating has something to do with the connotations it takes on in my native language. Three German glosses for the act of recognition come to mind: *Erkennen,* as in "I know these persons or objects when I see them" (cognition), *Wiedererkennen,* as in "I know them because I remember them" (memory), and *Anerkennen,* as in "I give them the recognition they deserve" (acknowledgment).

With all three connotations in mind, let me now turn to difficulties the explorers of central Africa had with recognizing others as persons. The more I read, the more appalled and intrigued I became by how little recognition (in the sense of *Erkennen* and *Anerkennen*) European travelers had for the Africans they met. More often than not, positive statements are partial ("beautifully built but cruel"): they rarely maintain what they affirm; they almost always hedge it or deny it in the same sentence. An example (out of many similar statements) is Wissmann's brief remark on his encounter with one of the most impressive East African chiefs, a conqueror and serious political player in a game that included Arab-Swahili colonizers: "At Mirambo's I had a most friendly reception (with two bottles of champagne and a slaughtered ox). This, the most important negro I met in Africa, is thoroughly misjudged [*verkannt:* lit., misrecognized] in Europe; I spent three extremely interesting days with this bellicose prince who must inspire respect even in a European" (*MAGD* 3, no. 4 [1883]: 253).

Prejudice, racism, and an obsession with maintaining superiority may account for such twisted, or strained, compliments ("even in a European"). The very people who, at great expense and often at the cost of their lives, ventured into Africa in order to study it deny its peoples recognition. In an earlier chapter, when we spoke of authority and command, we saw how vital it was for explorers to *receive* recognition. Some knew that a give-and-take was necessary to make this relationship work and said so. But even Becker, who went farther than most of his colleagues in this respect, eventually defends an outright colonialist position. Toward the end of his account, he reflects on the role of recognition (*reconnaissance*) in maintaining his position as the absolute chief of Karema. He concludes that any appeal to mutual recognition would undermine his authority and be incompatible with the European's mission as the emissary of a superior race (see 1887, 2:333–34). As far as I can tell, Torday was the only one to condemn colonization as an injustice. Apart from occasional fits of whimsy among others, all our travelers were convinced that their assignment to produce knowledge gained rather than lost by maintaining superiority and distance. It was not for them to ponder the epistemological consequences of the exercise of power.

Moving on to recognition as *Wiedererkennen,* we note in these travelogues an even more intriguing *denial* of recognition. For years I have told my students, perhaps a bit flippantly, that the kinds of things explorers and ethnographers sought and found in Africa and reported as strange customs—spectacular fertility rites, processions, harvest festivals, or masked dances—took place too ten miles outside Oxford or Cambridge, and certainly in the villages around Berlin, Brussels, or Vienna during the last third of the nineteenth century. If this view is even half accurate, explorers made strikingly little reference to déjà vu, recognition as *Wiedererkennen,* when they noted African peasants' countenance, speech, daily work, seasonal worries, or rituals. An exception to this rule is Wolff's recognition of the familiar in the strange when he compared races. A second example occurs early in his work, when the expedition passed Dahomey on its way to the Congo. He observed some "fetish priests" working on magical protection for the small boats crossing the dangerous surf that prevented larger ships from anchoring close to the coast. "I am firmly convinced," he says, "that these people have the same success as the processions that in many regions of Europe are supposed to pray to heaven for rain or otherwise favorable weather" (1889, 35).

Another example I found in a remarkable passage by Coquilhat relates to the topic of physiognomy below. Meanwhile we can consider his observation about drinking parties on the banks of the Congo: "These drinking contests sometimes take on gargantuan proportions and in that case, instead of ending like a scene in a picture by Teniers [the Flemish genre painter], they often finish with squabbles that degenerate into bloody fights" (1888, 267). Once again, recognition stated and taken back in the same breath. And were the scenes Teniers had in mind always as peaceful as genre painting made them appear?[9]

Finally, we come to the exceptional signs of recognition given by two German travelers. One, by Wolff, regards the custom of administering the ordeal to find out who might have caused the death of a person: "Terrible as this custom may at first seem, this sort of tribunal is by far less grisly than the witch trials that were fashionable among us for such a long time" (1889, 52). Böhm makes the same point in reverse when he qualifies African practices of pursuing sorcerers as expressing a primitive stage of development because they resemble what we have left behind (1888, 92). Wolff aligns himself with Africans; Böhm sets himself apart from them. Interestingly enough, on another occasion both authors use the same formula to designate similarities they see between African and European practices (past, in Böhm's case; present, in Wolff's). They call what Africans do *ländlich-sittlich*, literally rural-ethical, that is, acceptable by the standards of a rural society (1888, 69; 1889, 54).

Whereas they seem to suppress recognition (as *Wiedererkennen*) with regard to persons, practices, and institutions, travelers frequently recognize in foreign parts features of familiar landscapes. With the consistency of a topos, *recognition as remembering* is evoked in countless descriptions of the physical environment (which thereby turns into a recognizable landscape). Here are a few examples I happened to note in the reports of German travelers; one could easily find more in other sources. Gierow, who accompanied Schütt through parts of Angola, writes: "The country here has many meadows, rich with flowers, which remind us very much of our home country" (*MAGD* 3, no. 2 [1882]: 109). Or take Lt. Schulze recalling a road "accompanied by a long mountain range recalling in its form the Vosges [where he was stationed in the military]" (*MAGD* 4, no. 4 [1885]: 282). Lt. Kund writes, "No one would get the idea that he is in the tropics. He would first think of the least attractive places in the Marken [regions around Berlin], or of the high plains of the Hunsrück or Westerwald" (*MAGD* 4, no. 6 [1885]: 373). And later, "The country, especially when the clouds are very low as is the case today, reminds one of a European landscape. One could think of the upper parts of Lake Zurich, of course without the alpine background, rarely enough visible" (381).[10] A most intriguing example of this topos is reported by Büttner. His caravan came to a village in mountainous country: "The village, although located at a high altitude, is surrounded by mountains that are still higher. Kornelius insisted that one of them resembled the Pilatus [a mountain near Lucerne in Switzerland]" (1890, 125). Kornelius, remember, was Büttner's African companion from Ghana who had been to Europe. The episode also shows that the travelers exchanged and sometimes debated images of recognition.

That recognition could also become appropriation (and then take on a slightly crazy twist) appears from a passage in Böhm's letters. He observed that the mountain country of Usagara "gives the impression of southern Switzerland. Sometimes the African props are truly striking in a scenery that resembles so much European landscapes; the troupes of...black warriors, bands of monkeys, parrots, and hornbills don't really fit this frame" (1888, 56).

Not only landscapes caused recognition, but also the fauna and flora and even meteorologic events brought up memories ("a real Belgian rain," exclaims one of the Belgian writers). Recognition played a role when travelers described the people's physiognomy, another source of knowledge they liked to tap, occasionally to support their moral judgments but mostly to establish classificatory traits and types.[11] Although some among our authors may have been familiar with physiognomic theories popular at the time, I found no attempts to present relevant observations systematically. All of them associated physiognomy with character, race, and class—faces are qualified as more or less "negroid" or more or less noble. If we add, as the explorers often did, pairs of qualifiers such as stupid/intelligent, vulgar/refined, honest/shifty, the game of physiognomy had a large number of possible permutations that could be passed off as pseudo-specific observations. And this is not even counting the fact that physiognomic judgments could also depend on parts of the face (eyes, nose, mouth, forehead). Nor does it cover confusion and equivocation through failure to distinguish between the form of a face (its morphology, one could say) and the expression inferred from the way a face is "set" or used in communication. Also, many statements about faces are in fact interpretations of gaze (someone "looks" honest), that is, of intentions and messages expressed in situated contexts of interaction. In other words, they do not at all support the typecasting or generalization they occasion.

Because all recognition entails some form of reaching out, it is often not easy to draw a line that separates recognition from projection. The following (admittedly rather exceptional) passages by Coquilhat leave me with an eerie feeling of uncertainty—did he recognize the familiar in the strange, or did he cover the strange with familiar images? Juxtaposed, the two texts offer yet another example of unresolved contradictions in pronouncements about Africans. Coquilhat first addresses the notorious difficulties a European seems to have telling African faces apart. They all look alike. Not so, he says, "an extended study makes him see all the kinds of physiognomy which exist among us." As if sensing that he may have gone too far with this extraordinary admission, he continues with a *toutefois:* "Nevertheless, the gaze/expression of the Congolese from the interior generally indicates a certain degree of dissimulation, deceit, and defiance. I know of exceptions to this rule, but only very few" (1888, 330). Then, immediately following this paragraph, Coquilhat treats us to following gallery of portraits.

> To me, the Bangala express a series of well defined types. Mata Buiké represents, under ordinary circumstances, the subtle geniality of a peasant from Normandy, but when he is preoccupied with something disagreeable his fatherly face becomes uncommonly hard. Mata Monpinza recalls the placid disposition of a good justice of the peace. Mongonga has the rotundity of Roger Bontemps; in the manner of the well-to-do he deigns to laugh now and then, something that permits him to show off the beautiful teeth of the unbridled cannibal he is. Nyamalembe looks to be smiling and crying at the same time. Mata Ipéko has the cold correctness of a public prosecutor. Mata M'Popo is the good fellow and libertine. Monpata is a serious and energetic type. Monganga Doua has seen it all; his gait is solemn and he carries his head like the Holy Sacrament. N'Joko is a thirty-five-year-old dandy, at once good-hearted and a family man. Imbembé has the distinction of a well-bred plotter. Muélé has the external appearance of a tough businessman. N'Gélé expresses insolence without being conscious of it, and so on. As to the women, I easily discover, among the young ones, the coquettish type, the modest, the cold, the excitable, the dainty, the down-to-earth and, among the old ones, I immediately recognize the fusspot, the gossip, the harpy, the good housewife, the one who regrets her plumpness. (330)

At least as far as African men are concerned—all the persons named here are chiefs or notables Coquilhat had observed in endless meetings and negotiations—the text demonstrates the physiognomic method's dialectical capacity to make of individuals generic types and, in doing this, to restore to them a concreteness that enables the reader to relate to persons who would otherwise have remained indistinct cannibalistic Bangala. To some extent, this strategy works in its characterization of women; while they remain generic they are not presented as just one undifferentiated category.

My use of "generic" in this comment may appear inconsistent but reflects an epistemological position: genres structure practices of knowledge production as they structure practices of speaking or communicating. Genres are productive as long as they mediate between the general and the specific. If generic labels fail to mediate—as almost all designations of evolutionary stages, of race, of religion, and of ethnicity do— they have the opposite effect; they make the specific disappear. They cover up the specific practices explorers sought in their travels and we seek in our field research. An unexamined cultural tenet has us believe that abstraction is difficult, that it requires higher faculties (which explorers often denied to Africans) and special training. Not at all; as Hegel once argued, abstract thinking is most pronounced in the domain of popular images and stereotypes.[12] Explorers may have made sense, to themselves and their readers, when they deployed current concepts and theories. But when something in their experiences made them resist facile generalizations, they came up with insights we too find worth their efforts.

This last point brings me to two further aspects of recognition our authors noted. The first one reports bodily reactions to an event that demands recognition: Wolf is observing Africans. He describes this scene of the arrival of their caravan among the Kuba, who had never before seen a European riding an ox: "Some were speechless with astonishment and covered their mouth with a cupped hand, others ran around confused holding their spears while one woman stared at me with an expression of utmost surprise, forcefully pinching the folds of her belly such that the pain she inflicted on herself reflected in her face" (Wissmann et al. 1891, 227). The second relates a reaction of recognition that comes suddenly and creates understanding. Torday describes such an event. It reminds me of T. S. Kuhn's "instant paradigm switch," also described as conversion, though I would interpret it as a dramatic instance of coeval experience in the face of danger. On one of his earlier travels he had taken a boat ride down the rapids near the site that became Stanleyville/ Kisangani.

I think those seconds were the most glorious of my life and it came as a revelation to me that these negroes, for whom I had had the contempt that many
a civilised man feels towards savages, were giants compared to me, and from
that moment my heart went out to them. I do not mean to say that I was
aware of this sentiment at once; all I really felt was the admiration that no
man can withhold from the strong and the brave; and as with women pity is
often the first step on the path to love, with men admiration leads to sympathy and friendship. (Torday 1913, 29)

AESTHETIC JUDGMENTS
AND THE SUBVERSIVENESS OF BEAUTY

> The Mahenge...are a race evidently superior to the
> Wakhutu. They are much lighter in colour, and have
> far finer features. The men have good figures, though
> many are somewhat effeminate in this respect. Hair on
> their face and head is also unusually abundant, luxuri-
> ant beards being by no means uncommon. The women
> are short and stout, few or none being good-looking.
> Many, however, have not the pendent breasts so char-
> acteristic of East African women. (1:189)

Knowledge of Africa and Africans set up a grammar of oppositions: we
and they, civilized and savage, rational and superstitious, enterprising and
lazy—in sum, white and black. Such ultimately racist binarism characterized colonial discourse from its beginnings. We saw it in many examples.
True, our authors sometimes denied oppositions with whimsical expressions of doubt in the superiority of the white race. This did not mean that
ethnographic knowledge shook their convictions or led them to reject the
premises of colonialism. Set categories expressed themselves, to use a Kant-
ian phrase, in judgments a priori. To observe intelligent, often sympathetic men caught up in binary categorizing, condemned to rehearse these
oppositions over and over again, is a depressing experience for the reader.
Only now and then our explorers had their moments and rose above
stereotypical divisions.

In this context, it is interesting to bring together observations, some
predictable, others surprising, on a theme that appears in most of the
sources: the role of aesthetic judgments in producing knowledge about
Africans. Here is first a text that demonstrates how aesthetics served to
establish ethnic and racial distinction, one of the concerns of exploration
we discussed in the preceding chapter. It comes from the section titled
"Ethnographic Matters" in Büttner's report from the lower Congo. Citing H.H. Johnston (1884) as an authority, he develops an opposition be-

tween two racial types, "Bantu" and "negro." He starts on the coast and near the mouth of the Congo.

> [There he sees a] type that in Europe one is too easily inclined to ascribe to the entire dark-colored population of Africa, that is, to people with a skin color that is a dull black, with a sparse growth of hair, short hair on the head which is dense and woolly, bad musculature, an ill-proportioned build of the body, a rounded skull, and a facial expression that with its prognathous chin, thick prominent lips, and snub nose looks to us anything but sympathetic. Such types lead one to assume a mixing of *Bantu* tribes with real *negroes*, a more or less pronounced negrification of the *Bantu* type that can hardly be taken to present an improvement. (*MAGD* 5, no. 3 [1889]: 185–86)

Büttner finds the counterimage among the Mayakkalla, Bayanzi, and Bateke who live some distance from the coast.

> Outright classical figures are by no means rare. As if cast in bronze of different hues they present themselves in the most varied gradations of a warm velvety brown, well proportioned and, especially the men, strongly developed, with small feet, wonderfully arranged coiffure and facial expressions, people who, especially with regard to the shape of nose and lips, often resemble cultured peoples much more than one is inclined to think in Europe. Not only their better external appearance wins our sympathy, with their character, the purer *Bantu* also surpass the negrified *Bakongo* whose many contacts with the white race, furthermore, have not always been to their advantage. (186)

On the surface, Büttner uses a European concept of value—purity—to refute a European preconception—the ugliness of Africans. He presents the result (which leaves many of them ugly) as a scientific finding (complete with a reference to an authority). But his writing betrays a sensual appreciation of African hues ("velvety brown" evokes touch as well as sight) and interjects an aesthetic image. And admiration expresses some degree of identification: without guile Gierow, who had no scientific pretensions, admires Luba body art, something that other travelers would have taken to confirm rather than subvert that stereotype of the cannibal.

> The Tuschilanga are a well-built race, most of them still being cannibals. Among those who traveled with us, most were covered, from their foreheads to their ankles, even around the neck, with tattoos that were quite beautiful. Where parts of the body, such as the navel or nipples, offered a clue there were several concentric circles from which beautiful lines in the form of arabesques ran over the whole body, betraying considerable sense of beauty and talent for design. (*MAGD* 3, no. 2 [1882]: 117)

Here and elsewhere beauty opens a crack in the artifice of denigrating oppositions construed in the semantic space between white-black and clothed-naked. Several writers, reversing racist stereotypes, openly admired the naked black body. First, though the gender element may distract from the point I eventually want to make, are some statements by Becker about the context of aesthetic observations. Early on during his trip to Karema he admitted lack of understanding for M. Sergère's, his French companion's, penchant for black women. He would learn to see differences, he was told (1887, 1:75), and, as he admits not much later, such turned out to be the case: "Is M. Sergère's prediction beginning to come true? In this place I admired young negro women who are really beautiful, with attractive shapes. Their nudity, almost complete, makes it possible to admire their round and elegant shoulders, their firm bust, not pressed down by the use of wraps as is the case with the women from the coast, their arms of an exquisite cast" (92). Later he expresses what other travelers have felt (and said) about African nudity: "Compared to the undressed individuals who act in our operettas and pantomime-ballets, the naked African appears quite dignified and decent" (153).

In his report on travel among the Kuba, Wolf devotes several pages to describing the physical appearance of Africans, including variations of color and the occurrence of albinos: "With their light-skinned nudity they make a disagreeable impression, whereas black skin color without the cover of clothes usually does not offend aesthetic sensibility" (1891, 251). Similar feelings about black nudity, again without sexual undertones, occur in a reflection by Wissmann. It illustrates the alternative to blind projection of divisive racial stereotypes, namely a learning process leading to recognition that humanized the experience. This is how he describes a woman of some distinction, a member of the children of hemp, who had served as his guide on a trip to the Lomami River.

> [She had something] that made us forget that we had before us just a half-clothed negro woman from the savage interior, something that unconsciously made us behave toward her as to an elderly lady from our home country. The feeling of contempt which the European often has when he first deals with savages soon disappears, one no longer notices the peoples' nudity, and one also learns to distinguish faces, something that is very difficult in the beginning. (1889, 151)

Deviating once more from my resolve not to quote Thomson except in epigraphs, I offer the following passage as an extension, but also comment and interpretation, especially on Wolf's observation: "Nudity with a black skin never strikes me as strange or noteworthy; but with a white skin it is different. Indeed, I almost developed a morbid disinclination to look at myself, and once or twice I have even blushed to see my white skin. I became so afraid of being seen bathing even by my men, that it was only with the utmost secrecy that I ever attempted it" (1881, 271). Thomson was a prudish young man, or a prudish writer, but this remarkable admission of feeling shame for his white skin should not be written off as individual squeamishness or exaggerated ("morbid") modesty. Though it would not be unheard of for a true Victorian to blush at the sight of his own skin, I prefer a different interpretation. Thomson's shame was both more superficial and more profound: it was caused by an aesthetic perception—white, untanned skin, can look ugly—and by the realization that such ugliness could have endangered his position of authority over his men. Whiteness, in this case, was potential weakness.

If anything, descriptions of African nudity should have been irresistible to producers of a literary genre known for catering to the prurience of its readership. After all, ethnography was just about to become a major provider of soft pornography, especially in the "scientific" illustrations it provided for popular publications. Some of the travelogues contain such pictures but, strangely enough (or not at all, given the visual bias in these matters), I cannot readily come up with textual examples.[13]

Perhaps explorers were just off guard when they let appreciation of black beauty contradict what they had to say most of the time about dark, filthy savages, scrawny women with pendulous breasts, and fat, shifty-eyed potentates. Büttner comes to mind as an example. The passages about the appearance of Africans we quoted above, though not all negative, would not lead us to expect from him statements such as the following. When after a long period of travel he met the first whites again at Kinshasa station he notes: "Automatically one had the impression how unnatural and sick our color looks under this hot sun and among our brothers with their more or less dark brown and velvety skin!" (1890, 214).

Apparently aesthetic distinctions, except when they served to confirm racial prejudice, could not seriously endanger ideological assumptions that counted as scientific. Yet being entranced with beauty, something I would count among ecstatic experiences, subverted at least momentarily racist certainties that were irrational as well as unreasonable.

CONTRADICTIONS AND TRUTH

> We have no right as yet to come to rigid conclusions
> about the character of the negro, and what his capacity
> for improvement may be. Travellers who have made
> such sweeping denunciation of the negro have seen him
> as degraded from ages of exposure to the curse of slav-

> ery, ever fighting like a wild beast for his very exis-
> tence—his hand against every man, and every man's
> against him. I ask any one who knows anything about
> Africa to look over the land, and ask himself if there is
> not abundant proof if the improvability of the native.
> (1:140)

Even liberal-minded explorers spoke of African religious ideas as "contradictory superstitions" (Becker 1887, 2:294). Pronounced by nineteenth-century men of science who were prone to equate rationality with elementary logic, such indictments seemed to have at least the grace of simplicity: here is Western science, there is African thought, and we know what separates the two. Truth. Yet by now we have, perhaps to the point of becoming tedious, given scores of examples showing that directness and consistency are just about the last things we could attribute to the explorers' minds and their ways of reasoning.

Take the phrase just quoted—"contradictory superstitions." The attribute contradictory appears to express straightforward disapproval and dismissal following the rules of logic. But in fact it leaves in the dark what it qualifies as contradictory. Before superstitions can be said to contradict each other they must be recognized for what they are. And in the travelogues they were, above all, beliefs contradicting Christian religion. None of the authors, as far as I can see, would have admitted that using the term *superstition* committed him to a position that was ultimately theological. Or was the phrase tautological? Did contradiction make superstitions out of beliefs? Furthermore, was it enough for beliefs to contradict each other to make them superstitions or did they also have to contradict the assertions of science? Conversely, could beliefs in disagreement with science, but not among each other, really be called contradictory? This latter position was obviously hard for the explorers to maintain; sometimes they said Africans were perfectly logical, after all. Here is a statement by Kund on the question of canceling a pact: "To them, this is prohibited by the strictly logical way of thinking of this race—on that point as on many others I recommend not looking down on them as being inferior—because they feel quite strongly that there must be among people a form of promise that cannot be broken, because [if broken,] it would then immediately lose its value as the most valuable pledge possible" (*MAGD* 4, no. 6 [1885]: 388).

But why did such insights only in the rarest of cases shake an author's faith in the superior rationality of Western thought—and then only briefly—or have consequences for his overall outlook on African thought? Durkheim's discovery of a hyper-rationality, existing not in the assertions but in the function of "primitive religion," was yet to come. Meanwhile, explorers made do with the kind of *bricolage* we tried to document throughout this chapter on making sense—mouthing stereotypes, working what needed to be explained into received theories, giving examples of careful reasoning based on experiences and observations, and often doing all the above at the same time.

When I try to form a general view of the ways, and accomplishments, of "making sense" in these accounts I am led to conclude that meaning and understanding came to explorers in moments only and then mostly, at least in matters of culture, against and in spite of the scientific equipment and expectations they brought along. It is as if it took all the faith in scientific truth they could muster (and a few other faiths: in their superiority, in their sponsors, in their nations) to maintain their sanity and overlook the contradictions in the very premises of European exploration. Fundamental among them were the contradictory demands made by power and truth, not just in the abstract sense in which they constitute an ageless philosophical quandary, but in the concrete form of serving imperialist and colonialist designs and scientific projects.

Let us recall some basic facts: a minor European monarch, Leopold II of Belgium, pursuing his private desires and those of his allies in the world of finance, managed to set up an organization for the geographic exploration of central Africa, advertised as an enterprise in the service of humanity. The many expeditions sent out by the IAA and its German affiliate, supposedly complementing and aiding each other in a common undertaking, soon became part of a wild scramble for Africa, a competitive search for routes of communication, commercial prospects, natural resources, and territories to occupy. The men on the spot paid an incalculable price. Many of them died. Those who lived to accomplish their mission and tell their stories were constantly forced to betray the scientific ideals they may have had and to invent justifications for serving purposes, exploration and occupation, which many of them recognized as irreconcilable.

All this led only to madness and it is sobering to discover that the best among the explorers (the most insightful and productive, the ones we most readily see as our predecessors in the work of ethnography) also exhibited its most severe symptoms. Leaving aside cases that could be dismissed as individual pathologies (Buchner and his paranoia, Reichard and his killing spree come to mind), we have Becker and Coquilhat, Wissmann and Frobenius. Again it is Becker who offers the most explicit textual evidence of madness. Racist, imperialist statements and judgments appear in all the sources (even in Torday). Usually they are dispersed; often they come as obligatory or "involuntary" twitchings of colonial discourse. But an entire chapter in the second volume of Becker's travelogue (ch. 35) leaves us aghast with his willingness and capacity to make statements that are in glaring contradiction to what he says in other places, in fact, to the general picture we get of him as a careful observer and compassionate human being.

Much of that chapter astutely analyzes slavery from the point of view of those who practice and suffer it. Comparing what he found in Africa with what he knows from regimes of labor elsewhere, he reveals the hypocrisy of European anti-Arab, antislavery campaigns. But then he proceeds to destroy the gains in rational understanding he just made with a barrage of racist statements about the natural servility of Africans. Echoes of future colonialist ravings resound when he concludes: "In a country where the word freedom is interpreted as the right to laziness, servitude is the necessary and inescapable consequence of the entire race's indifference" (328–31).[14] As he goes on, the argument's tone grows shrill and, considering the many repetitive passages, its delivery becomes truly manic.

But then could anyone torn between the demands of comprehension and domination be consistently reasonable? Ultimately, I suspect, ethnographic reality appears less in a travelogue's verifiable propositions than in the changes it worked on explorers as rational human beings. And that is another thing modern ethnographers may have in common with their predecessors.

TEN

Presence and Representation

When I think of describing the sights of this day, I find that words fail me. Well-merited superlatives are at the tip of my pen; but of what use is it to besprinkle them over the page? They could convey to the reader no definite or adequate idea. They would only indicate how much I was impressed. (1:51)

As we near the end of our travels through the minds of travelers in central Africa, we come back to choices we made at the outset. Positing links between exploration in the past and ethnography in the present, we looked at one genre of writing, the travelogue addressed to a wide readership. The explorers' reports of ethnographic practices—published in their accounts and in the bulletins of one sponsoring organization (*MAGD*)—in turn allowed us to take part in the epistemological critique of ethnography.

Reflecting on "our minds"—in terms anthropologists have become familiar with during the recent literary turn taken by our discipline—I want to understand metonymic connections between exploration and ethnography. There are contiguous, albeit not necessarily continuous, links between past and present research practices and discursive habits.[1] Both have been part of the history of economic and political relations between Africa and the nations where most of us work in our profession today. Colonial relations are present now in routines and conventions of research and writing and in "high places," that is, in upper-level theoretical concepts such as science, knowledge, and rationality—the very rationality that guides our critical efforts. The inevitably political dimension of our work obliges us to ponder not just what we represent of, or imagine about, Africa but what we inflict on it, and us, when we formulate ethnographic knowledge. Whatever literary criticism we muster should help us understand our practices; we should not use it to get a free ride in a powerful and fashionable discipline.[2]

TEXTS AND GENRES:
THE MAKING OF TRAVELOGUES

Travelogues count as popular writing for two reasons, one legitimate, the other doubtful. The wide readership they have had for centuries justifies the attribute but not the charge of unsophisticated, scientifically useless writing, indulgent in form as well as content. True, travelogues have always been permeable to fantasy and fiction. As we saw earlier (in chapter 8), this was the case with at least one of our sources. Schütt's sponsors caught him faking the maps of a part of his trip (1881) that, though small, would have been important had he undertaken it. Although we know which part of the trip he invented, from a casual reading of the relevant portion of his travelogue I found it impossible to tell where the factual narrative ended and the fictive story started.

Disdain for such potentially disreputable company made leading theoreticians in anthropology in the nineteenth century cling to their armchairs and declare travelers their poor and dubious relatives, if they did not deny kinship altogether. Before the 1960s (when our discipline's historiography reached its current level), students were in essence told that anthropology became a science when it left the travelogue behind. That some of the classic texts of modern anthropology—canonical works by Boas, Malinowski, Bateson, and Mead—contained more than incidental traits of the travelogue did little to shake that conviction. Nor did it seem to bother anyone that the "expedition," the term for modern planned ethnographic research before it became scaled down, individualized, and routinized as "fieldwork," had a rather unsavory imperialist ancestry.

Expeditions and fieldwork produced monographs as the distinctive, canonic genre of scientific writing. The decisive break with the travelogue, probably unavoidable given the professionalization of the field, occurred when writing, often called writing-up, came to be regarded a mere instrument, a vehicle for communicating results, when it should have been recognized as an essential element in the production of ethnographic knowledge. Critique of that position has been the most valuable epistemological contribution made by anthropology's literary turn. Writing, as it were, has been rehabilitated; the monograph is no longer the canonic genre, and many recent ethnographies bear uncanny resemblances to travelogues, including their inevitably autobiographical cast.[3]

Many of our authors were keenly conscious of problems of literary form in the communication of knowledge. That has been one of the lessons of this study. At times we find flashes of insight that strike us as thoroughly modern, up to current standards of criticism. To illustrate them, I quote first from a work with close connections to our corpus (though I exclude it mainly for chronological reasons). This is the three-volume report by the German Loango expedition of 1874–76 (Güßfeldt et al. 1879–1907).[4] It was called a *Reisewerk,* a travelogue, on the title page, and in his preface to the first part Paul Güßfeldt defended this designation. "Knowledge, still too weak to be able to stand on its own feet, needs to lean on the means by which it was acquired and, by donning the modest garb of a descriptive travelogue, it does at least not sin with statements whose general validity still has to be demonstrated. These considerations were decisive for the form which the work was given in the following" (1879, [ii]).

Less specific but still aware of form and content, the preface to Wolff's work concludes: "The costume given to this little book is bright and cheerful. However one should not be led by such external appearance to infer a content that is light and indifferent. The author believes that a drab and boring form is not at all required to communicate serious matters and to discuss serious questions" (1889, iv).

Another example of such literary awareness, in this case touching on ethnography's autobiographical aspects, occurs in Torday's retrospective account: "My book has no pretensions of being a scientific treatise; it is a simple account of what I have seen, and, if it appears now and then egotistical, the reader will bear in mind that observations have to be judged according to the mood of the person who makes them. There is perhaps more of me in those parts of the book in which I speak of other people than in those in which I am the principal actor" (1925, 17–18).

These observations by Güßfeldt, Wolff, and Torday exemplify many less explicit but often quite specific statements in our sources that address connections between literary form and research practices. Some of these should have our attention now.

First a comment on one fascinating case that would deserve a separate study, the travelogue coauthored by Capelo and Ivens. I am sure philologists could detect who wrote what in the account that was published, but when the first person singular is used the reader practically never knows which of the two explorers is speaking; the personal pronouns "I" and "we" or references to "one of us" or "his companion" may occur on a single page. This peculiar literary trait, incidentally, reflects an extraordinary feature of exploration: the possibility of collective, indeed dialogic, production of knowledge. Reports of numerous episodes show the two travelers consulting about decisions to be made and courses of action to be taken, but also conversing about how a particular event, experience, or piece of information is to be understood (335). Capelo and Ivens must have been a remarkable pair. They acted together and suffered together; they even went together through the most serious bouts of fever. Of course, they also worked together to control their experiences by means of the preconceived ideas and defensive stereotypes we encountered among all the travelers. Other travelers report similar, though less intensive, interaction—positively, for instance, in the Belgian and German East Africa expeditions or negatively, often as conflict and disagreement, in the German Congo Expedition.

Capelo and Ivens's work invites comparison with another work on our list that had several authors (Wissmann et al. 1891). Though Wissmann's voice dominates (in volume, as it were) much of the book is a compilation of reports whose authors are identified. Most likely this also reflects the peculiar modus operandi of the enterprise, which repeatedly split into several expeditions (one resulted in a separate travelogue: von François 1888). In the case of Torday's and Hilton-Simpson's travelogues, separate books expressed differences in scientific status.

In some reports and travelogues, I came upon occasional remarks on the act of writing as such. One example (quoted earlier for a different purpose) I noticed in *MAGD*—not the kind of publication we might expect to indulge reflections on writing. Reichard, whom we got to know as a rather brutal man of action, ended one of his reports to the German association with these words: "Please excuse the hasty writing because right now I have no patience for good composition" (*MAGD* 4, no. 5 [1885]: 308). Reichard recognized "good composition" as a value and a goal to attain. Of course we also read the remark as a gesture of defiance toward the metropolitan sponsors: the explorer in the field cannot be bothered with literary form and refinement.

Introducing the long report to *MAGD* from which we quoted repeatedly, Büttner has this to say about literary form and the epistemological significance of tensions between narrative and monographic writing.

> Being limited by the narrow space of this publication, on the one hand, and following the desire to convey many new findings and visible results of my travels in West Africa during the years 1884–86, on the other, I find myself constrained to set aside the external form of presentation and to deliver essentially a simple compilation of observations and statements. So as not to report unimportant matters, I must often disregard temporal connections; to avoid repetition, I need to put the reader in medias res and refer him to earlier publications. (*MAGD* 5, no. 3 [1889]: 168–69)

Unlike the monograph with its fairly rigid rubrics and standard sequences of topics, the genre travelogue we have been examining always
turns out to be a varied, changing combination of (sub)genres. Remarkably, even the titles of our major sources have no consistent pattern. Many
books have long descriptive headings that echo those of the preceding centuries; others make do with laconic phrases such as "A Trip to ———,"
"Travels in ———," or simply "Life in Africa." Mention of the names of
geographic regions is inconsistent. When subtitles specify a literary form
we get a rather long list of genres, among them narrative, description, diary, report or record, account, observation, adventure, impression, survey—
everything but travelogue (*récit de voyage, Reisebeschreibung*).

Rather than refine a concept of genre that functions on at least two
different levels (genre and subgenre) at the same time or mixes forms of
writing, we need to consider the pragmatics of its use. (Recall that our
focus on knowledge production and chosen approach of a *lectio dificilior* put the voluminous body of writing about travel writing and literary analysis out of reach.) What we want to know is whether and how
generic constraints function in oral and written communication as well
as in the interpretation of documents produced by speech and writing.
Even more simply, how does the genre help us understand the pragmatics of travel writing (and reading)?

It is best to start with some elementary considerations on time, place,
circumstances, purposes, and whatever can count as context amid the
vagaries and contradictions in the practices of travel. And what the best
among our authors make us forget, at least now and then, is that the
composition of travelogues usually took place in the metropolitan countries where obligations to, or pressure from, their sponsors, ambition,
and sometimes economic need made them produce their works.

I said composition, not writing, because substantial parts of all our
texts consist of passages copied from diaries and journals that explorers
kept in the field. Sometimes the accounts include long quotations from
other travelogues along with portions of documents and reports from
the offices of the IAA, letters from Africa kept by friends and relatives,
and undoubtedly, though seldom marked as such, notes prepared for lectures to scholarly societies and the wider public. Remember also that one
work was edited by another person from the traveler's diaries (Schütt
1881) and another one compiled from letters written to family and
friends (Böhm 1888).

One of the major works had—as its author, Frobenius, intimates—
practically been completed by the time the author was ready to return

to Europe (and the publication date supports this). His seemingly bound-less energy and determination may account for such a feat. Or more likely, during the early part of his career, he never left behind his metro-politan frame of mind and, at any rate, did not need the distance from the events that seemed to be required to make writers of travelers. Al-though most authors were not quite so fast, all of them were in a hurry to get their works out, if only to beat their personal competitors or ful-fill their obligations toward their homelands engaged in the scramble for Africa. Quite a few mentioned imposed hastiness as an excuse for the shortcomings of their writing. "I have been compelled to finish the work as rapidly as possible," Thomson says in the preface, "and therefore to confine myself to a large extent to the simple narrative" (1887, 1:xi). Torday, who does not seem to fit this picture, perhaps took his time be-cause, as a Hungarian, he was less directly bound to his British spon-sors. One of his works on our list (1925) appeared almost twenty years after the events. Another example showing that quick publication was a rule with exceptions is Pechuël-Loesche, whose 1907 book came out more than thirty years after the expedition on which it was based. What could be called the economics of the travelogue should also be consid-ered. Other than a sedate outlet in scholarly articles and monographs, there was a sometimes lucrative market (in some instances extended by translations) in narratives, diaries, adventures. And this market contin-ued to be important. Especially after the era of imperial sponsors for ethnography as exploration, and before that of scientific foundations, anthropologists wrote travelogues to finance their field research.[5]

A major problem of composition was to integrate the modes of nar-ration and description: the genre's overall intent was to interest, sway, and entertain its general readers as it impressed and convinced the "ge-ographical" community of specialists. In the preface to his travelogue Becker faces the inevitable tensions between the two modes. The work's "true canvas" (or outline), he says, was furnished "by the copybooks to which I consigned every evening the big and small events, as well as the joyous and sad impressions of the day. After the fact, I augmented them with some retrospective memories. Ordinary daily facts I connected in-timately to ethnographic and anthropological considerations which the reader skips all too often when they make up the content of special chap-ters breaking the order and movement of the narrative" (1887, 1:xix).

Composition as combination was a characteristic trait of the trav-elogues. Without exception, they consisted of a mixture, or rather jux-taposition, of genres, sometimes between chapters, more often within the same chapter or within a report, as, for instance, in the one Büttner submitted to *MAGD*. The first two sections are titled "From the Diary and Travel Account" and "Ethnographic Matters," respectively (*MAGD* 5, no. 3 [1889]: 169–82; 182–93). Frequently, the authors felt the need to announce and justify breaks resulting when they switched from one form of presentation to another. Typically, they related these breaks to events that marked turning points in their progress through the countries they explored. This is how Thomson announces the "fault line" separating narration from description: "Having entered a new country, and among different people, we may now profitably take a retrospective glance at the country we have passed through, draw isolated facts together which may have been lost sight of in the narrative, and present a condensed view of the whole" (1887, 1:132).

A standard situation, aside from entering a new country or village, was the encounter with African rulers and other prominent interlocutors ("sorcerers," Arab-Swahili traders, fellow explorers, or missionaries). First comes a more or less extensive narrative of the ceremonies of arrival, greeting, and exchange of presents, along with the appearance of the persons or their entourage and dwelling. Next the writer often takes the occasion to note general information and reflections on his interlocutor's office and his political and economic importance. A meeting with a missionary may then produce a small treatise on the role of missions and a comparison of different methods of evangelization in central Africa; one with a Swahili trader makes the author reflect on the institution of slavery or the economics of the ivory trade.

Long before an explorer faced the task of writing his travelogue, he shifted modes as he wrote in the diary. Often the new mode accompanies the change from movement to stillness we examined in the second chapter. Forced immobility, caused by inclement weather or the need to negotiate passage or to restock food and trade goods, is a major occasion to interrupt the narrative of the expedition with monographic accounts of peoples and customs.

When we correlate generic breaks in a writer's account with events in the world, we run little risk of assigning too much reality to literary form. The correlations were real to our authors; witness one excerpt from Schütt's travelogue (in an unquestioned part of the book): "Unfortunately, we had to stay the next day on the same spot because a porter had run away with several things.... There was nothing to be done about it and...I used the rest to write some experiences made during the last days into my diary. These will now follow in a rather motley succession"

(1881, 89–90). The last phrase indicates that the general observations he is about to note down follow no particular order; they are nevertheless recognizable as ethnographic rubrics (palavers, sexual mores, making palm wine) he could fit into a monograph.

The text's fault lines thus point us back to practical conditions of travel and, by the same token, to those of knowledge production. Other influences, however, provide an even more explicit link to modern practices of keeping ethnographic records. Anthropologists advise students leaving for the field to keep both a continuous journal and a system of notes, preferably on index cards (or now, in databases on their laptops). If we follow Justin Stagl, to whom we owe some of the most interesting recent discoveries about the history of the social sciences (see chapter 8), we can trace these recommendations (and later habits) to procedures of double-entry bookkeeping. That these procedures came into use at about the time Europe began its global expansion was hardly a mere coincidence.

Cataloging its practices, we begin to acknowledge the diary's place as a genre of writing within the conflict-prone practices of exploration. Keeping a diary was both a deeply felt need *and* an imposed obligation. Furthermore, conflict was unavoidable between the essentially private nature of the activity and the ultimately public destination of the facts and thoughts recorded. Pogge, praised in his obituary in *MAGD* for reporting in the "honest" diary form, provides us with two puzzling illustrations, one truly enigmatic (noted in another context in chapter 7), the other just intriguing.

Pogge was dying in Loanda when the German vice-consul, I. Ph. W. Wenniger, visited him. The explorer asked that his diaries be burned. Wenniger informed the board of the German organization in a letter that he "resolutely" refused the request (*MAGD* 4, no. 4 [1885]: 208). Did he tell Pogge he would not do it? And if Pogge hoped either to preserve his privacy or to prevent information from getting into the wrong hands, why did he ask a public official? At any rate, "a dozen yellowed diaries of varying length, heavily damaged by the tropical climate, partly difficult to decipher," survived their author. Excerpts later appeared, edited and published in *MAGD*. Facing Pogge's mysterious request, the editor added a few more twists to the questions we just asked: "The reasons that made the dying explorer request that these last witnesses of his work should be destroyed and burned are a psychological riddle. Who could solve it? Was it his excessive modesty, perhaps the expectation that a stranger would get nothing out of these hastily jotted thoughts and inquiries, or was it only the effect of his fatal illness that drove him to take this extreme step? We have been unable to find a solution to that question" (*MAGD* 4, no. 4 [1885]: 228).

There was more about Pogge's diary that intrigued its editor: "For reasons that have remained totally unexplained, Pogge, back from Nyangwe in Mukenge, began and continued to keep his diaries in English instead of German. One can only guess that the traveler thought perhaps that he would be able to express his thoughts more precisely and succinctly in this language in which he was hardly more fluent than in his native tongue" (229).

Pogge's case illustrates something that other authors experienced and expressed less dramatically. All of them found themselves under obligation to keep diaries.[6] But certainly not all explorers brought the keeping of a diary along as a habit they had acquired before they faced the task of exploration (we first referred to it as an often dreaded chore of expeditionary travel). Their middle-class upbringing had prepared them for a genre of writing that was defined as private, intimate, hence secret. As such, the diary was destined to be an outlet for emotions and intuitions, in short, for a writer's "subjectivity." It transformed experience into memory, even when the diarist considered it a mere aide-mémoire.[7] In a complex relationship between past time and the concept of facts—a theme in anthropological discourse and a major ingredient of what I called its allochronic stance (Fabian 1983, 88–89)—the diary's private, subjective practice objectified knowledge. Incorporated or transformed into travelogues or ethnographies, the diary conformed to a conception of (scientific) knowledge that suppressed or carefully controlled immediate experience, imagination, and memory. It and other exercises of tropical hygiene we encountered throughout this study governed the presentation as well as the production of knowledge.

Accordingly, some authors felt the diary was a more objective mode of presenting knowledge than a descriptive or analytical presentation of results. Its immediacy precluded the construction, crafting, and fiction that make less personal narratives and monographic ethnographies coherent and convincing. The same Coquilhat whose knack for analysis and theorizing we documented in the preceding chapter states in the preface to his book: "The pages that follow were written without literary pretensions. Perhaps [the reader] will find too little method in the way pieces of information and impressions follow one another. As an excuse I would invoke the rule I set myself, that is, simply to exhibit, as they were, my daily notes in order to retrace as truthfully as possible the days I lived in the Congo" (1888, viii).

Another example—putting more emphasis on sincerity than on accuracy—comes from the preface to Becker's work: "As the only one who returned [from this expedition] I dare to submit to the public observations collected from one day to another during three years *lived* in regions where, for the European, everything is still mysterious and full of surprises" (1887, 1:xxi).

Reflections like these put recent discussion about realism as a characteristic of modern ethnography in a different light. In Coquilhat's reasoning (and not only in his) the diary was a more realistic mode of representation than edited narratives and descriptions. Capelo and Ivens, too, introduce a switch from general narrative to excerpts from their diary as follows: "We extract from the diary the notes of the two following days...for being jotted down at the time they will serve better than any narrative to enlighten our readers upon what an explorer has frequently to endure upon his march" (1882, 2:65). Consequently, moving away from the diary meant moving toward forms that were less realistic though more scientific. The paradox dissolves, however, if we trace realistic ethnography's mode to the literary style of realism that characterized nineteenth-century novels.[8]

Some writers were conscious of such connections, as the following text demonstrates. In a portion of his account that has the generic traits of descriptive ethnography, Becker mentions that before the Wagogo warrior goes away and after he comes back, he washes himself in his wife's urine, which he collects for that purpose. Reporting such unsavory detail seemed to require an apology: "I humbly apologize to my readers for entering into such realistic detail but at a time when the modern novel, without scruples, uses the most crude expressions and wallows in the most scabrous situations, simple travelers, who do not invent anything, must be permitted to keep abreast of the movement" (1887, 1:152).

If literary realism inspired our early ethnographers, then we face an interesting possibility: the move from subjective narrative ethnography toward monographic representation involves a greater, not a lesser, element of literary fiction. An escape from this conclusion—or the illusion of escape—is simple denial of any link between ethnographic writing and literature and, hence, fiction. Clifford Geertz (1988) had a major role in showing up the illusion. As far as I can tell, the writers of the travelogues we studied never had illusions about the (un)importance of writing. Even the short passages we quoted document a realistic conception of knowledge production that current anthropology attempts to regain.

Most of our authors were keenly aware of a more conventional distinction between fact and fiction, one that equates fiction with the made-up or purely imagined. In an earlier chapter I quoted a text where Becker, after recounting a particularly gory episode, invoked Hoffmann, Poe, and Verne, writers of the fantastic, to profess his own veracity and the realism of his writing (see chapter 4). Toward the end of his work, he recalls how he discovered the remains of one of his slain couriers, including a batch of letters addressed to him. In a reverie about this drama, he cites some contemporary authors (among them again Verne) whose incredible adventures are "more often than not surpassed by simple reality" (1887, 2:243).

Of course, our authors also must have known of a widespread tendency, probably as old as the travelogue, to suspect (writing) travelers of being "travel liars."[9] Hence the many statements professing veracity. Nevertheless, no one expected them to write a staid and strictly factual account of moving from here to there and back (and get it published).[10] A travelogue was expected to excite, entertain, and edify its readers and, in a sense, exploratory travel adapted to the literary form it was eventually to take. We cannot claim representation shaped the experience, but at the very least travel and its representation were part of one and the same practice. The dividing line between fact and fiction runs through all aspects of that practice and not only between travel and the travel account.

Among the travelogue's generic demarcation lines is one that separates the *story* of the main narrative from *stories* of extraordinary hardship (mostly about crossing natural obstacles: rivers, mountains, forests, deserts) or of strange or dangerous events, and *anecdotes* of remarkable or funny incidents.[11] Hunting stories in particular combine and display all these elements, and all the major sources in our corpus have examples of the genre. Implicit clues (for instance, a more consciously "literary" style) and explicit statements often suggest their crafting to meet generic expectations for tales of adventure: to entertain rather than merely inform. More than others, hunting stories could become vehicles of irony when they told of failure and, at times with obvious relish, recounted the author-hero's bungling ineptitude. And the recurrent motif of getting lost in the wilderness dramatizes the explorers' thorough dependence on guides and helpers. In other words, these stories dictated by conventions of literary fiction and in some cases even literally fictive could also serve critical and reflexive purposes.

What different authors made of that possibility can be documented by two contrasting examples. In the preceding chapter we read Büttner's disparaging comment on travelers approaching central Africa in search of game: he calls hunting an insignificant element of African travel. Becker, coming from the east where game was often plentiful and hunting actually helped feed a caravan, has a much more differentiated view of the matter, both of the activity and its literary representation. He fills about five pages of his book citing letters that his companion Roger, a passionate and efficient hunter, had sent to the secretariat of the IAA in Brussels (1887, 1:187–92). They consist almost entirely of hunting stories. His last comment here manages to denounce and valorize the genre in one breath: "Don't these details, narrated without pretension, have a taste of sincerity much more captivating than the pompous hunting stories sent by illustrious but vainglorious travelers?" (192).[12]

Finally, we should mention two minor (sub)genres: recorded native texts and reported dialogues. In earlier chapters we had occasion to comment on one or two of the texts of fables, songs, or proverbs presented in the original language and in translation. Of dialogues we get most often only brief examples, put in to enliven the account. But a few exceptions have a more literary quality, such as Coquilhat's substantial report of a palaver between his companion E. W. Hanssens and a local chief (1888, 90–94). By current standards, few of these texts qualify as literal transcripts of actual conversations, though several later travelers had the technology to make sound recordings. In a vast majority of cases, "authentic" texts and dialogues (much like the native terms spread throughout the narratives) were literary—hence fictional—marks of a realistic style of writing. Should we count as an ecstatic element the flourish and drama of literary conventions in the translation of experience into knowledge? They help explain why authors of exceptional literary accomplishment such as Becker and Coquilhat (and perhaps even Torday and Frobenius) strike us as the best ethnographers.[13]

I can now refine an observation I made about genre in the previous chapter. In a comment on Coquilhat's uses of physiognomy, I stated that one effect of generic description may be to lend authenticity to its subjects. In ethnographic accounts, as elsewhere, genre works through rules and constraints; conversely, obeying the rules of a genre gives the writer a certain authority, a kind of power. We can test the proposition in the following passage relating a meeting between Schütt and the Luba chief Mai: "In the evening we were brought to him and, while he once again assured us of his friendship, he consumed incredible quantities of palm wine. Afterward he even swore that he would be my friend forever whereby he rubbed my hand with *Pende* and he wanted me to baptize him" (1881, 151).

Elements of this fragment give it its "typical" character, hence its credibility: the drinking chief, the motif of a pact of friendship, the ritual use of *Pende* (probably a corruption of *pembe,* white clay) as a demonstration of peace and good intentions. After reading basically the same tale many times in other sources, we might even overlook Schütt's claim that the chief wanted to be baptized. It strikes a wrong note: no other traveler mentions such a thing (it was a generic trait of encounters between Europeans and Africans in earlier centuries). Yet we know that the author makes use of the generic's capacity to create a sense of reality here as he recounts an event that never took place, at least not with the person indicated. Meeting chief Mai was part of Schütt's travelogue that proved to be fiction in the sense of forgery.

WRITING AND READING

Many of our authors addressed their readers directly in the second person ("Dear reader") or in the third ("I ask the reader..."). Modern ethnographies seldom do. Even writers of fiction use these phrases nowadays only for flavor, to give their writings an antique gloss. But there is more to the disappearance of the "Dear reader" than changes in fashion. Modern conventions of ethnographic writing avoided narratives and stories and asked for reports, comments, explanations, and so forth. Its authors did not have to imagine readers or address them to keep them present in their writings. The scientific monograph's very form and content gave it a predestined readership. The rhetorical devices (claims and contestations mainly) that scientific authors nevertheless employed were expected to work in a disembodied space of scientific discourse; it was bad to be caught arguing ad hominem or addressing a person. How much science actually relies on personal solidarity, on groups and paradigms, still caught us by surprise two or three generations later when it was revealed by historians such as T. S. Kuhn.

Among our sources there is an interesting test case for assertions about the importance of readers, Böhm's posthumously edited letters (1888). They were presumably selected and arranged such that they amounted to a travelogue, that is, an ongoing narrative much like those we find in the other books.[14] The published letters are no more personal, intimate, or revealing than the travelogues, though the writer indulges somewhat more in hunting stories and especially in lengthy descriptions of nature. What makes them different is the influence of an intended addressee/reader on their form and content. In fact, a few sequences of letters have a "*Rashomon* effect," reporting the same event differently to different addressees.

Once again here the act of writing shows up as an integral part of knowledge production. Since different pragmatic situations may influence not only the form but also the content of travel accounts—explorers' experiences but also their insights and opinions—an author's political and ideological constraints become visible in single statements and in tendencies that develop over the course of a book. Take for instance Becker. Part of his account clearly consists of notes and reflections made "in the field"; that may account for their extraordinary freshness and directness. But the write-up, as we would say today, was done in the metropolitan country (notice his use of IAA archives). We must imagine the effects of political pressure in the latter setting: they demanded he create absolute distance between himself and the Africans he encountered. The pressure begins to show in increasing defensiveness about his position on the Arabs' role and what he considers the slave trade's true nature. He either fails or refuses to understand that the antislavery campaign is not primarily a moral or legal but a political and economic issue. At the latest toward the middle of the second volume (see its chap. 35), I detected a tendency to base generalizations about Africans on outright racist premises. As we saw, many of his own reported experiences and feelings conflict with and exacerbate the position he finds himself expressing at the home base. Similar qualifications apply to the many stereotypical colonialist and racist statements we found in other sources. Quite likely their madness must be seen as an artifact of presentation rather than a product of experience. This does not excuse bigotry and racism wherever it occurs; it does remind us that sacrifices for the comforts of conformity too often and too quickly replaced the gains in freedom and insight travelers made when they went beyond themselves in the field.

A somewhat subtler pressure relates to conventions of writing for an unspecified audience. Outside special fields, such as botany and geology, the writers of travelogues could not (yet) place their findings in fully established discursive space of a science of others (though we met emerging elements in the preceding chapter). At any rate, explorers had to assume that general readers would make sense of and share their ethnographic-anthropological theories and explanations. They had to build their specific authority on the fact that travel had brought them to the worlds they described. They "had been there" to observe, record, and collect.[15] It is this emphasis on (personal) presence that made narration the dominant mode of their writing. As narrators who told *their* story, they needed readers whom they imagined and sometimes addressed as persons. The travelers' own presence and authority were enhanced to the extent that they succeeded in taking their readers along on their travels by letting them participate in dangers, difficulties, doubts, troubles, and the intellectual work of making sense of experiences.

Authors turn to their public with sweeping promises, as Capelo and Ivens do at the beginning (of the report) of their voyage, following one of those generic descriptions of a caravan's departure we find in many of the travelogues: "And now...that the confused noises attending the starting of the caravan are ringing in our ears, we ask you, friendly reader, to bear us company in our journey westward, on our promise that, whatever the obstacles and annoyances that may start up by the way, we will endeavor to be cheerful and entertaining companions" (1882, 1:41). Or they make more specific requests for the reader's participation, as Torday does when he faces a problem with ethnic distinctions: "Why did I speak at all about the Badjok when I am only concerned with the Bushongo and their kindred? I want the reader to compare this people, who have for two hundred years been in contact with civilization, with the savage Bashilele; let him draw his own conclusions" (1925, 277).

The habit of addressing the reader explicitly and directly indicates a writer's intention. Much more numerous and pervasive are strategies that achieve this effect in less obvious ways. When I looked over Becker's account of the trip toward Mirambo's territory—this chief is one of the most powerful and impressive political figures we met—and his visit with Mirambo, what struck me was this episode's mutually reinforcing parts. Becker crafts a conspicuously vivid and positive tableau of a pleasant landscape and of the civilized settlements he traverses on his way to Mirambo. He prepares the reader for the thoroughly positive image he then paints of the ruler (1887, 2:156–57).

A parallel point occurred to me then, and I began to pay greater attention to descriptions of landscapes as projections of the writers' moods and as (unstated) messages to the readers. Many examples of such parallelism of inner states and outer shapes exist, though, unlike Becker's, they usually refer to experiences of hardship. But then so do most accounts of travel. A widespread interpretation (sometimes shared by the protagonists) has it that travel in foreign parts is a metaphor of the difficult and dangerous quest for self-understanding. In our case the metaphor has only the sense of a rhetorical figure useful in specific situations and for specific effects. True, our authors often contributed to the glorification of European exploration but—at least in the sources I examined—did not wallow in the metaphor of travel as a generalized ideological strategy. At any rate, our intent throughout has been to materialize and literalize travel by using the available accounts to recuperate historical lessons that the myths of exploration usually overwrite.

Writing and reading bring up an issue we referred to here and there: the role of reading in the choice to make a vocation of travel. In the preceding chapter we quoted Becker on the motive that drove him and others to Africa: it was nostalgia for the unknown—fueled by the *memory of reading travelogues* (1887, 2:352). It reminds us that before they became travelers and writers, they were readers. In current parlance, it brings up the intertextuality of writing about the exploration of central Africa. It also extends the simple image of a writer and his public to include a third party: other writers. All the sources refer to, argue with, or confirm the writings of other explorers. Authors cite famous predecessors to give their accounts weight and importance or to set their own stories apart from those of all earlier travelers. Others simply connect their reports to existing knowledge. The result is a rhetorical constellation rather more complex than we would expect from travelogues. Of course, such practices of citation and quotation have considerable historical depth; they range from obligatory references to authorities to outright plagiarism, a notorious trait of travel literature through the ages.

An interesting question, discussed in recent reflections on ethnographic fieldwork, is the importance of reading while traveling. Our explorers read letters, reports, and manuals—and odd items like a Swahili Bible in Latin script Wissmann saw in Kasongo (according to his Arab-Swahili hosts, Stanley himself left the book there [1889, 197]). But I found few reports of the kind we have from Malinowski (and others before and after him), namely of escaping the realities of research by reading works of fiction. We learn little about the reading habits or books travelers brought along to Africa. The early expeditions seem to have been particularly ill equipped in that respect. Pogge, for instance, tells us of whiling away evenings by playing a thumb piano, adding, "Unfortunately I had nothing to read. My library consisted of a small Portuguese-German pocket dictionary" (1880, 137–38). When Lieutenant Kund traveled on a steamer, in contrast, he praised his cabin, which had enough space "for sitting down comfortably, reading, and eating...[and for storing] books, maps, and instruments" (*MAGD* 4, no. 6 [1885]: 380).

Becker speaks of the lack of reading as a deprivation and takes this as an occasion to describe the contents of the library at Karema station.

> The library of the station will offer us precious resources for the days of con-
> finement the rainy season threatens to bring. It is quite well equipped with
> scientific books, not all of them unpacked as yet. Among them I notice the
> big *Dictionnaire encyclopédique* by Vorrepierre, the excellent *Dictionnaire
> de Médecine* by Littré, treatises of philosophy, mathematics, political econ-
> omy, geography, colonization, astronomy, natural history, travelogues, and
> so forth. Among these books, the work of M. Houzeau on the *intellectual
> faculties of animals* has a distinguished place. We also have a complete set of
> the Roret collection of manuals comprising all European crafts. (1887, 2:277)

This impressive enumeration of metropolitan expectations tells us little
in the absence of information of what travelers actually read. Becker does
begin to address the point: "A few entertaining works and some French
and English novels have managed to smuggle themselves into this learned
company. During hours of depression [*spleen*] they will be most welcome" (277–78). Without going far enough to document reading as escape, the hint confirms our earlier observations: in exploration almost
any activity, including writing and reading, was either valued as a means
to maintain health and sanity or deemed to be in need of control as part
of a regime of tropical hygiene.

TEXTS AND IMAGES: WORDS AND ILLUSTRATIONS

An image—the intrepid European traveler who rides at the head of his
caravan (Figure 3)—was a point of departure for our attempt to debunk
the simple myths of exploration lodged in our minds. We expect that illustrations, memorable images of explorers and explored, were a prominent feature of the genre travelogue—as they are in a majority of our
sources. Yet in five works of our corpus they are almost entirely absent:
Thomson, if we ignore portraits of the two explorers in the frontmatter,
and the books by Böhm, Büttner, Schütt, and Wolff. Illustrations fill all
the others, images of landscapes, incidents, people, plants and animals,
and a host of other items, including ethnographic objects and samples
of fauna and flora collected. However, an assessment of these images'
significance for the presentation of knowledge is beyond the scope of this
study. In order to discuss recent critiques of anthropology's "visional-
ism" and of ethnographic objects exhibited in fairs, museums, on the
printed page, and on the screen—or even to comment extensively on the
images found in our travelogues—it would need to be twice as large (and
add more than that to the cost of production).

Such practical limitations dispose of one problem as they raise another.
Does a failure to provide close and detailed interpretations of images

FIGURE 3. The caravan (White Fathers 1884, 194).

printed in these travelogues affect the essence of our project? To begin with some cursory and general observations, the illustration of travel accounts is yet another aspect of our sources that appears to lack rhyme and reason.

In current debates on travel illustration we assume that its purpose, or at least its effect—apart from making the books commercially attractive—was to give the reader "typical" and stereotypical images, icons of the newly acquired knowledge of central Africa. Images have power; they may not argue or prove anything, yet they impress and convince. Such a perspective can be interesting and valid, especially when it concentrates on a single picture or a small number of them. But it risks projecting the interpreter's semiotic astuteness and hermeneutic subtlety onto practices of illustration, giving them a rationality and unity of purpose they never had. This is an insight I took away from compiling an inventory of images presented in our sources.[16] Here are some of the results.

Even allowing for changes in the technology of recording and reproducing images during the period we cover, number, kind, source, and placement of illustrations vary enormously. Except in a few specific areas (for instance, multiple ethnographic objects arranged as if in a museum's display cases [Figure 4]), I noted no conventional patterns to suggest standardized practices of illustration.

First, the number of images: Frobenius holds the record, with 352 images spread over 468 pages. The average of the other 10 illustrated sources is about 65 per work (with a range from 3 to 194). Without being able to assess the technology of reproduction's finer details, I found a similar degree of variation in the kinds of images. Woodcuts and engravings are predictably more frequent in earlier books, such as Becker and Coquilhat; photographs (halftones) appear in the later Frobenius, Hilton-Simpson, and Torday. Most have reproductions of pencil and pen drawings, of oil sketches and watercolors, and a few color lithographs (in Bastian and Pechuël-Loesche, the latter including charts for the classification of skin color). Throughout, and most often in some earlier publications, photographs served as models for many images—or so the captions indicate. Yet a photographic original is hard to imagine behind these frequently highly stylized illustrations: in Pogge, von François, and Capelo and Ivens, for instance. Africans, their physiognomy, their body posture, and often their cultural and natural surroundings appear in the style of earlier centuries (Figure 5), and often as realistic and idealized images within a single work (Figures 6 and 7). Again, it would take specialists to identify what exactly characterizes each style, but there can be no doubt that the line between them is not the one between pictures that are based on photographs and those that are not.

FIGURE 4. "Ethnological this-and-that" (Wissmann 1891, facing 136).

FIGURE 5 (*top*). "Women from Bokeri" (von François 1888, 99).   FIGURE 6 (*left*). A realistic portrait: an Ambaca gentleman (Capelo and Ivens 1882, 2:41). FIGURE 7 (*right*). A stylized portrait: a Tshokwe warrior (Capelo and Ivens 1882, 1:214).

Photographs bring up the sources of images. Again, these are so varied that it is impossible to generalize. As far as I can see, all expeditions (Thomson's excepted) carried photographic equipment. Those reported on by Becker and Wissmann included members designated as photographers. Torday and Frobenius were accompanied by professional artists (Norman Hardy, a "well-known painter of native life," and Hans Martin Lemme, *Kunstakademiker,* trained at an art academy) who doubled as photographers. Several travelers had their own sketches and paintings reproduced. However, of the vast amount of images collected by expeditions only a small portion appeared in the published travelogues. In other words, we cannot assume that the printed images adequately represent the importance of an expedition's use of visual means and modes to gather knowledge.[17] Therefore we need to qualify what I called practices of illustration. The making of visual records was probably fairly uniform; it belonged to the routine work of exploration. In contrast, the placing of illustrations in travelogues was often so varied as to strain the notion of an established practice. It presents problems not unlike those we had with applying the concept of genre to the travelogue.

Though I cannot demonstrate this proposition, I would even go as far as to suggest that the discrepancies we note (here and below) express an awareness that text and images were different creatures altogether; they only cohabited in the book. What, we may ask, are our habits of "reading" illustrations in travelogues? Do we really stop and ponder semiotic messages and relations? Or do we let pictures affect us much as the typesetting, the paper, or the binding do, that is, as material, sensual aspects of a book? If the latter is the case, we may find in the illustration of travelogues an aspect of the presentation of knowledge that resisted rational control. Though simplifying and fundamentalist interpretations of visual representation of Africa and Africans as products of the "imperial eye" work for single images—and there are plenty of those in our sources—they fail for illustrations. The latter show much the same vagaries, tensions, and contradictions we discovered in the practices of exploration.

Inconsistencies become visible when we consider the placement of images in a narrower sense. Printing technologies (requiring, for instance, a special kind of paper) may account for a major distinction between illustrations in the text and others, usually designated as plates, that command a full page (sometimes, but not always, numbered as pages). But technology of reproduction cannot be the only reason for making such distinctions. In several works, engravings and halftones occur both in the text and as plates. The difference may have been one of semiotic function: depicting the message printed in the text as opposed to offering tableaux, or evocative images without direct links to the message (a similar distinction can be made between images that narrate and others that symbolize). But, then, often plates do illustrate portions of the text (sometimes with page references given). And occasionally images in the text have little detectable connection to that page's message, maybe because the designer or printer has other criteria for placing pictures—spreading them evenly throughout the book, perhaps. Design also accounts for illustrations that appear in the manner of initials at the beginning of a chapter (Figure 8). As a rule, however, images come with captions that spell out connections to the text and often also identify the source.

The topic of illustration, finally, raises questions about the role of art, or artistic quality, in "imaging" the exploration of central Africa. On the whole, the pictures in these travelogues seem to have functional (depicting) and expressive (evoking) properties (though their choice itself is problematic: we seldom know who made it). Curiously enough, the sources facing us made little use of the images produced by the two professional artists who were members of expeditions. Photography may already have won out as the true, scientific mode of depicting reality, as Frobenius suggests when he comments on Lemme's work. He puts two images (from a series of four) of Richthofen Falls together on one page (Figures 9 and 10).

> To me, it seems interesting to reproduce also on 388 the painting that my draftsman, Herr Lemme, made of these falls in Europe. He had done the preliminary studies exactly at the place were I took the [photographic] picture marked "Illustration 3." I was struck already from the sketch that, in order to improve the effect of the picture, he had somewhat overestimated the relationships of height. In the finished painting he has now created a presentation that no longer has anything to do with the facts....I would never dare to criticize the artistic value of transformations such as Lemme's, but I must point out, that it is not possible to use these transformations for scientific purposes. (1907, 395–96)[18]

The samples of Lemme's and Hardy's work reproduced in the travelogues show craftsmanship, but most of them can hardly count as examples of art if we reserve that term to creations that transform, intensify, exalt, or degrade rather than simply reproduce objects and events. And if we go on Frobenius's remarks, one principle of selection was to exclude works judged to be too artistic.

Of course, not even the most prosaic pictures of implements were mere reproductions of objects (and any reproduction is always a matter

CAPITEL II.

Lingster „Ngo".

Erste Eindrücke an der Loangoküste. — Banana. — Die „Afrikaansche Handels-Vereeniging". — Wohnstätten der Weissen und der Schwarzen. — Crumanos und freie Arbeiter. — Der Markt. — Gefangene. — Handelsproducte. — Tauschartikel. — Congomündung. — Strand. — Versammlungshalle. — Die Loangoküste als Terra incognita. — Die Portugiesen der Küste. — Das Reisen in der Hängematte. — Von Banana nach Vista. — Das erste Negerdorf. — Eine Handelsfactorei. — Der Lingster. — Wasserpassagen. — Kabinda. Frühere und jetzige politische Zustände. — Die Bai von Kabinda. — Fischerei. — Die Savane zwischen Futila und Tschimfime. — Eine Fetischceremonie. — Africanische Flusslandschaft. — Canoefahrt. — Tschiloango. — Landana. — Zusammentreffen mit Dr. Bastian.

Die ersten Eindrücke, die man in Banana erhält, sind die einer unerwarteten Grossartigkeit; man verdankt dieselben nicht der Natur, die hier dürftiger sich zeigt als an irgend einem andern Puncte der Loangoküste, sondern den Schöpfungen eines aus kleinen Anfängen hervorgegangenen Rotterdamer Hauses, der „Afrikaanschen Handels-Vereeniging". Dieses Haus besitzt an der Küste, welche unseren Operationen als Basis gegeben war, und südlich davon, eine grosse Anzahl von Factoreien, in denen direct von der eingeborenen Bevölkerung eingekauft wird. Banana ist für alle die Centralstelle: von hier giebt der Hauptagent seine Weisungen, von hier aus werden die europäischen Tauschwaaren, die conservirten Lebensmittel und was sonst

FIGURE 8. An initial illustration: the interpreter Ngo (Güßfeldt et al. 1879–1907, 1:29).

FIGURE 9 (*top*). Richthofen Falls, photograph (Frobenius 1907, 388). FIGURE 10 (*bottom*). Richthofen Falls, oil painting by H.M. Lemme (Frobenius 1907, 388).

of degree). Every "illustration"—or "illumination," to use a telling term from an earlier period—directs the reader-viewer's gaze by bringing some objects, some scenes, to the light and leaving others in the dark. I am sure close inspection of graphic reproductions of photographs would show the choices at work. We need not dwell on the complex interplay of focus, light, and frame, of posing and arranging, that goes into ethnographic or geographic photography: all illustrations hide while they reveal. Rather than ponder what individual pictures hide, it would be more interesting to look at practices of illustrating exploratory travel. Not having made a detailed study of these practices, I offer only a general impression: however haphazard illustration was, visual images lend to the presentation of scientific knowledge in these travelogues an aura of realism and credibility that smoothes over the rough spots, breaks, and outright contradictions we found, again and again, in the texts.

Though the illustration of travelogues generally fell short of qualifying as art, accuracy demands the mention of two remarkable exceptions, one pertaining to Becker's work as a whole, the other to one kind of image in Frobenius's account. The title page of Becker's *La vie en Afrique* announces that its two volumes contain a frontispiece, a portrait, an etching, and a photogravure and are "enriched" by 150 "original pictures [*dessins*]...signed" by no fewer than 33 artists (Figure 11).[19] As Becker notes in the preface to his work, "the elite of the Belgian School spontaneously offered to enrich it with original pictures"[20] (1887, 1:xxii). Some of the images are fairly conventional, but many are obviously efforts to achieve artistic quality by, what I am told, the most modern standards of the period, among them some symbolic-allegorical tableaux that strike us as rather quaint (Figure 12; see Figure 13 for a similar image in Wissmann). The artistic oeuvre assembled here advertises in its entirety the importance of exploration. In this case, illustration could make a political statement.

The second example is a series of thirteen caricatures by Lemme (Frobenius 1907, 278–93). The genre trades artistic refinement and realistic representation for visual and rhetorical appeal to parody and irony or—and here art touches morals or politics—derision. More obviously than other illustrations, caricatures rely for their effect on captions. In this case they consist of two elements, a general designation repeated with each picture ("Exercises in the humoristic contemplation of the negro" [Figure 14]) and a phrase describing what the picture shows: handling a spoon or straining coffee. As may be expected, the humoristic effect superficially derives from incongruities between image and legend;

LA

VIE EN AFRIQUE

ou

TROIS ANS DANS L'AFRIQUE CENTRALE

PAR

JEROME BECKER

Lieutenant du 5e Rég. d'Artillerie de Belgique

avec Préface du Cte GOBLET D'ALVIELLA

Président de la Société royale belge de Géographie

ET APPENDICES

Comprenant : Un Projet de Gymnases d'Exploration et de Colonisation; un Vade-Mecum du Voyageur en Afrique ; les résumés des Conférences données, sur la région du Tanganika, par les Capitaines Cambier et Storms ; ainsi que les voyages, séjours etc., de MM. Crespel, Maes, Wautier, Dutrieux, Popelin, Van den Heuvel, Burdo et Roger d'après les documents les plus authentiques et les plus récents.

DEUX VOLUMES

Enrichis d'un FRONTISPICE de J. Dillens ; d'un PORTRAIT a L'EAU-FORTE par Gustave Vanaise ; d'une PHOTOGRAVURE, d'après un portrait de Léon Herbo; d'une CARTE-ITINÉRAIRE, dressée par le capitaine L. Van de Velde,

ET DE

150 DESSINS ORIGINAUX

Signés : Abry, Bertrand, Broerman, Courtens, Dell'Acqua, Dierickx (O. et J), Dillens, De Rudder, Duyck, Farasyn, Frédéric, Heins, Herbo, Houben, Hubert, Lagae, Lambeaux, Lamorinière, Mols, Portaels, Serrure, Simons, Smits, Vanaise, Van Camp, Van Engelen, Van Kuyck, Van Leemputten, Verhaert, Verlat, Verstraete et Wytsman.

TOME I

J. LEBÈGUE & Cie, ÉDITEURS

PARIS	BRUXELLES
25, rue de Lille, 25	46, rue de la Madeleine, 46

1887

FIGURE 11. Title page (Becker 1887, vol. 1).

FIGURE 12. "The union of the three races" (Becker 1887, 2:329).

FIGURE 13. Untitled allegory (Wissmann [1890], facing viii).

Übungen in der humoriſtiſchen Betrach=
tung des Negers: Der Boy reicht Dir
einen Löffel.

Übungen in der humoriſtiſchen Be=
trachtung des Negers: Der Boy
ſeiht Dir den Kaffee durch ſeinen
Lendenſchurz.

FIGURE 14. "Exercises in the humoristic contemplation of the negro: the Boy hands you a
spoon; the Boy strains your coffee through his
loincloth" (Frobenius 1907, 283, 286).

on a deeper level, these cartoons presuppose a complaisant audience for
smug generalizations about the lack of understanding Africans have for
civilization. Intended to endear themselves to readers, Lemme's caricatures celebrate white superiority.

One other factor makes this example especially interesting. Most writers say little or nothing about the importance they gave to illustrations
and even less about the role they themselves played in picking the ma-

terial. In this case, Frobenius tells us the decision to put these particular images in this particular place of his travelogue was his own. It has always struck me as one of the craziest twists of the colonial mind. Frobenius puts them in chapter 16, where for the most part he exposes and denounces the atrocities he had witnessed in regions where the infamous rubber-collecting Compagnie du Kasai operated.[21] As we read these outrageous stories and gaze at the sketches, our puzzlement and horror grow. At last the author explains: "It is not without reason that I illustrate this tragic chapter with gay little pictures from the life of the Boys. These are sketches conceived by the expedition's draftsman after humorous experiences in daily life" (1907, 293).

Visually supported by caricatures, all of them asserting the white man's superiority, and phrased in contemptuous language—even if the "Boys" he refers to are his servants and literally children—this statement introduces Frobenius's reflections on the importance of humor for the African traveler (quoted and commented on in chapter 4). He intends the passages to be engaging, to express a human reaction to inhuman situations. They are to bring relief, not from the horror of atrocities committed against Africans, but from the "cruel aggravations" suffered by Europeans in their daily dealings with their African personnel. For us, recommendations of humor as a measure of hygiene and control add insult to injury.

Ending this chapter on presence and representation with comments on illustrations we found in our sources brings us back to our point of departure, the myth of exploration we keep alive above all in visual images. Iconoclasm, as we know from a long history of movements of protest and renewal (the children of hemp, we remember, are part of it), has been an ecstatic element of social and political critique, and we need feel no compunction about smashing idols as we retraced the exploration of central Africa. What remains now is to sum up this arduous enterprise's gains for our understanding of ethnography—this, after all, was the reason we embarked on it.

ELEVEN

Epilogue

Did we bring home what we promised at the beginning of this journey through travelogues of the exploration? Scholarly books should end with conclusions that restate their goals and then summarize, chapter by chapter, the arguments that confirmed or refuted them. But if I take the idea of a journey (and a story) seriously, I cannot report its results in a few paragraphs that refract its premises. A measure of journeys is that travelers may return to the point of departure but are no longer the same when they get there. This is why an epilogue, a "word after," seems appropriate as an end to this study.

As I return to questions that always intrigued me or came up as I widened and deepened my reading of the sources, I know I will not be able to condense my findings to a single major point. In fact, I begin to see this book as a continuation of what I attempted in *Time and the Other:* its only point, I sometimes thought, was to intrigue. Apparently it did. Here too I hope to intrigue and stir up the ways many think about anthropology.

A STORY AND ITS PROTAGONISTS

More than once I spoke of telling stories or hearing protagonists report and comment on what happened. These figures of speech helped keep me from falling into an abstract critical disquisition on the conditions and vagaries and the merits and limits of knowledge about a part of

Africa, produced during the rallying time of Western imperialism and the beginnings of colonial rule. For if my narrative had a form, it was that of an epic succession of small, pointed inquiries to confront the sources with critical questions. Some drew on current critiques of ethnography. Most arose whenever the travelogues' premises and conclusions, programs and activities, ideologies and concrete actions gave rise to doubts or proved manifestly inconsistent, contradictory, and simply incoherent. But I came away from my readings convinced that these writings (and presumably the practices they report) are by no means of antiquarian interest only. They already contain the elements we can assemble for critical interpretation today. And if this study amounts to a critique—incomplete and unsystematic because historically situated—of ethnographic practices at their early stages, then my story makes sense.

If "telling stories" was a figure of speech, so was talk of protagonists. Explorers appeared as authors of statements or as actors in their own reports chosen and quoted to provide information and support arguments we can apply to our critiques. As the story unfolded most of the travelers took on individual traits; they became moral and intellectual subjects who demanded moral and intellectual responses, rather than classification according to some system of sociological types or literary categories. I thought of my role as that of one reader among others, a role that allowed me to show my admiration and contempt, appreciation and disagreement. In this I followed a rule I have tried to respect in my ethnographic work with contemporary interlocutors as well as in interpretations of historical documents.

Having said this, I must reiterate the point about the protagonists of my story being figures of speech. All these explorers of central Africa appear as subjects only during the short episodes documented in the travelogues. I cannot do biographical justice to any one of them; what I said about them as intellectuals and human beings is valid only within the frame I defined. A limited knowledge of their further careers leads me to suspect that a cumulative biography would pick up the pervasive pattern of contradictions, incongruities, and—indeed—madness that made up the plot of my story. Even the little information I can give now will make the point. Here is what I have been able to find out about the life of those who survived their involvement with exploration.

Becker sacrificed an almost certainly splendid colonial career to the loyalty he had for his Arab-Swahili friends and lived in Belgium under a cloud of suspicion and accusations until he met his prosaic death from a fall he took on one of the squares of Antwerp. The sensitive, critical

Coquilhat seems to have embraced King Leopold's dubious enterprise wholesale, becoming one of his trusted counselors and eventually vice-governor-general of the Congo Free State. Yet there is more than a touch of mad despair in his accepting this assignment against the advice of his doctors, in a state of failing health that made him last less than a year before he died in Boma. Pogge, as we saw, ended his life with the request that all his notes and diaries be destroyed. Schütt absconded to Japan, presumably because he knew that his faking the most important part of his journey would inevitably be uncovered. Buchner, whose ravings and rantings made us doubt his sanity, finished his career as director of the ethnological museum in Berlin (making him a successor of the great Bastian). Büttner taught secondary school, Wolff returned to medical practice; neither made much of the capital they accumulated as explorers. Staid and sober von François went on to become one of the terrifying agents of colonial oppression in German Southwest Africa as commander of a campaign that under his successors ended in the near-extermination of the Herero. So, in a way, did Wissmann, who was one of the first to deploy the Maxim gun in putting down the Bushiri revolt in East Africa.[1] His accomplishments gained him, still during the period we covered, an impressive volume of appraisal and praise as "Deutschlands größter Afrikaner" (Germany's greatest African [Becker et al. 1907]). He rose to the office of governor but his colonial career eventually evaporated, possibly because of divided loyalties and his disagreement with official policies. His life ended with an accident that invites comparison with the gunshot that took Hemingway's life. The much-quoted and almost lovable young Thomson went on to accomplish more exploratory feats, yet he finished as a typical Victorian racist. According to his biographer, "Thomson, the gentle, humane, seemingly sensible explorer of the early 1880s, devoted the last years of his young life to...irresponsible fulminations and propagation of commonplace analyses of Africa and its inhabitants" (Rotberg 1970a, 317).

Apart from Buchner, who remained inconspicuous, only Frobenius and Torday became Africanists of considerable fame. Yet neither achieved full academic recognition during his lifetime. Frobenius's almost manic activities and productivity earned him grudging acceptance until he was promoted by L. Sedar Senghor and others as one of the few Europeans ever to understand and appreciate the genius of African cultures. In the end only Torday emerges as an untainted figure, a liberal, careful, and respected ethnographer of the Kuba whose loyalties to his native country apparently barred him from finding a place among the great British anthropologists who contributed to the professionalization of our discipline.[2]

MYTH AND REALITY

Readers will recall that this project began with images of drunken or otherwise intoxicated encounters between European travelers and African potentates, meetings that at the same time counted as crucial events of exploration. Histories of these inquiries carried out while "under the influence" dismiss the context as accidental and in any case extraneous to the production of knowledge about other peoples that was to develop into ethnography, the empirical basis of anthropology. But my experiences as an ethnographer in contemporary Africa caused me to take a dim view of the possibility of a "pure" science of other peoples based on the ideals of positivism, and these instances of uncontrolled, ecstatic behavior on the part of "scientific travelers" intrigued me. Could ecstasis, defined more broadly than by the overspecific instances that first caught my attention, have actually been a productive element? Should it, under certain circumstances, count as a condition rather than an impediment for rational inquiry? After all, the object of inquiry here was not nature—its laws are the same everywhere—but human beings, whose history and culture were distinct and different from ours.

The next step was to identify what made the drunken encounters so intriguing. They contradicted other larger and more powerful—often very "visual" and specific—images of exploration as myth: a parable of Western scientific inquiry we absorbed mainly through the vastly popular literary genre of the travelogue that recorded the exploits of exploration. Of course, this possibility has occurred to others. Anthropologists have quite emphatically distanced themselves from the stories told by travelers. Here, for instance, is Lévi-Strauss's devastating way of dealing with the myth enshrined in travelers' writings. He denies precisely what I affirm, namely that it played, and continues to play, a significant role in the emergence of a science of others: "Society shows total indifference to what one would like to call the rational results of these adventures. It [travel writing] is not about scientific discovery, nor about poetic and literary enrichment, since the evidence is most often shockingly poor. It is the fact of the attempt that counts, not its object" (1955, 42).

He then went on to write *Tristes tropiques,* a book Clifford Geertz summed up as follows: "In the first place, it is, of course, and despite the ironic and self-reflexive denial of the famous opening passage, a travel book in a very recognizable genre. I went here, I went there; I saw this strange thing and that; I was amazed, bored, excited, disappointed; I got boils on my behind, and once, on the Amazon...—all with the implicit undermessage: Don't you wish you had been there with me and could do the same?" (1988, 33–34). Geertz goes on to name four other categories in which the book could be situated: ethnography, philosophical text, reformist tract, literary text. They definitely make *Tristes tropiques* a close relative of our sources, a point that recurs in the many examples of all the above within the fragmentary texts we quoted. At the very least, the same good reasons that made Geertz read Lévi-Strauss cause us to take the travelogues of central African exploration seriously: these works help us gain critical understanding of anthropology as it is now.

Though I paid much attention to exploration as writing, as the making of texts, our approaches differ in that I decided on a reading of travelogues that would debunk the myth of exploration. That is what we should do with myths (or this kind of myth) whenever we run into one;[3] it is especially appropriate and irresistible when myths turn out to have fooled us about a question that still matters to us: what makes ethnography, begotten in an age of Enlightenment but born under the auspices of imperialism, worth pursuing in these postcolonial times? Now, if our thesis holds—that the myth of exploration has been a centerpiece among the images of Western scientific rationality—it follows that a critique of that myth should and could be an enterprise I have always felt close to: a critique of reason. Notwithstanding its impressive history from Kant, Hegel, Marx, Nietzsche, the Frankfurt school to Jürgen Habermas (and Richard Rorty and Charles Taylor too) and, closer to home, again notwithstanding Frantz Fanon, V. Y. Mudimbe, Anthony Appiah, Gayatri Spivak, and many others, the philosophical critique of reason is only now beginning to class discourses and practices of the making of the Other among the vital and central problems it calls "perennial." To avoid biting off more of this huge cake than I can chew, I limited the field and embarked on this exploration of "our minds" in the exploration of central Africa.

What we now have is, I believe, both simple enough to describe in general terms and too complex and diffuse to cast into a few summarizing conclusions. It is relatively easy to state what we discovered when we confronted the myth of exploration with concrete, specific information contained in the same sources that enacted and fed that myth. We found that an ideal, and ideological, story of scientific inquiry as a highly individual, controlled, indeed heroic enterprise, devoted to rational purpose and as yet relatively free of disciplinary routine, contained its own counterstory in the abundant evidence we detected of conditions and structures that controlled every step a traveler to central Africa took during his peregrinations. Metropolitan plans and instructions ran into and, more often than not, got bogged down in local circumstances. Political and economic realities inevitably mixed with (and, in the views of its adepts, contaminated) pure science. What should have been a matter of carrying out well-circumscribed tasks almost always turned into a battle for mere survival, with death the outcome almost as often as not. Natural and human objects that should, according to the explorers' ideals of natural history, have been there to be observed turned out to be engaged in intricate relations of interaction and resistance. The simplest trappings and habits of science—instruments, measurements, classifications, maps—either did not work at all or had to be made to work by suspending and often violating basic rules of inquiry and inference. Even the staunchest naturalists among the travelers were frequently seduced and sometimes overcome by what they encountered. Forced to join the dance of circumstances, explorers often conducted their activities as spectacular theatrical performances not previously imagined even by those who admitted they had come to Africa also in search of adventure.

If these emissaries of imperialism and missionaries of a superior civilization had one pervasive experience, it was of dependency. Travelers depended on things—funds, equipment, and commodities—and the more things they had, the more they had to struggle with problems of logistics. And they depended on people. Especially during their first journeys, they were amateurs at African travel compared to their guides, interpreters, and porters. The more professional these helpers were, the more dependent the explorers became on their knowledge, even before they themselves were ready to produce the kind of knowledge they were expected to bring back. Add to all that the whims of local rulers and the vagaries of the climate and physical environment. One experience came to all these young, able-bodied men, and it epitomizes the rest: dependency on their bodies. Fatigue, minor sores and major illness, accidents and not-quite-lethal wounds caused suffering of heroic proportions and, again, prosaic dependency on the goodwill of their companions and auxiliaries.

As if all these determinations and constraints were not enough, there was the expectation of self-control. Individually and collectively, the explorers followed an encompassing regime of tropical hygiene that regulated all imaginable activities from taking care of their feet to keeping a diary. Even learning a language and compiling vocabularies could come

under the rubrics of hygiene: they maintained health and only incidentally let scientists communicate with the people they had come to study.
The pressures of self-discipline and self-control inevitably left them little
tolerance for the constant challenges, playful and serious, that Africans
put up against their authority as the leaders of caravans. Even the most
scientific travelers resorted to physical violence—trying to match self-
control with control of others in order accomplish their mission—and, as
some of them knew, found themselves even further from their goals.

Finally, though most explorers wanted to believe they served science
and thereby humanity in an enterprise that had to be honest by definition, few were able to close their eyes to evidence they had of their imperial sponsors' duplicity. Organizing a geographic conference for "scientific exploration," Leopold II gave them a means to prepare the
occupation of future colonies. Slavery was a test case—after the Brussels
conference, its eradication also became the moral legitimation for imperialism—for the travelers' relations with the Arab-Swahili traders and
colonists on whose cooperation most of the expeditions operating from
the east depended. Becker, Thomson, and others acknowledged Arab culture and hospitality, and several of them established close personal
friendships and lasting loyalties. In the end Becker embraced wholesale
condemnation of Islam as "plague" as a sort of counterimage to the
heroic metaphor of "fever" that, as it were, sanctified Western exploration of Africa.

Entanglement in imperial designs has worried anthropology ever
since. From our sources we know that such inherent contradictions, especially also the constant pressure to compete with the representatives
of other nations and to rush through their assignments when serious scientific inquiry would have required time and extended stays, drove some
to the brink of madness or, at any rate, made them behave in ways toward, and say things about, Africans that strike us as somehow demented. Many took refuge in racist judgments and most often couched
them in moral terms.

CONTROL AND ECSTASIS

Ecstasis started us off and became a frequent topic in the most varied
contexts in almost every chapter. Why is it that, as I come to the end of
my efforts, the prospect of having to take stock of the concept and spell
out what our findings could mean for anthropology seems so difficult?
Perhaps my reaction is appropriate; perhaps a coherent account of what

were of necessity brief moments of freedom, abandonment, and surrender would cancel its purpose. Nevertheless, readers will expect some kind of concluding statement; here is what I am able to put into words.

Let me begin with two suppositions I made when I began to think about the issue. First, as a form of scientific inquiry, exploration has two elements in common with ethnography: the Self as an irreplaceable agent in the production of knowledge and an Other as the human object of inquiry.[4] Individual researchers may form teams—explorers did and ethnographers do. But if the knowledge sought is to be that of a human Other, exploration as well as ethnography depends on communication between individuals. Language, the most social and super-individual of human inventions, cannot be activated except by individual speakers. Even the explorers, who, almost without exception, subscribed to a natural history view of observation as the scientific activity par excellence, had to realize this. Unlike observation, communication does not come "naturally." Beyond the exchange of certain universally understood signals, verbal or nonverbal communication demands specific, cultural competences. Our authors differed greatly with respect to their awareness of these connections: some communicated with Africans and others didn't.

In gaining knowledge of Others—knowledge that we can state discursively, or knowledge that shapes our understanding—we must pass cultural boundaries to reach common ground. Both sides to the exchange travel back and forth between different positions. Put in dialectical terms, communication across cultural boundaries creates a problem of identity. Because action needs an agent, we must maintain our identity. And we must abandon it, because no action—certainly not the action of exploration and ethnography—is possible if we keep a rigid hold on our identity. But if we think of identity as a process rather than a property or state, we resolve the apparent contradiction. Except in limit cases that may be pathological, human beings everywhere engage in individual and collective activities and processes that form and change their identity. Our action makes identity, of Self as well as Other, a precarious matter and may explain why in Western thought—if we may use this summary notion to cover a vast variety of individual and collective processes—identity requires control.

My second major presupposition about scientific inquiry as a cultural practice (as most philosophers and historians of science now agree it is) was that of the need for (self-)control, again individually as well as collectively. Throughout this study I asked a simple two-pronged question: *is* science a controlled practice, and *should* science be a controlled practice? Rather than address these questions to science in general, I focused on the practices that concern us as anthropologists: ethnography and its historical predecessor, exploration. If the only possible alternatives to control were total anomie or randomness, a negative answer would be hard to imagine. Yet what we said about identity must also apply to control. It is a stultifying concept unless we think of it dialectically, as an assertion that must include its negation. We conceived such negation as ecstasis: it is not the theoretical, logical opposite of control but becomes its pragmatic and existential negation. As such it does not remain a matter of cogitation but can become the object of inquiry, in this case, into practices of knowledge production. Which takes us back to the starting point of these reflections: what have we learned about ecstasis as an element of scientific inquiry from our reading of accounts of the exploration of central Africa?

I cannot help but think of the children of hemp, whose story constitutes a pivotal chapter not only in the organization of this study. For there, localized and limited in time, a movement of modernization, inspired ritually, ideologically, and physically by a consciousness-altering drug, met an exploratory expedition representing the *oeuvre civilisatrice*. That expedition was in desperate shape—out of control owing to desertion, illness, and lack of means. Pogge's and Wissmann's incorporation in the hemp cult and their obviously genuine friendship with Mukenge and Meta involved an exchange of minds beyond the call of needs and interests. In my view it was a paradigmatic event, expressive of the potential of ecstatic experiences, and a glimpse at a utopian meeting of the West and Africa on equal terms. Of course, eventually control took over: the expedition reorganized itself to perform its imperial tasks, to instrumentalize friendship, and finally to betray it, forcing whatever knowledge it gained to serve the establishment of colonial rule. A similar and basically tragic turn brought Becker across cultural and ideological boundaries to firm friendship with Tipo Tip. Though, unlike Wissmann, he always stood by his insights and loyalties and in the end sacrificed his career to them, the potential of the meeting of minds between the explorer and the Swahili trader and political genius quickly vanished in the course of colonial history. Coquilhat had his moments of deep comprehension; the impetuous Wolff and the pedantic Büttner had extraordinary possibilities offered to them, especially by their African guide and mentor, David Kornelius Bardo. Similar breaks—I think this is an appropriate expression considering the effects they had in cracking personal and cultural shells—were offered to many explorers by the children they employed and the women they met.

Aside from these sometimes dramatic forms, tied to events that travelers experienced, ecstasis played a role in exploration in countless other ways in which loss of control because of illness (and medication), desperate situations, fits of rage and violence, moments of seduction, and purposeless conviviality induced more or less lasting states of detachment from imperial projects and from the rules of scientific inquiry (both of them embodied in the regime of hygiene). Ecstasis, reflecting theoretically and practically on the wealth of evidence we found in our sources, was a dimension of experiencing Africa and of whatever knowledge explorers finally produced. The point of this, if it still needs to be made, is not that we should be able to sort out kinds of knowledge gained through controlled activities as distinct from others produced ecstatically. What we found—and we should apply this to our critical reflections on the nature of ethnography—is that being "out of our minds" is a dimension, indeed a condition of possibility, of disciplined knowledge about Others that exists within physical, social, and political circumstances.

NON SEQUITUR

I end with two conclusions readers should not draw. One regards the methodological implications of what we found about ecstasis, the other the larger historical and political significance of the picture we painted of the exploration of central Africa.

Ecstasis, like empathy, communication, and dialogue, as well as age, gender, social class, and relations of power, belongs to concepts that impose themselves when we reflect critically about what makes us succeed or fail in our efforts to produce knowledge about Others. We recognize them as conditions and as integral dimensions of ethnographic inquiry yet—such is the strength of the positivist tradition—tend to ascribe success to method and consequently mistake conditions and dimensions for ways and means. True, certain methodological choices reflect critical insights: we can prepare ourselves with linguistic competences; we can pick sites and topics we somehow find congenial; we can allot time and energy to conversing and recording our conversations; we can even to some extent let things happen around us while we are in the field rather than rush to line up informants and cover topics according to plans we had to present to our sponsors. On another level, we may realize that all ethnography is inevitably contingent, historically and autobiographically situated. But as we take a critical distance from positivist methods or methodologism—that core of misunderstood modernity in all forms of scientism—we must not try to turn empathy or dialogue or any other condition or dimension of knowledge we discern after the fact into a method for producing knowledge. It would be ironic indeed if critical anthropology were to reproduce, once removed, all the follies of method that made us lose faith in Newtonian science as a paradigm for anthropology in the first place. Ecstasis is not something to pursue in the practice of ethnography—getting drunk or high, losing one's mind from fatigue, pain, and fever-induced delirium, or working oneself into a frenzy—as a method of field research. Seeking such experiences (and often controlling them carefully, by the way) is the privilege of mystics, perhaps of artists, but the knowledge they are after is not what we seek.

The second non sequitur concerns the rationality of exploration in practice. What struck us in many minor incidents and at some major junctures was the contradictory, indeed mad, nature of the enterprise. But we cannot let imperialism—not even the part of it that was early ethnography—off the hook by a plea of insanity. What our findings should help us do is move the critique of colonialism from questions of guilt to questions of error; error not just in the sense of making mistakes but of failing to acknowledge the demands of reason (reason itself being a constant object of critical reflection). What I have been after, and what I hope to have shown, was a kind of failure that reaches beyond individuals in the past: a failure that we can still ascribe, presently and collectively, to ethnography, hence to being "out of *our* minds."

What else can we learn from this study? An ability to approach ethnography critically does not in principle distinguish us from our forbears. To be sure, their writings had no organized discourses on epistemology and literary critique (though there are interesting exceptions). What counts is that they had all the elements and were aware of them. And that their writings prompt our critical questions today.

But surely historical hindsight puts us in a different, privileged position? Yes, but the lessons of history do not come to us automatically, just because time has passed. Nor do I believe in the positivist article of faith that its history justifies a scientific discipline. The fact of its presence today cannot legitimate anthropology's existence. Ours is an exercise in remembering: in reminding ourselves of our beginnings; in using our own memories to select what, in these accounts, reminds us of what. Far from aiming for a definitive history or critique of the beginning of central African ethnography, I am remembering the present.

Expeditions

Some Overviews

MEMBERS AND MAJOR REPORTS

GERMAN EXPEDITIONS

Sponsored by Deutsche Gesellschaft zur Erforschung des äquatorialen Afrikas (founded in Berlin, April 19, 1873) and its successors

Pogge (1874–76).[1] Report in Paul Pogge (1880)
Schütt (1878–79). Report in Otto H. Schütt (1881)
Buchner (1878–81). Reports in *MAGD*
German East African Expedition (1880–84).[2] Baron von Schöler, Richard Böhm, Emil Kaiser, Paul Reichard. Reports in *MAGD*, Böhm ([posthumous] 1888)
Pogge-Wissmann (1880–83).[3] Reports in *MAGD*, Hermann Wissmann (1889)
German Congo Expedition (1884–86).[4] Eduard Schulze, Richard Büttner, Wilhelm Albert Wolff, Richard Kund, Hans Tappenbeck. Reports in *MAGD*, Wolff (1889), Büttner (1890)

BELGIAN EXPEDITIONS

Sponsored by the Brussels committee of the International African Association (Association internationale africaine)

IAA First Expedition (1877–79). Louis Crespel, Ernest Cambier, Pierre Dutrieux
IAA Second Expedition (1879). Emile Popelin, Theodore van den Heuvel
IAA Third Expedition (1880–82). Jules Ramaeckers, Jérôme Becker
IAA Fourth Expedition (1882–83). Popelin, Roger, Emile Storms
IAA Fifth Expedition (1883–84).[5] Report in Becker (1887)
Upper Congo Expedition (1882–85).[6] Report in Camille Coquilhat (1888)
Wissmann (1883–85).[7] Report in Wissmann et al. (1887)

TRAVELS IN THE CONGO FREE STATE

Wissmann (1886–87). Reports in Wissmann ([1890], 1891 [in English])
Frobenius (1904–6). Report in Leo Frobenius (1907)
Torday–Hilton-Simpson (1907–9). Reports in M.-W. Hilton-Simpson (1911),
   Emil Torday (1913)

OTHER EXPEDITIONS

Johnston-Thomson (1878–79). Report in Joseph Thomson (1881)
Capelo and Ivens (1877–79). Report in Hermingildo Capelo and Roberto Ivens
   (1882)

YEARS OF DEPARTURE

YEAR	GERMAN AND OTHERS	BELGIAN	FREE STATE
1874	Pogge		
1877	Capelo and Ivens	First IAA: Crespel, Cambier, Dutrieux	
1878	Schütt Buchner Johnston-Thomson		
1879		Second IAA: Popelin, van den Heuvel	
1880	German East African: Schöler, Böhm, Kaiser, Reichard Pogge-Wissmann	Third IAA: Ramaeckers, Becker	
1882		Fourth IAA: Popelin, Roger, Storms Upper Congo: Coquilhat	
1883	Wissmann: Wissman, Wolf, von François, H. Müller, F. Müller	Fifth IAA: Becker	
1884	German Congo: Schulze, Büttner, Wolff, Kund, Tappenbeck		
1886			Wissmann
1904			Frobenius
1907			Torday–Hilton-Simpson

OVERLAP OF OPERATIONS BEFORE 1900

	1874	1875	1876	1877	1878	1879	1880	1881	1882	1883	1884	1885	1886	1887
Pogge	x	x	x											
Capelo and Ivens				x	x	x								
First IAA				x	x	x								
Johnston-Thomson					x	x								
Schütt					x	x								
Buchner					x	x	x	x						
Second IAA						x								
German East African							x	x	x	x	x			
Pogge-Wissmann							x	x	x	x				
Third IAA							x	x	x					
Fourth IAA									x	x				
Upper Congo										x	x	x		
Fifth IAA										x	x			
Wissmann										x	x	x		
German Congo											x	x	x	
Wissmann													x	x

Notes

ONE

1. Shaba and Zaire were the official names throughout most of the time I worked in this region. Recent political developments resulted in the country's reverting to the name it had when I started my fieldwork in the 1960s: the Democratic Republic of the Congo. When referring to the colonial past or the recent present, I use the names Katanga and Congo instead of Shaba and Zaire (as the context requires).

2. I listed and counted only what linguists call "types," that is, the items of a (presumed) lexicon. In speech and writing a given type may yield any number, sometimes large numbers, of "tokens," or occurrences, and these I did not count. Now, after a second careful reading of Becker, I find that I had overlooked a substantial number of tokens, perhaps as many as fifty, which increases my earlier vocabulary by some 10 percent.

3. Luc de Heusch explored this motif in a study of the origin of the state in Africa (1972).

4. For a recent critique of this resistance perspective and its consequences for conceptions of ethnography, see Ortner 1995.

5. Mark Hobart formulated a similar demand, if I understand him correctly, in a witty, acerbic essay titled "Ethnography as a Practice" (1996). His mythopoetic place is Bali, not central Africa, and his perspective on developments in American anthropology is somewhat more European and more negative than mine, but his arguments are congenial to what I hope to accomplish in this study.

6. Works too numerous to cite here have contributed to a history of ethnography as part of the history of anthropology, an endeavor led by George W. Stocking. But only a few of their authors (such as Marshall Sahlins and Jan Vansina) have done ethnographic research themselves. Also relevant for episte-

mological approaches to the history of anthropology is work in the history and philosophy of science that uses ethnographic methods.

7. Notice that his injunction does not problematize "experience," which is precisely what we want to do. The rule refers to the empiricist element in positivism. Experience should be understood as whatever enters the Lockean "empty cabinet" of the mind through the senses, with the eye as the most reliable, hence most "noble," of the senses (on this visualist orientation in anthropology see Fabian 1983, ch. 4).

8. See, for instance, Michael Taussig's *Mimesis and Alterity* (1993). I take the opportunity to acknowledge much overlap in our approaches to the effects of colonialism on the production of knowledge.

9. *Notes and Queries,* first published in 1874—at the beginning of the period we cover—will be discussed in chapter 8.

10. Readers who want to know more about my notion of positivism may consult my critical essays (Fabian 1991b) and the book by Leszek Kolakowski that helped me clarify my understanding (1969).

11. As far as I recall, the suggestion came from Philippe Marechal, a historian at the Royal Museum of Central Africa in Tervuren, who was then working on his thorough study of the Belgian anti-Arab campaign (1992).

12. Just as this manuscript went to press I received from Beatrix Heintze a copy of her work on German explorers in Angola (1999a); a condensed version of it appeared in English just before my study went to the printer (1999b). Apart from interpretive essays, the book contains short biographies, selections of texts, and extensive bibliographies, which may be consulted to fill the gaps left in my less detailed account. Heintze covers all the German travelers mentioned here, as well as others outside the period of my study. As may be expected, Heintze's much wider corpus of sources (which, unlike mine, is not limited to published travelogues) and our different theoretical interests and polemic temperaments lead us to different readings and evaluations of some of the protagonists and their work. It was encouraging to see that a scholar for whom I have the greatest respect has found a similar, in many ways complementary, undertaking worthwhile.

13. The East Central African Expedition was organized and initially led by Keith Johnston, a geographer and cartographer trained in Britain and Germany who had field experience in Paraguay. He soon became seriously ill and died on June 28, 1879. Thomson called him one of the "geographical martyrs who have attempted to break through the barriers of disease and barbarism which make the interior almost impenetrable" (1881, 149).

14. I made a similar choice in my *Language and Colonial Power,* as I explain there (1991a, 11).

15. See *Exploration* 1 (1876): 2, 5.

16. On the foundation of the Afrikanische Gesellschaft in Deutschland and its prehistory, see *MAGD,* no. 1 (1878): 1–3 and 18–21; on its dissolution, *MAGD* 5, no. 3 (1889): 133.

17. The literature on Leopold II and the Congo Free State is vast. For a fairly recent biography of the king in English, see Emerson 1979. Scores of works were published around 1985, when several international meetings commemorated the

centennial of the Berlin Conference and of Leopold's colony. Pakenham 1991 is a voluminous yet readable account of the African activities of the imperial powers and their agents, detailing the major campaigns and conquests from 1876–1912 that constituted "the scramble for Africa." But none of the sources I will be using figure in Pakenham's account. The most recent scholarly treatment of the period is Wesseling 1996.

18. See the autobiography of the great trader and traveler Tipo Tip (Hamed bin Mohammed el Murjebi), who met many of our protagonists. The most richly documented edition and translation of this document is Bontinck and Janssen 1974 (in French), which includes a history of the text.

I should point out that the term *Arab,* as used in our sources, sometimes refers to people who either came from or traced their origins to regions such as Oman and Muscat and who continued to speak Arabic in Africa. Most often, however, the term designates persons of mixed Arab and African descent who spoke Swahili, the linguistic medium of a distinctive east coast culture and, in its vehicular varieties (as trade or work idioms) from the coast to the upper Congo, a means of communication. I follow the sources in using *Arab* whenever the meaning is clear from the context; otherwise I specify Arab-Swahili or simply Swahili.

19. See Hibbert 1982, as well as Rotberg 1970b, a collection of historical essays on the major figures of that period.

20. The United States played an important role in the emergence of the Congo Free State, something often overlooked, though well documented in Bontinck 1966.

21. See Bastian 1874–75, 1:ix; and *MAGD,* no. 1 (1878): 18.

22. I thank Beatrix Heintze for bringing Essner's book to my attention.

TWO

1. A few lists of regulations were eventually authored by some of our protagonists. Remarkable examples are the appendixes to Becker's work (1887, 1:457–90; 2:498–500); Société d'études coloniales 1896; and Wissmann 1895. We will address this literature in chapter 8.

2. Published in an appendix to vol. 1 (457–90), Becker's vade mecum is by far the most complete logistical document in our sources. For many years, my favorite literary text on exploration has been Per Olof Sundman's classic (and epistemological) novel, *The Expedition* (1967). Inspired by Stanley's writings, he vividly describes the intricate, often mathematical nature of the problems of logistics the explorers faced.

3. These are appellations in Swahili that were used mostly in expeditions departing from the east coast. But Zanzibaris were also employed in operations starting from the lower Congo. Caravans departing from the Portuguese Loango coast seem to have been somewhat less clearly structured, to judge from descriptions in the sources.

4. It took an exceptionally open-minded person such as Willy Wolff to appreciate Kornelius's intellect and wisdom. He devotes an entire chapter to the latter's views on European education (1889, 23–28); elsewhere he notes Kor-

nelius's critical remarks on the missions and the motivation of European colonialism (108, 109–10). From Wolff we learn that in Europe Kornelius "at one time also let himself be seen as a savage at fairs" (23).

5. Wissmann, for instance, says that women rarely came along on expeditions (1889, 14), yet he himself provides contrary evidence (see the role of the children of hemp, both men and women, discussed in chapter 7).

6. See *MAGD* 2, no. 4 (1881): 212, and no. 5 (1881): 221–22, for the German complaints; and Becker 1887, 1:47, 75, 92, 102, 116–17, 165, 439–40, 451; and 2:90.

7. See Pogge 1880 and especially Schütt 1881, who describes the brothers as educated and multilingual; he found them to be excellent informants who would also give travelers credit if they ran out of funds.

8. See Wissmann 1889, 11; similar meetings were reported by Becker and Coquilhat.

9. On African auxiliaries (mainly in East African operations) and on the point made in this section see Donald Simpson's *Dark Companions* (1975). He speaks of Mabruki Speke several times (see index), but not of his service under Roger and Burdo, and he mentions Zaidi, the boatman (122). Livingstone's and later Thomson's Chuma (or Juma) rates a crowded entry in the index.

10. A comparable situation obtained in the east with the establishment of German colonies. Because after 1885 the east coast no longer served as point of departure for travel to central Africa in the restricted sense of the Congo Basin, I ignore reports of East African travel conducted after the Berlin Conference.

11. Although (or because?) the caravan has a large role in the myth of exploration, it has had little scholarly attention apart from two studies, one by Beidelman (1982) on missionary caravans, another one by Spittler (1987) on explorers' caravans in the western Sudan during the first half of the nineteenth century. Neither discusses caravan travel's incongruities and contradictions, but Beidelman's complements and confirms the picture I draw.

12. Hunting—what the British called sports—as a source of food was negligible on the almost gameless western approach, but there was still much to shoot in East Africa. Later chapters will comment on the value attached to sports as a strong motive for travels in Africa.

13. Perhaps these *rugaruga* were a structural concomitant of state formation, much like the groups of *balungu* in central Africa recently described in a provocative study by Rik Ceyssens (1998).

14. On Grenfell see Johnston 1908, commissioned by the Baptist Missionary Society and compiled with Torday's help; the book is a remarkably informative and richly illustrated account of Grenfell's role in establishing the Congo Free State. Other missionaries of the period mentioned by our travelers, such as Weeks (1914) and especially Bentley (1900), also published lengthy memoirs showing their contribution to the knowledge of country and people.

15. Hinde 1897 and Marechal 1992 document in great detail how much of the Arab-Swahili colony had to be removed so that the Belgians could set up theirs. In some places new stations were built with bricks recuperated from destroyed Arab residences.

THREE

1. The Congolese painter-historian Tshibumba Kanda Matulu documents popular memory of exploration when he condenses African recollections in images that appear to be inspired by the European myth of exploration. He depicts African versions of first encounters and covers the gamut of possibilities when he opposes Livingstone and Stanley as two extremes. Livingstone inquires among and converses with the people; he dies in the arms of Africans. Stanley moves about but never makes contact with the villagers, who flee wherever he shows up (see Fabian 1996, 24–31).

2. Elsewhere (Fabian 1991b, ch. 8) I sketched its religious roots and hence its capacity to keep open "passages" (another notion I borrow from Michel Foucault) between colonization's religious and secular discourses.

3. Other comprehensive terms for the "tropical condition" do as yet not compete with *fever: spleen* in English and apparently adopted in French (see the quotation from Becker in chapter 10, where I translate it as "depression"); especially the German *Tropenkoller* (with connotations of raving madness) is conspicuously absent from the sources.

4. Control of alcohol was raised, but not much discussed, at the Berlin Conference of 1884–85 and debated at length in 1890 at the Brussels antislavery conference and several later international meetings (see Pan 1975).

5. Torday assigns (1913, 75) this epithet to Frobenius and the expedition's artist, Lemme.

6. Frobenius's term, *kneipen,* comes from student jargon and refers to occasions when corporations would gather, in full colors, for beer-drinking bouts.

7. I'm tempted to compile an explorer's cookbook from the many menus and detailed descriptions in our sources—it would be entertaining as well as educational.

8. Half of the roughly twenty travelers most frequently mentioned in our sources (authors of travelogues, contributors to *MAGD,* and their companions) died in Africa during the period we cover. A mortality figure of 25 percent each year for Congo Free State personnel was mentioned earlier. Figures for members of the Belgian army (29 percent between 1877 and 1908) and of Scandinavian military in the service of the Congo Free State (38 percent between 1878 and 1904) were even higher (see Force publique 1952, 505–6).

FOUR

1. The European explorers in our corpus were an all-male cast. Though the sources mention homosexual relations between Europeans and Africans, they offer no evidence that one or another of our protagonists lived out or made efforts to control homoerotic inclinations.

The only European woman to travel at the western edge of the area during the 1890s was Mary Kingsley (not counting an unknown number of female missionaries who began to reside in the Congo). Kingsley is the focus of Alison Blunt's study on travel, gender, and imperialism (Blunt 1994). This work and others in a growing literature on colonialism and sexuality (e.g., McClintock

1995 and Young 1995) form a background to this chapter's more modest and focused purposes.

2. Somewhat later, and perhaps when Becker used the term, *menagères* described African women who lived with European colonial agents.

3. On the page facing this passage is one of the book's few illustrations of sparsely clad African women in poses that are not suggestive: the chief of Konko with one of her *demoiselles d'honneur.* As for Becker's companions, Sergère was the French partner in a firm of traders and outfitters of caravans (Sergère and Sewa; see chapter 2); Captain Baron von Schöler was then still the head of the German East African expedition and very shortly returned to Europe, probably for reasons of health (he drops out of *MAGD*'s reports).

4. Heintze found (1999, 90–91) that only one German traveler, Pechuël-Loesche, had an African *Zeitfrau* (temporary wife), who was also one of his chief informants. The information comes from his diary, not his published account.

5. See recent attempts to bring not only gender in general but sex into the light of debates about the practice of ethnography (Kulick and Willson 1995).

6. Clifford Geertz called (1973, 347) the design of *Tristes tropiques* "in the standard form of the Heroic Quest" that held a "combination of autobiography, traveler's tale, philosophical treatise, ethnographic report, colonial history, and prophetic myth"—ingredients we find in our sources (and in Becker's case perhaps, similarly blended).

FIVE

1. The hemp test replaced the traditional poison ordeal among the Bene Diamba in the Lulua-Kasai region; more about them in chapter 7.

2. I am not sure where to class fireworks. Apart from their appearance in the abbé Debaize's stores inventoried at the outset of this chapter, rockets (*Raketen*) turned up among supplies Pogge had left with Saturnino Machado in Quimbundu, where Schütt (1881, 134) found them years later.

3. Thomson's is the most extensive account in our sources of the abbé Debaize's follies (2:92–95). Later he tells of listening to Debaize's "hurdy-gurdy" (190–91) and describes his reaction in terms almost identical to Becker's (to be quoted presently).

4. Hilton-Simpson recalled an evening, most likely one of many such evenings, when he and Torday sat together, had a drink, and listened to music on the phonograph (1911, 33).

5. He may be referring to the band of the Lukokesha, the female chief, which consisted of xylophones, drums, and a large slat drum (*Holzpauke*) (1880, 154).

6. See the seminal study of African drumming by John Chernoff (1979), who, it appears, also had reason drummed into his ears. Inspired by Nietzsche's *Geburt der Tragödie aus dem Geiste der Musik* (Birth of tragedy from the spirit of music [1872]), he demonstrates that scholarly study and participation in performance combine to produce knowledge that goes far beyond the usual ethnomusicological collecting and bookkeeping.

7. Wissmann's first impressions of Mirambo (1889, 256–61) agree with Becker's.

8. Reproduced on the cover of Fabian 1991a.

SIX

1. Recall Becker's remarks on language learning through "joyful and frequent exchanges with the *dames d'honneur* of the chief of Konko, our increasingly intimate relations with the natives" (1887, 2:51), quoted in chapter 4.

2. On Böhm see his obituary (*MAGD* 4, no. 5 [1885]: 295); Fabian 1991b gives an overview of manuals for Swahili and other languages in the early phase of Belgian colonization (on 85, 87).

3. Gierow, of Schütt's expedition, had no compliments for him, either; he called him a coward and a liar (*MAGD* 3, no. 2 [1882]: 123, 126). Schütt (1881) recognized that Germano's service was important to his expedition.

4. For a composite portrait of the *ambaquista*, the "African Bohemian" (with an illustration, titled "An Ambaca Gentleman" [Figure 6 of this book]), see Capelo and Ivens 1882, 2:39–41.

5. A process described in great detail by William Samarin in his seminal work, *The Black Man's Burden* (1989). Swahili was used also on the lower Congo as long as many of the auxiliaries were recruited on the east coast.

6. One such case was an "Oriental," the Lybian Mohammed Biri, hired by the IAA Third Expedition (Becker 1878, 1:37). He had served Ramaekers in North Africa and followed him to Brussels—picking up the nickname Bamboula—and back to Africa. He later represented the expedition in Tabora and was accused of mismanaging its funds (2:396–98, 446–47). The peccadilloes of another interpreter and factotum, a certain Boniface (a lapsed Christian who converted or reverted to Islam; see 1:195, 307–8), amused Becker but he spoke of the Lybian with uncharacteristic contempt.

7. Société d'études coloniales 1896; for quotations and comments see Fabian 1991b, 160–61.

8. In the introduction I referred to the discrepancy and its role in getting me started on this project.

9. Incidentally, I could not find the original transcripts or recordings of these folktales in the Frobenius-Institut archives—a glaring absence, and all the more intriguing because my search turned up a typed draft of the *Dichtkunst* introduction with the author's corrections. The archivist assured me that several manuscripts of Frobenius's books were destroyed as soon as the works were printed.

10. See Fabian 1991a, 75, where I quote a sample contract from the Belgian colonial archives.

11. Torday devotes several pages (and a photo) to his trusted helper (1913, 222–26).

12. Relations between Torday's two accounts are difficult to establish. I assume that Buya (mentioned in 1913) and Meyey (in 1925) are the same person. Torday bought his servant from a chief who had a legal hold on the child. Meyey

stayed with him for two years, had his keys and access to all his goods, and talked back to his master but never once gave cause for complaints.

13. On the employment of children as servants and interpreters see chapter 2's section on auxiliaries and intermediaries.

14. Kashawalla appears again as "der alte Bizerra" (old Bizerra) when Schütt's expedition reaches Kimbundu (1881, 134). Presumably this Bizerra is identical with "unser Führer Casavalla" (our guide Casavalla [145]), who gives Schütt the first coherent story about the Bashilange (see the next chapter).

15. Becker also found out that a little laudanum passed out to the porters would help to make them "a little more docile" (1887, 1:94, 111).

16. The section on time and timing in chapter 3 also has quotations relevant to the present topic.

17. Société d'études coloniales 1896, 86. Later I used it to introduce the section on hygiene in an essay on religious and secular colonization (Fabian 1991b, ch. 8).

18. Including Thomson's. In the preface he proudly claims (1881, vii) the expedition uniquely free of internal strife and trouble—but later records scores of more or less serious incidents.

19. My translation leaves open the possibility that cracking the man's skull did not kill him. But the same phrase could also mean "I blow his brains out with a shot from my revolver."

20. From his second trip Wissmann reports a similar incident in which, he believes, laughter saved the situation ([1890], 88–89).

21. See *MAGD*, no. 4–5 (1879): 235; 2, no. 1 (1880): 44, 46, 47. Notice that these reports are published in a quasi-official bulletin.

22. Kaiser was the first explorer sponsored by the German society to die in Africa, the obituary states (*MAGD* 4, no. 1 [1883]: 1).

23. The Hoover Institute bibliography (Hess and Coger 1972) has twenty-one entries of writings by Reichard, four of them coauthored with his colleagues Kaiser and Böhm.

24. See Frobenius 1907, 281–92 (the rubber company), 267, 275 (beating Africans), and 170–75 (military action)—though he apparently had no military background, he formed his own uniformed police force ("meine Polizeitruppe"; see photos, 270, 271).

25. The explorers shared their attitudes toward corporal punishment of children with the best among their contemporaries. But we may still question their argument for treating Africans like children. Neither evolutionism nor paternalism but a justification of force and often violence was the logic behind such reasoning.

SEVEN

1. Zetterström's monograph (1966) is the most concise modern compilation of known facts and received interpretations I found (in a highly respected but hardly popular Swedish series); it draws on our principal sources: the writings of Pogge and Wissmann in their travelogues and their reports submitted to *MAGD* (one important work he includes on the later history of the children of

hemp [De Clercq 1928] falls outside our period and focus). Ceyssens 1998, an imaginative study of political dynamics in central Africa, gives the children of hemp and the Wissmann-Pogge expeditions a prominent role.

The spelling of both elements of the name Bene Diamba varies (*bena, riamba, liamba, niamba;* see Zetterström 1966, 154n. 7); those for hemp are phonological varieties or artifacts of transcription. The version I opt for has its counterpart in ethnic designations of the type *bene* + label, signifying commonality usually traced to ancestry or origin. Here I translate the term *bene* as children; it is neither gender-specific (like Wissmann's "sons of hemp") nor simply generic (as in "descendants" or "belonging to the clan of").

2. Having to choose the first reports on the Bene Diamba from a wealth of texts for the next section, I often took quotations from *MAGD* because they are fresher, closer to the ethnographic experiences made by the authors, and less accessible than the travelogues.

3. I follow Wissmann's spelling except in quotations. In their early uncertain use of prefixes, Pogge and Wissmann often used the Lunda or Tshokwe forms *tu-* and *ka-*, obviously not always realizing that the latter marked the singular, the former the plural. Much later, Pogge offers an explanation for this Lunda-ized use: "The local people do not like the appellation *Tusselange,* as they are called by the *Kioko* and our porters. They want to be called *Baluba,* sing. *Muluba*" (*MAGD* 4, no. 1 [1883]: 66n.). Wissmann, incidentally, stuck to *Bashilange* (see [1890], 242–54, especially 243n. of his ethnographic summary).

4. He was Wissmann and Pogge's interpreter; see chapter 6's section on language, politics, and rhetoric. And in August 1881, when Pogge hired "Johannes Biserra," he identified him as "the same man who accompanied Schütt to Kiluata but then fell from grace with him and was fired." Biserra/Kashawalla then went to "Casselange," where he stayed for two years as a trader with chief Mukenge (*MAGD* 3, no. 2 [1882]: 147).

5. In his preface Paul Lindenberg explains why Schütt had him edit his travelogue: in the spring of 1880 Schütt took up service for the Japanese government (1881, v).

6. A third party of German explorers, Major von Mechow and his companions Theus and Bugslag. attended the meeting but apparently left no published records except for a brief notice in *MAGD* and a short report in the transactions of the German Society of Geography (see titles 4069 and 4070 in the Hoover Institute bibliography [Hess and Coger 1972]).

7. For an overview I refer readers to Zetterström 1966 and note 1 above.

8. See Vansina 1966, ch. 3, on the empires that emerged at about the same time Europeans began to establish trade and political connections in the sixteenth century.

9. He took office in 1874, Pogge says, and suggests that it took his sister Sangula Meta some time to convert him to the cult (*MAGD* 4, no. 1 [1883]: 69).

10. Historical accounts usually credit a certain Mwamba Mputu (*Mputu* is a widespread term for Europeans, derived from "Portuguese"), who started a hemp cult around 1861 with features of a cargo cult—the movement was awaiting the return of ancestors who would bring the weapons and goods of civiliza-

tion. Contact with Tshokwe traders seems to have been a triggering factor (see, e.g., Vansina 1966, 220).

11. Pogge also notes that the Lunda notables somehow prevent the ruler from drinking and smoking so that he will keep a clear head.

12. Capelo and Ivens heard the name (in 1879) when they met a Bangala caravan near the Cuanza River in present-day Angola. The traders came "from Lubuco or Luba territory" but were unwilling—Capelo and Ivens thought, unable—to give exact information about that region (1882, 2:217–18). Ceyssens, brushing aside Pogge and Wissman's translation, links *lubuku* to Luba terms for divination and stresses Kalamba's authority as a diviner or prophet (Ceyssens 1998, 152–59 for his summary of traits). Divination was certainly present (though more in Sangula Meta) but not as the movement's foremost characteristic.

Pogge mentions another—and far from otherworldly—connotation of *lubuku:* a trading transaction based on credit (*MAGD* 4, no. 1 [1883]: 72); other sources point out the Bene Diamba's sharp trading practices.

13. The sources say little about the diet of the Bashilange. Possibly the prohibitions were a recent experiment, relatively easily abandoned; the one on goats may have been an attempt to change customs related to bride wealth, where goats figured as payment (as noted by Pogge, *MAGD* 4, no. 5 [1885]: 260).

14. He notes in passing, "The well-known traveler and trader Silva Porto from Bihé made, at the same time as ours, a trip to Kabao" (a major ivory market on the Lulua in the country of the Kete [Pogge calls them *Tukettes*], 220; on Silva Porto see also Capelo and Ivens 1882, 1:17). Traders took part in exploration but rarely left written reports; one exception was Carl Wiese ([1891–92] 1983).

15. The explorers could not have had time for serious inquiry before Wissmann made his categorizations. See also my remarks in an essay on Galton's travels (Fabian 1987); in both cases the categorizations had long-lasting effects in an interplay between local interests and colonial imposition. Among the explorers, the only "trained ethnographers"—holding a degree and an academic position—were Bastian, a founder of German *Völkerkunde*, and, de facto (though not de jure), Torday and Frobenius, whose writings are part of the canon of African ethnology, even though their authors never had regular academic careers.

16. Wissmann gives no reason for his qualification (a matter of faithful translation or ethnographic accuracy? or, more likely, of the Bene Diamba's belief in the fable's accuracy?).

17. At least once, at the Bene Diamba's insistence, members of the Wissmann expedition actually ingested hemp (mentioned below).

18. Credit goes also to the oxen the travelers rode—Pogge to Nyangwe and back and Wissmann all the way to the coast (*MAGD* 4, no. 1 [1883]: 73).

19. Katende (his title; his name was Kapanga Munene) stayed in German custody and was eventually released to his country (191).

20. On the treaties with local chiefs (in German) concluded by von François and countersigned by the expedition's interpreter, José Maria Germano, on behalf of the IAA (copies are in the Belgian colonial archives in Brussels), see Ceyssens (1998, 244–47 in facsimile; also treaties between Hans Müller and Kalamba and Tshingenge, 248–49).

21. Wissmann's speech refers to his reincarnation: Kabassu Babu too returned from the sea.

22. The cover illustration Essner (1985) or her publisher put—by choice or accident?—on her study of German African explorers shows members of Wissmann's second expedition together with Sangula Meta, Kalamba, and Tshingenge. Notice Wissmann's hands on Sangula Meta's shoulders and what appears to be a hemp pipe at Kalamba Mukenge's feet.

23. Vansina gave his account of Mukenge's historical role in this Lulua perspective (1966, 220–22); see also Mabika Kalanda (1959) and Libata Musuy-Bakul (1987).

EIGHT

1. As described in Lepenies 1976. On early traveling "naturalists" and knowledge of Africa see Duchet 1971, 47–53; on observation, a key concept of natural history, and the beginnings of anthropology see Moravia 1973, and Leclerc 1979 on the concept's persistence in the social sciences during colonial times; on observation, vision, and modernity in the nineteenth century see Crary 1990.

2. See Stafford 1984, a monumental study of travel accounts from 1760 to 1840. I am not aware of a work of similar scope for our period.

3. Böhm was an ornithologist but, remarkably, the only professional geographer was Keith Johnston, the leader of Thomson's expedition who died early on in the enterprise (it seems geography was a metropolitan, armchair discipline based on observations the travelers provided).

4. Unlike Pogge, Capelo and Ivens apparently never experienced African musical performances as anything but "horrid noise" and "insufferably monotonous" (1882, 1:62, 70; they document one [139] that includes a transcription of a song melody accompanied by xylophone and drums and a picture of a xylophone).

5. Buchner was one of the few travelers who became a professional anthropologist and, in 1887 (at about the time Frobenius was preparing for his trip), director of the ethnological museum in Munich (1985, 187).

6. Wolf put his anthropological observations and measurements of 48 Baluba in an appendix (Wissmann et al. 1891, 436–43).

7. Because my study of curios draws on the sources I use here (Fabian 1998a), I summarize my findings below and add a few relevant points and texts.

8. Rather than assert a strict historical sequence, I view the process as a back-and-forth between observation and categorization but not as totally open induction.

9. See 1898, plates facing 62, 90, and an illustration on 128.

10. See 1888, 61, 72, 85, 107, 135, 137, 159, 173, all of them displays of numerous and numbered or lettered objects.

11. An exhibition and book based on objects collected in northeastern Congo toward the end of our period document this change (see Schildkrout and Keim 1990).

12. Buchner's collection (except items he brought back personally) was lost in a shipwreck off the English coast (*MAGD* 3, no. 2 [1882]: 82). That of the

German East African Expedition was destroyed in a fire (see chapter 4) and Reichard, the only European survivor of that expedition, later reports that he had to burn and throw away three loads of "beautiful ethnographic collections" (from his trip to Bunkeya in Katanga) because the porters were needed to carry food (*MAGD* 4, no. 5 [1885]: 305).

13. See the monograph by John Mack (n.d.) accompanying a recent exhibition and essays by Mack and others in Schildkrout and Keim 1998.

14. They do provide thirty pages of vocabularies in six languages in an appendix (1882, 2:304–34). More than other authors of travelogues (except Böhm 1888), Capelo and Ivens also liked to display their command of Latin taxonomic labels for specimens of zoology and botany.

15. Recent work on popular historiography shows that names of persons and places trigger the most vivid memories of the colonial past: see Fabian 1990 (on a document that calls itself a "vocabulary"!) and 1996, 22–24.

16. For a more extended treatment of this aspect and further references, see Fabian 1991b, ch. 8, and 1991a.

17. I quoted this passage in an essay on curios and curiosity (Fabian 1998a, 99) to point to analogies between the collecting of objects and the compiling of vocabularies.

18. See *MAGD*, nos. 4–5 [1879]: 173, 179, 181, 187, 192, 196; also earlier, where it is said to signify "sea" (111).

19. Tshibumba reflects on this (mis)understanding in his history of Zaire (Fabian 1996, 22–23).

20. Wissmann notes that the name the Basonge gave them is Bena Kalunga, "children of the sea" (1889, 121, 123); it may relate to Pogge and Wissmann's role in the Bene Diamba movement (see chapter 7).

21. For an investigation of maps and the spatial focus of colonial discourse (in the German occupation of what is now Namibia), see Noyes 1992. And on the "verbalization of space" that mapping and travel narratives always involve, see the detailed and comprehensive study by Lorenza Mondada (1994).

22. The most comprehensive treatment of this history is a collection of essays by Justin Stagl (1995), the rediscoverer of the *ars apodemica* and its Ramist roots.

23. See the section on the "philosophical traveler" in Fabian 1983, 2–11.

24. In a section where Coquilhat compiles his findings on the ethnography of the Bangala, he mentions "Notes sur l'ethnographie de la partie orientale de l'Afrique équatoriale" by Dr. Jacques and Captain Storms, "published in the memoirs of the Anthropological Society of Brussels" (1888, 361). As for Becker's reference to a manual (1887, 1:389), I cannot identify it; it is not the *Manuel* published by Société d'études coloniales (1896). A later publication (Ministère des colonies 1909) is outside our period but may have circulated in earlier versions.

25. According to Mack (n.d., 29) the Congo Free State sponsored this version, titled *Questionnaire ethnographique,* published by the Belgian Institut de Sociologie in 1905, and "intended [it] as a device by which to get the machinery of the incipient colonial administration functioning." We can infer its use in Torday's writings, to organize ch. 11 of his *Camp and Tramp in African Wilds*

(1913). Torday's collaborator, Joyce, also used the questionnaire to check his notes.

26. Indirectness but without tricks is what Torday recommends: "The thing to do is to provoke discussions amongst the natives, in this way alone can reliable evidence be accumulated"(1913, 105).

NINE

1. In 1885 Stanley's account of the founding of the Free State was simultaneously published in French and in English.

2. In the original edition I consulted, the pagination jumps from 1 to 10.

3. As far we can tell, only the zoologist Böhm of the German East African Expedition had formal training in evolutionist thought: as we noted, he wrote his dissertation under the direction of the evolutionist Ernst Haeckel in Jena (*MAGD* 4, no. 5 [1885]: 295).

4. If magic posed no threat, travelers could accept its use. From the east, Böhm and Kaiser, for instance, describe a ritual of protective magic for their caravan, detailing its texts in Swahili, Kiwende, and a German translation (*MAGD* 3, no. 3 [1882]: 206–7). Büttner reports a similar case from the west, a ritual of mutual protection between a local chief and the explorer's caravan (*MAGD* 5, no. 3 [1889]: 178).

5. Becker's fanciful transcription of the name gives a strange, exotic flavor to a perfectly ordinary Swahili soubriquet: *kangelengele* (or *kangerengere*): he with the little bells, probably referring to a *nganga*'s paraphernalia.

6. Like the rest of our sources and other travelers reporting on roughly the same area and populations, Hilton-Simpson wrote his account for a popular readership and came up with reports of cannibalism that are quite similar (see, e.g., Wissmann [1890], 43). Unlike them, he did not claim the status of explorer.

7. The forest is an ambivalent symbol (along with other topoi and stereotypes). After this chapter, "With the Bankutu Cannibals," comes "The Peoples of the Great Forest." For the most part it discusses the expedition's encounters with the Tetela, calling them open and friendly and noting the expedition's "roaring trade in curios" (1911, 168).

8. In the following I draw on Fabian 1999. See also my observations on collecting artifacts in chapter 8.

9. Contrast such refusal of recognition with earlier colonial practices, such as the fanciful titles of nobility (kings, dukes, counts) by which sixteenth-century Portuguese "recognized" the status of African officeholders. Was their naive projection of European titles part of a phase when denial of recognition was not crucial to the encounter?

10. Anthropologists may remember Bronislaw Malinowski's diary entry on seeing the Carpathians in Melanesia.

11. On traits and types in northern Cameroon see Aissato Bouba (1996), an essay rich in detail.

12. See Hegel's essay titled "Wer denkt abstrakt?" (Whose thinking is abstract? [1970, 575–81]).

13. There is one exception, a long and graphic passage where Coquilhat describes a public wrestling match between two young women (1888, 150–51).

14. Incidentally, the illustration this statement frames is our Figure 12, a sentimental tableau (Becker 1887, 2:329): an explorer holds the IAA's flag (later the Free State's flag), an Arab rests his arm on an African's shoulders, and all three join hands.

TEN

1. See a short essay on the the ethnographic account as a genre in central Africa by Jan Vansina (1987). This is an occasion to cite two special issues of the journal *Paideuma* that provide much background information on the history of ethnographic research in Africa during the period covered in this study: Heintze and Jones 1987; and Jones and Streck 1996.

2. For elaborations of this position see Fabian 1991b, "Presence and Representation" and "Dilemmas of Critical Anthropology."

3. James Clifford most impressively documents and demonstrates these changes with a focus on travel (1997), noting its persistence as a practice and a metaphor in current anthropology.

After this manuscript had gone to the copyeditor, my colleague Peter Pels brought to my attention a book by Deborah Root (1996)—a disconcerting discovery because it came too late to receive here the attention it deserves. According to the table of contents, its historical and geographical scope is broader, but at times our two works show a considerable convergence of topics raised.

4. The expedition set out in 1874; its sponsor was the Deutsche Gesellschaft zur Erforschung des äquatorialen Afrikas (see also the introduction).

5. Paul Schebesta's several popular works on the Bambuti, for instance, appeared also in English and later made it into the anthropological canon, while his monographs and articles in German, French, and Czech went uncited (and unread).

6. I distinguish between individual travelers' diaries and the expeditions' logbooks, which at least some of the expeditions led by teams presumably also kept, but cannot tell from the sources whether individual travelers made that distinction.

7. Occasionally the diaries quoted in travelogues have entries that consisted only of a date and remarks such as "nothing special happened"—bare assertions of a writer's presence and the continuity (or "reality") of travel; occasionally they found their way into the published travelogue.

8. See my brief discussion of epistemological vs. literary realism, with a reference to the pertinent essay by Marcus and Cushman (1982) in Fabian 1991b, ch. 11. See also Clifford and Marcus 1986, index under "realism." For an interesting study of the research diary and its many facets in modern anthropology and sociology, see Lourau 1988.

9. Thus the title of Percy Adams's classic essay on the topic (1980, first published in 1962).

10. Some travelers did attempt a strictly factual account: one example is von François's report of river travel on the Congo, Tshuapa, and Lulongo (1888).

11. An instance is Becker's shift to a genre that could be called "strange events" (1887, 2:228–32).

12. My guess is that Roger's sponsors used the letters for propaganda and popularization of their enterprise.

13. Kund wrote a long, Conradesque report on river travel in the diary form (*MAGD* 4, no. 6 [1885]: 379–91), but its promised continuation was not ready when the last issue of *MAGD* went into print (5, no. 3 [1889]: 134).

14. We omit another example of the genre, Dupont 1889, a compilation of letters with the subtitle "narrative of a scientific journey."

15. On presence and related matters raised here see Clifford's essay on ethnographic authority (1988, ch. 1).

16. The inventory of illustrations includes a few works that have been marginal as sources of our account (Bastian; Güßfeldt et al.) and (usually small) reproductions of maps that occur in the text as well as larger, often fold-out maps placed at the end of all travelogues. Given the number of items, it may also have a small margin of errors.

17. On many of these issues see the well-documented catalog by Gisela Stappert (1996) for an exhibition of images from the Frobenius-Institut archives, the bulk of it coming from the Frobenius-Lemme expedition of 1904–6; see too the richly illustrated book on Torday as a collector and ethnographer by Mack (n.d.).

18. The German original's wordplay gets lost in translation: *Umwertung* (transformation) and *Verwertung* (use). The two images are reproduced and Frobenius's comments discussed in Stappert (1996, 42–43).

19. My own count was 127 illustrations, a discrepancy I cannot explain.

20. I translate *dessins* as pictures (rather then drawings) because these illustrations reproduce a great variety of originals (etchings, engravings, woodcuts, drawings, watercolors, and others I am unable to identify). In a standard dictionary of Belgian romantic painters (Flippo 1981) I found all but two of the names of artists, most of them described as landscape or genre painters and affiliated with the art academy in Antwerp.

21. In this same chapter 16 a nauseatingly "objective" description of an African being beaten to death led me to write an essay on white humor (Fabian 1992). See also Stappert's comments on Lemme's caricatures and Frobenius's sense of humor (1996, 37–40).

ELEVEN

1. Wissmann's travelogue published in 1890 makes several references to his military experiences in the east (in 1888–89).

2. On Torday and his Kuba collection see Mack (n.d.), and on Frobenius see Stappert 1996. After I finished this study, a biography of Frobenius appeared (Heinrichs 1998), documenting his career and intellectual trajectory but lacking a coherent critique of either person or oeuvre—which may or may not be the biographer's fault.

3. An anthropologist who recommends debunking myth may raise a few eyebrows. Our discipline's injunction to treat myths where they are alive in the cultures we study with utmost respect is one of its accomplishments and also ex-

plains why anthropology and reason are equally appropriate targets of our critique. More about this presently.

4. What we call social and cultural research today was always only a part of
exploration; for some natural scientists among the travelers it was a burden. But
the natural history approach prevalent at the time made differences between natural and cultural phenomena less important than they are now.

APPENDIX

1. Initially headed by Major Alexander von Homeyer, this expedition to the
Lunda also included the Austrian first lieutenant Anton Lux and the botanist
Hermann Soyaux. All of them left for health reasons before the caravan reached
the interior.

2. Baron von Schöler was the leader until the expedition reached Tabora, and
he left for Germany.

3. Pogge was the leader but did not continue with Wissmann beyond
Nyangwe on the Lualaba.

4. Lieutenant Schulze, the appointed leader, died early on in Saõ Salvador.
After that the expedition split in three, led by Büttner, by Wolff, and by Kund
and Tappenbeck.

5. Recognition of the Congo Free State at the Berlin Conference of 1884—
85 preempted a Belgian eastern approach, and this expedition never left the coast.

6. Coquilhat's extraordinary report prompted us to include this exploration-
occupation of the Congo first headed by Stanley. Straining the idea of an expedition, it set up riverain stations from the coast to the upper Congo and
employed agents of many nationalities; the enterprise was the immediate predecessor of the Congo Free State.

7. This expedition also split into several separate undertakings. Two Belgian
officers, Paul Le Marinel and de Macar, were temporarily associated with the
expedition. When Wissmann left for health reasons, Ludwig Wolf became its
commander.

Bibliography

PRIMARY SOURCES

Bastian, Adolf. 1859. *Afrikanische Reisen: Ein Besuch in San Salvador, der Hauptstadt des Königreiches Congo; Ein Beitrag zur Mythologie und Psychologie.* Bremen: Heinrich Strack.

———. 1874–75. *Die deutsche Expedition an der Loango-Küste, nebst älteren Nachrichten über die zu erforschenden Länder: Nach persönlichen Erlebnissen.* 2 vols. Jena: Hermann Costenoble.

Becker, Jérôme. 1887. *La vie en Afrique; ou trois ans dans l'Afrique centrale.* 2 vols. Brussels: J. Lebègue.

———. 1889. *La troisième expédition belge au pays Noir.* Brussels: J. Lebègue.

———. N.d. *Avec Jérôme Becker en Afrique orientale.* Digestes congolais no. 1. Namur: Editions "Grands Lacs."

Böhm, Richard. 1888. *Von Sansibar zum Tanganjika: Briefe aus Ostafrika von Dr. Richard Böhm.* Nach dem Tode des Reisenden mit einer biographischen Skizze herausgegeben von Herman Schalow. Leipzig: F. A. Brockhaus.

Büttner, Richard. 1890. *Reisen im Kongolande.* Leipzig: Hinrichs.

Capelo, Hermingildo, and Roberto Ivens. 1882. *From Benguella to the Territory of Yacca: Description of a Journey into Central and West Africa; Comprising Narratives, Adventures, and Important Surveys of the Sources of the Rivers Cunene, Cubango, Luando, Cuanza, and Cuango, and of Great Part of the Course of the Two Latter.* 2 vols. London: Sampson Low, Marston, Searle and Rivington.

Coquilhat, Camille. 1888. *Sur le Haut-Congo.* Paris: J. Lebègue.

François, Curt von. 1888. *Die Erforschung des Tschuapa und Lulongo: Reisen in Centralafrika.* Leipzig: F. A. Brockhaus.

Frobenius, Leo. 1907. *Im Schatten des Kongostaates: Bericht über den Verlauf der ersten Reisen der D. I. A. F. E. von 1904–1906, über deren Forschungen und Beobachtungen auf geographischem und kolonialwirtschaftlichem Gebiet*. Berlin: Georg Reimer.

Güßfeldt, Paul, Julius Falkenstein, and Eduard Pechuël-Loesche. 1879–1907. *Die Loango-Expedition: Ausgesandt von der Deutschen Gesellschaft zur Erforschung Aequatorial-Afrikas 1873–1876; Ein Reisewerk*. 3 vols. Leipzig: Paul Frohberg.

Hilton-Simpson, M. W. 1911. *Land and Peoples of the Kasai: Being a Narrative of a Two Years' Journey Among the Cannibals of the Equatorial Forest and Other Savage Tribes of the the South-Western Congo*. London: Constable.

MAGD = Mittheilungen der Afrikanischen Gesellschaft in Deutschland. *Published in Berlin, 1878–89 (5 vols.)*.

Pogge, Paul. 1880. *Im Reiche des Muata Jamwo: Tagebuch meiner im Auftrage der Deutschen Gesellschaft zur Erforschung Aequatorial-Afrika's in den Lunda-Staaten unternommenen Reise*. Beiträge zur Forschungsgeschichte Afrika's. Pt. 3. Berlin: Dietrich Reimer.

Schütt, Otto H. 1881. *Reisen im südwestlichen Becken des Congo: Nach den Tagebüchern und Aufzeichnungen des Reisenden bearbeitet und herausgegeben von Paul Lindenberg; Mit 3 Karten von Dr. Richard Kiepert*. Berlin: Dietrich Reimer.

Thomson, Joseph. 1881. *To the Central African Lakes and Back: The Narrative of the Royal Geographical Society's East Central African Expedition, 1878–80*. 2 vols. London: Sampson Low, Marston, Searle and Rivington.

Torday, Emil. 1913. *Camp and Tramp in African Wilds: A Record of Adventures, Impressions, and Experiences during many years spent among the Savage Tribes round Lake Tanganyika and Central Africa, with a description of Native Life, Character, and Customs*. London: Seeley, Service.

———. 1925. *On the Trail of the Bushongo: An Account of a Remarkable & Hitherto Unknown African People, Their Origin, Art, High Social & Political Organization & Culture, Derived from the Author's Personal Experience Amongst Them*. London: Seeley, Service.

White Fathers. 1884. *A l'assaut des pays nègres: Journal des missionnaires d'Alger dans l'Afrique équatoriale*. Paris: Oeuvre des écoles d'orient.

Wissmann, Hermann. 1889. *Unter deutscher Flagge quer durch Afrika von West nach Ost: Von 1880 bis 1883 ausgeführt von Paul Pogge und Hermann Wissmann*. Berlin: Walther und Apolant.

———. [1890]. *Meine zweite Durchquerung Aequatorial-Afrikas vom Congo zum Zambesi während der Jahre 1886–1887*. Frankfurt an der Oder: Trowitzsch und Sohn.

———. 1891. *My Second Journey Through Equatorial Africa from the Congo to the Zambesi in the Years 1886 and 1887*. Trans. Minna J. A. Bergmann. London: Chatto and Windus.

Wissmann, Hermann von, Ludwig Wolf, Curt von François, Hans Müller. 1891. *Im Innern Afrikas: Die Erforschung des Kassai während der Jahre 1883, 1884, und 1885*. 1887. Third printing, Leipzig: F. A. Brockhaus.

Wolff, Willy [Wilhelm Albert]. 1889. *Von Banana zum Kiamwo: Eine Forschungsreise in Westafrika, im Auftrage der Afrikanischen Gesellschaft in Deutschland*. Oldenburg: Schulze.

REFERENCES CITED

Adams, Percy G. 1980. *Travelers and Travel Liars 1660–1800.* 1962. Reprint, New York: Dover.

Aissato Bouba. 1996. "Lauter breite Negergesichter": Die Darstellung der äußeren Erscheinung einiger nicht-moslemischer Ethnien aus Deutsch-Kamerun in der Vorkolonial- und Kolonialzeit. *Paideuma* 42:63–83.

Becker, A., C. von Perbandt, G. Richelmann, Rochus Schmidt, W. Steuber. 1907. *Hermann von Wissmann: Deutschlands größter Afrikaner.* Berlin: Alfred Schall.

Beidelman, Thomas O. 1982. The Organization and Maintenance of Caravans by the Church Missionary Society in Tanzania in the Nineteenth Century. *International Journal of African Historical Studies* 15:601–23.

Bentley, W. Holman. 1900. *Pioneering on the Congo.* 2 vols. London: Religious Tract Society.

Blunt, Alison. 1994. *Travel, Gender, and Imperialism: Mary Kingsley and West Africa.* New York: Guilford Press.

Bontinck, François. 1966. *Aux origines de l'état indépendant du Congo.* Louvain: Nauwelaerts.

Bontinck, François, with K. Janssen, ed. and trans. 1974. *L'Autobiographie de Hamed ben Mohammed-el-Murjebi Tippo Tip (ca. 1840–1905).* Brussels: Académie royale des sciences d'outre-mer.

British Association for the Advancement of Science. 1874. *Notes and Queries in Anthropology, for the Use of Travellers and Residents of Uncivilised Lands.* London.

Casati, Gaetano. 1891. *Zehn Jahre in Äquatoria und die Rückkehr mit Emin Pascha.* Bamberg: Buchner.

Ceyssens, Rik. 1998. *Balungu: Constructeurs et destructeurs de l'état en Afrique centrale.* Paris: L'Harmattan.

Chavanne, Josef. 1887. *Reisen und Forschungen im alten und neuen Kongo-Staate in den Jahren 1884 und 1885.* Jena: H. Costenoble.

Chernoff, John Miller. 1979. *African Rhythm and African Sensibility: Aesthetics and Social Action in African Musical Idioms.* Chicago: University of Chicago Press.

Clifford, James. 1988. *The Predicament of Culture: Twentieth-Century Ethnography, Literature, and Art.* Cambridge, Mass.: Harvard University Press.

————. 1997. *Routes: Travel and Translation in the Late Twentieth Century.* Cambridge, Mass.: Harvard University Press.

Clifford, James, and George E. Marcus, eds. 1986. *Writing Culture: The Poetics and Politics of Ethnography.* Berkeley: University of California Press.

Crary, Jonathan. 1990. *Techniques of the Observer: On Vision and Modernity in the Nineteenth Century.* Cambridge, Mass.: MIT Press.

De Clercq, A. 1928. Le chanvre chez les Bena Lulua, Congo: Origine, signification et influence de l'usage du chanvre. *Congo* 1:504–14.

De Heusch, Luc. 1972. *Le roi ivre; ou, l'origine de l'état.* Paris: Gallimard. Published in English as *The Drunken King; or, the Origin of the State,* trans. Roy Willis (Bloomington: Indiana University Press, 1982).

Delcommune, Alexandre. 1922. *Vingt années de vie africaine: Récit de voyages et d'exploration au Congo belge 1874–1893*. 2 vols. Brussels: Veuve Ferdinand Larcier.

Duchet, Michèle. 1971. *Anthropologie et histoire au siècle des lumières*. Paris: Maspéro.

Dupont, Edouard. 1889. *Lettres sur le Congo: Récit d'un voyage scientifique entre l'embouchure du fleuve et le confluent du Kasaï*. Paris: C. Reinwald.

Emerson, Barbara. 1979. *Leopold II of the Belgians: King of Colonialism*. London: Weidenfeld and Nicolson.

Essner, Cornelia. 1985. *Deutsche Afrikareisende im neunzehnten Jahrhundert: Zur Sozialgeschichte des Reisens*. Wiesbaden: Steiner.

Exploration: Journal des conquêtes de la civilisation sur tous les points du globe. Published in Paris, 1876–84 (18 vols.).

Fabian, Johannes. 1983. *Time and the Other: How Anthropology Makes Its Object*. New York: Columbia University Press.

———. 1984. *Language on the Road: Notes on Swahili in Two Nineteenth-Century Travelogues*. Beiheft Sprache und Geschichte in Afrika. Hamburg: H. Buske Verlag.

———. 1987. Hindsight: Thoughts on Anthropology upon Reading Francis Galton's *Narrative of an Explorer in Tropical South Africa* (1853). *Critique of Anthropology* 7:37–49.

———. 1990. *History from Below: The "Vocabulary of Elisabethville" by André Yav*. Amsterdam: John Benjamins.

———. 1991a. *Language and Colonial Power: The Appropriation of Swahili in the Former Belgian Congo, 1880–1938*. Cambridge: Cambridge University Press, 1986. Reprint, Berkeley: University of California Press.

———. 1991b. *Time and the Work of Anthropology: Critical Essays 1971–1991*. Philadelphia: Harwood Academic Publishers.

———. 1992. White Humor. *Transition*, no. 55:56–61.

———. 1995. On Ethnographic Misunderstanding and the Perils of Context. *American Anthropologist* 97:1–10.

———. 1996. *Remembering the Present: Painting and Popular History in Zaire*. Berkeley: University of California Press.

———. 1998a. Curios and Curiosity: Notes on Reading Torday and Frobenius. *In* Schildkrout and Keim 1998, 79–108.

———. 1998b. *Moments of Freedom: On Popular Culture in Africa*. Charlottesville: University Press of Virginia.

———. 1999. Remembering the Other: Knowledge and Recognition in the Exploration of Central Africa. *Critical Inquiry* 26:49–69.

Flippo, Willem G., ed. 1981. *Lexicon of the Belgian Romantic Painters*. Antwerp: International Art Press.

Force publique. 1952. *La Force publique de sa naissance à 1914: Participation des militaires à l'histoire des premières années du Congo*. Brussels: Institut royal colonial belge.

Frobenius, Leo. 1928. *Die Dichtkunst der Kassaiden*. Jena: Eugen Diederichs.

Galton, Francis. 1972. *The Art of Travel; or, Shifts and Contrivances Available in Wild Countries*. London: J. Murray, 1855. Reprint, New Abbot: David and Charles Reprints.

Geertz, Clifford. 1973. *The Interpretation of Cultures*. New York: Basic Books.

———. 1988. *Works and Lives: The Anthropologist as Author*. Stanford: Stanford University Press.

Glassman, Jonathon. 1995. *Feasts and Riot: Revelry, Rebellion, and Popular Consciousness on the Swahili Coast, 1856–1888*. London: James Currey.

Hegel, G. W. F. 1970. *Jenaer Schriften*. Vol. 2 of *Werke*, ed. Eva Moldenhauer and Karl Markus Michel. Frankfurt am Main: Suhrkamp.

Heinrichs, Hans-Jürgen. 1998. *Die fremde Welt, das bin ich. Leo Frobenius: Ethnologe, Forschungsreisender, Abenteurer*. Wuppertal: Hammer.

Heintze, Beatrix. 1999a. *Ethnographische Aneignungen: Deutsche Forschungsreisende in Angola*. Frankfurt am Main: O. Lembeck.

———. 1999b. Ethnographic Appropriations: German Exploration and Fieldwork in West-Central Africa. *History in Africa* 26:69–128.

Heintze, Beatrix, and Adam Jones, eds. 1987. *European Sources for Sub-Saharan Africa before 1900: Use and Abuse*. Wiesbaden: Franz Steiner.

Hess, Robert L., and Dalvan M. Coger. 1972. *A Bibliography of Primary Sources for Nineteenth-Century Tropical Africa as Recorded by Explorers, Missionaries, Traders, Travelers, Administrators, Military Men, Adventurers, and Others*. Stanford: Hoover Institution Press.

Hibbert, Christopher. 1982. *Africa Explored: Europeans in the Dark Continent 1769–1889*. New York: W. W. Norton.

Hinde, Sidney Langford. 1897. *The Fall of the Congo Arabs*. London: Methuen.

Hobart, Mark. 1996. Ethnography as a Practice, or the Unimportance of Penguins. *Europaea* 2:3–36.

Hobsbawm, Eric, and Terence O. Ranger, eds. 1983. *The Invention of Tradition*. Cambridge: Cambridge University Press.

Hochschild, Adam. 1998. *King Leopold's Ghost: A Story of Greed, Terror, and Heroism in Colonial Africa*. New York: Houghton Mifflin.

Johnston, Harry. 1908. *George Grenfell and the Congo: A History and Description of the Congo Independent State and Adjoining Districts of Congoland etc.* 2 vols. London: Hutchinson.

Jones, Adam, and Bernhard Streck, eds. 1996. *Zur Geschichte der Afrikaforschung*. Stuttgart: Franz Steiner.

Kalanda, Mabika. 1959. *Baluba et Lulua: Une ethnie à la recherche d'un nouvel équilibre*. Collection Etudes congolaises no. 2. Brussels: Editions de Remarques congolaises.

Kolakowski, Leszek. 1969. *The Alienation of Reason: A History of Positivist Thought*. Trans. N. Guterman. New York: Doubleday.

Kulick, Don, and Margaret Willson, eds. 1995. *Taboo: Sex, Identity, and Erotic Subjectivity in Anthropological Fieldwork*. London: Routledge.

Leclerc, Gérard. 1979. *L'observation de l'homme: Une histoire des enquêtes sociales*. Paris: Seuil.

Lepenies, Wolf. 1976. *Das Ende der Naturgeschichte*. Munich: Hanser.

Lévi-Strauss, Claude. 1955. *Tristes tropiques*. Paris: Plon.

Libata Musuy-Bakul. 1987. Regroupement des Baluba et ses conséquences géo-politiques dans la périphérie de Luluabourg (1891–1960). *Annales Æquatoria* 8:99–129.

Lindqvist, Sven. 1996. *"Exterminate All the Brutes": One Man's Odyssey into the Heart of Darkness and the Origins of European Genocide.* Trans. Joan Tate. New York: New Press.

Lourau, René. 1988. *Journal de recherche: matériaux d'une théorie de l'implication.* Paris: Méridiens Klincksieck.

Lux, Anton E. 1880. *Von Loanda nach Kimbundu: Ergebnisse der Forschungsreise im Äquatorialen West Afrika, 1875–1876.* Vienna: E. Hölzel.

Mack, John. N.d. *Emil Torday and the Art of the Congo 1900–1909.* Seattle: University of Washington Press.

Marcus, George E., and Dick Cushman. 1982. Ethnographies as Texts. *Annual Review of Anthropology* 11:25–69.

Marechal, Philippe. 1992. *De "Arabische" campagne in het Maniema-gebied (1892–1894): Situering binnen het kolonisatieproces in de Onafhankelijke Kongostaat.* Tervuren: Royal Museum of Central Africa.

McClintock, Anne. 1995. *Imperial Leather: Race, Gender, and Sexuality in the Colonial Contest.* New York: Routledge.

Mecklenburg, Adolf Friedrich, Herzog von. 1909. *Ins innerste Afrika: Bericht über den Verlauf der deutschen wissenschaftlichen Zentral-Afrika-Expedition.* Leipzig: Klinkhardt und Bierman.

Ministère des colonies. 1909. *Plan de documentation pour aider à l'élaboration d'études ethnographiques sur les peuplades du Congo belge.* N.p.

Mondada, Lorenza. 1994. Verbalisation de l'espace et fabrication du savoir: Approche linguistique de la construction des objets de discours. Ph.D. diss., University of Lausanne.

Moravia, Sergio. 1973. *Beobachtende Vernunft: Philosophie und Anthropologie in der Aufklärung.* Munich: Hanser.

Noyes, John. 1992. *Colonial Space: Spatiality in the Discourse of German South West Africa 1884–1915.* Philadelphia: Harwood Academic Publishers.

Ortner, Sherry B. 1995. Resistance and the Problem of Ethnographic Refusal. *Comparative Studies in Society and History* 37:173–93.

Pakenham, Thomas. 1991. *The Scramble for Africa: White Man's Conquest of the Dark Continent from 1876 to 1912.* New York: Avon.

Pan, Lynn. 1975. *Alcohol in Colonial Africa.* Helsinki: Finnish Foundation for Alcohol Studies, no. 22. Uppsala: Scandinavian Institute of African Studies.

Pechuël-Loesche, Eduard. 1907. *Volkskunde von Loango.* Stuttgart: Strecker und Schröder.

Pratt, Mary Louise. 1992. *Imperial Eyes: Travel Writing and Transculturation.* London: Routledge.

Reichard, Paul. 1891. *Deutsch-Ostafrika: Das Land und seine Bewohner, seine politische und wirtschaftliche Entwicklung.* Leipzig: O. Spamer.

Root, Deborah. 1996. *Cannibal Culture: Art, Appropriation, and the Commodification of Difference.* Boulder, Colo.: Westview Press.

Rotberg, Robert I. 1970a. Joseph Thomson: Energy, Humanism, and Imperialism. *In* Rotberg 1970b, 295–320.

————, ed. 1970b. *Africa and Its Explorers: Motives, Methods, and Impact.* Cambridge, Mass.: Harvard University Press.

Said, Edward W. 1978. *Orientalism.* New York: Random House.

Samarin, William J. 1989. *The Black Man's Burden: African Labor on the Congo and Ubangi Rivers, 1880–1900.* Boulder, Colo.: Westview Press.

Schildkrout, Enid, and Curtis A. Keim. 1990. *African Reflections: Art from Northeastern Zaire.* New York: American Museum of Natural History.

————, eds. 1998. *The Scramble for Art in Central Africa.* Cambridge: Cambridge University Press.

Schweinfurth, Georg August. 1878. *Im Herzen von Afrika: Reisen und Entdeckungen im Centralen Aequatorial-Afrika während der Jahre 1868–1871.* 1874. New ed., Leipzig: F. A. Brockhaus.

Scott, James C. 1985. *Weapons of the Weak: Everyday Forms of Peasant Resistance.* New Haven: Yale University Press.

Simpson, Donald. 1975. *Dark Companions: The African Contribution to the European Exploration of East Africa.* London: Paul Elek.

Société d'études coloniales. 1896. *Manuel du voyageur et du résident au Congo.* Part 2, *Renseignements pratiques.* Brussels: A. Lesigne.

Soyaux, Hermann. 1879. *Aus West-Afrika, 1873–76: Erlebnisse und Beobachtungen.* 2 vols. Leipzig: F. A. Brockhaus.

Spittler, Gerd. 1987. European Explorers as Caravan Travellers in the West Sudan: Some Thoughts on the Methodology of Journeys of Exploration. *Paideuma* 33:391–406.

Stafford, Barbara Maria. 1984. *Voyage into Substance: Art, Science, Nature, and the Illustrated Travel Account.* Cambridge, Mass.: MIT Press.

Stagl, Justin. 1995. *A History of Curiosity: The Theory of Travel, 1550–1800.* Philadelphia: Harwood Academic Publishers.

Stanley, Henry Morton. 1885. *The Congo and the Founding of Its Free State.* 2 vols. New York: Harper; London: Sampson Low, Marston, Searle and Rivington. Published in French as *Cinq années au Congo, 1879–1884: Voyages, explorations, formation de l'état indépendant du Congo* (Brussels: Institut national de géographie, 1885).

Stappert, Gisela. 1996. *Afrika EthnoGraphisch: Eine Bildausstellung des Frobenius-Instituts.* Frankfurt am Main: Frobenius-Institut an der Johann Wolfgang Goethe-Universität.

Stocking, George W., Jr. 1992. *The Ethnographer's Magic and Other Essays in the History of Anthropology.* Madison: University of Wisconsin Press.

Sundman, Per Olof. 1967. *The Expedition.* Trans. Mary Sandbach. London: Secker and Warburg.

Taussig, Michael. 1987. *Shamanism, Colonialism, and the Wild Man: A Study in Terror and Healing.* Chicago: University of Chicago Press.

————. 1993. *Mimesis and Alterity: A Particular History of the Senses.* London: Routledge.

Vansina, Jan. 1966. *Kingdoms of the Savanna: A History of Central African States until European Occupation.* Madison: University of Wisconsin Press.

————. 1987. The Ethnographic Account as Genre in Central Africa. *Paideuma* 33:433–44.

Weeks, John H. 1914. *Among the Primitive Bakongo: A Record of Thirty Years'
Close Intercourse with the Bakongo and Other Tribes of Equatorial Africa,
with a Description of Their Habits, Customs and Religious Beliefs.* London:
Seeley, Service.

Wesseling, H. L. 1996. *Divide and Rule: The Partition of Africa, 1880–1914.*
Westport, Conn.: Praeger.

Wiese, Carl. 1983. *Expedition in East-Central Africa, 1888–1891.* Ed. Harry W.
Langworthy; trans. Donald Ramos. Norman: University of Oklahoma Press.

Wissmann, Hermann von. 1895. *Afrika: Schilderungen und Rathschläge zur Vor-
bereitung für den Aufenthalt und den Dienst in den Deutschen Schutzge-
bieten.* Berlin: S. Mittler.

Young, Robert J. C. 1995. *Colonial Desire: Hybridity in Theory, Culture and
Race.* London: Routledge.

Zetterström, Kjell. 1966. Bena Riamba: Brothers of Hemp. *Studia Ethnograph-
ica Upsaliensia* 26 (2): 151–66.

Index

Personal, geographical, and ethnic names that appear only in quotations are listed in the form given in the sources.